Frommer's

Moscow &
St. Petersburg

1st Edition

by Angela Charlton

WILEY
Wiley Publishing, Inc.

About the Author

Angela Charlton first went to Russia a few weeks after the collapse of the Soviet Union in 1991, and spent the better part of the ensuing decade living and working there as a journalist. She was a Moscow-based correspondent for the Associated Press for six years, and she also studied in St. Petersburg and worked in Kiev. She is currently a freelance writer living in France.

Published by:

Wiley Publishing, Inc.

111 River St.
Hoboken, NJ 07030-5774

ISBN-13: 978-0-7645-8899-0
ISBN-10: 0-7645-8899-0

Editor: Christine Ryan, with Alexis Lipsitz Flippin
Production Editor: Ian Skinnari
Cartographer: Nicholas Trotter
Photo Editor: Richard Fox
Production by Wiley Indianapolis Composition Services

Front cover photo: Moscow: Monument to Minin and Pozharsky and St. Basil's Cathedral
Back cover photo: St. Petersburg: Peterhof Park, Grand Cascade, canals and waterworks

For information on our other products and services or to obtain technical support, please contact our Customer Care Department within the U.S. at 800/762-2974, outside the U.S. at 317/572-3993 or fax 317/572-4002.

Wiley also publishes its books in a variety of electronic formats. Some content that appears in print may not be available in electronic formats.

Manufactured in the United States of America

5   4   3   2   1

Contents

List of Maps

To Marina and Maxim

Acknowledgements

Many thanks to all those who influenced this book and my relationship with Russia. To the Pimkins, the first Russian family to open their home to me, in the days when sugar and hot water were precious commodities; to the late Sander Thoenes, for sharing his love of Russia and his boundless curiosity, and for countless biking and skiing trips in and around Moscow; to all those Russian officials who told me *"nyet,"* encouraging me to dig deeper; and to the coat-check clerk at the Russian Museum who mended my wayward buttons. I owe extra gratitude to Anna and Alexander Potekhin, for their guidance around and insight into St. Petersburg, for their generosity and copious tea and caviar; and to fact-checker Irina Krasnova. Thanks to Vera Chamoux for her moral support and interpretation of Russian culture, and to Christine Ryan and all the other Frommer's editors for their patience and diligence. Thanks to the friends and family whose frank suggestions and tolerance of my work schedule helped make this possible. Most of all, thanks to Yegor, my husband, for his love and inspiration, and for ensuring that I have a lifelong connection to Russia.

An Invitation to the Reader

In researching this book, we discovered many wonderful places—hotels, restaurants, shops, and more. We're sure you'll find others. Please tell us about them, so we can share the information with your fellow travelers in upcoming editions. If you were disappointed with a recommendation, we'd love to know that, too. Please write to:

Frommer's Moscow & St. Petersburg, 1st Edition
Wiley Publishing, Inc. • 111 River St. • Hoboken, NJ 07030-5774

An Additional Note

Please be advised that travel information is subject to change at any time—and this is especially true of prices. We therefore suggest that you write or call ahead for confirmation when making your travel plans. The authors, editors, and publisher cannot be held responsible for the experiences of readers while traveling. Your safety is important to us, however, so we encourage you to stay alert and be aware of your surroundings. Keep a close eye on cameras, purses, and wallets, all favorite targets of thieves and pickpockets.

Other Great Guides for Your Trip:

Frommer's Europe
Frommer's Scandinavia

Frommer's Star Ratings, Icons & Abbreviations

Every hotel, restaurant, and attraction listing in this guide has been ranked for quality, value, service, amenities, and special features using a **star-rating system.** In country, state, and regional guides, we also rate towns and regions to help you narrow down your choices and budget your time accordingly. Hotels and restaurants are rated on a scale of zero (recommended) to three stars (exceptional). Attractions, shopping, nightlife, towns, and regions are rated according to the following scale: zero stars (recommended), one star (highly recommended), two stars (very highly recommended), and three stars (must-see).

In addition to the star-rating system, we also use **seven feature icons** that point you to the great deals, in-the-know advice, and unique experiences that separate travelers from tourists. Throughout the book, look for:

Finds	Special finds—those places only insiders know about
Fun Fact	Fun facts—details that make travelers more informed and their trips more fun
Kids	Best bets for kids and advice for the whole family
Moments	Special moments—those experiences that memories are made of
Overrated	Places or experiences not worth your time or money
Tips	Insider tips—great ways to save time and money
Value	Great values—where to get the best deals

The following **abbreviations** are used for credit cards:

AE	American Express	DISC	Discover	V	Visa
DC	Diners Club	MC	MasterCard		

Frommers.com

Now that you have the guidebook to a great trip, visit our website at **www.frommers.com** for travel information on more than 3,000 destinations. With features updated regularly, we give you instant access to the most current trip-planning information available. At Frommers.com, you'll also find the best prices on airfares, accommodations, and car rentals—and you can even book travel online through our travel booking partners. At Frommers.com, you'll also find the following:

- Online updates to our most popular guidebooks
- Vacation sweepstakes and contest giveaways
- Newsletter highlighting the hottest travel trends
- Online travel message boards with featured travel discussions

The Best of Moscow & St. Petersburg

Russia breathes superlatives: the world's biggest country; its largest supplier of natural gas and second-largest oil producer; and home of the planet's longest railroads, busiest subway system (Moscow's), and one of its deepest, biggest, and oldest lakes (Baikal, in Siberia). It even boasts balmy beach resorts (on the Black Sea), though the Kremlin and the snowcapped cupolas of its cathedrals seem truer reflections of this northern nation's might and mysticism.

What the country lacks in climatic warmth, Russians make up for with their bottomless generosity and jovial hospitality. Survivors of despots from Ivan the Terrible to Stalin, Russians place high value on keeping their home worlds safe from the perils of without and stocking the larders with homemade jams, pickles, and desserts. The past decade has been rough on Russians, but it's sharpened their adaptation skills. Today's Russian university graduates know more languages, more about financial markets, and more about text messaging than many of their Western counterparts.

There is much for travelers to experience in Russia's two most popular cities. The rigorous traditions of the Bolshoi Theater coexist with some of Europe's most cutting-edge DJs. Hip restaurants fashion mouthwatering delicacies that put a twist on traditional Russian meat pies and cabbage soup. The Hermitage Museum is a fortress of fine art from around the world; and just down the street, the Russian Museum overflows with works by local artists from throughout the centuries. Explore Russia's contributions to the exploration of the universe by taking a "ride" in a space shuttle in Gorky Park or wandering the Cosmonautics Museum, a tribute to the tireless scientists and engineers who sent the first man—and woman—into space.

Russia's tourism infrastructure, alas, is still catching up with the rest of the changes, but Moscow and St. Petersburg are well on their way. Take along some pluck and flexibility and have a look at the best Russia has to offer.

1 Most Memorable Russian Experiences

- **View Red Square at Night** (Moscow): The crimson-and-ivy-colored domes of St. Basil's Cathedral rise in a dizzying welcome to this most majestic of Russian plazas. The red stars on the Kremlin towers twinkle above one side of the square, making the medieval fortress seem festive instead of forbidding. Lenin's Mausoleum in nighttime shadow is appropriately eerie. Stand on the rise in the center of the square and feel a part of Russia's expanse.

- **Experience White Nights in St. Petersburg:** Two weeks of festivities in late June celebrate the longest day of the year, when the northern sun never dips below the horizon. The

Russia

Russia's enormous size (6,592,846 square miles or 17,075,400 square kilometers, covering 11 different time zones) makes it difficult to map; in this drawing, North follows the meridians (lines of longitude) that converge near the top center of the map.

White Nights are more than just a party; they're a buoyant, carefree attitude of summer-ness liberated after the city's long hibernation. Watch at midnight as residents picnic with their kids or play soccer in the courtyards. Then take a nighttime boat ride through the canals as the sunset melts into a languorous sunrise, and you'll never want to go south again.

- **Steam Your Stress Away at the Banya:** Thaw your eyelashes in January or escape snow flurries in May in the traditional Russian bath house, something between a sauna and a Turkish hammam. The pristine Sandunovsky Baths in Moscow are a special treat, with Greek sculptures and marble baths. Watch expert banyagoers beat themselves with birch branches, plunge into icy pools, exfoliate with coffee grounds, and sip beer while waiting for the next steam. **Sandunovsky Baths (Sandunovskiye Banyi)** are at 14 Neglinnaya, Moscow (© 095/925-4631). See p. 141.

- **Watch the Drawbridges Open Along the Neva River** (St. Petersburg): An unforgettable outing during White Nights, or anytime, involves perching yourself on the quay very early at 2am to watch the city's bridges unfold in careful rhythm to allow shipping traffic through the busy Neva. Just be careful not to get caught on the wrong side of the river from your hotel.

- **Take the Trans-Siberian Railroad:** This winding link between Europe and Asia offers a sense of Russia's scale. Seven days from Moscow to Beijing, or from Moscow to Vladivostok on the Pacific Coast, the journey provides plenty of time for reflection and making acquaintances. Lake Baikal and the Altai Mountains are stunning interruptions in the masses of pine and birch forests.

- **Picnic at Kolomenskoye** (Moscow): This architectural reserve boasts the breathtaking 16th-century Church of the Assumption and the wooden house where Peter the Great sought refuge before assuming the throne. The surrounding lawns and groves beckon visitors to stretch out with caviar or cucumber sandwiches and a thermos of strong Russian tea. The hilly paths wind through apple orchards. Historic folk festivals are staged here throughout the year.

- **Pay Your Respects at Novodevichy Cemetery and Convent** (Moscow): The intricately original graves of the Russian eminences buried here—writers Anton Chekhov and Nikolai Gogol, Soviet leader Nikita Khrushchev and Stalin's suicidal wife among them—are allegories more than headstones. The tranquil grounds of the convent above witnessed bloody palace intrigues, and many a powerful woman in Russian history was exiled there. Today its restored cathedrals and adjacent pond exude a quiet serenity.

- **Sip Baltika Beer at Patriarch's Ponds** (Moscow): This prestigious neighborhood inspired writer Mikhail Bulgakov. It's still a prime spot in which to sink onto a bench with a bottle of local beer (Baltika is a popular choice) or other beverage and watch Moscow spin by. Whimsical statues of characters from Ivan Krylov's fables will entertain kids, and the pond is a skating rink in winter.

- **Take Tea at a Luxury Hotel:** A cup of steaming tea from an antique samovar is a treat for anyone, and even those on tight budgets should find something affordable at top-end hotels. To accompany the tea, try jam-filled *bliny* (thin Russian pancakes), fruit- or meat-filled *pirozhki* (pies), or caviar on toast. (For more information, see the listings for Moscow's Le Royal Meridien National or Metropol hotels (chapter 5) or St. Petersburg's Grand Hotel Europe (chapter 13).

- **Sample Wild Mushrooms:** Mushroom-picking in the countryside is a national pastime, and homemade mushroom dishes are heavenly though not without risks. Restaurant-approved mushrooms are nearly as good and much safer: succulent cepes in soup; chanterelles sprinkled on pork chops; or *zhulien,* any wild mushroom baked with cheese and sour cream.

- **Enjoy a Night Out at the Bolshoi Theater** (Moscow): Locals bemoan falling standards and rising prices at Russia's premier ballet and opera house, but the performers remain top class. Even seats on the fourth-level balcony offer views of the opulent 18th-century interior. The Mariinsky (formerly The Kirov) is St. Petersburg's no less impressive version.

2 Best Luxury Hotels

- **Baltschug Kempinski** (Moscow; ✆ 800/426-3135; www.kempinski-moscow.com): The hotel's views of St. Basil's Cathedral, Red Square, and the Kremlin are so breathtaking that TV networks set up here for their stand-ups. The brunch is fit for a czar, and the understated elegance of the rooms complements the facade's pastel ornamentation. See p. 91.

- **Le Royal Meridien National** (Moscow; ✆ 095/258-7000; www.national.ru): The National (a Royal Meridien hotel) has hosted legions of foreign and Russian dignitaries, including Vladimir Lenin before he moved into the Kremlin across the street. Now Russia's capitalist multimillionaires make it their home away from home. See p. 82.

- **Metropol** (Moscow; ✆ 095/927-6040; www.metropol-moscow.ru): The intricate Art Nouveau mosaic circling its crown is just one reason to delight in Moscow's century-old

Metropol. The chandeliers eclipse all else. The Bolshoi Theater lies across the square. See p. 82.

- **Grand Hotel Europe** (St. Petersburg; ✆ 812/329-6000; www.grandhoteleurope.com): This baroque confection in central St. Petersburg charmed Tchaikovsky and Bill Clinton, among other dignitaries. The winter garden stays lush even during St. Petersburg's dimmest months. The harpist and the plush furniture of the mezzanine cafe provide respite from a day of touring. See p. 211.

- **Corinthia Nevsky Palace** (St. Petersburg; ✆ 812/380-2001; www.corinthia.ru): Bursting with amenities too rare in Russia's second city, this thoroughly modern hotel is housed in a 19th-century landmark on central Nevsky Prospekt. Its heated garage, aromatherapy sessions, and sunbathing terrace compete with its in-house theatrical museum for customer raves. See p. 210.

3 Best Affordable Accommodations

- **Pulford Apartments** (St. Petersburg, ✆ 812/325-6277; www.pulford.com): A British company rents out these furnished, renovated flats with views of St. Petersburg's greatest monuments. A range of room sizes and services is available, including cleaning and airport transfers. Moscow apartments are also available. See p. 207.

- **Sovietsky Hotel** (Moscow; © 095/ 960-2000; www.sovietsky.ru): The soaring ceilings and cornice work of this behemoth in northern Moscow infuse it with grandeur. The service is no longer as Soviet as its name. Downstairs, the renowned Yar restaurant serves up elegant Russian fare. See p. 93.

- **G&R Hostels** (Moscow; © 095/ 378-0001; www.hostels.ru): Several floors of a drab Soviet hotel have been transformed into clean, comfortable accommodations. Services include cars with drivers and visa invitations (see "Entry Requirements," in chapter 2). While the location is not central, it's right next to a metro station. See p. 95.

4 Best Dining Experiences

- **Best Aristocratic Atmosphere:** Plunge into the refined opulence of 19th-century Russia at **Cafe Pushkin** (Moscow; 26a Tverskoi Bulvar.; © 095/229-5590), as you spear a bite of suckling pig or sip fine tea from a silver samovar. Though it only opened in 2000, the three-story restaurant's careful design and immediate popularity have made it seem an old landmark. See p. 105.

- **Best Comfort Food:** One of the most reliable, reasonable Russian menus in Moscow is at the basement restaurant/bar **Uncle Vanya** (Moscow; 16 Pyatnitskaya; © 095/951-0586). Literary and musical memorabilia line the walls, and the place mats teach you the Russian alphabet. Favorites are their dumplings (*pelmeni* or *vareniki*) with meat, potato, or berry fillings; and the buckwheat kasha. See p. 113.

- **Best Fusion:** Leading restaurateur Anton Novikov has capitalized on Russia's growing obsession with Asian cuisine without surrendering to it, at **Vanil** (Moscow; 1 Ostozhenka; © 095/202-3341). The menu is relentlessly fresh; a recent option was a soup of duck livers and oysters. The soaring ceilings and massive chandeliers seem built to the scale of the staggering Christ the Savior Cathedral across the street. See p. 114.

- **Best Fresh Fish:** The spare stone arches of St. Petersburg's **Staraya Tamozhnya** (St. Petersburg; Old Customs House; 1 Tamozhenny Pereulok; © 812/327-8980) evoke the building's history as an 18th-century Customs House, but its elegant lines and French chef keep things thoroughly modern. The unobtrusive salad bar offers marinated Russian specialties. The fish is so fresh you can forget any fears and indulge. See p. 232.

- **Best Georgian Fare:** The generous cuisine of Georgia, in the herb- and sheep-covered Caucasus Mountains, is best sampled at **Genatsvale** (Moscow; 12/1 Ostozhenka; © 095/ 202-0445). Exposed wood and lace curtains provide the perfect homestyle setting for cheese-filled *khachapuri* loaves or lamb marinated in pomegranate juice. Georgia's southern climes also produce spicy vegetable dishes sorely lacking in Russian cuisine. The same family runs **Mama Zoya** and another Genatsvale locale. See p. 115.

- **Best Literary Dive:** Just a small streetlight above the entrance marks the bohemian basement cafe **Idiot** (St. Petersburg; 82 Moika Canal; © 812/315-1675), named after a Fyodor Dostoyevsky novel. Mulled wine warms visitors in the winter months; lightly fermented *kvas* cools you in July. Pick a book in English from the cafe's eclectic library to peruse while you sip. See p. 230.

- **Best Kitschy Theme Dining:** Three elaborate and pricy Moscow restaurants plumb the stereotypes and cuisines of Russia's neighbors. **Shinok** (Moscow; 2 Ulitsa 1905 Goda; Ⓒ 095/255-0888), a Ukrainian farm with a chicken coop, is hidden on one of the city's hippest streets. Aromatic borscht is served here 24 hours. **Prisoner of the Caucasus** (Moscow; Kavkazkaya Plennitsa; 36 Prospekt Mira; Ⓒ **095/280-5111**) offers grilled lamb and garlicky eggplant. Waiters are decked out as mountain warriors. **White Sun of the Desert** (Moscow; Beloye Solntse Pustyni; 29/14 Neglinnaya St.; Ⓒ **095/209-7525**) offers central Asian cuisine like lamb pilaf and spicy dumplings. See pp. 116, 115, and 111, respectively.

- **Best Quickie Meal: Yolki-Palki** is a Russian chain with basic sit-down service in a country kitchen setting. It's also kid-friendly, a rarity on Russia's otherwise up-to-date dining scene. See p. 108.

5 Best Views

- **Lookout Point at Sparrow Hills** (Moscow): With the Stalin Gothic skyscraper of Moscow State University at your back, the capital spreads out beneath you in its enormity. Watch newlyweds pose and embrace at the lookout, leaving empty champagne bottles on the ledge.

- **Resurrection Gate Entrance to Red Square** (Moscow): Get ready to gasp when the cacophonous onion domes of St. Basil's Cathedral greet you at this cobblestone hilltop square. Resurrection Gate, itself resurrected in the 1990s, forms a perfect frame.

- **Strelka** (St. Petersburg): If you stand on this spit of land on Vasilevsky Island, you'll get a panorama of nearly every major landmark and monument in St. Petersburg, while the Neva River laps at your feet. It's also a window onto the classical conformity of the city's architecture.

- **The Sail Up to the Petrodvorets Palace** (Peterhof): The dense forests along the Baltic shore suddenly part and the gilded palace emerges, atop cascading fountains and sculpted gardens. Any boat from St. Petersburg to the imperial summer residence offers this vista. Hydrofoils leave from the Winter Palace/Hermitage in the warmer months.

6 Best Architecture

- **The Kremlin** (Moscow): This red brick fortress encloses a complex of 15th-century cathedrals that serve as Russia's best-preserved window onto that era, with their gold domes and pointed arches. Surrounding them are palaces where Russia's President Vladimir Putin and his predecessors have reigned, from the flowered columns of the Grand Kremlin Palace to the classical triangular Senate Building. See p. 119.

- **Palace Square** (St. Petersburg): The Russian baroque Winter Palace looks across this square—the stage for the Russian Revolution—toward the Alexander Column (celebrating the victory over Napoleon) and the curved facade of the General Staff building. Though its parts were erected at different times, Palace Square demonstrates the ensemble architecture that gives this planned city its consistency. See p. 238.

- **Stalin Gothic Skyscrapers** (Moscow): These seven towers raised in the 1940s to 1950s soar above the capital, looking grandiose from afar and eerie up close. Two of the towers house private apartments, two house government buildings, two are hotels, and one is Moscow State University. See p. 66.

- **Kolomenskoye museum reserve** (Moscow): The towering tented spires of the 16th-century Church of the Ascension share this reserve with the quirky wooden house in which Peter the Great once stayed, among other architectural treasures. See p. 137.

- **Moscow's Metro Stations** (Moscow): The spotless marble and granite floors of the subway are as remarkable as the intricate artwork and regal columns that adorn the stations. Favorites include the bronze statues at Ploshchad Revolutsii, the aviation mosaics at Mayakovskaya, and any stop on the opulent Circle Line.

7 Best Museums

- **State Hermitage Museum** (St. Petersburg; 1 Palace Sq.; © 812/110-9079): The museum holds one of the world's best and biggest collections of fine art, from Egyptian carvings to Rembrandt to Impressionist masterpieces. A controversial hall holds so-called trophy art seized from the Germans after World War II. The museum is located in the Winter Palace, stormed in 1917 by revolutionaries arresting Czar Nicholas II's government. See p. 234.

- **Armory Museum** (Moscow; Kremlin; © 095/302-3776): Fabergé eggs, coronation robes, royal carriages, and jewels have filled what was once the czarist weapons storehouse. The Armory, the Kremlin's main museum, also holds an impressive collection of armor and weaponry. Admission is limited to four sessions per day. See p. 122.

- **Tretyakov Gallery** (Moscow; 10 Lavrushinsky Pereulok; © 095/230-7788): The largest collection of Russian art, this museum is treasured by locals but underappreciated by visitors. Chagall and Kandinsky share space with penetrating medieval icons. Vrubel's Style Moderne and Levitan's smoky landscapes are pleasant discoveries. See p. 131.

- **Peter and Paul Fortress** (St. Petersburg; Hare's Island or Zaichy Ostrov): This island fort holds the cathedral where the remains of Russia's last royal family are interred, as well as a former mint and several small galleries. It was here that Peter the Great started his project to build this northern capital. See p. 240.

- **Museum of Cosmonautics** (Moscow; Prospekt Mira 111; © 095/283-7914): Housed beneath a sculpture of a rocket shooting off into the cosmos, this museum traces the formidable industry that put the Soviets head-to-head with the United States in the Space Race. Exhibits include moon rocks and the evolution of spacesuits. See p. 131.

- **Literary Museums:** Moscow and St. Petersburg have wonderful small museums devoted to Pushkin, Tolstoy, Dostoyevsky, Bulgakov, Gorky, and scores of other Russian writers, though signage is often in Russian only. See p. 137.

8 Best Gifts to Bring Home

- **Linens:** Delicately embroidered tablecloths, pillowcases, and women's or children's traditional tunics made from local linen are great buys.
- **Lacquer Boxes:** Different schools produce different styles of boxes, usually in black wood decorated with images from Russian folk tales.
- **Vodka:** Russky Standart and Flagman are two top-quality choices unavailable outside Russia.

- **Nesting Dolls:** *Matryoshka* dolls can be tacky or tasteful, and kids love them. Adults like the political ones portraying Russian or U.S. leaders stacked inside each other.
- **Stones from Siberia:** Malachite, charoite, and radonite are set into jewelry hard to find anywhere else in the world.

9 Best Oddball Attractions

- **Lenin's Mausoleum** (Moscow): The red-and-black granite mausoleum on Red Square is no longer the pilgrimage site it once was, and its future is in question—which is all the more reason to go see Vladimir Lenin's embalmed body now. A visit allows you access to the graves of all the other Soviet leaders (except Khrushchev) along the Kremlin wall. See p. 126.
- **Art MUSEON** (Moscow, behind the Central House of Artists; 10 Krymsky Val): A collection of Lenin heads and other Soviet monuments toppled in the early 1990s lay abandoned in Gorky Park until the pieces were unofficially resurrected and lined up in a garden behind Moscow's modern art museum. The place is a fitting commentary on Russia's political tumult of the last 15 years. See p. 130.

- **Kunstkamera** (St. Petersburg; 3 Universitetskaya Naberezhnaya; © 812/ 328-1412): Peter the Great's museum of 18th-century scientific curiosities is not for viewing after lunch. Among exhibits of the foremost technical developments of his day, the museum boasts pickled animals and human heads. See p. 244.
- **Buryan space shuttle in Gorky Park** (Moscow): The amusement section in Gorky Park is fun for kids but feels generic—until you bump into the Buryan. This space shuttle abandoned during the Soviet Union's waning years has been turned into a ride along the Moscow River, with gyrating chairs meant to make your stomach lurch as in a real rocket blastoff. The effect is mediocre, but the up-close view of the shuttle is worthwhile. See p. 134.

2

Planning Your Trip to Moscow & St. Petersburg

Russia vaults across two continents and spans 11 time zones, yet its territorial vastness is easily forgotten in the crush of rush-hour metro rides and in crowded urban apartments. This chapter helps you figure out how to tackle your trip: where and when to go; how to get there; what precautions to take; and how to save money.

Moscow is almost a country unto itself, a metropolis of 12 million people enjoying the fruits of Russia's booming oil economy. Despite Russians' innate conservatism, today's Moscow is a 24-hour city that pulses with change, from the ruthlessly competitive restaurant and club scenes to the volatile financial markets and the clamor for the latest top-of-the-line cellphone. In the background, tented spires and golden cupolas of medieval cathedrals beckon, Stalin's neo-Gothic skyscrapers soar, and the imposing authority of the Kremlin lords over it all.

St. Petersburg occupies a world of architectural order forged out of a swamp at a forbidding latitude. Peter the Great's invention cost the lives of thousands of workers sent to make the Baltic Sea delta inhabitable 300 years ago. But his vision lives on— even new buildings adhere to the symmetry and classicism of Peter's day. The sea-green Winter Palace overlooking the Neva River houses the Hermitage Museum's staggering collection of fine art, and sumptuous royal estates dot the surrounding forests. St. Petersburg's reputation as Russia's intellectual and cultural center has not brought the city the prosperity that today's Moscow enjoys, but Petersburg has better hotel choices and a restaurant scene nearly as vibrant as the capital's.

1 Entry Requirements & Customs

ENTRY REQUIREMENTS

International visitors' first experience of Russia is the clumsy, often frustrating process of getting a visa. Brace yourself, and remember that the rest of your Russian experience—the exhilarating White Nights, the gilded bell towers, the salmon tartlets following iced vodka—will be worth the hassle.

All visitors to Russia need a visa, with the exception of residents of a few former Soviet republics. Package tours usually take care of visas, though you will need to give the travel agency your passport for submission to the nearest Russian embassy or consulate.

For independent travelers, visa applicants must provide proof of hotel reservations in an official letter from a hotel or travel agency. Travelers staying in private homes need an official invitation from a Russian organization. Two places that offer this service for a fee are www.waytorussia.net; and Sindbad's Hostel, www.sindbad.ru (© **812/331-2020**). Fees for the visa (in addition to any fees for the

---

Tips **Passport Savvy**

Allow plenty of time before your trip to apply for a passport, especially since you will need your passport to start the lengthy visa process. Processing of passports normally takes 3 weeks but can take longer during busy periods (especially spring). Keep in mind that if you need a passport in a hurry, you'll pay a higher processing fee. When traveling, safeguard your passport and visa in an inconspicuous, inaccessible place like a money belt, and keep a copy of the critical pages with your passport number in a separate place. If you lose your passport, visit the nearest consulate or embassy of your native country as soon as possible for a replacement. If you lose your Russian visa, contact your hotel administrator or the nearest police station.

---

invitation) range from $60 to $350, depending on how quickly you need it, how long you need it for, and how many times you want to enter the country. For example, a single-entry, 3-month tourist visa costs $100 in the United States. Start the process several weeks before you leave. If you do not live near a Russian embassy or consulate, you can apply by mail, but you will have to send your passport to them via Federal Express. Anyone applying for a visa for more than 3 months must provide proof of a recent HIV test, a discriminatory and futile effort to cope with Russia's growing AIDS/HIV problem.

Once you get your visa, which is either a separate piece of paper or a sticker affixed to your passport, make a copy of it in case of emergency. You will need the original visa to leave the country as well as to enter it, and for as long as you're in Russia. While in Russia you will also need to **register your visa** with the local authorities. Most hotels will do this automatically for you the first day, but ask to be sure. If they don't offer this service, check with the visa agencies listed above.

Contact your nearest Russian embassy for rules in your country:

UNITED STATES: Embassy: 2641 Tunlaw Rd. NW, Washington, DC (© 202/939-8907, 202/939-8913, or 202/939-8918; www.russianembassy.org).

Consulates: 9 E. 91 St., New York, NY (© 212/348-0926); 2790 Green St., San Francisco, CA (© 415/928-6878); 2322 Westin Building, 2001 6th Ave., Seattle, WA (© 206/728-1910).

BRITAIN: 5 Kensington Palace Gardens, London W8 4QS (© 0870/005-6972).

CANADA: 52 Range Rd., Ottawa, Ontario K1N 8G5 (© 613/594-8488).

AUSTRALIA: 78 Canberra Ave., Griffith, Canberra, ACT 2603 (© 02/6295-9474).

IRELAND: 186 Orwell Rd., Rathgar, Dublin (© 01/492-3492).

For an up-to-date, country-by-country listing of passport requirements around the world, go to the "Foreign Entry Requirement" Web page of the U.S. State Department at **http://travel.state.gov/foreignentryreqs.html**.

CUSTOMS
WHAT YOU CAN BRING INTO RUSSIA

Visitors can bring in most things other than weapons, drugs, and livestock. If you have cash in any currency worth more than $1,500; anything antique; or valuable jewelry, laptop computers, cameras, or other electronics, then fill out a Customs declaration form upon entry and go through the **Red Channel** at airport Customs. That way you won't have any problem taking the items home with you when you leave. The declaration form will be stamped and returned to you, and you must present it again upon departure. You can take up to $10,000 if you declare it. Otherwise, you can pass through the **Green Channel** without filling out any forms. You can also register items that can be readily identified by a permanently affixed serial number with your home Customs office before you leave. Take the items to the nearest Customs office or register them with Customs at the airport from which you're departing. You'll receive, at no cost, a Certificate of Registration, which allows duty-free entry for the life of the item. If you go through the Red Channel, be aware that if the amount of cash you take out of Russia is larger than the sum you declared upon entry, you may be questioned on suspicion of abetting capital flight.

WHAT YOU CAN TAKE HOME FROM RUSSIA

Most souvenirs are safe to take home, except antiques, artwork, and caviar. Overfishing has shriveled the population of Caspian Sea sturgeon, the main source of the world's black caviar. Travelers are currently allowed to take 250 grams (10 oz.) out of the country, though Americans should be aware that U.S. Customs forbids importing fish products. The rules on artwork and antiques change with puzzling frequency; they most often affect religious icons, old samovars, and artwork worth over $1,000. In some cases, the item cannot be exported at all; in others, export is permitted but only with special Culture Ministry certification. Fortunately, most vendors can complete the export certification for these items for you. Tourists wishing to export anything valuable or anything made before 1960 (including books or Soviet memorabilia) should have the store certify it or clear it

themselves with the **Russian Ministry of Culture's Assessment Committee** (in Moscow, © 095/921-3258; in St. Petersburg, © 812/310-1454). Applications are cheap (about $10), but export duties can run up to 100% and the process is tedious. Demand receipts when buying anything valuable, even items from open-air markets.

Until recently, visitors were prohibited from taking rubles out of the country. Now a small amount can be taken, but the limit is indexed to the official minimum wage and therefore changes often, so stick to small sums to be safe. Bear in mind that you cannot exchange them back for dollars when you get home, since the ruble is not internationally convertible.

Returning **U.S. citizens** who have been away for at least 48 hours are allowed to bring back, once every 30 days, $800 worth of merchandise duty-free. You'll be charged a flat rate of duty on the next $1,000 worth of purchases. Any dollar amount beyond that is dutiable at whatever rates apply. On mailed gifts, the duty-free limit is $200. Be sure to have your receipts or purchases handy to expedite the declaration process. *Note:* If you owe duty, you are required to pay it upon your arrival in the United States, either by cash, personal check, government or traveler's check, money order or, in some locations, Visa or MasterCard.

With some exceptions, you cannot bring fresh fruits and vegetables into the United States. For specifics on what you can bring back, download the invaluable free pamphlet *Know Before You Go* online at **www.cbp.gov**. (Click on "Travel," and then click on "Know Before You Go! Online Brochure.") Or request the pamphlet from the **U.S. Customs & Border Protection (CBP),** 1300 Pennsylvania Ave. NW, Washington, DC 20229 (© 877/287-8667).

For a clear summary of **Canadian** rules, write for the booklet *I Declare,* issued by the **Canada Customs and Revenue Agency** (© **800/461-9999** in Canada, or 204/983-3500; www.ccra-adrc. gc.ca). Canada allows its citizens a C$750 exemption, and you're allowed to bring back duty-free one carton of cigarettes, one can of tobacco, 40 imperial ounces of liquor, and 50 cigars. In addition, you're allowed to mail gifts to Canada valued at less than C$60 a day, provided they're unsolicited and don't contain alcohol or tobacco (write on the package "Unsolicited gift, under $60 value"). All valuables should be declared on the Y-38 form before departure from Canada, including serial numbers of valuables you already own, such as expensive foreign cameras. *Note:* The $750 exemption can be used only once a year and only after an absence of 7 days.

U.K. citizens returning from **a non-E.U. country** have a Customs allowance of: 200 cigarettes; 50 cigars; 250 grams of smoking tobacco; 2 liters of still table wine; 1 liter of spirits or strong liqueurs (over 22% volume); 2 liters of fortified wine, sparkling wine, or other liqueurs; 60cc (ml) perfume; 250cc (ml) toilet water; and £145 worth of all other goods, including gifts and souvenirs. People under 17 cannot have the tobacco or alcohol allowance. For more information, contact HM Customs & Excise at © **0845/010-9000** (from outside the U.K., 020/8929-0152), or consult their website at www.hmce.gov.uk.

The duty-free allowance in **Australia** is A$400 or, for those under 18, A$200. Citizens can bring in 250 cigarettes or 250 grams of loose tobacco, and 1,125 milliliters of alcohol. If you're returning with valuables you already own, such as foreign-made cameras, you should file form B263. A helpful brochure available from Australian consulates or Customs offices is *Know Before You Go.* For more information, call the **Australian Customs Service** at © **1300/363-263;** or log on to www.customs.gov.au.

The duty-free allowance for **New Zealand** is NZ$700. Citizens over 17 can bring in 200 cigarettes, 50 cigars, or 250 grams of tobacco (or a mixture of all three if their combined weight doesn't exceed 250g); plus 4.5 liters of wine and beer, or 1.125 liters of liquor. New Zealand currency does not carry import or export restrictions. Fill out a certificate of export, listing the valuables you are taking out of the country; that way, you can bring them back without paying duty. Most questions are answered in a free pamphlet available at New Zealand consulates and Customs offices: *New Zealand Customs Guide for Travellers, Notice no. 4.* For more information, contact **New Zealand Customs,** The Customhouse, 17–21 Whitmore St., Box 2218, Wellington (© **04/473-6099** or 0800/428-786; www.customs.govt.nz).

2 Money

Though capitalism has brought Russia more in line with the economies of the West, money matters continue to vex visitors. Caviar, symphony tickets, and haircuts can barely dent your wallet; rubbery pizza and roach-ridden hotels can drain it. Russia can be quite cheap, though visitors on escorted tours may not notice, as accommodations are often overpriced and tour operators charge a premium. Cash is by far the most popular form of payment among Russians, but credit cards are increasingly accepted. ATMs are widely available in Moscow and St. Petersburg and are generally reliable.

CURRENCY

Russia's **ruble** is still not technically a "hard" currency, which means very few banks abroad will sell you rubles (in cash or traveler's checks) before you leave home or buy them back from you when you return. The U.S. dollar was the de facto second currency in the 1990s as the ruble lost all credibility among Russians. In recent years the ruble has remained quite stable, and inflation has calmed down considerably, though Russians still prefer to keep their savings in dollars or euros. If you're not queasy about carrying cash from home, change it at the currency exchange booths found at all airports, hotels, and most street corners. Exchange booths in town offer more competitive rates than do hotels and airports and do not charge commissions, though most buy only U.S. dollars and euros. Be sure

to have crisp, new bills, as exchange booths often refuse well-worn notes or those printed pre-1995. Note that prices listed on menus and in shops are often in dollars or euros, though only rubles are accepted as payment. This is a remnant of the 1990s, when the ruble's value plunged daily. For an explanation of the "monetary units" used on some price lists, see the "Currency Confusion" box on p. 83.

Most prices listed in this book are in U.S. dollars, following Russian hotel and restaurant practice, or in rubles with the rough dollar equivalent following.

The site www.xe.com/ucc is a universal currency converter that gives up-to-the-minute exchange rates. Current rates are:

The Ruble, the Dollar & the Pound

Ruble	US$	£
1 ruble	3.5¢	2 pence
28 rubles	$1.00	10 shillings
100 rubles	$3.50	1.93 pounds sterling
1000 rubles	$35.00	19.31 pounds sterling

ATMS

The easiest way to get cash in Moscow and St. Petersburg is from an ATM. The **Cirrus** (© **800/424-7787**; www.master card.com) and **PLUS** (© **800/843-7587**; www.visa.com) networks span the globe; look at the back of your bank card to see which network you're on. Most Russian ATMs accept both. Be sure you know your personal identification number (PIN) before you leave home, and be sure to find out your daily withdrawal limit before you depart. Also keep in mind that many banks impose a fee every time a card is used at a different bank's ATM; that fee can be higher for international transactions than for domestic ones. On top of this, the Russian bank from which you withdraw cash may charge its own small fee. For international withdrawal fees, ask your bank. To limit these

charges, take out as much money as you're comfortable with at once.

You can also get cash advances on your credit card at an ATM. Credit card companies try to protect themselves from theft by limiting the funds you can withdraw outside your home country, so call your credit card company before you leave home. And keep in mind that you'll pay interest from the moment of your withdrawal, even if you pay your monthly bills on time.

TRAVELER'S CHECKS

Few places in Russia accept traveler's checks outside major hotels and restaurants, and those that do usually only accept American Express. If you have checks from elsewhere, call your hotel in advance to see if they're accepted. Currency exchange booths in the major hotels generally accept traveler's checks, but most other exchange booths do not.

Traveler's checks are something of an anachronism from the days before the ATM made cash accessible at any time. Traveler's checks used to be the only sound alternative to traveling with dangerously large amounts of cash. They were as reliable as currency but, unlike cash, could be replaced if lost or stolen. These days, traveler's checks are less necessary because most cities have 24-hour ATMs that allow you to withdraw small amounts of cash as needed. However, keep in mind that you will likely be charged an ATM withdrawal fee if the bank is not your own.

You can get traveler's checks at almost any bank. **American Express** offers denominations of $20, $50, $100, $500, and (for cardholders only) $1,000. You'll pay a service charge ranging from 1% to 4%. You can also get American Express traveler's checks over the phone by calling © **800/221-7282;** Amex gold and platinum cardholders who use this number are exempt from the 1% fee.

Visa offers traveler's checks at Citibank locations nationwide, as well as at several other banks. The service charge ranges between 1.5% and 2%; checks come in denominations of $20, $50, $100, $500, and $1,000. Call © **800/732-1322** for information. American Automobile Association members can obtain Visa checks

without a fee at most AAA offices or by calling © **866/339-3378. MasterCard** also offers traveler's checks; call © **800/223-9920** for a location near you.

If you choose to carry traveler's checks, be sure to keep a record of their serial numbers separate from your checks in the event that they are stolen or lost. You'll get a refund faster if you know the numbers.

CREDIT CARDS

Credit cards are welcome in nearly all Russian hotels and many restaurants, but many museums and train stations take only cash. Cards most commonly accepted in Russia are American Express, Visa, MasterCard, and Eurocard. Places that take Diners Club are rare, and those that take Discover are nearly nonexistent.

Credit cards are a safe way to carry money. They also provide a convenient record of all your expenses, and they generally offer relatively good exchange rates. You can also withdraw cash advances from your credit cards at banks or ATMs, provided you know your PIN. If you've forgotten yours, or didn't even know you had one, call the number on the back of your credit card and ask the bank to send it to you. It usually takes 5 to 7 business days, though some banks will provide the number over the phone if you tell them your mother's maiden name or some other personal information. Keep in mind that when you use your credit card

---

⸂Tips Dear Visa: I'm Off to Russia!

Some credit card companies recommend that you notify them of any impending trip abroad so that they don't become suspicious when the card is used numerous times in a foreign destination, and block your charges. Even if you don't call your credit card company in advance, you can always call the card company if a charge is refused. Keep in mind that 1-800 toll-free numbers listed on the back of the card can't be dialed from Russia—a good reason to find out the company's standard toll number. Perhaps the most important lesson here is to carry more than one card with you on your trip; a card might not work for any number of reasons, so having a backup is the smart way to go.

abroad, most banks assess a 2% fee above the 1% fee charged by Visa, MasterCard, or American Express for currency conversion on credit charges. But credit cards still may be the smart way to go when you factor in exorbitant ATM fees and higher traveler's check exchange rates (and service fees).

3 When to Go

Frost-tinged, wind-whipped, ice-glazed. Snow blankets much of Russia for most of the year, and Moscow and St. Petersburg usually see flurries in May and September. Understandably, prices are lower September through May and tourist sites less crowded. Hotel and airline rates spike around the New Year's holiday, the main event in the Russian calendar.

Most visitors favor summer, both in Moscow and subarctic St. Petersburg, with sunsets that linger until sunrise, balmy temperatures, and all-night activity that makes you forget it's 3am and you haven't slept. Russians shed layers, sunbathe on park benches, and let loose after their long hibernation. Festivals and open-air concerts make up for the summer departure of the major opera and dance companies such as the Bolshoi and Mariinsky (formerly the Kirov) theaters. Summer weather in both cities can be unpredictable, though, with spells of heavy heat (and rare air-conditioning) or drizzly cold. Bring layers and an umbrella no matter when you go.

Autumn is a few idyllic weeks in late September and early October when the poplars and oaks shed their leaves and the afternoon sun warms you enough to help you through the cooling nights. Spring, a few weeks in April, is slushy and succinct in Moscow and St. Petersburg.

If a winter wonderland is your fantasy, Russia in December won't disappoint you. The northern sun shines softly low on the horizon, and snow masks garbage-strewn courtyards and muffles the sound of traffic. Cross-country skiing fans can wind through forests within Moscow city limits or skate-ski along the frozen Gulf of Finland in St. Petersburg. Skaters have frozen ponds galore for ice season fun. The downside, other than a suitcase weighted with sweaters, is that many country palaces and other outdoor sites close for the winter.

Businesses and government agencies slow down considerably because of vacations the first 2 weeks of January, the first 2 weeks of May, and much of August. These are calmer times to visit Russia but can prove a nightmare if you have visa problems or other administrative needs. When a public holiday falls on a weekend, the nearest weekday is given off in compensation.

CALENDAR OF EVENTS

All dates below are official holidays unless noted. December 25 is not a holiday in Russia.

For other festivals and sports championships, see "The Performing Arts" in chapters 9 and 17 and "Spectator Sports" in chapters 7 and 15.

January 1–2: New Year's Day. This is the major holiday of the Russian year, a family event centered around a fir tree, a huge feast, and gift-giving traditions transferred by Soviet leaders from Christmas to the more secular New Year's Day. Even the smallest of children stay up to ring in midnight. Both January 1 and 2 are holidays.

January 7: Russian Orthodox Christmas. Ignored in Soviet times, this is now a primary religious holiday, with many people attending midnight Mass and more festive meals.

January 14: "Old" New Year. Not an official holiday, but celebrated nonetheless. It's left over from the pre-revolutionary days when Russia followed the

Butter Week

Known as Maslenitsa in Russian, Butter Week began as a pagan festival celebrating the end of winter. The arrival of the Orthodox calendar didn't extinguish this week of revelry, but turned it into a pre-Lenten party, a sort of Russian version of Carnival or Mardi Gras. The name comes from the butter used for pancakes eaten throughout the week—pancakes whose golden warmth and roundness is meant to represent the sun and impending springtime. The butter also refers to the upcoming Lent, when Orthodox believers are expected to refrain from dairy products and other luxuries. To store up for this austere period, Russians indulge greedily in rich foods during Maslenitsa. Pancakes are stuffed with soft farmers' cheese, ham, or caviar. Eggy desserts grace the table, not to be seen again until Easter.

Maslenitsa was a major event in Moscow and St. Petersburg before the revolution, but the grand citywide festivals vanished in Soviet times. Today, festivities are again staged at parks such as **Kolomenskoye** in Moscow (p. 137) and the **Summer Gardens** in St. Petersburg (p. 246), as well as in villages and country estates on the cities' outskirts. A key part of the ritual is the burning of one or several straw scarecrows representing winter. They're paraded around a snow-covered field and then set alight as onlookers cheer, chant, and dance. At Kolomenskoye, performers in embroidered costumes revive traditional songs and children's games, and build ice forts for mass snowball fights. Everyone is treated to honey from nearby hives, and barrels of mead—a warm, fermented honey drink—are prepared just for the occasion.

Dates of Butter Week vary from year to year, since it's linked to Orthodox Easter, but it usually falls between late February and late March. The original rituals have been adapted to modern times, with the big parties usually held on Saturday and Sunday to accommodate work schedules. Each day of the week has a significance. Thursday, for example, is **Cleansing Day,** when Russians are expected to clean out their cupboards and lives for the coming spring. Sunday is **Forgiveness Day,** and even in Soviet times it was common for long-feuding siblings to phone each other on that day to mend their differences. According to some traditions, Monday morning is teeth-cleaning day, when men are expected to drink large amounts of vodka to cleanse the remnants of fatty foods from their teeth.

If you're visiting Russia during this season, tracking down a Maslenitsa party is a great way to boost your mood and distract you from the cold slushiness all around. Some Russian travel agencies arrange special Maslenitsa tours. Check with your hotel concierge; see www.maslenitsa.com/english for a calendar of Moscow Maslenitsa events; or check *The St. Petersburg Times* website (www.sptimes.ru) for St. Petersburg parties.

The Biggest Party of the Year

Presents under a fir tree, a copious family feast, and a big man with a long white beard—for a Russian, these traditions conjure up not Christmas, but New Year's Eve. The atheist Soviet government wiped religious holidays off the official calendar, but they couldn't suffocate the midwinter holiday spirit. Stalin, recognizing the people's unwillingness to abandon Christmas traditions, encouraged their shift to the more secular New Year's holiday. Even today, a decade and a half after the collapse of Soviet Communism, New Year's remains the primary event on the Russian calendar. Russian Orthodox Christmas—celebrated on January 7, according to the Julian calendar in use before the revolution—has re-assumed some of its former significance, but it's seen as a day for attending Mass and singing hymns instead of gift-giving and family celebration. Those rituals are reserved for December 31, when even the smallest children stay up to ring in the New Year.

Some restaurants and clubs are tapping into Western New Year's rituals with expensive all-night parties drenched in champagne, but the majority of Russians consider it an at-home, family event. The appetizers emerge in early evening, when relatives squeeze around the over-burdened table. For the next several hours, people eat, drink, tell stories, and dance to favorite songs. Father Frost, or Dyed Moroz, delivers gifts sometime around midnight. Because most Russians live in apartment buildings, the whole coming-down-the-chimney tradition plays no role here, and family members pull presents from cupboards or from under beds. In fairy tales, Dyed Moroz is assisted by a Snow Maiden, Snegurochka, and some families dress up as the two characters.

Menu items reflect the end of the pre-Christmas fast called for by Orthodox custom, 40 days of refraining from meat and dairy products: Beef and pork roasts dripping with fatty sauces, cured meats, veal in aspic, salads packed with diced ham and egg and heaped with mayonnaise, buttery pancakes heaped with caviar. . . . To drink, men stick to vodka; women either

Julian calendar, which was about 2 weeks behind the one used by the Western world.

February 23: Defenders of the Motherland Day (Armed Forces Day). With the military draft still mandatory, many Russians see this as a general "Men's Day," involving much vodka and stories of hazing and corrupt commanding officers.

February/March: Maslenitsa, or Butter Week. Not an official holiday. The week before Orthodox Lent is traditionally a time to eat lots of buttery *bliny* (crepelike pancakes) and other rich foods that believers will forego for the next 40 days. Each day of the week has a significance, such as Cleansing Thursday when Russians purge over-stuffed closets, and Forgiveness Sunday when people forgive wrongs committed over the past year. The origins of the holiday are pagan, and many towns stage raucous Maslenitsa festivals. It's join in or sip *nastoika,* a homemade liqueur made of vodka brewed with berries, herbs, or roots. Pre-revolutionary aristocrats introduced fine French champagne to their Christmas feasts; the Soviets spread the tradition to the masses with the production of cheap sparkling wine that is still a staple of the New Year's table. The most popular brand is Sovietskoye (if you run across it, be aware that all categories but the *brut* are quite sweet).

Since the 1970s, many Russian families have incorporated the TV set into their New Year's rituals, with the annual showing of the film *The Irony of Fate, or Have a Good Steam (Ironiya Sudby, ili S Lyokhim Parom).* The film centers around a man who goes to the sauna on New Year's Eve with friends and wakes up not in his Moscow apartment but in an identical flat at the same address in Leningrad. The comedy pokes fun at the uniformity of Brezhnev-era life and quickly became a cult classic.

The New Year's celebrations peak with a midnight fireworks display over Red Square, broadcast nationwide. The crowds of mostly young revelers in the square are so dense that few of them notice the freezing temperatures. In St. Petersburg, the biggest fireworks are shot over the Neva River across from the Hermitage. Back at home, many families celebrate well into the night, or go outside to set off their own small firecrackers. The first day of the year is a day of rest and lots of leftovers.

If you visit Moscow or St. Petersburg over New Year's, be sure to check in advance online or through your travel agent for special holiday events at your hotel. If you can't get invited to a Russian home, try one of the elaborate parties at traditional Russian restaurants such as One Red Square, Baltschug Kempinski hotel, or Le National hotel (all have great views of the Moscow fireworks). Meal service starts at 10pm or later. Seats are expensive and must be booked well in advance. For English-language listings on New Year's parties, see *The Moscow Times* newspaper (www.themoscowtimes.com) or *The St. Petersburg Times* (www.sptimes.ru). And practice saying "S Novym Godom!" (Happy New Year!)

not Carnival or Mardi Gras, but it's lively.

March 8: International Women's Day. Begun by U.S. feminists in the 1920s, the holiday became a Soviet banner for gender equality. Today's Russian women lament that men get pampered 364 days a year and women only get appreciated on Vosmovo Marta (Mar 8). It's a sacred holiday nonetheless, and every Russian male is expected to present flowers or chocolates to his wife, mother, daughters, and female colleagues.

April/May: Orthodox Easter. The date varies, but it's usually 1 or 2 weeks after Catholic/Protestant Easter. The following Monday is a state holiday, though Good Friday is not. The day has taken on greater significance since the collapse of Soviet atheism, and on Easter morning, every Orthodox church has lines of people waiting to have their traditional Easter cakes blessed. The holiday feast is the richest on the Russian calendar, with eggs a major theme.

April/May: Easter Arts Festival (Moscow). A weeklong event showcasing St. Petersburg's Mariinsky Company orchestra in Moscow and small choral ensembles performing in the city's cathedrals following Orthodox Easter. Bell-ringing is a major part of the event.

May 1–2: Labor Day/Spring Festival. May Day parades under red Communist banners still wend through Moscow's streets, though they're no longer allowed on Red Square, site of the tremendous Soviet-era demonstrations of Kremlin-enforced proletarian solidarity.

May 9: Victory Day. The Soviet Union lost more people than any other nation in World War II, and even 6 decades later the day commemorating Hitler's defeat is a major Russian holiday. Every Russian has a relative or friend who served in what they call the Great Patriotic War, and the sight of elderly veterans pinning on rusting medals for a day is a poignant reminder of one of the most impressive feats of the Soviet era.

June 12: Russian Independence Day. On this day in 1990, the Russian Federation declared itself independent from the Soviet Union, a symbolic move inspired by nationalist movements in the Baltics and eastern Europe. Few Russians today know what the holiday commemorates.

Late June/early July: White Nights. Two weeks around the summer solstice, St. Petersburg puts on concerts, film festivals, all-night boat tours, and other events to celebrate the northern light. It's peak tourist season.

November 7: Day of Reconciliation and Accord. For 70 years this was called Revolution Day, marking the 1917 events that brought the Soviets to power. The post-Soviet government didn't have the heart to take away the holiday, so they renamed it. A dwindling number of Communist die-hards still gather around Red Square, visiting Lenin's tomb and lamenting the demise of his brainchild.

December 12: Constitution Day. Marks the 1993 referendum that approved Russia's first post-Soviet constitution.

Last week in December: White Days Festival (St. Petersburg). The city boosters' efforts to lure tourists during the snowy months, this festival includes winter carnivals in the city parks and a dense program of dance, opera, and orchestral performances. See www.whitedays.ru for more information.

Moscow's Average Temperatures

	Jan	Feb	Mar	Apr	May	June	July	Aug	Sept	Oct	Nov	Dec
Temp (°F)	10	14	25	41	55	61	66	63	55	43	32	16
Temp (°C)	−12	−10	−4	5	13	16	19	17	13	6	0	−9

St. Petersburg's Average Temperatures

	Jan	Feb	Mar	Apr	May	June	July	Aug	Sept	Oct	Nov	Dec
Temp (°F)	14	18	25	39	54	59	66	63	54	43	32	19
Temp (°C)	−10	−8	−4	4	12	15	19	17	12	6	0	−7

4 Travel Insurance

Check your existing insurance policies and credit card coverage before you buy travel insurance. You may already be covered for lost luggage, canceled tickets, or medical expenses. The cost of travel insurance varies widely, depending on the cost and length of your trip, your age and health, and the type of trip you're taking, but expect to pay between 5% and 8% of the vacation itself.

TRIP-CANCELLATION INSURANCE Trip-cancellation insurance helps you get your money back if you have to back out of a trip, if you have to go home early, or if your travel supplier goes bankrupt. Allowed reasons for cancellation can range from sickness to natural disasters to the State Department declaring your destination unsafe for travel. (Insurers usually won't cover vague fears, though, as many travelers discovered who tried to cancel their trips in Oct 2001 because they were wary of flying.) In this unstable world, trip-cancellation insurance is a good buy if you're getting tickets well in advance—who knows what the state of the world, or of your airline, will be in 9 months? Insurance policy details vary, so read the fine print—and make sure that your airline or cruise line is on the list of carriers covered in case of bankruptcy. A good resource is **"Travel Guard Alerts,"** a list of companies considered high-risk by Travel Guard International (see website below). Protect yourself further by paying for the insurance with a credit card—by law, consumers can get your money back on goods and services not received if you report the loss within 60 days after the charge is listed on your credit card statement.

Note: Many tour operators, particularly those offering trips to remote or high-risk areas, include insurance in the cost of the trip or can arrange insurance policies through a partnering provider, a convenient and often cost-effective way for the traveler to obtain insurance. Make sure the tour company is a reputable one, however: Some experts suggest you avoid buying insurance from the tour or cruise company you're traveling with, saying it's better to buy from a "third party" insurer than to put all your money in one place.

For more information, contact one of the following recommended insurers: **Access America** (© 866/807-3982; www.accessamerica.com); **Travel Guard International** (© 800/826-4919; www.travelguard.com); **Travel Insured International** (© 800/243-3174; www.travelinsured.com); or **Travelex Insurance Services** (© 888/457-4602; www.travelex-insurance.com).

MEDICAL INSURANCE For travel overseas, most health plans (including Medicare and Medicaid) do not provide coverage, and the ones that do often require you to pay for services upfront and reimburse you only after you return home. Even if your plan does cover overseas treatment, most Russian and other out-of-country hospitals make you pay your bills upfront, and send you a refund only after you've returned home and filed the necessary paperwork with your insurance company. As a safety net, you may want to buy travel medical insurance, particularly if you're traveling beyond Moscow and St. Petersburg to a remote or high-risk area of Russia where emergency evacuation is a possible scenario. If you require additional medical insurance, try **MEDEX Assistance** (© 410/453-6300; www.medexassist.com) or **Travel Assistance International** (© 800/821-2828; www.travelassistance.com; for general information on services, call the company's Worldwide Assistance Services, Inc., at © 800/777-8710).

LOST-LUGGAGE INSURANCE On domestic flights, checked baggage is covered up to $2,500 per ticketed passenger.

On international flights (including U.S. portions of international trips), baggage coverage is limited to approximately $9.07 per pound, up to approximately $635 per checked bag. If you plan to check items more valuable than the standard liability, see if your valuables are covered by your homeowner's policy, get baggage insurance as part of your comprehensive travel-insurance package, or buy Travel Guard's "BagTrak" product. Don't buy insurance at the airport, as it's usually overpriced. Be sure to take any valuables or irreplaceable items with you in your carry-on luggage, as many valuables (including books, money, and electronics) aren't covered by airline policies.

If your luggage is lost, immediately file a lost-luggage claim at the airport, detailing the luggage contents. For most airlines, you must report delayed, damaged, or lost baggage within 4 hours of arrival. The airlines are required to deliver luggage, once found, directly to your house or destination free of charge.

5 Health & Safety

STAYING HEALTHY

No vaccinations are necessary to visit Russia, though there have been cases of diphtheria and cholera in provincial areas in recent years, and tuberculosis is a major problem in prisons. Most visitors' biggest health challenges are digestive, either from St. Petersburg's bacteria-ridden water or dubiously prepared street food. Bottled water is cheap and widely available. HIV is a growing problem, and prevention and public information campaigns are sorely inadequate.

GENERAL AVAILABILITY OF HEALTH CARE

Soviet health care was universal and nearly free, though clinics were chronically short of equipment. State subsidies shriveled in the 1990s and shortages worsened; doctors remain dismally paid and depend heavily on bribes from patients. But competition is slowly emerging, and Moscow and St. Petersburg have several private clinics that offer high-standard care and English-speaking personnel, though at high prices.

Bring any prescriptions with you, and Imodium or other anti-diarrhea medication. All-night pharmacies are common in Moscow and St. Petersburg, and over-the-counter medications are easily available, though generics are rarer. Foreign brands are often of better quality and always more expensive than their Russian equivalents. For the bold, even penicillin and IUDs can be purchased without a prescription.

Tips   Tricks of Transliteration

Because the Russian language uses the Cyrillic alphabet, confusion often abounds when Russian names are translated—or more precisely, transliterated—into the Latin alphabet. There are several accepted systems for transliterating into English, as well as a French and German system. In this book we've stuck to the Revised American system, with a few exceptions made to aid pronunciation. Famous names such as Tchaikovsky and Gorbachev are spelled as they're most commonly known, not as they would be properly transliterated. See appendix B, at the back of this book, for the Russian spelling and pronunciation of several key words, phrases, place names, and menu items.

Contact the **International Association for Medical Assistance to Travelers (IAMAT;** © **716/754-4883,** or 416/652-0137 in Canada; www.iamat.org) for tips on travel and health concerns in the countries you're visiting, and for lists of local, English-speaking doctors. The United States **Centers for Disease Control and Prevention** (© **800/311-3435;** www.cdc.gov) provides up-to-date information on health hazards by region or by country and offers tips on food safety.

COMMON AILMENTS

DIETARY RED FLAGS Moscow's water is potable but can be risky for foreigners. St. Petersburg's water contains the bacteria *giardia lamblia* and should be avoided (beware of tooth-brushing and iced drinks). Many St. Petersburg hotels have their own water filtration system. Cheap bottled water is widely available. Avoid fried meat pies sold on the street and meat sold outdoors. Vegetarians are finding more and more options in Russia, mainly at restaurants that specialize in Japanese or American cuisine. However, nearly all restaurant soups are made with meat stock, and vegetable side dishes are often prepared in lard. Although Russia has substantial Muslim and Jewish minorities, very few restaurants cater to those with religious dietary restrictions.

RESPIRATORY ILLNESSES Tuberculosis, virtually wiped out by Soviet health campaigns, has resurfaced in recent years, largely among prison populations. The disease is treatable but some strains have grown resistant to standard medicines. Another respiratory challenge is air quality, which is dismal in most Russian cities. Fuel emissions are restricted but the restrictions are barely enforced.

EXTREME WEATHER EXPOSURE Though Russia is no doubt a cold place, most travelers do not spend enough time outdoors in the winter to risk hypothermia or its milder cousin, frostbite. Visitors engaging in a lot of outdoor winter activity should carry many layers of clothing and thermoses of warm liquid.

WHAT TO DO IF YOU GET SICK AWAY FROM HOME

Any foreign consulate can provide you with a list of area doctors who speak English. If you get sick, consider asking your hotel concierge to recommend a local doctor—even his or her own. You can also try the emergency room at a local hospital. Finding doctors or all-night pharmacies can be hard in Moscow and St. Petersburg if you know no Russian, and is much easier with a Russian helper or hotel concierge. You will pay as you go no matter where you seek help, and prices can vary from a few dollars in a public clinic for emergency care to hundreds of dollars in a private one. Foreigners are sometimes charged more just because they are assumed to have more money than Russians. See "Hospitals" and "Emergencies" in "Fast Facts: Moscow" (chapter 4) and "Fast Facts: St. Petersburg" (chapter 12).

If you suffer from a chronic illness, consult your doctor before your departure. For conditions like epilepsy, diabetes, or heart problems, wear a **MedicAlert identification tag** (© **888/633-4298;** www.medicalert.org), which will immediately alert doctors to your condition and give them access to your records through MedicAlert's 24-hour hot line.

Pack **prescription medications** in your carry-on luggage, and carry prescription medications in their original containers, with pharmacy labels—otherwise they won't make it through airport security. Also bring along copies of your prescriptions in case you lose your pills or run out. Don't forget an extra pair of contact lenses or prescription glasses. Carry the generic name of prescription medicines, in case a local pharmacist is unfamiliar with the brand name.

Avoiding "Economy Class Syndrome"

Deep vein thrombosis, or as it's know in the world of flying, "economy-class syndrome," is a blood clot that develops in a deep vein. It's a potentially deadly condition that can be caused by sitting in cramped conditions—such as an airplane cabin—for too long. During a flight (especially a long-haul flight), get up, walk around, and stretch your legs every 60 to 90 minutes to keep your blood flowing. Other preventative measures include frequent flexing of the legs while sitting, drinking lots of water, and avoiding alcohol and sleeping pills. If you have a history of deep vein thrombosis, heart disease, or another condition that puts you at high risk, some experts recommend wearing compression stockings or taking anticoagulants when you fly; always ask your physician about the best course for you. Symptoms of deep vein thrombosis include leg pain or swelling, or even shortness of breath.

6 Security Concerns

WHAT ABOUT TERRORISM?

This is a sadly pertinent question for travel almost anywhere in this post-9/11 world. Russia's experiences with terrorism date back to the 19th century, when revolutionary bombers assassinated Czar Alexander II. The source of more recent terrorist attacks has been the war in Chechnya, where a 10-year conflict between Russian troops and Chechen guerrillas has simmered for much of the decade. Two major terrorist attacks outside Chechnya in recent years—the Moscow theater siege in 2002 and the Beslan school massacre in 2004—terrified the world and hardened Russian opposition to the Chechen cause. With no end to the conflict in sight, the Chechen problem will continue to cast a shadow over Russia's post-Soviet progress.

The provinces in the northern Caucasus Mountains neighboring Chechnya are at the most risk of spillover violence that could affect tourists. Moscow, 1,000km (600 miles) to the north, is sheltered from everyday Chechnya-related violence, but as the seat of Russia's government, it is at risk of rare attacks like the theater siege. Like terrorist acts in other European cities, these are nearly impossible to predict and avoid. Most experts judge the terrorism risk in Moscow as no higher than in other major capitals, though if an attack occurs, Russian security services are likely to handle it more ruthlessly than their European counterparts would. St. Petersburg is considered largely free of any terrorism risk.

See the U.S. State Department's Advisory website www.travel.state.gov for recent warnings, though be aware that they tend to be more alarmist than the travel advisories posted by other governments. If you notice a suspicious abandoned bag on the metro or in a public place, report it to the nearest metro official or police officer.

STAYING SAFE

The notorious Russian "mafia" made for good movie villains in the 1990s, but its reputation is rather exaggerated and it is not a serious threat to foreign visitors. The victims of most crimes are Russian millionaires and powerful tycoons who have much more to lose than the average American tourist. Pickpockets and over-friendly drunks are the main annoyances to today's traveler; both can be avoided by being alert, traveling in groups, and sticking to well-lit areas after dark. Prostitution and drug use are illegal but widespread, and not worth a run-in with the Russian police. Drunk-driving laws are strict, forbidding drivers from having even one drink, but traffic police readily accept payoffs for overlooking minor infractions.

DEALING WITH DISCRIMINATION

The Soviet Union was one of the most ethnically diverse places on the planet, and Russia is still home to hundreds of nationalities. Few Russians can claim to be 100% Slavic, after centuries of mingling with people of Turkic, Nordic, and Mongol blood. However, the two wars in Chechnya over the past decade have fueled a blanket suspicion of anyone from the Caucasus region, and there have been sporadic incidents of skinhead violence against ethnic minorities in recent years, especially immediately following a terrorist attack. Foreigners with "southern" features—dark eyes and hair and olive skin—can occasionally suffer reluctant service and suspicious looks, unless it's clear that you're a tourist and not a terrorist. Africans from fellow socialist states were welcomed in the Soviet era, but periodic waves of nationalist sentiment in the post-Soviet era have resulted in backlashes against anyone with black skin. Tourists rarely suffer from this hostility, especially those traveling in groups.

Most Russians are eager to criticize the U.S. government for something, but the comments are purely political—a way of making conversation and demonstrating their knowledge of world events, as opposed to a personal attack. Most interlocutors are happy to talk to a foreigner about current events, even if your views differ, and you'll find pro-Western sentiment is as common as anti-Western sentiment.

7 Specialized Travel Resources

TRAVELERS WITH DISABILITIES

Most disabilities shouldn't stop anyone from traveling. There are more options and resources out there than ever before. That said, Russia remains a formidable destination for anyone in a wheelchair. Only the biggest and priciest hotels and restaurants are accessible. Many of Moscow's wide streets can only be crossed underground without ramps. Even some tourist destinations that claim to be accessible have a few stairs leading up to the cash desk, or into the church. Call every place you plan to visit before you go and be sure they can accommodate you.

Many travel agencies offer customized tours and itineraries for travelers with disabilities. **Access-Able Travel Source** (© **303/232-2979;** www.access-able.com) offers extensive access information and advice for those traveling around the world with disabilities. **Avis Rent a Car** has an "Avis Access" program that offers such services as a dedicated 24-hour toll-free number (© **888/879-4273**) for customers with special travel needs; special car features such as swivel seats, spinner knobs, and hand controls; and accessible bus service. Organizations that offer assistance to disabled travelers include **Moss-Rehab** (www.mossresourcenet.org), which provides a library of accessible-travel resources online; and **SATH** (Society for Accessible Travel & Hospitality; © **212/447-7284;** www.sath.org; annual membership fees: $45 adults, $30 seniors and students), which offers a wealth of travel resources for all types of disabilities and informed recommendations on destinations, access guides, travel agents, tour operators, vehicle rentals, and companion services.

GAY & LESBIAN TRAVELERS

Soviet statutes barring homosexual acts were at last lifted in 1993, and Russia's gays and lesbians have been celebrating

Chechnya

Chechnya is an uncomfortable subject, and objective information is nearly impossible to come by. Even calling the blood-spilling that goes on there daily a "war" can provoke hours of debate. The fate of this region in the Northern Caucasus Mountains is the most controversial subject in today's Russia—and in many ways, the most important.

Chechens make up one of nearly 100 ethnic groups with no relation to Slavic Russians scattered in the mountains and valleys of the Caucasus Mountains. Russians fought for dominance over the region for decades in the 18th and 19th century, and technically "won" in 1859, but Chechens in particular continued to bristle at Russian rule, and guerrilla bands repeatedly attacked Russian colonizers. During the Russian Revolution and ensuing civil war, the Bolsheviks won over many Chechens with promises of greater autonomy and religious freedom. These promises were quickly forgotten, however, and Chechens staged uprisings against Soviet rule.

Stalin was so panicked by Chechen hostility toward Moscow that he accused the entire Chechen population of collaborating with the Nazis, and in a fit of paranoia and despotism, exiled them all to concentration camps in Kazakhstan in 1944. They were allowed to return home only under Khrushchev's thaw 13 years later, to find Chechnya "Sovietized," with an ethnically diverse population, a university, and a busy airport. The Chechens assimilated back into their homeland, which was by then a province within the Russian Soviet Federated Socialist Republic. But the indignity of exile remains seminal in Chechens' modern memory, and pent-up rage over that and other Russian offenses simmered for decades. The late-1980s independence movements in other Soviet republics fueled the ambitions of a few Chechens, led by Dzhokhar Dudayev, to establish their own sovereign state. But Chechnya remained a republic within Russia when the Soviet Union collapsed. Dudayev encouraged resistance against Russian police, and amid increasing violence in the region, Boris Yeltsin ordered troops into Chechnya in December 1994.

Neither side seemed ready for what happened next. The Russian army turned out to be so demoralized and financially crippled that its troops succumbed in battle after battle to ragtag Chechen bands. The Russian populace

ever since. Still, Russia's conservative society remains suspicious of same-sex couples, and openly gay public figures remain rare, outside the performing arts. Russian women, regardless of sexual preference, often hold hands and embrace in public, but public intimacy between gay men can provoke taunts or worse. Gay-friendly venues, including clubs, restaurants, business groups, and public pick-up spots, are numerous in Moscow and St. Petersburg.

The website www.gay.ru is a solid starting place for gay and lesbian visitors to Russia, with accommodations suggestions and extensive club listings. **The International Gay and Lesbian Travel Association (IGLTA; © 800/448-8550** or 954/776-2626; www.iglta.org) is the trade association for the gay and lesbian travel industry, and offers an online directory of gay- and lesbian-friendly travel businesses; go to their website and click was horrified by the war and the deaths of underfed, underpaid teenage conscripts in pointless firefights. Even Dudayev's death in 1996 didn't improve the Russian forces' lot, and in August that year the two sides signed a peace deal allowing Chechnya greater autonomy. Yet the Chechens proved unprepared to govern themselves, and the republic sank into lawlessness. Reconstruction funds were blatantly embezzled, and kidnapping for ransom became the engine of the Chechen economy (in addition to siphoning oil from pipelines leading out of the Caspian Sea). No outsider dared enter the region, whether federal official, journalist, or aid worker.

In August 1999, Chechen bands raided the neighboring Russian republic of Dagestan and seized several villages, pledging to create a regionwide Islamic state. Soon afterward, apartment bombings in Moscow and two other cities killed 300 civilians and terrified the nation. Yeltsin sent troops back to Chechnya, and his new prime minister, Vladimir Putin, successfully "sold" the war to the Russian people, who by then were eager for determined leadership and an end to Chechen crime and terrorism. Putin's popularity soared amid early successes for Russian troops, and within months he had replaced Yeltsin as president.

And the war rages on. Chechnya's remaining warlords continue to stage terrorist attacks on civilian targets, including the hostage-taking in a Moscow theater in 2002 and the seizure of a school in Beslan in 2004, both of which left scores of dead. Such attacks only strengthen Russian resolve against peace talks. The Chechens' funding, which appears steady, is believed to come from various Islamic groups. A decade ago most Chechens were casual in their observance of Islamic custom, but the war has changed that. Many now sport long beards, forgo alcohol, and adhere to sharia law.

The Kremlin has claimed for years that Chechnya is "normalized," but Russian police and the Chechens who cooperate with them are killed daily in guerrilla raids on mountain roads, and Chechen families suffer routine torture in Russian "cleanup operations" on villages thought to harbor rebels. International pressure has failed to get Putin to rethink his Chechnya policy, especially in this era of worldwide terrorism.

on "Members." *Out and About* (© 800/929-2268; www.outandabout.com) offers guidebooks and a newsletter ($20 per year; 10 issues) packed with solid information on the global gay and lesbian scene. *Gay Travel A to Z: The World of Gay & Lesbian Travel Options at Your Fingertips* by Marianne Ferrari (Ferrari International; Box 35575, Phoenix, AZ 85069) is a very good gay and lesbian guidebook series.

SENIOR TRAVEL

Russians have great respect for their elders, but the country's modern history has been brutal to them, wiping out their savings, shriveling the value of their pensions, and leaving them without cheap health care just when they need it most. Russians over 60 qualify for discounts everywhere, including reduced admission on public transport and to many museums and other attractions. However, many tourist sites offer this discount only to Russians, and charge all foreigners a separate, inflated price. Also note that Russian sightseeing requires a lot of walking and ubiquitous stairs.

Mention the fact that you're a senior when you make your travel reservations. Many hotels still offer discounts for seniors. **INTRAV** (© **800/456-8100;** www. intrav.com) is a high-end tour operator that caters to the mature, discerning traveler, not specifically seniors, with trips around the world that include guided safaris, polar expeditions, private-jet adventures, and small-boat cruises down jungle rivers. Recommended publications offering travel resources and discounts for seniors include: the quarterly magazine *Travel 50 & Beyond* (www.travel50and beyond.com); *Travel Unlimited: Uncommon Adventures for the Mature Traveler* (Avalon); *101 Tips for Mature Travelers,* available from Grand Circle Travel (© **800/221-2610** or 617/350-7500; www. gct.com); and *Unbelievably Good Deals and Great Adventures That You Absolutely Can't Get Unless You're Over 50* (McGraw-Hill), by Joann Rattner Heilman.

FAMILY TRAVEL

Russia can be a daunting place with kids but an unforgettable experience for them. A major challenge is the Cyrillic alphabet—but you can turn that it to a family game by setting out to learn its 33 letters together (many are the same as in English), and then sounding out street signs together ("Look, PECTOPAH means restaurant!"). Travel with small children is difficult, since few restaurants have high chairs, and nothing is stroller-friendly—even the pharmacies have steps and unwieldy doors. Because Russians travel infrequently with their children, there are few hotels with specifically kid-friendly services, though that doesn't mean they're hostile to families. Also be prepared for unsolicited child-rearing advice from well-meaning Russian grandmothers, who always seem to think that children are underdressed no matter what the temperature. Russian **circuses** are world-renowned, and the **Moscow Zoo** (p. 138) and **Gorky Park** (p. 134) are good family destinations. There are several puppet theaters in Moscow and St. Petersburg.

Recommended family travel Internet sites include **Family Travel Forum** (www. familytravelforum.com), which offers customized trip planning and advice for Moscow and St. Petersburg; **Traveling Internationally with Your Kids** (www. travelwithyourkids.com), a comprehensive site offering sound advice for long-distance and international travel with children; and **Family Travel Files** (www. thefamilytravelfiles.com), which offers an online magazine and a directory of off-the-beaten-path tours and tour operators for families, including Russian destinations.

WOMEN TRAVELERS

There are no restrictions on women's travel or activity in Russia. Soviet planners succeeded at employing women in every sector of the economy, but failed to change traditional views on gender. As a result, Russian women go to work all day *and* do all the cooking, cleaning, child care, and shopping. Russian men retain traditions such as opening doors for women, carrying women's bags (even strangers'), and picking up the check when in a restaurant or bar. Women traveling alone should be careful walking the streets at night, as you could be mistaken for a prostitute or otherwise hassled. Check out the award-winning website **Journeywoman** (www.journey woman.com), a "real life" women's travel information network where you can sign up for a free e-mail newsletter and get advice on everything from etiquette and dress to safety; or look through the travel guide **Safety and Security for Women Who Travel** by Sheila Swan and Peter Laufer (Travelers' Tales, Inc.), which offers common-sense tips on safe travel.

8 Planning Your Trip Online

SURFING FOR AIRFARES

Cheap fares to Russia can be found, but the choice is limited by the relatively small number of carriers that serve the country. None of the major low-cost carriers do, and the only U.S. airline that flies into Russia is Delta, with flights to Moscow and St. Petersburg. Few Russian airlines fly international routes other than Aeroflot, which serves several U.S. and European cities. Most visitors use the major European airlines such as British Airways, Air France, or KLM.

The "big three" online travel agencies, **Expedia.com, Travelocity.com,** and **Orbitz.com,** sell most of the air tickets purchased on the Internet. (Canadian travelers should try Expedia.ca and Travelocity.ca; U.K. residents can go for Expedia.co.uk and Opodo.co.uk.) Each has different business deals with the airlines and may offer different fares on the same flights, so it's wise to shop around. Expedia and Travelocity will also send you **e-mail notification** when a cheap fare becomes available to your favorite destination. Of the smaller travel agency websites, **SideStep** (www.sidestep.com) has gotten the best reviews from Frommer's authors. It's a browser add-on that purports to "search 140 sites at once," but in reality only beats competitors' fares as often as other sites do.

Also remember to check **airline websites.** Even with major airlines, you can often shave a few bucks from a fare by booking directly through the airline and avoiding a travel agency's transaction fee. But you'll get these discounts only by **booking online:** Most airlines now offer online-only fares that even their phone agents know nothing about.

Great **last-minute deals** are available through free weekly e-mail services provided directly by the airlines. Most of these are announced on Tuesday or Wednesday and must be purchased online. Most are only valid for travel that weekend, but some (such as Southwest's) can be booked weeks or months in advance. Sign up for weekly e-mail alerts at airline websites or check mega-sites that compile comprehensive lists of last-minute specials, such as **Smarter Travel** (www.smartertravel. com). For last-minute trips, **site59.com** and **lastminutetravel.com** in the U.S. and **lastminute.com** in Europe, often have better air-and-hotel package deals than the major-label sites. A website listing numerous bargain sites and airlines around the world is **www.itravelnet.com**.

If you're willing to give up some control over your flight details, use what is called an **"opaque" fare service** like **Priceline** (www.priceline.com; www. priceline.co.uk for Europeans) or its smaller competitor **Hotwire** (www.hotwire. com). Both offer rock-bottom prices in exchange for travel on a "mystery airline" at a mysterious time of day, often with a mysterious change of planes en route. The mystery airlines are all major, well-known carriers—and the possibility of being sent from Philadelphia to Chicago via Tampa is remote; the airlines' routing computers have gotten a lot better than they used to be. But your chances of getting a 6am or 11pm flight are pretty high. Hotwire tells you flight prices before you buy; Priceline usually has better deals than Hotwire, but you have to play their "name our price" game. If you're new at this, the helpful folks at **BiddingFor-Travel** (www.biddingfortravel.com) do a good job of demystifying Priceline's prices and strategies. Priceline and Hotwire are great for flights within North America and between the U.S. and Europe. But for flights to other parts of the world, consolidators will almost always beat their fares. *Note:* In 2004 Priceline added non-opaque service to its

Surfing the "Ru-net" Before You Go

Soviet programmers created their own interactive "web" back in the 1980s, and today's Runet (*roo*-net), as the Russian-language Internet world calls itself, is as vibrant as any online community. More and more Russian sites have English-language pages, and below are a few worth checking out before you go. The sometimes clumsy translations are compensated for by the information and guidance. And, of course, don't forget www.frommers.com, especially the advice from other travelers on the Russia destination forum.

Museums

- **www.hermitagemuseum.org:** Official site of Hermitage Museum, good for planning your visit to the museum ahead of time.

- **www.rusmuseum.ru:** Site of St. Petersburg's Russian Museum, a good introduction to Russian art.

- **www.tretyakov.ru:** Site of Moscow's Tretyakov Gallery, another good introduction to Russian art.

- **www.kremlin.ru/eng:** Official Kremlin website, with history of the Kremlin complex itself and excerpts from President Vladimir Putin's daily schedule.

News

- **www.themoscowtimes.com:** Site of English-language daily newspaper *The Moscow Times*. News, weather, exchange rates, entertainment, and restaurant listings.

- **www.sptimes.ru:** Site of English-language semiweekly paper *The St. Petersburg Times*.

- **www.cdi.org/russia/johnson/default.cfm:** Johnson's Russia List is a compilation of articles and commentary about Russia from the English-language and Russian press, updated daily.

- **www.exile.ru:** Best known for its thorough, audacious listings on Moscow nightlife and for its caustic, often X-rated commentary on Russian society.

Listings/General Information

- **www.ru:** Calls itself "original Russian Web directory." Information-packed and searchable in English, but rather unwieldy.

- **www.infoservices.com:** The Travelers' Yellow Pages for Moscow and St. Petersburg, with searchable telephone and address listings in English, including nearest metro station and opening hours.

- **www.waytorussia.net:** Company offering advice and listings, aimed at expatriates in Russia but useful for tourists, too.

roster. You now have the option to pick exact flights, times, and airlines from a list of offers—or opt to bid on opaque fares as before.

SURFING FOR HOTELS

Shopping online for hotels is generally done one of two ways: by booking through the hotel's own website, or by booking

- **www.expat.ru:** Forum for English-speaking expats, mostly in Moscow.

- **www.cheap-moscow.com:** Irreverent site with tips on how to live in Moscow on little money.

- **www.eng.menu.ru:** Moscow restaurant reviews and listings, most but not all in English.

- **www.cityguide.spb.ru:** Site of the *City Guide,* an English-Russian quarterly available at St. Petersburg hotels and restaurants.

Airlines/Airports

- **www.aeroflot.com:** Site of Russian airline Aeroflot, with schedules and fares.

- **www.transaero.ru/english:** Site of airline Transaero.

- **http://eng.pulkovo.ru:** Site of St. Petersburg's Pulkovo International Airport, with updated flight information.

- **www.sheremetevo-airport.ru:** Site of Moscow's Sheremetevo International Airport.

Visa Information:

- **www.russianembassy.org:** Site of Russian Embassy in the United States, with visa applications and information and links to embassies and consulates in other countries.

- **www.myrussianvisa.com:** U.S. company that arranges invitations for travelers not with a group.

- **www.visatorussia.com:** Can issue invitations for travelers from nearly any country in the world. (*Note:* Fees for visa invitations—sometimes called "visa support"—are **in addition** to the fees you must pay the embassy for the visa itself.)

Maps:

- **www.infoservices.com/moscow/map/index.html:** Maps of Moscow neighborhoods and sights.

- **http://www.infoservices.com/stpete/map/index.html:** Maps of St. Petersburg neighborhoods and sights.

- **www.yell.ru/map:** Interactive maps of Moscow and St. Petersburg.

Images:

- **www.ivan.ru:** Photos of Moscow sights with amusing commentary.

- **www.livecam.spb.ru:** Webcam of St. Petersburg sights.

through an independent hotel agency (or a fare-service agency like Priceline; see below). These Internet hotel agencies have multiplied in mind-boggling numbers of late, competing for the business of millions of consumers surfing for accommodations around the world. This competitiveness can be a boon to consumers who have the patience and time to shop and compare the online sites for good deals—but shop you must, because prices can vary considerably from site to site. And keep in mind that hotels at the top of a site's listing may be there for no other reason than that they paid money to get the placement.

Three Russian-specialty sites to try are www.hotels-russia.net, www.bnb.ru, and www.waytorussia.net. Of the "big three" sites, **Expedia** offers a long list of special deals and "virtual tours" or photos of available rooms so you can see what you're paying for (a feature that helps counter the claims that the best rooms are often held back from bargain-booking websites). **Travelocity** posts unvarnished customer reviews and ranks its properties according to the AAA rating system. Also reliable are **Hotels.com** and **Quikbook.com.** An excellent free program, **TravelAxe** (www.travelaxe.net), can help you search multiple hotel sites at once, even ones you may never have heard of—and conveniently lists the total price of the room, including the taxes and service charges. Another booking site, **Travelweb** (www.travelweb), is partly owned by the hotels it represents (including the Hilton, Hyatt, and Starwood chains) and is therefore plugged directly into the hotels' reservations systems—unlike independent online agencies, which have to fax or e-mail reservation requests to the hotel, a good portion of

which get misplaced in the shuffle. More than once, travelers have arrived at the hotel, only to be told that they have no reservation. To be fair, many of the major sites are undergoing improvements in service and ease of use, and Expedia will soon be able to plug directly into the reservations systems of many hotel chains—none of which can be bad news for consumers. In the meantime, it's a good idea to **get a confirmation number** and **make a printout** of any online booking transaction.

In the opaque website category, **Priceline** and **Hotwire** are even better for hotels than for airfares; with both, you're allowed to pick the neighborhood and quality level of your hotel before offering up your money. Priceline's hotel product also covers Europe and Asia, though it's much better at getting five-star lodging for three-star prices than at finding anything at the bottom of the scale. On the downside, many hotels stick Priceline guests in their least desirable rooms. Be sure to go to the BiddingForTravel website (see above) before bidding on a hotel room on Priceline; it features a fairly up-to-date list of hotels that Priceline uses in major cities. For both Priceline and Hotwire, you pay upfront, and the fee is nonrefundable. *Note:* Some hotels do not provide loyalty program credits or points or other frequent-stay amenities when you book a room through opaque online services.

9 The 21st-Century Traveler

INTERNET ACCESS AWAY FROM HOME

Travelers have any number of ways to check e-mail and access the Internet on the road. Of course, using your own laptop, PDA (personal digital assistant), or electronic organizer with a modem gives you the most flexibility. If you don't have a computer, you can still access your e-mail and your office computer from cybercafes.

WITHOUT YOUR OWN COMPUTER

In Moscow and St. Petersburg, cybercafes are concentrated around the tourist attractions such as the Kremlin and Nevsky Prospekt. Russian **public libraries** often offer Internet access free or for a small charge. Avoid **hotel business centers** unless you're willing to pay exorbitant rates. For a listing of cybercafes around the world, see www.cybercaptive.com and www.cybercafe.com. For specific suggestions, see "Fast Facts: Moscow" (chapter 4) and "Fast Facts: St. Petersburg" (chapter 12).

WITH YOUR OWN COMPUTER

Wi-Fi (wireless fidelity) is the buzzword in computer access, and more and more hotels, cafes, and retailers are signing on as wireless "hot spots" from where you can get high-speed connection without cable wires, networking hardware, or a phone line. You can get Wi-Fi connection one of several ways. Many laptops sold in the last year have built-in Wi-Fi capability (an 802.11b wireless Ethernet connection). Mac owners have their own networking technology, Apple AirPort. For those with older computers, an 802.11b/**Wi-Fi card** (around $50) can be plugged into your laptop. You sign up for wireless access service much as you do for cellphone service, through a plan offered by one of several commercial companies that have made wireless service available in airports, hotel lobbies, and coffee shops, primarily in the U.S. (followed by the U.K. and Japan). **Boingo** (www. boingo.com) and **Wayport** (www.wayport. com) have set up networks in airports and high-class hotel lobbies. iPass providers (see below) also give you access to a few hundred wireless hotel lobby setups. Best of all, you don't need to be staying at the Four Seasons to use the hotel's network; set yourself up on a nice couch in the lobby. The companies' pricing policies can be byzantine, with a variety of monthly, per-connection, and per-minute plans, but in general you pay around $30 per month for limited access—and as more and more companies jump on the wireless bandwagon, prices are likely to get even more competitive. The site http://www.wayto russia.net/Practicalities/Business/Internet. html lists spots in Moscow and St. Petersburg with Wi-Fi access.

In addition, major Internet Service Providers (ISP) have **local access numbers** around the world, allowing you to go online by simply placing a local call. Check your ISP's website or call its toll-free number and ask how you can use your current account away from home, and how much it will cost.

If you're traveling outside the reach of your ISP, the **iPass** network has dial-up numbers in most of the world's countries. You'll have to sign up with an iPass provider, who will then tell you how to set up your computer for your destination(s). For a list of iPass providers, go to www.ipass.com and click on "Individual Purchase." One solid provider is **i2roam** (© **866/811-6209** or 920/235-0475; www.i2roam.com).

Wherever you go, bring a **connection kit** of the right power as well as phone adapters, a spare phone cord, and a spare Ethernet network cable—or find out whether your hotel supplies them to guests.

Electric current in Russia is 220 volts (as opposed to 110 volts in the United States), and older hotels will require a five-pronged Russian phone adapter, available in Russian hardware stores or from hotel staff. Newer hotels will have standard phone jacks.

USING A CELLPHONE

The three letters that define much of the world's **wireless capabilities** are GSM (Global System for Mobiles), a big, seamless network that makes for easy cross-border cellphone use throughout Europe and dozens of other countries worldwide. In the U.S., T-Mobile, AT&T Wireless, and Cingular use this quasi-universal system; in Canada, Microcell and some Rogers customers use GSM, and all Europeans and most Australians use GSM.

If your cellphone is on a GSM system, and you have a world-capable multiband phone such as many Sony Ericsson, Motorola, or Samsung models, you can make and receive calls across civilized areas on much of the globe, from Andorra to Uganda. Call your wireless operator and ask for "international roaming" to be activated on your account. Unfortunately, per-minute charges can be high—usually $1 to $1.50 in western Europe and up to $5 in places like Russia and Indonesia.

That's why it's important to buy an "unlocked" world phone from the get-go. Many cellphone operators sell "locked" phones that restrict you from using any other removable computer memory phone chip card (called a **SIM card**) other than the ones they supply. Having an unlocked phone allows you to install a cheap, prepaid SIM card (found at a local retailer) in Russia. (Show your phone to the salesperson; not all phones work on all networks.) You'll get a local phone number—and much, much lower calling rates. Getting an already locked phone unlocked can be a complicated process, but it can be done; call your cellular operator and say you'll be going abroad for several months and want to use the phone with a local provider.

For many, **renting** a phone is a good idea. Renting a cellphone is possible in Moscow and St. Petersburg but not in smaller cities (try www.go-russia.com for more information). Rates run from $12 to $20 per day and at least $50 per week; all incoming calls and local outgoing calls cost about 20¢ to 30¢ per minute, and outgoing international calls cost from 50¢ to $2 per minute.

Russia's major cellphone companies (both in Moscow) are **MTS** (© 095/766-0177; www.mts.ru) and Bee-Line (© 095/974-8888; www.beeline.ru).

You can also rent phones before you leave home. That way you can give loved ones and business associates your new number, make sure the phone works, and take the phone wherever you go—especially helpful for overseas trips through

several countries, where local phone-rental agencies often bill in local currency and may not let you take the phone to another country. Phone rental isn't cheap. You'll usually pay $40 to $50 per week, plus airtime fees of at least a dollar a minute. Shop around.

Two good wireless rental companies are **InTouch USA** (© 800/872-7626; www.intouchglobal.com) and **RoadPost** (© 888/290-1606 or 905/272-5665; www.roadpost.com). Give them your itinerary, and they'll tell you what wireless products you need. InTouch will also, for free, advise you on whether your existing phone will work overseas; call © 703/222-7161 between 9am and 4pm EST, or go to http://intouchglobal.com/travel.htm.

For trips of more than a few weeks spent in one country, **buying a phone** becomes economically attractive, as Russia and many other countries have cheap, no-questions-asked prepaid phone systems. Once you arrive at your destination, stop by a local cellphone shop and get the cheapest package; you'll probably pay less than $100 for a phone and a starter calling card. Local calls may be as low as 10¢ per minute, and with some Russian providers incoming calls are free.

True wilderness adventurers, or those heading to less-developed areas of Russia, should consider renting a **satellite phone** ("satphone"), which is different from a cellphone in that it connects to a satellite rather than to a ground-based tower. A satphone is more costly than a cellphone but works where there's no cellular signal and no towers. You can rent satellite phones from **RoadPost** (© 888/290-1606 or 905/272-5665; www.roadpost.com). InTouch USA (see above) offers a wider range of satphones but at higher rates. Per-minute call charges can be even cheaper than roaming charges with a regular cellphone, but the phone itself is more expensive (up to $150 a week) and, depending on the service you choose, people calling you may incur high long-distance charges. At press time, satphones are amazingly expensive, so purchasing one isn't a realistic option for most travelers.

Online Traveler's Toolbox

Veteran travelers usually carry some essential items to make their trips easier. Following is a selection of handy online tools to bookmark and use.

- **Airplane Seating & Food.** Find out which seats to reserve and which to avoid (and more) on all major domestic airlines at www.seatguru.com. And check out the type of meal (with photos) you'll likely be served on airlines around the world at www.airlinemeals.com.
- **Foreign Languages for Travelers** (www.travlang.com). Learn basic terms in more than 70 languages and click on any underlined phrase to hear what it sounds like.
- **Intellicast** (www.intellicast.com) and **Weather.com** (www.weather.com). Both give weather forecasts for all 50 states and for cities around the world.
- **Mapquest** (www.mapquest.com). This best of the mapping sites lets you choose a specific address or destination and, in seconds, it will return a map and detailed directions.
- **Subway Navigator** (www.subwaynavigator). Download subway maps and get savvy advice on using subway systems in dozens of major cities around the world, including Moscow.
- **Time & Date** (www.timeanddate.com). See what time (and day) it is anywhere in the world.
- **Travel Warnings** (http://travel.state.gov/travel_warnings.html, www.fco. gov.uk/travel, www.voyage.gc.ca, www.dfat.gov.au/consular/advice). These sites report on places where health concerns or unrest might threaten American, British, Canadian, and Australian travelers. Generally, U.S. warnings are the most paranoid; Australian warnings are the most relaxed.
- **Universal Currency Converter** (www.xe.com/ucc). See what your dollar or pound is worth in more than 100 other countries.
- **Visa ATM Locator** (www.visa.com), for locations of PLUS ATMs worldwide, or **MasterCard ATM Locator** (www.mastercard.com), for locations of Cirrus ATMs worldwide.
- **Weekly Events** (www.themoscowtimes.com, www.sptimesrussia.com, russiatravel-pdtours.netfirms.com). *The Moscow Times* and its sister paper *The St. Petersburg Times* have comprehensive listings of music, art, dance, and theater events, as well as restaurant reviews and unusual museum exhibits. Patriarshy Dom offers listings of its English-language tours.
- **Expat Advice** (www.expat.ru). See what Moscow's English-speaking expatriates are up to, or ask them for advice before you go.

10 Getting There

BY PLANE

Russia's chief international carrier remains Aeroflot, the former Soviet behemoth. Delta is the only major U.S. airline that flies into Russia, though all major European carriers serve Moscow and St. Petersburg. You can often find good deals through British Airways, Air France, and KLM. For a cheaper option, try the Eastern European airlines, such as Poland's LOT, or Hungary's Malév; or Asian carriers such as Air India that use Moscow as a fueling stop. Moscow's Sheremetevo-2 airport is the main port of entry for international flights and is in need of a facelift. Be prepared for lengthy waits to go through passport control. The much more pleasant Domodedovo airport has been recently renovated and is starting to lure some European carriers. St. Petersburg's Pulkovo-2 airport is where international flights to that city land, and is friendlier than Sheremetevo but still has a Soviet-era feel.

For contact information for these and other airlines flying to and from Moscow and/or St. Petersburg, see Appendix C.

For internal flights in Russia, such as between Moscow and St. Petersburg, the luggage weight limit is 20 kilograms (44 lb.); sometimes carry-ons are weighed as well. Above that weight, you'll have to pay a fee, usually at a separate cash desk apart from the check-in counter.

For advice on getting into town from the airports, see "Arriving" in chapter 4 and "Arriving" in chapter 12.

GETTING THROUGH THE AIRPORT

With the federalization of airport security, security procedures at U.S. airports are more stable and consistent than ever. Generally, you'll be fine if you arrive at the airport **1 hour** before a domestic flight and **2 hours** before an international flight; if you show up late, tell an airline employee and she'll probably whisk you to the front of the line.

Bring a **current, government-issued photo ID** such as a driver's license or passport. Keep your ID at the ready to show at check-in, the security checkpoint, and sometimes even the gate. (Children under 18 do not need government-issued photo IDs for domestic flights, but they do for international flights to most countries.)

In 2003, the Transport Security Administration (TSA) phased out **gate check-in** at all U.S. airports. And **e-tickets** have made paper tickets nearly obsolete. Passengers with e-tickets can beat the ticket-counter lines by using airport **electronic kiosks** or even **online check-in** from your home computer. Online check-in involves logging on to your airline's website, accessing your reservation, and printing out your boarding pass—and the airline may even offer you bonus miles to do so! If you're using a kiosk at the airport, bring the credit card you used to book the ticket, or bring your frequent-flier card. Print out your boarding pass from the kiosk and proceed to the security checkpoint with your pass and a photo ID. If you're checking bags or looking to snag an exit-row seat, you will be able to do so using most airline kiosks. Even the smaller airlines are employing the kiosk system, but always call your airline to make sure these alternatives are available. **Curbside check-in** is also a good way to avoid lines, although a few airlines still ban it; call before you go.

Security checkpoint lines are getting shorter than they were during 2001 and 2002, but some nasty ones remain. If you have trouble standing for long periods of time, tell an airline employee; the airline will provide a wheelchair. Speed up security by **not wearing metal objects** such as big belt buckles. If you've got metallic body parts, a note from your doctor can prevent a long chat with the security screeners. Keep in mind that only **ticketed passengers** are allowed past security, except for people escorting disabled passengers or children.

Federalization and globalization have stabilized **what you can carry on** and **what you can't.** The general rule is that sharp things are out, nail clippers are okay, and food and beverages must be passed through the X-ray machine—but that security screeners can't make you drink from your coffee cup. Bring food in your carry-on rather than checking it, as explosive-detection machines used on checked luggage have been known to mistake food (especially chocolate, for some reason) for bombs. Travelers in the U.S. are allowed one carry-on bag, plus a "personal item" such as a purse, briefcase, or laptop bag. Carry-on hoarders can stuff all sorts of things into a laptop bag; as long as it has a laptop in it, it's still considered a personal item. The TSA has issued a list of restricted items; check its website (www.tsa.gov/public/index.jsp) for details.

Airport screeners may decide that your checked luggage needs to be searched by hand. You can now purchase luggage locks that allow screeners to open and re-lock a checked bag if hand-searching is necessary. Look for Travel Sentry certified locks at luggage or travel shops and Brookstone stores (you can buy them online at www.brookstone.com). These locks, approved by the TSA, can be opened by luggage inspectors with a special code or key. For more information on the locks, visit www.travelsentry.org. If you use something other than TSA-approved locks, your lock will be cut off your suitcase if a TSA agent needs to hand-search your luggage.

FLYING FOR LESS: TIPS FOR GETTING THE BEST AIRFARE

Passengers sharing the same airplane cabin rarely pay the same fare. Travelers who need to purchase tickets at the last minute, change their itinerary at a moment's notice, or fly one-way, often get stuck paying the premium rate. Here are some ways to keep your airfare costs down.

- Passengers who can book your ticket **long in advance,** who can **stay over Saturday night,** or who **fly midweek** or at **less-trafficked hours** may pay a fraction of the full fare. If your schedule is flexible, say so, and ask if you can secure a cheaper fare by changing your flight plans.
- You can also save on airfares by keeping an eye out in local newspapers for **promotional specials** or **fare wars,** when airlines lower prices on their most popular routes. You rarely see fare wars offered for peak travel times, but if you can travel in the off-months, you may snag a bargain.
- Search **the Internet** for cheap fares (see the section "Planning Your Trip Online," earlier in this chapter).
- Try to book a ticket **in its country of origin.** For instance, if you're planning a one-way flight from Bombay to Moscow, an India-based travel agent will probably have the lowest fares. For multi-leg trips, book in the country of the first leg; for example, book New York–London–Amsterdam–Moscow–New York in the U.S.
- **Consolidators,** also known as bucket shops, are great sources of international tickets. Start by looking in Sunday newspaper travel sections; U.S. travelers should focus on the *New York Times, Los Angeles Times,* and *Miami Herald.* For less-developed destinations, small travel agents who cater to immigrant communities in large cities often have the best deals. *Beware:* Bucket shop tickets are usually nonrefundable or rigged with stiff cancellation penalties, often as high as 50% to 75% of the ticket

price, and some put you on charter airlines, which may leave at inconvenient times and experience delays. Several reliable consolidators operate worldwide and are available on the Net. **STA Travel** is now the world's leader in student travel, thanks to their purchase of Council Travel. It also offers good fares for travelers of all ages. **FlyCheap** (© **800/FLY-CHEAP;** www.1800flycheap.com) is owned by package-holiday megalith MyTravel and so has especially good access to fares for sunny destinations. **Air Tickets Direct** (© **800/778-3447;** www.airticketsdirect.com) is based in Montreal and leverages the currently weak Canadian dollar for low fares; it'll also book trips to places that U.S. travel agents won't touch, such as Cuba.

- Join **frequent-flier clubs.** Accrue enough miles, and you'll be rewarded with free flights and elite status. It's free, and you'll get the best choice of seats, faster response to phone inquiries, and prompter service if your luggage is stolen, your flight is canceled or delayed, or if you want to change your seat. You don't need to fly to build frequent-flier miles—**frequent-flier credit cards** can provide thousands of miles for doing your everyday shopping.

LONG-HAUL FLIGHTS: HOW TO STAY COMFORTABLE

Long flights can be trying; stuffy air and cramped seats can make you feel as if you're being sent parcel post in a small box. But with a little advance planning, you can make an otherwise unpleasant experience almost bearable.

- Your choice of airline and airplane will definitely affect your legroom. Find more details at www.seatguru. com, which has extensive details about almost every seat on six major U.S. airlines. For international airlines, research firm Skytrax has posted a list of average seat pitches at www.airlinequality.com.

- Emergency-exit seats and bulkhead seats typically have the most legroom. Emergency-exit seats are usually held back to be assigned on the day of a flight (to ensure that the seat is filled by someone able-bodied); it's worth getting to the ticket counter early to snag one of these spots for a long flight. Many passengers find that bulkhead seating (the row facing the wall at the front of the cabin) offers more legroom, but keep in mind that bulkheads are where airlines often put baby bassinets, so you may be sitting next to an infant. *Note:* At press time, some airlines had begun charging extra for emergency-row seating.

Travel in the Age of Bankruptcy

Airlines go bankrupt, so protect yourself by **buying your tickets with a credit card**—the U.S. Fair Credit Billing Act guarantees that you can get your money back from the credit card company if a travel supplier goes under (and if you request the refund within 60 days of the bankruptcy). **Travel insurance** can also help, but make sure it covers "carrier default" for your specific travel provider. And be aware that if a U.S. airline goes bust mid-trip, a 2001 federal law requires other carriers to take you to your destination (albeit on a space-available basis) for a fee of no more than $25, provided you rebook within 60 days of the cancellation.

Coping with Jet Lag

Jet lag is a pitfall of traveling across time zones. If you're flying north-south and you feel sluggish when you touch down, your symptoms will be caused by dehydration and the general stress of air travel. When you travel east to west or vice versa, however, your body becomes thoroughly confused about what time it is, and everything from your digestion to your brain gets knocked for a loop. Traveling east, say, from Chicago to Paris, is more diffi-cult on your internal clock than traveling west, say from Atlanta to Hawaii, as most peoples' bodies find it more acceptable to stay up late than to fall asleep early.

Here are some tips for combating jet lag:

- **Reset your watch** to your destination time before you board the plane.
- **Drink lots of water** before, during, and after your flight. Avoid alcohol.
- **Exercise and sleep well** for a few days before your trip.
- If you have trouble sleeping on planes, **fly eastward on morning flights.**
- **Daylight** is the key to resetting your body clock. At the website for **Out-side In** (www.bodyclock.com), you can get a customized plan of when to seek and avoid light.
- If you need help getting to sleep earlier than you usually would, some doctors recommend taking either the hormone **melatonin** or the sleeping pill **Ambien**—but not together. Some recommend that you take 2 to 5 mil-ligrams of melatonin about 2 hours before your planned bedtime—but again, always check with your doctor on the best course of action for you.

Call ahead to find out if the airline you are flying has instituted this practice.

- To have two seats for yourself in a three-seat row, try for an aisle seat in a center section toward the back of coach. If you're traveling with a com-panion, book an aisle and a window seat. Middle seats are usually booked last, so chances are good you'll end up with three seats to yourselves. And in the event that a third passenger is assigned the middle seat, he or she will probably be more than happy to trade for a window or an aisle.
- Ask about entertainment options. Many airlines offer seatback video systems that let you choose movies or play video games—but only on some of their planes. (Boeing 777s are your best bet.)

- To sleep, avoid the last row of any section or a row in front of an emer-gency exit, as these seats are the least likely to recline. Avoid seats near highly trafficked toilet areas. Avoid seats in the back of many jets—these can be more narrow than those in the rest of coach class. You also may want to reserve a window seat so that you can rest your head and avoid being bumped in the aisle.
- Get up, walk around, and stretch every 60 to 90 minutes to keep your blood flowing. This helps avoid **deep vein thrombosis,** or "economy-class syndrome," a potentially deadly con-dition that can be caused by sitting in cramped conditions for too long. Other preventative measures include drinking lots of water and avoiding

alcohol (see next bullet). See the "Avoiding 'Economy Class Syndrome'" box under "Health & Safety," earlier in this chapter.

- Drink water before, during, and after your flight to combat the lack of humidity in airplane cabins—which can be drier than the Sahara. Bring a bottle of water on board. Avoid alcohol, which will dehydrate you.

- If you're flying with kids, don't forget to carry on toys, books, pacifiers, and chewing gum to help them relieve ear pressure buildup during ascent and descent. Let each child pack his or her own backpack with favorite toys.

BY TRAIN

Rail travel into and around Russia is romantic and often comfortable, but time-consuming. The most direct train route from London to Moscow, for example, takes 48 hours. Be prepared for a lengthy wait at Russia's borders while the wheels are changed to fit the wider eastern tracks. Customs procedures are unpredictable on trains, sometimes messier but sometimes smoother than in airports. If you're traveling through Belarus, you will need a transit visa; contact your nearest Belarusian embassy or consulate for details.

Flying with Film & Video

Never pack film—developed or undeveloped—in checked bags, as the new, more powerful scanners in U.S. airports can fog film. The film you carry with you can be damaged by scanners as well. X-ray damage is cumulative; the faster the film, and the more times you put it through a scanner, the more likely the damage. Film under 800 ASA is usually safe for up to five scans. If you're taking your film through additional scans, U.S. regulations permit you to demand hand inspections. In international airports, you're at the mercy of airport officials. On international flights, store your film in transparent baggies, so you can remove it easily before you go through scanners. Keep in mind that airports are not the only places where your camera may be scanned: Highly trafficked attractions are X-raying visitors' bags with increasing frequency.

Most photo supply stores sell protective pouches designed to block damaging X-rays. The pouches fit both film and loaded cameras. They should protect your film in checked baggage, but they also may raise alarms and result in a hand inspection.

You'll have little to worry about if you are traveling with **digital cameras**. Unlike film, which is sensitive to light, the digital camera and storage cards are not affected by airport X-rays, according to Nikon. Still, if you plan to travel extensively, you may want to play it safe and hand-carry your digital equipment or ask that it be inspected by hand.

Carry-on scanners will not damage **videotape** in video cameras, but the magnetic fields emitted by the walk-through security gateways and handheld inspection wands will. Always place your loaded camcorder on the screening conveyor belt or have it hand-inspected. Be sure your batteries are charged, as you may be required to turn the device on to ensure that it is what it appears to be.

Tips **Important Visa Information**

Passengers who participate in St. Petersburg shore excursions or arrange for private transportation through the ship's shore-excursions desk (see "Coming Ashore & Getting Around," below) do not need to obtain a visa.

Those who wish to go ashore on their own, however, do have to obtain a tourist visa prior to departure. To receive a Russian visa, you must have a valid passport that remains valid at least 30 days past the last day of the cruise. For more information on obtaining a visa, see "Entry Requirements & Customs," earlier in this chapter.

For details on what to do upon arrival, see the "Orientation" section in chapter 4 for Moscow, or in chapter 12 for St. Petersburg.

BY CAR

Automobile transport is Russia's least convenient mode of getting around, and the country's vast expanse makes arriving by car a daunting proposition. Roads outside central Moscow and St. Petersburg are dismal, signage is poor and often only in the Cyrillic alphabet, and roadside services—including gas stations—are extremely scarce. For the hardy who want to drive into Russia, be sure you have international documentation for the car, including registration, insurance, and an international driver's license. Your visa should be in order and should indicate you are bringing a car into the country. You must leave the country with the same car to avoid paying duties on it. Prepare for long waits at the borders, especially around holiday season, and have plenty of small bills ready for "fines" levied by traffic police along the way. You will need transit visas if you plan to cross Ukraine or Belarus. Renting a car once you arrive—or even better, a car with a driver—is a much more reliable and pleasant option.

BY BUS

Several European tour companies offer bus trips to Moscow, usually from Germany; or to St. Petersburg, usually from Finland. The journey from Berlin to Moscow is long, about 2 days, and involves poorly maintained Russian highways and long waits at the borders. You will need transit visas if you travel through Belarus, as most Moscow-bound routes go. The Helsinki-to-St. Petersburg journey takes about 7 hours and is often included on Scandinavian-based tours. For details on what to do when you arrive, see the "Orientation" section in chapter 4 for Moscow or in chapter 12 for St. Petersburg.

BY CRUISE SHIP

St. Petersburg, one-time capital of imperial Russia and the second-largest city in Russia, is the country's largest port. It's also become a popular cruise-ship destination. Shore excursions to St. Petersburg include visits to top sights like the Hermitage Museum, which has one of the richest art collections in the world (p. 234); the Peter & Paul Fortress, the burial place of the Romanov dynasty (p. 240); and St. Isaac's Cathedral, the fourth-largest cathedral in the world (p. 242). Cruise lines also typically offer nighttime shore excursions to see ballet, opera, folk performances, or circuses.

COMING ASHORE & GETTING AROUND

The main cruise terminal is about a 20-minute drive from the city center. Small ships can come right into town up the

Neva River, but you are still best off taking a **taxi**, especially at night. Official taxis are usually four-door Volvo sedans. Russia also has what is known as the "private" taxi. "Private," in this case, means virtually anyone can stop and pick you up, and you enter such a cab at your own risk (there have been robberies). If you want to tour the city without having to join a shore excursion, you are best off hiring a car, limo, or van with a **private guide.** Your cruise line shore-excursion desk will be able to arrange this for you. A private car with a guide will carry four passengers and cost about $375 for a half-day, $700 for a full day. Vans may also be available for bigger groups (you can get several couples together and save).

THE BEST SHORE EXCURSIONS

In addition to excursions to St. Petersburg, the cruise line may offer day trips to Moscow. The tours, including round-trip flights, run from about $615 to $675 per person.

City Tour (3–3½ hr.; $40–$55): This introductory tour includes a view of the Peter and Paul Fortress with its gilded spire; the cruiser *Aurora,* the ship that fired a blank round in 1917 that signaled the start of the October Revolution; and the Winter Palace, which houses the Hermitage. You will see the famous Bronze Horseman statue depicting the city's founder, Peter the Great; the exquisitely decorated Church of the Spilled Blood; and magnificent St. Isaac's Cathedral, one of the world's largest domed structures (it took 40 years to construct and was used as a museum under the Soviet regime; it's now an active church again). Some tours include a stop at 18th-century Smolny Convent, a crowning achievement of the renowned architect Rastrelli. Others include a stop

at the Summer Palace, a beautiful example of 18th-century architecture.

The Hermitage (3½–4 hr.; $56–$76): Take a short drive along the banks of the Neva River to the Winter Palace for a guided tour through parts of the vast Hermitage Art Museum. The former home of the imperial family, this 18th-century baroque palace and four adjacent buildings now house one of the most outstanding art collections in the world.

Peterhof (4 hr.; $50–$60): Drive 35km (22 miles) through the suburbs of St. Petersburg to Peterhof, the former summer home of Peter the Great, built to rival Versailles. Construction began 300 years ago and spanned 2 centuries. The massive estate encompasses seven parks and more than 20 smaller palaces and pavilions. Your guided tour will include the grand staircase and a walk through some of the palace's lavish rooms, as well as the grounds. The 120-hectare (300-acre) park and spectacular fountains, some 129 in total, were designed by Peter himself.

Pushkin (Tsarskoye Selo) (4 hr.; $45–$56): Drive 27km (17 miles) south of St. Petersburg to Pushkin (the village of Tsarskoye Selo was renamed Pushkin in 1937 after Russia's favorite poet, Alexander Pushkin) for a visit to the opulent summer residence of Catherine the Great. The estate was presented as a gift from Peter the Great to his wife in 1710 and was the main summer residence of the imperial family from Peter's reign until the fall of the monarchy in 1917. The palace was almost totally destroyed during World War II but has been magnificently restored to its former splendor. You'll take a guided tour of several lavish rooms, including the Great Blue Room, Picture Gallery, and Amber Room. The surrounding park features Italian-designed grounds with numerous marble statues.

11 Packages for the Independent Traveler

Before you start your search for the lowest airfare, you may want to consider booking your flight as part of a travel package. Package tours are not the same as escorted tours. Package tours are simply a way to buy the airfare, accommodations, and other elements of your trip (such as car rentals, airport transfers, and sometimes even activities) at the same time and often at discounted prices—kind of like one-stop shopping. Packages are sold in bulk to tour operators—who resell them to the public at a cost that usually undercuts standard rates.

A few tour companies to try are **Eastern Tours,** run by Russian émigrés and focusing on reasonably priced tours to Moscow, St. Petersburg, and Kiev (www.traveltorussia.com; © **800/339-6967**); and **Cosmos Tours,** which includes several Russian packages (© **800/276-1241;** www.cosmos.com). Be sure to read reviews of their tours by former clients on www.frommers.com or other independent websites.

One good source of package deals is the airlines themselves. Most major airlines offer air/land packages. Several big online travel agencies—Expedia, Travelocity, Orbitz, Site59, and Lastminute.com—also do a brisk business in packages. If you're unsure about the pedigree of a smaller packager, check with the Better Business Bureau in the city where the company is based, or go online at www.bbb.org. If a packager won't tell you where they're based, don't fly with them.

Many of the mainstream packagers haven't caught on to Russia yet, so the choices are more limited. Russia-based packages are cheaper but riskier than those

based in your home country; be sure to get as much insurance and guaranties as you can. Places to check include **Tour Vacations To Go** (© **800/680-2858;** www.tourvacationstogo.com) and **Budget Travel** (www.budgettravel.com). Russia-based agencies include **Russia Info-Center** (© **095/939-1605;** www.russia-ic.com); and **www.homestays.ru**, which offers high-end hotels as well as homestays.

Package tours can vary by leaps and bounds. Some offer a better class of hotels than others. Some offer the same hotels for lower prices. Some offer flights on scheduled airlines, while others book charters. Some limit your choice of accommodations and travel days. You are often required to make a large payment upfront. On the plus side, packages can save you money, offering group prices but allowing for independent travel. Some even let you add on a few guided excursions or escorted day trips (also at prices lower than if you booked them yourself) without booking an entirely escorted tour.

Before you invest in a package tour, get some answers. Ask about the **accommodations choices** and prices for each. Then look up the hotels' reviews in a guidebook and check their rates online for your specific dates of travel. You'll also want to find out what **type of room** you get. If you need a certain type of room, ask for it; don't take whatever is thrown your way. Request a nonsmoking room, a quiet room, a room with a view, or whatever you fancy.

Finally, look for **hidden expenses.** Ask whether airport departure fees and taxes, for example, are included in the total cost.

12 Escorted Tours

Russia's tourism industry is only beginning to tap the travel possibilities across the world's largest country. No roads exist

across much of the territory, and hotels and services in small towns are often little better than gulags. All this makes an escorted tour—with a group leader, including airfare, hotels, meals, admission costs, and local transportation—quite appealing. The chief benefit is that the tour company negotiates the hassle of getting a visa; it's also handy to have tour guides navigate museums and street signs labeled in Russian only. The main drawback of an escorted tour is its high cost.

For general-interest tours, **Escorted Russian Tours** (© **800/942-3301;** www.escortedrussiantours.com) provides a range of offerings focusing on Moscow and St. Petersburg, as do the U.K.-based **Russian Gateway** (© **07050-803-160;** www.russiangateway.co.uk) and the Russian-based **www.tourstorussia.com**.

Several special-interest trips are also available, such as the "World War II Battlefield" tour, "Opera" tour, and "Silk Road" tours offered through **www.biztravel.com**. One popular excursion is a **cruise from St. Petersburg to Moscow.** It takes your boat about 10 days to wind through rivers and canals, with stops at the island monastery at Valaam, the fairy tale–like wooden village of Kizhi, lakes Ladoga and Onega, and the Volga river towns of Yaroslavl and Kostroma. **Russian Tours** (www.rustours.com) and **Russiana** (www.russiana.co.uk) are two places to start.

BEFORE YOU BOOK

Many people derive a certain ease and security from escorted trips. Escorted tours—whether by bus, motorcoach, train, or boat—let travelers sit back and enjoy your trip without spending lots of time behind the wheel or worrying about details. You know your costs upfront, and there are few surprises. Escorted tours can take you to the maximum number of sights in the minimum amount of time with the least amount of hassle—you don't have to sweat over the plotting and planning of a vacation schedule. Escorted tours are particularly convenient for people with limited mobility. They can also be a great way to make new friends.

On the downside, an escorted tour often requires a big deposit upfront, and lodging and dining choices are predetermined. You'll get little opportunity for serendipitous interactions with locals. The tours can be jam-packed with activities, leaving little room for individual sightseeing, whim, or adventure—plus they often focus only on the heavily touristed sites, so you miss out on the lesser-known gems.

Before you invest in an escorted tour, ask about the **cancellation policy:** Is a deposit required? Can the company cancel the trip if it doesn't get enough people? Do you get a refund if the company cancels? If *you* cancel? How late can you cancel if you are unable to go? When do you pay in full? *Note:* If you choose an escorted tour, think strongly about purchasing trip-cancellation insurance, especially if the tour operator asks you to pay upfront. See the section on "Travel Insurance" earlier in this chapter.

You'll also want to get a complete **schedule** of the trip to find out how much sightseeing is planned each day and whether enough time has been allotted for relaxing or wandering solo.

The **size** of the group is important to know upfront. Generally, the smaller the group, the more flexible the itinerary, and the less time you'll spend waiting for people to get on and off the bus. Find out the **demographics** of the group as well. What is the age range? What is the gender breakdown? Is this mostly a trip for couples or singles?

Discuss what is included in the **price.** You may have to pay for transportation to and from the airport. A box lunch may be included in an excursion, but drinks might cost extra. Tips may not be included. Find out if you will be charged if you decide to opt out of certain activities or meals.

Before you invest in an escorted tour, get some answers. Ask about the **accommodations choices** and prices for each.

Then look up the hotels' reviews in a Frommer's guide and check their rates online for your specific dates of travel. You'll also want to find out what **type of room** you get. If you need a certain type of room, ask for it; don't take whatever is thrown your way. Request a nonsmoking room, a quiet room, a room with a view, or whatever you fancy.

Finally, if you plan to travel alone, you'll need to know if a **single supplement** will be charged and if the company can match you with a roommate.

13 Getting Around Russia

BY TRAIN

The most pleasant, romantic, and historic way to travel around Russia is by train. The Moscow–St. Petersburg route is the most frequented and best maintained. Travelers choose between a leisurely 8-hour night trip in a comfortable sleeping compartment (about $45 per person in a four-bed cabin; $85 per person in a two-bed cabin), and a 5-hour day trip (same price). A snack and beverages are included in the price, though you sometimes have to pay the conductor for the bed linens (about $2).

Trains from Moscow to St. Petersburg leave from Moscow's Leningradsky Station and arrive at St. Petersburg's Moskovsky Station. Both are in the center of town and easily accessible. Arranging train tickets before you arrive, for example through your travel agent at home, is the safest way to go, but is often more expensive. Most hotels can arrange train tickets to major cities. It is cheaper to buy from the train stations themselves, though the lines are chaotic and interminable.

Commuter trains (called *elektrichki*) with hard benches and rock-bottom prices serve many of the country estates and other sights just outside the big cities.

BY PLANE

Given Russia's size, plane travel is crucial for reaching more distant destinations such as Lake Baikal or Vladivostok. The Russian airlines Aeroflot and Pulkovo dominate the Moscow–St. Petersburg route, and prices for a one-way ticket run $60 to $100.

Flights on this route are nearly all on large, sturdy Soviet-era jets (not the flimsy twin-propeller Soviet planes that crash with alarming frequency), and although the upholstery is badly outdated, the service is steadily improving. See www.aeroflot.ru, www.pulkovo.ru, or www.eastline-tour.ru.

BY CAR

If you're not on a tour bus, renting a car can be a reasonable way to get around Moscow or St. Petersburg. However, a strongly recommended alternative is to rent a car with a driver. It can cost no more than a standard rental, and you don't have to worry about the challenges presented by Russian driving. Roads are riddled with holes, signage is often poor, gas stations and services are sparse. Russian drivers are ruthless, especially with the indecisive. Moscow's traffic is overwhelming much of the day, and traffic police are hostile to anyone behind the wheel and rely heavily on on-the-spot "fines" for their incomes. Most sidewalks or walkways are fair game for parking, and there are very few parking garages. Knowledge of the Cyrillic alphabet is strongly recommended for anyone driving in Russia, in order to decipher street signs.

For rental without a driver, see Avis (www.avis.com), Hertz (www.hertz.com), or Europcar (www.europcar.com). For cars with drivers, try www.moscow-taxi.com.

BY BUS

Russian-run tourist buses offer day trips to cities on the Golden Ring outside Moscow and several sights around St.

Petersburg, and are generally comfortable. Vendors often hawk tours on loudspeakers at central spots such as St. Petersburg's Nevsky Prospekt metro station and Moscow's Red Square. Otherwise, hotels can often arrange bus tours.

14 Tips on Accommodations

Hotel options in Russia have come a long way from the days of the state agency Intourist's monopoly on serving foreigners, but the country still has far too few mid-range hotel rooms to satisfy demand. Luxury chains were quick to recognize this new market and opened several top-class hotels in the 1990s, some opting for renovating elegant old hotels while others started from scratch. The most active chains in the luxury market are Marriott, InterContinental, Radisson, Sheraton, and Renaissance (now part of the Marriott chain). Holiday Inn (now part of the InterContinental hotel group) and Best Western have also entered the scene with somewhat cheaper offerings.

Even the highest-end locations sometimes offer deep discounts through online or traditional travel agencies or their own websites, up to 60% off the official or "rack" rate. It definitely pays to shop around. Most package tours rely on well-established Soviet-era hotels, usually enormous, architecturally bleak buildings offering the key services tourists need but with limited enthusiasm. The good news is that several of these hotels are renovating one floor at a time, and the increased price for the new rooms is usually well worth the fresh plumbing and improved service.

The best Russian hotel development in recent years is the flowering of the "mini-hotel" market in St. Petersburg. Dozens of hotels of 12 to 30 rooms have opened up, often occupying a few renovated floors of an apartment building. Most are centrally located and inexpensive, and offer eager, individual service that the big hotels lack. Unfortunately, Moscow's powerful hotel industry has kept this phenomenon largely at bay in the capital.

Hostels and traditional bed-and-breakfasts are rare though growing. Several companies rent out furnished apartments at rates much lower than the hotel rates. Quality varies widely, with some offering warm and helpful English-speaking hosts, others offering daily maid service and hotel-style assistance, and still others offering nothing but a key. Get the opinions of previous guests through websites such as www.frommers.com or www.virtual tourist.com before booking.

Russian hotels tend to be emptier in winter and busier in summer, especially around St. Petersburg's White Nights festival from late June to early July. Rates usually reflect this. Be aware of any big festivals or holiday events that might fill up hotels (see the "Calendar of Events" earlier in this chapter for guidance).

Neither Moscow nor St. Petersburg offers an official reservations service, and your chances of just showing up and getting a room are slim, even in hostels. You are strongly recommended to reserve in advance by phone or online; the cost is usually lower that way as well. Another advantage of reserving ahead is that most hotels will arrange for your visa, and register it once you arrive (see "Entry Requirements & Customs" earlier in this chapter).

Hotels often have "floor monitors" employed round-the-clock who in the Soviet era often acted as KGB informers; now they're basically nosy chambermaids and sometimes they'll make guests tea.

Russia's star-rating system is only gradually adjusting to the international standard and is an unreliable source of judging quality.

BED & BREAKFASTS, HOMESTAYS & APARTMENT RENTAL

Opting for less conventional accommodations can inject your trip with individuality and flexibility—or it could tangle you in scams and unfulfilled promises. If you choose wisely, these three options can offer comfort, charm, and a convenient location at a reasonable price. Be aware that they lack many of the security features and financial guarantees of big hotels, and that rates and quality vary widely.

Just because a Russian hotel calls itself a "bed-and-breakfast" doesn't mean it will look anything like what you'd expect. Russian tourism gurus have taken the term to mean just about anything: an upscale urban hotel, a room in a student dormitory, a spotless apartment serviced by a real estate agency, or a cramped room in a family's apartment vacated just for the duration of your stay. There is no single body regulating who or what can call itself a B&B. The website www.bnb.ru, for example, is a portal for Russian accommodations of any category, from high-end Marriott hotels to long-term real estate deals. The main thing to keep in mind is that in Moscow and St. Petersburg, bed-and-breakfasts are urban experiences, not village cottages with fruit fresh from the orchard. Russian B&Bs usually occupy a single apartment or a floor of an apartment building. Some were once communal apartments, with entire families sharing single rooms and the whole floor sharing a single bathroom and kitchen, but today they are entirely renovated and quite comfortable. To help you avoid misunderstanding, the reviews in chapters 5 ("Where to Stay in Moscow") and 13 ("Where to Stay in St. Petersburg") are as thorough as possible.

In St. Petersburg, you'll see lots of places advertised as **"mini-hotels."** These are often a renovated floor of an apartment building, and they offer more services than most bed-and-breakfasts but are less expensive and more intimate than the massive Soviet-era hotels most tour groups prefer.

Renting a **private apartment** for your stay is also popular, opening up more options in price and location than the hotel industry can. This is especially convenient during high seasons, such as the White Nights, when hotels fill up fast. The safest bet is to use a real estate agency that services the apartment and is available for assistance at all hours in case of emergency. Many individual apartment owners also advertise rentals online or hover around international airports and train stations, but most of these are risky propositions.

If you're seeking a closer look at day-to-day Russian existence, or want to learn or practice Russian, a **homestay** can be a good option. The ideal homestay is an apartment with a family history and a family member eager to tell you about it, as opposed to someone merely renting out a room for extra cash. Your room will probably be packed with the family's stuff, a library's worth of books, and a few generations' worth of knickknacks. Your host will clear out a shelf in the overstuffed closet for your belongings, but little more. The best way to determine what you're getting into is to call your hosts before you reserve, or at least before you pay. (This is also a good way to check how well they speak English.)

Note: With any of the above options, be sure to find out *before you reserve* whether they can arrange your **visa invitation.** If not, you'll need to find a reputable travel agency to take care of that for you, which could cost up to $100 more and takes at least 2 weeks.

In addition to the reviews in the "Where to Stay" chapters, the following companies can help you with less traditional accommodations.

Russian Travel Service (www.123russia.com): This service arranges homestays in St. Petersburg with English-speaking or Russian-only hosts. Rates start at $20 per night. They'll ask you about your animal and food allergies and arrange your visas.

Host Families Association (www.hofa.ru): This service arranges homestays in both Moscow and St. Petersburg, with either Russian or English-speaking hosts. Rates start at $25 per night.

City Realty (www.cityrealtyrussia.com): This company provides serviced apartments of all categories in Moscow and St. Petersburg, from $50 per night.

SAVING ON YOUR HOTEL ROOM

The **rack rate** is the maximum rate that a hotel charges for a room. Hardly anybody pays this price, however, except in high season or on holidays. To lower the cost of your room:

- **Ask about special rates or other discounts.** Always ask whether a room less expensive than the first one quoted is available, or whether any special rates apply to you. You may qualify for corporate, student, military, senior, or other discounts. Mention membership in AAA, AARP, frequent-flier programs, or trade unions, which may entitle you to special deals as well. Find out the hotel policy on children—do kids stay free in the room or is there a special rate?

- **Dial direct.** When booking a room in a chain hotel, you'll often get a better deal by calling the individual hotel's reservation desk rather than the chain's main number.

- **Book online.** Many hotels offer Internet-only discounts, or they supply rooms to Priceline, Hotwire, or Expedia at rates much lower than the ones you can get through the hotel itself. Shop around. And if you have special needs—a quiet room, a room

with a view—call the hotel directly and make your needs known after you've booked online.

- **Remember the law of supply and demand.** Resort hotels are most crowded and therefore most expensive on weekends, so discounts are usually available for midweek stays. Business hotels in downtown locations are busiest during the week, so you can expect big discounts over the weekend. Many hotels have high-season and low-season prices, and booking the day after "high season" ends can mean big discounts.

- **Look into group or long-stay discounts.** If you come as part of a large group, you should be able to negotiate a bargain rate, since the hotel can then guarantee occupancy in a number of rooms. Likewise, if you plan a long stay (at least 5 days), you might qualify for a discount. As a general rule, expect 1 night free after a 7-night stay.

- **Avoid excess charges and hidden costs.** When you book a room, ask whether the hotel charges for parking. Use your own cellphone, pay phones, or prepaid phone cards instead of dialing direct from hotel phones, which usually have exorbitant rates. And don't be tempted by the room's minibar offerings: Most hotels charge through the nose for water, soda, and snacks. Finally, ask about local taxes and service charges, which can increase the cost of a room by 15% or more. If a hotel insists upon tacking on a surprise "energy surcharge" that wasn't mentioned at check-in, or a "resort fee" for amenities you didn't use, you can often make a case for getting it removed.

- **Book an efficiency.** A room with a kitchenette allows you to shop for groceries and cook your own meals. This is a big money saver, especially for families on long stays.

LANDING THE BEST ROOM

Somebody has to get the best room in the house. It might as well be you. You can start by joining the hotel's frequent-guest program, which may make you eligible for upgrades. A hotel-branded credit card usually gives it owner "silver" or "gold" status in frequent-guest programs for free. Always ask about a corner room. They're often larger and quieter, with more windows and light, and they often cost the same as standard rooms. When you make your reservation, ask if the hotel is renovating; if it is, request a room away from the construction. Ask about nonsmoking rooms; rooms with views; rooms with twin, queen- or king-size beds. If you're a light sleeper, request a quiet room away from vending machines, elevators, restaurants, bars, and discos. Ask for a room that has been most recently renovated or redecorated.

If you aren't happy with your room when you arrive, ask for another one. Most lodgings will be willing to accommodate you.

15 Recommended Reading

Histories of Russia tend to be either murky or politicized, depending on prevailing world views at publication time. *The Icon and the Axe* by Library of Congress director James Billington is a broad and readable history. For a peek into czarist life that reads like historical fiction, try Robert Massie's lively *Peter the Great* and *Nicholas and Alexandra.* The most renowned reference on the Stalin era is Robert Conquest's *Great Terror,* and his very anti-Soviet *Reflections on a Ravaged Century* is based on decades of meticulous research for his numerous books. For a view from the other side, try Karl Marx's *Das Kapital,* which still provides food for thought even for the most die-hard capitalist. John Reed's *Ten Days That Shook the World* is an intricate report on the 1917 revolution by an American radical journalist, who is the only foreigner buried along the Kremlin wall. For a chilling account of the nearly 3-year siege of Leningrad by Hitler's army, Harrison Salisbury's *The 900 Days* is a must. *Moscow: An Architectural History* by Kathleen Berton gives insight into why St. Basil's Cathedral looks nothing like its contemporaries. Tamara Talbot Rice's *Concise History of Russian Art* is rather superficial but serves as a good introduction, covering early Kievan Rus up through the Soviet era.

Books about today's Russia tend to paint a bleak or sinister picture of its economic, political, and environmental prospects. David Remnick is one of the more optimistic observers in *Resurrection* and its predecessor, *Lenin's Tomb,* about the fall of the USSR. Prostitution, narcotics, organized crime, and corrupt judges are laid bare in *The Exile: Sex, Drugs and Libel in the New Russia* by Mark Ames and Matt Taibbi, founders of the weekly publication *eXile.*

Osip Mandelstam's *Noise of Time* portrays life in St. Petersburg in the early 20th century, before the author's persecution and death in 1938.

The long airline flight may be the perfect time to discover—or rediscover— Tolstoy and Dostoyevsky. Russia's world-famous authors plumb their nation's violent side and its ponderous one, bringing Russia alive through the icy battlefields of *War and Peace* and the foggy St. Petersburg canals of *Crime and Punishment.* Alexander Pushkin holds a dearer place in Russians' hearts, with his lyrical poems infused with love and dissent. The stories of Anton Chekhov and Nikolai Gogol are satires of the Russian

The Russian Silver Screen

An excellent way to prepare for your Russia trip would be to watch at least one movie from the Soviet era and one movie made since then. There are few better ways to glimpse how the country has changed over the past generation. Soviet filmmakers were heavily censored but free of commercial constrictions; post-Soviet filmmakers face the opposite problem, desperate for money but free to produce movies as political, tasteless, or shallow as the viewers will bear. The selection of Russian movies available abroad is limited, and those that are available are often too dense or tragic for Western audiences, but a few suggestions are listed below.

Russian film in the 20th century mirrored Russian politics more closely than any other medium. Vladimir Lenin quickly recognized the new "moving picture" as an excellent propaganda tool. But early filmmakers were crippled by the devastation to the country's basic infrastructure (including reliable electricity) wrought by World War I and the ensuing revolution and civil war, and by the loss of top performers and writers who fled abroad to escape the Communist regime. Eventually, a new artistic community emerged eager to define Soviet film as something more experimental than the commercial products coming out of capitalist America. Sergei Eisenstein was the most well-known of this group, and his *Battleship Potemkin*, released in 1925, became an international classic. Short propaganda films known as *agitki* were carried to towns and villages from Siberia to central Asia to advertise the wonders of modern technology—and by extension, of Soviet rule. Communist Party leaders became increasingly restrictive, however, and the 1930s and 1940s saw few artistic breakthroughs. The thaw under Khrushchev led to some internationally acclaimed films, but was followed by 2 more decades of stagnation under Brezhnev, an era dominated by bland dramas and goofy comedies. Gorbachev's *glasnost* produced some of the best Russian films to date, though most are pretty grim, reflecting the uncertain state of the USSR and the whole Communist experiment.

Russian film today is on the upswing, and movie selections look more and more like those in stable European countries: sci-fi blockbusters packed with special effects, psychological crime dramas, romantic teen comedies, and esoteric art films honored at international festivals. Russian animation—both for children and adults—has long been a strong genre that tends to be edgier than western animation, so if you have a chance to see some Russian animated shorts at a film festival near you, seize it.

sort, often more tragic than comical, and their descriptions of aristocratic feasts are as delectable and voluminous as the meals they depict.

For a taste of 21st-century Russia, turn to Viktor Pelevin, an irreverent author of novels such as *Generation P* and *Buddha's Little Finger* with a cynical yet giddy

A few favorite Soviet films:

The Cranes Fly (Letyat Zhuravli), 1957: Tale of a musician who goes to war, and the romantic turmoil he leaves behind.

Ballad of a Soldier (Ballada o Soldate), 1959: Tender and heartbreaking account of a soldier on leave in the few days before he's killed in World War II.

Solaris, 1972: Psychological science fiction journey by Andrei Tarkovsky; remade by Hollywood in 2003.

Seventeen Instants of Spring (Semnadstat Mgnovenii Vesny), 1973: Tale of a Soviet spy in wartime Germany carefully balancing his dual identity; Stirlitz became a hero and anti-hero for Soviet jokes for decades.

Moscow Doesn't Believe in Tears (Moskva Slezam ne Verit), 1979: Bittersweet tale of three young women from small towns who arrive in Moscow to pursue their dreams.

Nostalgia, 1984: Soviet-Italian chronicle of a couple's relationship, one of the most accessible films of Andrei Tarkovsky.

Repentance (Pokoyaniye), 1987: Surreal and tragicomic saga of Stalinist repression in his homeland of Georgia, suppressed by censors for years.

Little Vera (Verochka), 1988: Account of a young woman's coming of age amid the social drift, shortages, and alcoholism in provincial Gorbachev-era Russia.

And post-Soviet Russian films:

Burnt by the Sun (Utomlyonnoye Solntsem), 1994: Oscar-winning account of a sun-kissed summer and the cold-blooded, Stalin-era secret police.

Prisoner of the Caucasus (Kavkazky Plennik), 1996: Moving, nuanced portrait of Russians and Chechens during the first Chechnya War.

East-West (Vostok-Zapad), 1999: Russian-French film about a Russian-French couple whose marriage and lives fall apart after they're lured back to Stalin's repressive Soviet Union.

The Wedding (Svadba), 2000: Painfully authentic drama about small-town romance and limited opportunity.

Nightwatch (Nochnoi Dozor), 2003: Big-budget thriller featuring vampires, darkness, and strong special effects.

view of the future and the past. Tatyana Tolstaya's essays on the political and personal offer insights from a Russian well-acquainted with the West. Boris Akunin has garnered a mass following among Russians with his series of well-crafted detective novels set at various times in Russian history, starting with *Azazel.*

3

Suggested Moscow Itineraries

Moscow's grand scale means that any good glimpse of the city requires a fair amount of travel, but these itineraries aim to keep the walking and metro- or car-riding to a minimum. When touring on your own, bear in mind the travel time between sights or neighborhoods. The tours below seek to balance the massive with the cozy, the modern with the ancient, and give a sense of what makes Moscow sizzle.

1 The Best of Moscow in 1 Day

Capturing Moscow in one day means hitting Red Square early and branching out from there. Bring good walking shoes and as much energy as you can muster. This itinerary takes you inside the Kremlin walls, gives you a glance at bustling Tverskaya Street, and leaves you the evening to explore the artsy Arbat neighborhood. *Note:* Try to do this tour on a day when the Kremlin is open (it's closed on Thurs). Otherwise, use those extra morning hours for wandering the Kitai-Gorod neighborhood on the other side of Red Square (see "The Neighborhoods in Brief" in chapter 4). *Start: Metro to Ploshchad Revolutsii, Okhotny Ryad, Alexandrovsky Sad, or Teatralnaya—then head to Red Square.*

❶ Red Square (Krasnaya Ploshchad) ✦✦✦

The city and country spread out from this sloping plaza, whose "red" ("kras-naya") label has nothing to do with the Communists, but dates from the Middle Ages, when the word meant "beautiful." For the full effect, enter the square from the Resurrection Gates, directly south of Tverskaya Street. Though the gates date only from the 1990s, they provide a stunning frame for the square. Sunrise over Red Square is particularly breathtaking. Soviet founder Vladimir Lenin lies embalmed in the mausoleum on the west side of the square, despite his wish to be buried.

❷ St. Basil's Cathedral (Khram Vasiliya Blazhennogo) ✦✦✦

No trip to Red Square is complete without a peek inside this onion-domed landmark that has formed the backdrop for "Live From Moscow" international TV spots for decades. The interior of the 16th-century church has little in common with its famous and festive exterior; dark and narrow passages wind up steep stairs to mystical, musty chapels and nooks. See p. 123 for details.

❸ The Kremlin ✦✦✦

This citadel ringed by red brick walls and towers has been the seat of Russian power for most of the past millennium. Some of its grounds and five of its cathedrals are

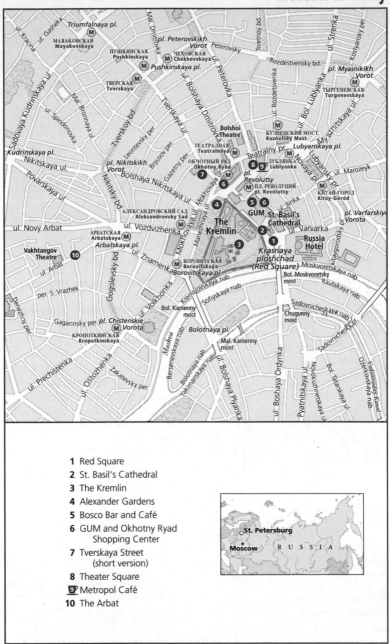

1 Red Square

2 St. Basil's Cathedral

3 The Kremlin

4 Alexander Gardens

5 Bosco Bar and Café

6 GUM and Okhotny Ryad
   Shopping Center

7 Tverskaya Street
   (short version)

8 Theater Square

9 Metropol Café

10 The Arbat

open to tourists, along with the collections of czarist treasures in the Armory and the Diamond Fund. The tourist entrance is on the north side of the Kremlin, at the Borovitsky Gates. Lines are rarely long, but allow at least 2 hours for the Kremlin experience just in case. The president's offices are off limits, but you may see a motorcade or two pass through the gates during your visit. See "The Kremlin" in chapter 7 for more information.

❹ Alexander Gardens (Alexandrovsky Sad)

After you emerge from the Kremlin, take some time to rest on a bench or wander through the greenery of Alexander Gardens, which run along the fortress's north wall. This used to be a river that helped protect the fortress from invaders, but in the 19th century it was filled in. Nearer to Red Square is the Tomb of the Unknown Soldier, a solemn spot where veterans and newlyweds often pay tribute. The cities listed around the tomb are those honored for their valiance and suffering during World War II.

> **❺ BOSCO CAFÉ AND BAR** ☞
>
> The employees are too gorgeous to be true and know it; ignore them and enjoy the view on Red Square instead. The bold design and comfy couches of this cafe inside the GUM department store are key parts of its appeal. Try the exotic salads or rich ice cream. Portions are delicate, so if you've worked up a good appetite, try the less romantic but heartier options in the Okhotny Ryad shopping center (see next stop). GUM, 3 Red Square; ✆ **095/927-3703.** See p. 102 for a full review.

❻ GUM & Okhotny Ryad Shopping Center

For shoppers and non-shoppers alike, these Russian "trading centers" deserve a look. GUM (p. 154), which stands for State Department Store (even though it's now a capitalist paradise), is the ornate

building that runs the full west side of Red Square. The 19th-century gallery boasts footbridges and skylights and a full array of international luxury brands. The Okhotny Ryad shopping center (p. 155) extends three floors underneath the plaza just north of Red Square. Less than a decade old, it houses shops with prices to fit all pocketbooks, as well as several cafes.

❼ Tverskaya Street (short version)

Even if you don't have time to explore the length of Tverskaya Street, you can afford a quick stroll up the first block of this crucial Moscow artery, which extends straight north from Red Square. At the top of the first block, turn around and take in the view of the Kremlin and everything else you've seen so far.

❽ Theater Square (Teatralnaya Ploshchad)

West of Tverskaya Street, along Okhotny Ryad, you'll first pass the State Duma (the lower house of parliament). Then the unforgettable facade of the Bolshoi Theater comes into view. Its pale pink portico is once again under renovation—as is its repertoire. If you can't squeeze in a performance, at least take a look at the miniature version of the theater's interior on display near the ticket office. For a reminder of the not-so-distant Soviet past, look across the fountained plaza in front of the Bolshoi at the statue across the street: It's Karl Marx, etched with the phrase PRO-LETARIAT OF THE WORLD UNITE.

> **❾ METROPOL CAFÉ** ☞☞
>
> For a quick pick-me-up or leisurely snack, settle into one of the deep armchairs of this cafe in the 19th-century hotel landmark on Revolution Square. Atmosphere is key here, so take a moment to wander the hotel lobby to admire chandeliers and Art Nouveau designs. Desserts are divine and tea is served with a ceremonial touch of the imperial age. Metropol Hotel, 1/4 Teatralny Proyezd; ✆ **095/927-6040.**

⑩ The Arbat

Walk or take the metro from Ploshchad Revolutsii (behind the Engels statue) one stop to the Arbatskaya station. Follow the crowds and the kiosks and you'll end up at the Arbat, a pedestrian street packed with shops, cafes, bars, buskers, and street vendors. The souvenirs inside the shops are of better quality and usually have better prices than those outside. Sure, it's touristy, but locals love it, too. If you're feeling adventurous, explore the lanes that sprout from the Arbat; they once housed Russian literary and artistic giants. The Pushkin House near the other end of the street is a small museum, and the Vakhtangov Theater hosts drama, dance, and other performances. The Arbat is a perfect place to wrap up the day.

2 The Best of Moscow in 2 Days

Use your second day in Moscow to immerse yourself in Russian art at the Tretyakov Gallery, wander the canals of Zamoskvarechye, and explore the cathedrals and historic neighborhood of Kitai-Gorod. Reserve the evening for Pushkin Square and a fuller glimpse of Tverskaya Street, where you'll find more than enough dining and entertainment to keep you busy. *Note:* Make this a day when the Tretyakov is open (it's closed on Mon). *Start: Metro to Tretyakovskaya or Novokuznetskaya.*

① Tretyakov Gallery (Tretyakovskaya Galereya) 🎭🎭🎭

This treasure trove of Russian art traces the country's 1,200-year history, covering everything from the earliest Orthodox icons to the floating figures of Chagall and jarring images of socialist propaganda. The Vrubel Room is a haven of Art Nouveau whimsy; newcomers to works by this 19th-century artist never fail to be impressed. The guided tour in English is well worth it. See p. 131.

② Lavrushinsky Lane & Canal Fountains

This little pedestrian street heads north from the Tretyakov to a footbridge over the Vodootvodny Canal in a cozy part of town called Zamoskvarechye (see stop 4 on this tour). The Bolotnaya Square on the other side of the canal, with its statue of artist Ilya Repin, was a public execution site in the 16th and 17th centuries; now it's a favorite rest and play spot for local residents, within walking distance of major Moscow sights yet usually devoid of tourists.

> ③ **UNCLE VANYA** 🎭🎭
> Artsy and accessible, this restaurant has an extensive menu of Russian comfort food throughout the day. Try the hot and cold soups, the meat or fruit dumplings, or just a good pot of tea. It has no real relation to Chekhov's play of the same name, but its alphabet placemats and bookshelves give it a literary feel. 16 Pyatnitskaya Ulitsa (entrance in courtyard); ✆ 095/951-0586.

④ Zamoskvarechye (Land South of the Moscow River)

This awkward name applies to the hump of land across the river from the Kremlin, a neighborhood where Ivan the Terrible sent his best guards to live while fending off threats from the south. The one- and two-story architecture is uncluttered by office blocks and high-rises, making the area feel intimate and accessible even though it's at the center of modern Moscow. Pyatnitskaya Street boasts the most commerce, with plenty of cafes and some less touristy craft shops.

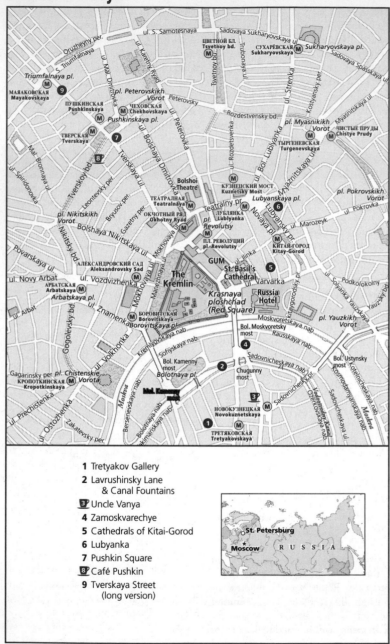

1 Tretyakov Gallery
2 Lavrushinsky Lane
  & Canal Fountains
3 Uncle Vanya
4 Zamoskvarechye
5 Cathedrals of Kitai-Gorod
6 Lubyanka
7 Pushkin Square
8 Café Pushkin
9 Tverskaya Street
  (long version)

⑤ Cathedrals of Kitai-Gorod

Heading back across the Bolshoi Moskvaretsky Bridge toward Red Square, you'll arrive at the neighborhood of Kitai-Gorod. Once a bustling community of traders and nobles, its top sights today are the churches and merchants' houses along Varvarka Street, a showcase of Russian architecture from the 15th to 17th centuries. The adjacent streets house government ministries and agencies. See the "Walking Tour" in chapter 7; the first five stops of the tour take you through the Kitai-Gorod neighborhood.

⑥ Lubyanka

No Russian responds indifferently to the dull yellow building overlooking Lubyanka Square—the headquarters of the KGB in Soviet times, and its successor, the FSB, today. Foreigners need not fret anymore, however. The imposing statue of Soviet secret police founder Felix Dzerzhinsky was torn down in 1991, and the KGB museum was even open to tourists for a while. The bald-looking plaza in front of the institution livens up a few times a year, when it hosts New Year's Eve concerts and other events. Take note of the small plaque off to the side of the square honoring those repressed by the Soviet regime (see stops 7 and 8 in chapter 7's "Walking Tour").

⑦ Pushkin Square (Pushkinskaya Ploshchad)

Alexander Pushkin is Russia's favorite poet, and even though he died in 1837, his likeness oversees Muscovites' favorite meeting spot. Though Pushkin Square throngs with activity all day, year-round, the statue of Pushkin himself retains an atmosphere of reverence. The McDonald's on the square was the world's largest when it opened in 1989, but it still wasn't big enough to accommodate the endless lines of people curious about the capitalist Big Mac. It's a good source of reliable restrooms. You can get here by taking the metro one stop from the Lubyanka to the Pushkinskaya station.

🍽 CAFE PUSHKIN 🐟🐟

This is a prime way to treat yourself after a long day, while remaining in the mood of bygone Russian aristocracy. A three-story, post-Soviet creation made to look a century older, this Russian restaurant has cuisine as elegant as it is satisfying. Dressed-up versions of Russian staples such as sturgeon and *bliny* share the menu with more innovative items such as shellfish and avocado salad. 26a Tverskoi Bulvar; ✆ 095/229-5590.

---

⑨ Tverskaya Street (long version)

Evening is a great time to experience Moscow's main drag in full. Wrought-iron street lamps, monstrous TV screens, and neon signs advertising a planet of international brands illuminate the dark sky. On ground level, shops are open late, and sushi bars, coffee shops, and top-scale eateries—many of them busy 24 hours a day—line Tverskaya. You'll pass the columned red facade of City Hall, the statue of city founder Yuri Dolgoruky (a 12th-c. prince), the former Revolution Museum, and plenty of plaques indicating where Soviet-era dignitaries once lived. See chapters 6 and 9 for restaurant and nightlife options along Tverskaya.

---

3 The Best of Moscow in 3 Days

The luxury of a third day in Moscow is best enjoyed at a more leisurely pace. Spend the morning at Novodevichy Convent and Cemetery, a secluded spot that feels miles from the downtown rush. Then take a car or the metro to Gorky Park. After lunch, head to the Pushkin Museum of Fine Arts, and spend the evening on a bus tour that hits sights farther afield and wraps up the Moscow experience. *Start: Metro to Sportiv-naya, then a 10-minute walk to the convent.*

---

❶ Novodevichy Convent and Cemetery (Novodevichy Monastyr) ⚑⚑

This complex, nestled on a leafy peninsula overlooking the Moscow River, was built in the 16th century and housed many exiled or self-exiled royal wives, daughters, and lovers. Its cathedrals form a stunning window onto Russian architecture. The cemetery below holds the intricate and unusual graves of many of Russia's most famous and talented literary, artistic, musical, and political figures. See p. 127.

❷ Gorky Park (Park Kultury i Otdkykha Imeni M. Gorkovo) ⚑

This is not Moscow's prettiest park or its greenest, but it is the most famous and the most lively. Ice sculptures and iced-over alleys offer skating pleasure in winter, and concerts and children's festivals keep things lively in summer. The small amusement park along the river includes a real Buran space shuttle that now offers riders a chance to feel like they're blasting off. See p. 134.

> **❸ MAMA ZOYA ON THE WATER** ⚑⚑
> This kitschy-looking boat-restaurant boasts some fine Georgian cuisine and a surprisingly homey atmosphere. Mama Zoya's original basement cafe was so popular that she branched out to this dock across from Gorky Park. Try Georgian specialties like grilled lamb *shashlyk* or ground-beef kebabs, or the hearty redbean-and-garlic *lobio* stew. On the docks across from 4/6 Frunzenskaya Naberezhnaya; ✆ 095/325-3421.

❹ Pushkin Museum of Fine Arts ⚑⚑

This impressive collection of international art from the ancients to the present is often overshadowed by the Hermitage Museum, but the Pushkin is a masterpiece of its own. Don't miss the Impressionists and the controversial "trophy art"—works taken from European Jews by the Nazis, then later seized by victorious Soviet troops. The Museum of Private Collections across the street shows rotating exhibits of top quality and varying tastes. You can walk here from Gorky Park down picturesque Ostozhenka Street, or take the metro one stop from Gorky Park to Kropotkinskaya. See p. 133.

❺ Christ the Savior Cathedral ⚑

This dominant feature of Moscow's skyline has a history as striking as its facade. First built over several decades in the 19th century, the massive cathedral was razed by Stalin in the 1930s and became a public swimming pool. Muscovites were chagrined when the popular pool was gutted in 1994, due to the mayor's decree that a bigger, better Christ the Savior Cathedral be erected in its place. Its newness is palpable, especially after the mystical and musty St. Basil's. See p. 127.

❻ Peter the Great Monument

You don't have to cross the river to get a good look at this bronze tribute to Peter the Great; it's so enormous you can study it from the platform of Christ the Savior Cathedral. The oddly proportioned monument, to a czar who detested Moscow and built his own capital on the Baltic Sea, has remained controversial since its 1997 appearance. The Moscow mayor's favorite sculptor, Zurab Tsereteli, perched the nautical Peter atop a ship on an island jutting into the Moscow River. Catch a whiff of chocolate from Red October Candy Factory next door.

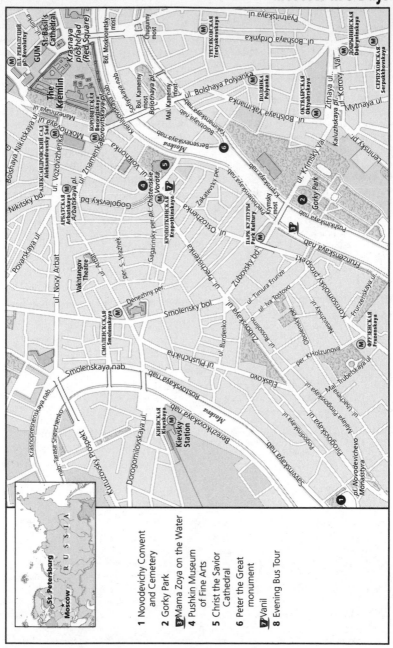

1 Novodevichy Convent
  and Cemetery
2 Gorky Park
3 Mama Zoya on the Water
4 Pushkin Museum
  of Fine Arts
5 Christ the Savior
  Cathedral
6 Peter the Great
  monument
7 Vanil
8 Evening Bus Tour

7 VANIL ★★

Pamper yourself in this sleek restaurant that represents some of Moscow's finest and most adventurous cuisine. (It also serves steak and baked fish for the conservative diner.) The clientele is almost too fashionable to stomach, but the European-Asian food and stunning design make up for your dining partners. 1 Ostozhenka; ✆ 095/202-3341. See p. 114.

8 Evening Bus Tour ★★

By now you no longer need to get your bearings, but a bus tour is a great way to take a step back and see the city as a collaboration of remarkable sights. A tour is also a convenient way to reach more distant spots on Moscow's tourist map—those that from the city are little more than parts of a good view. Highlights to look for are Moscow State University in the Sparrow Hills, and Victory Park. If a bus tour isn't available, consider renting a car with a driver. Evening is an ideal time for a tour because traffic thins and darkness hides the city's impurities, while streetlamps highlight its beauty. See "Organized Tours" in chapter 7.

4

Getting to Know Moscow

Moscow has matured over a millennium into a richly layered, ever-expanding, and never-sleeping metropolis. Its sporadic growth has left it without a compact downtown, which means that great sights, hotels, and restaurants can be found in nearly any corner of the city. Its vast territory requires a good bit of walking and plenty of rides via metro (subway), taxi, or tour bus. Take along a copy of *War and Peace* for distraction during traffic jams or long subway rides.

Below are tips for how to view, explore, and handle the city without letting it overwhelm you.

1 Orientation

ARRIVING
BY PLANE

The main port of entry for international flights is **Sheremetevo-2 Airport** (✆ 095/956-4666 or 095/578-4727; www.sheremetyevo-airport.ru), a dingy gray terminal built for the 1980 Olympics, 30km (18 miles) north of downtown. The passport control lines are formidable, as the border officers inspect every passport and visa. Luggage carts are free, though they sometimes run short in number, so grab one as soon as you see the baggage carousel. Porters hawk their services for exorbitant rates. A currency exchange booth and ATM are available after you've cleared Customs; rates are better in town but most travelers have no choice. An information desk with English-speaking personnel is in the main arrivals hall, along a row of car-rental desks and airline ticket offices.

Package tours generally include transport to and from Russia's airports. Individual travelers should be prepared for an odorous herd of taxi drivers accosting passengers as you emerge from Customs. The best option is to arrange a taxi in advance. **Moscow Taxi** (www.moscow-taxi.com) and **Taxi Blues** (✆ 095/789-6654) offer good English-speaking services. If you arrive without a ride, push your way to the official taxi desk near the exit. Rates are determined by a zone map, and a ride to the city center runs about $30, payable in dollars or rubles. The freelance cabbies will try to convince you that $60 is your cheapest option.

There is no train service to downtown, but buses leave from the airport parking lot and stop at Rechnoi Vokzal metro station (bus no. 551) or Planernaya metro station (bus no. 517). The fare, about $5 (143 rubles), must be paid in rubles to the driver. Allow yourself 45 minutes to reach downtown in a taxi, and at least 90 minutes by bus and metro.

A few European airlines now arrive at the bright, renovated **Domodedovo Airport** (✆ 095/933-6666 or 095/363-3064; www.domodedovo.ru), 50km (28 miles) south of the center. Domodedovo has all the same services as Sheremetevo but in a friendlier setting, and has two major advantages: It runs a train direct to Paveletsky station, just south of the city center; and it has a clear, fair, and computerized taxi service greeting passengers as they exit. Taxis from Domodedovo to the center take about an hour and cost $30 to $50 (856–1,427 rubles), payable in rubles. The train ride to Paveletsky is 40 minutes and costs 100 rubles ($3.50). Two metro lines meet at Paveletsky station, where taxis are available.

Flights from St. Petersburg usually arrive at **Sheremetevo-1** (© 095/578-9101), adjacent to Sheremetevo-2 but smaller. Taxis from there cost slightly less than from the international terminal. Other domestic Russian flights come into **Vnukovo** (© 095/155-0922), 30km (18 miles) southwest of the city. Taxis to the center of the city cost about $30 to $40.

BY TRAIN

The St. Petersburg–Moscow train route is the country's best-maintained and most romantic. An overnight ride on a sleeper brings you into Leningradsky station and costs $30 to $90 depending on the train's class and hour. The pricier rides come complete with slippers, in-cabin television, and a late-night meal. Leningradsky, like all of Moscow's train stations, is conveniently located on the Circle Line of the metro. Western European trains generally arrive in Belorussky station, barely north of the city center and within walking distance of the hotels on busy Tverskaya Street. A second-class ticket in a sleeping car from Warsaw takes 24 hours and costs about $70; from farther west the time and cost rise accordingly. Most European trains travel through Ukraine or Belarus, both of which require a transit visa. Contact the Ukrainian or Belarusian embassy in your country for details, or pick a route through the Baltic states or Scandinavia. The train from Beijing takes 5 days and costs about $250. *Note:* Rail passes that serve the rest of Europe do not serve Russia.

BY CAR

For those rare arrivals by car, take the vehicle straight to your hotel and inquire about secure parking. Unfortunately, no current maps in English indicate one-way streets or other details for drivers. The Travellers Yellow Pages map in English, otherwise quite good, is available at www.infoservices.com and at major Moscow hotels. Do not underestimate Moscow traffic, which has mushroomed in the past decade and can leave visitors trapped in a labyrinth of jammed one-way streets, especially from 8 to 10am and 5 to 7pm. Watch out, too, for the traffic police who, always eager for pocket money, can stop you just to make sure your documentation is in order. Garages are rare despite rising demand. Muscovites park on sidewalks and in doorways if they can't find free spaces, but theft is common so this is not advised. Renting a car with a driver is a more reliable and often cheaper option.

BY BUS

Several European tour companies offer bus trips to Moscow, usually departing from Germany. However, the journey is long (2 days from Berlin) and along poorly maintained highways, and the waits at the borders are significant. For any trip traveling through or originating in Ukraine or Belarus, you must get a transit visa from those countries. Buses arrive at **Tsentralny Avtovokzal (Central Bus Terminal)** at 2 Uralskaya Ulitsa (© 095/468-0400). The Shcholkovskaya metro station is adjacent. Taxis from the terminal take about 30 minutes to reach the center at a rate of $15.

Tips **Map Confusion**

Beware of maps and guidebooks printed before the mid-1990s, which may include the Soviet-era names of many streets and metro stations instead of the new ones.

VISITOR INFORMATION

Moscow has lacked a network of official tourist offices since the demise of the Soviet era. **Intourist,** formerly the government tourist agency, can still be useful and has offices in the Kosmos Hotel at 150 Prospekt Mira (© **095/730-1919;** www. intourist.ru) and closer to downtown at 15 Stoleshnikov Pereulok (© **095/925-3434**). Hotel concierges and tour desks are likely to have as much information as Intourist, or more. Most hotels and many newspaper kiosks in the center of town sell maps in English (ask for a Karta na angliiskom, pronounced "*kar*-ta na ahn-*glees*-kom"). Pick up a copy of the free English-language daily *The Moscow Times* for weather, exchange rates, entertainment listings, and more. The newspaper is not sold at newsstands, but most of the hotels listed in chapter 5 (particularly the high-end ones) carry copies.

CITY LAYOUT

At Moscow's heart and nearly its geographical center lies the Kremlin, from which the rest of the city has expanded in roughly concentric circles: the Boulevard Ring, the Garden Ring, and the Third Ring. The last circle, the Moscow Ring Road, is the bypass around the city limits. The expansion continues apace and Moscow is now an unwieldy megalopolis of 12 million people encompassing 1,000 sq. km (386 sq. miles)—nearly 10 times bigger than Paris or Manhattan.

The Moscow and Yauza rivers curve through the city, delineating neighborhoods. Visitors are often struck by Moscow's broad boulevards and vast squares, as well as the city's large swaths of green space (which turns to white space during the 6-month winter). Yet housing remains concentrated in cramped apartment blocks.

All major airports are well out of town (see above). Train stations are scattered around a circle that generally corresponds to the Garden Ring Road and the metro system's Ring Line. Trains from the west arrive at Kievsky station or Belorussky station on the northwest side of town, and trains from the north arrive at Leningradsky station or Rizhky station on the northeast side.

THE NEIGHBORHOODS IN BRIEF

Moscow is divided into six districts, or *okrugs,* with most of the activity focused on the Central District. The best way to view the city is as a daisylike flower, with neighborhoods stretching like petals from the center core toward the "ring roads" outlined above. Most historical buildings and key sights are within the Boulevard Ring; museums are within the Garden Ring; and hotels, restaurants, and shopping for all budgets are found everywhere. The area from the Kremlin to the Boulevard Ring was known historically as the "Bely Gorod," or "White Town," because of the white stone walls that encircled it to fend off outsiders. The area between the Boulevard and Garden rings was called "Zemlyanoi Gorod," or "Earth Town," after its earthen ramparts.

Moscow Neighborhoods

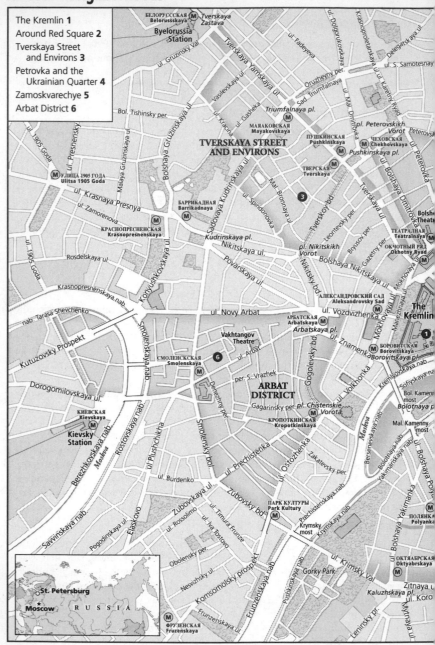

The Kremlin **1**

Around Red Square **2**

Tverskaya Street
and Environs **3**

Petrovka and the
Ukrainian Quarter **4**

Zamoskvarechye **5**

Arbat District **6**

БЕЛОРУССКАЯ Ⓜ *Tverskaya*
Belorusskaya *Zastava*

**Byelorussia
Station**

ul. Fadeyeva

ul. Dolgorukovskaya

Delegatskaya ul.

Krasnoproletarskaya ul. ul. Karetny Ryad

ul. S. Samotesnay

Oruzheyny per.

Sad. Triumfalnaya ul. Mal. Dmitrovka

Tverskaya Yamskaya ul.

Vasilevskaya ul.

ul. Gruzinsky Val

Tverskaya-Yamskaya ul.

Triumfalnaya pl.

pl. Peterovskikh
Vorot

Peterov

ul. Gasheka

Bol. Tishinsky per.

Bolshaya Gruzinskaya ul.

ul. Kracina

МАЯКОВСКАЯ
Mayakovskaya

ПУШКИНСКАЯ
Pushkinskaya

ЧЕХОВСКАЯ Ⓜ
Chekhovskaya

Pushkinskaya pl.

ul. Presnensky

Ⓜ УЛИЦА 1905 ГОДА
Ulitsa 1905 Goda

**TVERSKAYA STREET
AND ENVIRONS**

Malaya Gruzinskaya ul

ТВЕРСКАЯ Ⓜ
Tverskaya

Bolshaya Dmitrovka

ul. Krasnaya Presnya

ul. Zamorenova

БАРРИКАДНАЯ Ⓜ
Barrikadnaya

Sadovaya Kudrinskaya

ul. Spiridonovka

❸

Tverskoy-bd.

Leontevsky per.

Bryusov. per.

Tverskaya ul.

Tverskoy per.

ul. Bolshaya Dmitrovka

Bolshe
Theat

ТЕАТРАЛЬНАЯ
Teatralnaya Ⓜ

КРАСНОПРЕСНЕНСКАЯ
Krasnopresnenskaya ul.

Kudrinskaya pl.

Nikitskaya ul.

pl. Nikitskikh
Vorot

Gazetny per.

ОХОТНЫЙ РЯД Ⓜ
Okhotny Ryad

ul. 1905 Goda

Rosdelskaya ul

Konyushkovskaya ul.

Povarskaya ul

Bolshaya Nikitskaya ul

Nikitsky-bd.

Mokhovaya

АЛЕКСАНДРОВСКИЙ САД
Aleksandrovsky Sad

Krasnopresnenskaya nab.

nab. Tarasa Shevchenko

ul. Novy Arbat

ul. Vozdvizhenka

**The
Kremlin**

АРБАТСКАЯ Ⓜ
Arbatskaya
Arbatskaya pl.

Mokhovaya ul.

Manezhnaya

❶

Kutuzovsky Prospekt

Smolenskaya-nab.

Smolenskaya-nab.

**Vakhtangov
Theatre**

ul. Arbat

Gogolevsky-bd.

ul. Znamenka

БОРОВИТСКАЯ Ⓜ
Borovitskaya
Borovitskaya pl

СМОЛЕНСКАЯ Ⓜ
Smolenskaya

❻

Kremlevskaya-nab.

Sofiyskaya-nab.

Dorogomilovskaya ul.

per. S. Vrazhek

**ARBAT
DISTRICT**

ul. Volkhonka

Bol. Kameni
most
Bolotnaya pa

Rostovskaya nab.

Denezhny per.

Gagarinsky per. pl. Chistenskie
Vorota

Mal. Kamenny
most

КИЕВСКАЯ
Kievskaya

КРОПОТКИНСКАЯ
Kropotkinskaya

Zakatevsky per.

**Kievsky
Station**

Rostovskaya nab.

ul. Plushchikha

ul. Prechistenka

ul. Ostozhenka

Prechistenskaya nab.

Bersenevskaya nab.

Bolotnaya nab.

ul. Bolshaya Polya

Berezhkovskaya nab.

Savvinskaya nab.

ul. Burdenko

Smolensky bol.

ПОЛЯНКА
Polyanka Ⓜ

Pogodinskaya ul.

Elanovo

Zubovskaya nab.

Zubovsky bd.

Prechistenskaya nab.

Bolshaya Yakimanka

ul. Rossolimo

ul. Timura Frunze

ПАРК КУЛТУРЫ
Park Kultury

Yakimanskaya nab.

Obolensky per.

ul. Iva Tostovo

*Krymsky
most*

Krymskaya nab.

ul. Krimsky Val

Kaluzhskaya pl.

ОКТЯБРСКАЯ
Oktyabrskaya Ⓜ

Zitnaya u

ul. Koro

★ St. Petersburg

★ **Moscow**

R U S S I A

Nesvizhsky per.

Komsomolsky prospekt

Pushkinskaya nab.

Frunzenskaya nab.

Gorky Park

Leninsky pr.

Mytnaya u

ФРУЗЕНСКАЯ Ⓜ
Fruzenskaya

Frunzenskaya ul

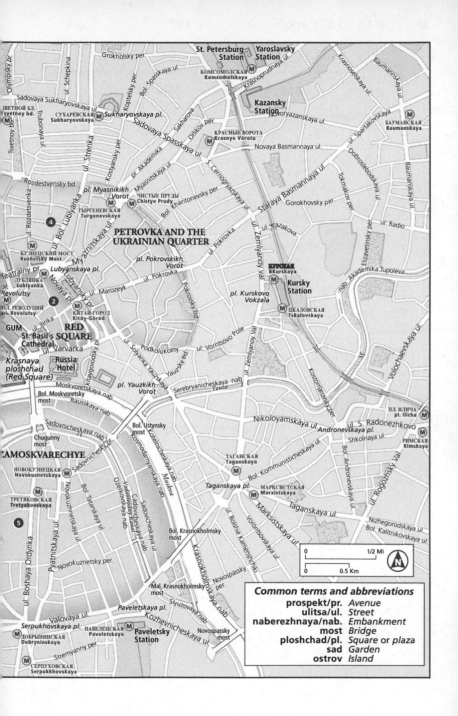

Common terms and abbreviations

prospekt/pr.	*Avenue*
ulitsa/ul.	*Street*
naberezhnaya/nab.	*Embankment*
most	*Bridge*
ploshchad/pl.	*Square* or *plaza*
sad	*Garden*
ostrov	*Island*

Stalin's Seven Sisters

By the end of your first day in Moscow, you're bound to have noticed at least one of these sky-scraping, turreted castles to Communism. Seven of them cut into the city skyline, immediately differentiating the city from any other in the world. Initiated under Stalin, Moscow's "Seven Sisters" emerged in the 1950s and came to embody an architectural style dubbed "Stalin Gothic" that was emulated in buildings throughout the Communist world.

The buildings are immediately recognizable by their tapered towers, glass spires, and solid stone enormity. Architecturally, they combine features of Russian 17th-century churches, Western Gothic cathedrals, and American skyscrapers of the 1930s. Many were built by German prisoners of war. The grandest example is the main building of **Moscow State University,** lording it over the city from the peak of Sparrow Hills. Containing 32km (20 miles) of corridors, this 5,000-room building is best viewed at a distance, ideally from the lookout platform above the Moscow River. Another impressive sister is the **Kotelnicheskaya apartment building** (1 Kotelnicheskaya Naberezhnaya), which housed the Communist elite in decades past and now includes some of the city's priciest real estate, even if its infrastructure is in need of an upgrade. A second apartment building, **Krasnaya Presnya Tower** at Kudrinskaya Square, once housed Soviet aviation elite. Two more of the Stalin Gothic buildings are hotels (**Hotel Ukraina,** 2/1 Kutuzovsky Prospekt; and **Hotel Leningradskaya,** near the Leningradsky Train Station at 21/40 Kalanchevskaya Ulitsa). The remaining two are government buildings (the **Foreign Ministry** on Smolenskaya Sq., and the **Transport Ministry** on the Garden Ring Rd. at Krasniye Vorota). Even modern developers have caught the Stalin Gothic bug: The biggest real estate project in recent years is the **Triumph Palace** apartment complex in northwest Moscow, which will be Europe's tallest building—you're sure to spot it on your way in from the airport.

The biggest castle of all—and the one that served as a boilerplate for the others—never reached fruition. The **Palace of Soviets** was intended to be the most elaborate ode to Communist power that Stalin could conceive, planned for the site of the razed Christ the Savior Cathedral (p. 127). The plans were sabotaged by infighting and later by World War II, and the site became a public swimming pool, and remained so until the end of the Soviet era. Today a new cathedral stands on the site, one so grandiose that some call it an Orthodox version of the Palace of Soviets. Original designs of the Palace of Soviets are among the exhibits at **Shchusev Museum of Architecture** at 5 Vozdvizhenka Ulitsa (© **095/291-2109;** Metro: Biblioteka Imeni Lenina; admission 50 rubles/$1.75). It's open Saturday to Thursday from 11am to 6pm.

At the center is **The Kremlin,** a village unto itself, with cathedrals, palaces, an enormous concert and congress hall, and of course the seat of presidential power—all surrounded by imposing red brick walls that extend for 2.5km (1½ miles). On its east side is **Red Square,** the epicenter of the city and the country. The square abuts a small neighborhood called **Kitai-Gorod.** This is almost like an annex to the Kremlin, with a dense collection of churches, old merchants' courtyards, and administrative buildings clustered on quiet streets overlooking the Moscow River. Its name today translates as "Chinatown," but more likely comes from an old Russian term for battlements because of its proximity to the Kremlin. The area boasts many restaurants but few hotels.

The primary petal of Moscow's daisy is undoubtedly **Tverskaya Street,** shooting north from Red Square in the direction of Russia's other imperial city, St. Petersburg. Moscow's most important thoroughfare, Tverskaya throbs with commerce, cafes, and nightclubs, and the columns of City Hall oversee it all. Tverskaya and its environs include key hotels and museums, and offer close-up views of Moscow's breakneck post-Soviet evolution. Hotels right on Tverskaya suffer from its 24-hour schedule, while those on the side streets are calmer but farther from the action.

The more true-to-tradition **Petrovka** district slopes eastward from Tverskaya. It includes several old and new restaurants, boutiques, and (mostly upmarket) hotels, in addition to two monasteries and a historic bath house. Curving southeast from there is the **Ukrainian Quarter,** whose steep and crooked lanes unveil architectural treasures tucked behind embassies and run-down government buildings. Accommodations here are limited, but the area is great for wandering. As you continue to circle Red Square clockwise, you cross the Moscow River to the Zamoskvarechye neighborhood on the opposite bank (see the box "The Land Beyond the Moscow River," above). Moving northwest, you come to aristocratic Ostozhenka and Prechistenka streets and the **Arbat District,** centered around the pedestrian Arbat Street lined with souvenir shops and cafes. Touristy but colorful, the Arbat is surrounded by alleys rich in literary legend and by a few convenient, reasonably priced hotels.

Outside the **Garden Ring Road** lie many hotels, as well as former "country mansions" now museums or concert halls surrounded by urbanism. Basing yourself beyond the center means you'll need more travel time to see city sights, but if your hotel is close to a metro station, the distance shouldn't be a hindrance.

Tips **Address Advice**

Finding addresses in Russia can be challenging, especially for buildings tucked in a courtyard or down a footpath. Russians usually list the house number after the street name. The number may include dashes or slashes or have an addendum like "building 2" or "wing 3." Big apartment buildings rarely have one central entrance; instead, apartments are reached by separate entrances called *podyezdy,* making it crucial to know which entrance you need. For example, to find Kutuzovsky Prospekt 7/4, building 3, entrance 1, apartment 16:

Locate no. 7/4 between nos. 5 and 9 (ignore the "/4"), walk through the parking lot, and search for building no. 3. Then find entrance no. 1 and check the list in the elevator to locate apartment no. 16's floor.

The Boulevard Ring

The innermost of Moscow's concentric circles is both a main traffic artery and one of the world's most oddly shaped parks. The Boulevard Ring, actually a semicircle tracing a hump through central Moscow, is a road split down the middle by a 9.7km-long (6-mile) green space. It's lined with paths and benches, and interrupted by a couple of playgrounds, a pond, several monuments, and busy intersections. If you have a free afternoon and the weather cooperates, wander one or more segments of the "bulvar"—an activity that Muscovites call the cheapest amusement in town.

The lines of the boulevard date back to the 14th century, when ramparts were erected to defend the city that had grown up between here and the Kremlin. White stone walls were installed in the 16th century, giving the settlements within the ramparts the nickname "Bely Gorod" or "White Town." Towers, chapels, and gates marked the spots where major intersections now throng with traffic and pedestrians, and the current names of some crossings reflect that era, such as Nikitsky Gates and Sretensky Gates. The ramparts were razed piece by piece in the 18th century and replaced with leafy alleys and wrought-iron lampposts much like those standing today. When Napoleon's army entered an abandoned and charred Moscow in 1812, soldiers chopped down many of the boulevard's trees for fuel. Today, it is lined with linden and poplar trees, and if you wander the ring in June, you may be sprinkled by white poplar tufts that Russians call their "summer snow."

A few key spots on the ring worth visiting are: **Pushkin Square,** on either side of Tverskaya Street, a major gathering place and the most energized of the boulevard's intersections; the two **statues of author Nikolai Gogol,** one triumphant and prominent on Arbat Square, the other contemplative and intriguing in a courtyard on Nikitsky Bulvar; and **Chistiye Prudy (Clean Ponds),** actually a single pond at the far eastern end of the ring that serves as an outdoor skating rink in winter and boating pond in summer.

2 Getting Around
BY PUBLIC TRANSPORTATION

The **Moscow Metro** is an attraction unto itself (see the review on p. 130), and well worth a visit just to view a few stations even if you have other transport. It's clean and efficient, with trains running every 90 seconds or so during the day. Station entrances are marked with a letter M. The Circle Line runs around the center, with nearly a dozen radial lines crossing it. Color-coded maps are posted at every station entrance and in every train car, and most are now printed in English as well as Russian. The signs in the stations directing you to platforms are in Russian, however, so it helps to know what the name of your station looks like printed in the Cyrillic alphabet. The system is slowly expanding but has not kept up with population growth. Trains are nearly always crowded, and stops are too few and far between. Opening and closing times vary from station to station but are roughly 5:30am to 1am.

Paper tickets with a magnetic strip are sold in each station, for one trip (13 rubles/50¢), two trips (26 rubles/$1), five trips (60 rubles/$2.20), or 10 trips (105 rubles/$3.80). No senior or student discounts are available. You insert the ticket into the side of the machine, then retrieve it from the top before you're allowed to pass.

The Land Beyond the Moscow River

The neighborhood of Zamoskvarechye (Za-moss-kva-*reh*-cha), which translates as "the land beyond the Moscow River," abuts the very heart of Moscow, even though its name makes it sound like it's in the city's nether reaches. The area does feel different from the rest of town, however, making it well worth a wander at some point on your trip. Situated on a bell-shaped cluster of islands south of the Moscow River, it spreads from the embankment opposite the Kremlin's southern wall down to the Garden Ring. Settlements in Zamoskvarechye date back to at least the 13th century, when Mongol envoys camped here during visits to exact tribute from their Muscovite subjects. The Muscovites themselves eventually moved into the neighborhood, setting up fortified compounds to house the *streltsy* (palace guards), who served as a buffer protecting the Kremlin from raids from the south.

With the end of Mongol domination, the area began attracting craftsmen, who settled in walled compounds. Each housed a different guild—tanners, weavers, barrel-makers, sheepskin curers—and was run by a council of elected elders called a *mirsky soviet*. As the guilds flourished, they began building the neighborhood's churches, many of which remain standing. Their modest lines contrast with the designs of more resplendent cathedrals elsewhere in town.

Merchants trading in the Kitai-Gorod district across the river "discovered" Zamoskvarechye in the 19th century, building mansions there and sponsoring neighborhood artists and artisans—eventually creating the country's first art museum, Tretyakov Gallery. By the early 20th century Zamoskvarechye had become a major industrial district, but its factories grew up alongside the homes and churches instead of subsuming them. The district was touched by uglier episodes in Russian history, too: Bolotnaya Ploshchad (Marshy Square) was once the site of public executions, though it now houses a tranquil park and a statue of painter Ilya Repin. The House on the Embankment (the enormous gray complex on Bersenevskaya Naberezhnaya) was transformed from a prestigious residence for the Communist elite into a house of terror during Stalin's purges. Overall, the neighborhood's character remains artsy and more low-key than the rest of town, with galleries, antiques dealers, and cafes its major draw. Highlights include **Tretyakov Gallery** (p. 131), the **Obvodny Canal fountains** around Luzhkov Bridge, **Pyatnitskaya Street**, and **Red October Chocolate Factory**. The nearest metro stations are Novokuznetskaya, Tretyakovskaya, and Polyanka.

Babushkas

The word *babushka* technically means "grandmother" in Russian, but the term encompasses much more, a whole mindset and layer of the Russian population. You'll see the babushka everywhere: guarding a museum, running a coat check, patrolling the metro escalators, sweeping Red Square, or suspiciously eyeing your untucked shirt. She may or may not be wearing the brightly flowered headscarf often associated with the word "babushka" in the West. She may not have grandchildren, or may not be particularly old. But if she has the attitude, she's a babushka.

The babushka considers it her responsibility to keep the world dressed warmly, well-nourished, free of infection, and properly groomed. She'll give you an earful if you're out hatless in winter. She'll berate a young woman for sitting on cold concrete ("It will harm your women's parts, dear"). She'll huff if you hand her a coat to check that's wrinkled or missing a button—and she may even mend it for you.

Sadly, the skills and traits that made babushkas so crucial to Russia's social fabric are losing their relevance in today's Russia. Fast food and supermarkets are reducing the family's reliance on her cooking and resourceful shopping tricks. Her home remedies are losing their appeal amid a flood of imported medicines. Increased housing options mean fewer and fewer young Russians live with grandma. Men die so much younger than women (male life expectancy is just 60, female life expectancy is 72) that many babushkas are on their own, unable to support themselves on shriveled pensions.

If you speak no Russian, you may not notice the critiques babushkas send in your direction. If you understand Russian or if a babushka upbraids you in English, stay cool. You may find it intrusive, but she wants what's best for you, even if she's never seen you before in her life. In other words, she wants you to feel right at home.

Trams are second-best to the metro if there's a tram route near your hotel or destination. The stops are on the sidewalk, even where the tram tracks are in the middle of the street. Three of the best lines (A, 3, and 39) run along the picturesque Boulevard Ring before crossing the Moscow River, offering a stunning view of the Kremlin and winding toward Moscow State University and Danilovsky Monastery, among other sights. **Trolleybuses,** attached to electrical lines overhead, are a good option for travel around the Garden Ring Road or along Novy Arbat Street. Rush hour is crowded and the timing between trolleybuses is unpredictable. **Buses** are the least convenient and most overcrowded form of public transport.

Tickets for trams, trolleybuses, and buses cost 11 rubles (40¢) and are available from the driver or sometimes from a conductor who roams the vehicle selling them. **Passengers must punch their own tickets** in the little red contraptions posted throughout the vehicle (watch other passengers and imitate). Failure to do so makes your ticket worthless, and you risk earning a fine. Maps are posted inside the vehicles,

Moscow Metro

1 Sokolnicheskaya
2 Zamoskvoretskaya
3 Artbatsko-Pokrovskaya
4 Filevskaya
5 Koltsevaya
6 Kaluzhko-Rizhskaya
7 Tagansko-Krasnopresnenskaya
8 Kalininskaya
9 Serpukhovsko-Timiryazevskaya
10 Lyublinskaya
11 Kakhovskaya
Under Construction
Transfer station

and routes are often listed at the stops, but in Russian only. Bus stops are marked by signs with the letter A, trolley stops with the letter T, and tram stops with the letters TP. Some stops serve all three. Waiting time can be from 5 to 40 minutes, depending on the hour and the traffic. The three forms of transportation run from 6am to midnight.

Route taxis, or *marshrutky,* are minivans that take up to 10 people along several routes that bigger buses don't serve. Fares vary but are always less than a dollar. The destinations are marked on the front of the van in Russian only. To get off. yell "Stop!" to the driver. The minivans are more convenient than buses, trams, or trolleys, but the drivers are often reckless and there are no seat belts.

BY TAXI

Official taxis are hard to come by in Moscow, except at train stations and major hotels. But "gypsy" cabs are available anywhere, anytime, offering an experience that combines hitchhiking with bargaining at the bazaar. If you stand on a corner and stick out your hand to hail a taxi, the majority of cars that stop will be those of private drivers with spare time and a need for your cash. They'll ask where you're going and then propose a price, and you're free to negotiate. This is not a recommended option if you don't speak Russian or if you're traveling alone, or if you're afraid to travel in old Ladas

---

The World Underground

The *perekhod,* or underground walkway, is one of those things that leaves you thinking: "Only in Russia. . . ." Soviet city planners built the walkways to allow passage across the extra-wide boulevards they so favored, without disrupting aboveground traffic. Post-communism, the *perekhods* turned into thriving commercial centers lined with kiosks, shops, buskers, pharmacies, and cafes. They also provide shelter on blustery days or during rainstorms, and are often used as wintertime meeting places ("Meet me under Pushkin Square at 8pm"). They're invariably crowded but are often useful: for getting rubles at a currency exchange booth, for buying a cool drink or quick snack, or for finding an emergency umbrella (or shampoo, or batteries, or aspirin, or a DVD, or a bunch of wildflowers, or a fur hat . . .). As a pedestrian, you're bound to encounter plenty of them in Moscow and St. Petersburg. When trying to cross major avenues, you may have to walk some distance to find the next *perekhod,* but making the extra journey is much wiser than trying to jaywalk across an eight-lane road clogged with fearless Russian drivers. The commercially busiest *perekhods* are at central intersections or along major thoroughfares such as Moscow's Tverskaya Street and St. Petersburg's Nevsky Prospekt. Many also serve as auxiliary entrances to metro stations, though the thicket of kiosks sometimes makes it hard to find the metro doors. There's nothing sinister about this underground world during the day, but after the shops shut down at night, some *perekhods* attract drug dealers and drunken brawls. Avoid them after dark if you're alone.

with slack seat belts. A safer (though more expensive) bet is to order a cab through a taxi company. Some charge by the kilometer, some charge by the clock, and a few offer set rates for certain zones. Reliable options in Moscow include **Moscow Taxi** (online only at www.moscow-taxi.com); **City Taxi** (① **095/789-3232**); and **Taxi 232** (① **095/232-1111**).

BY CAR

Driving your own car is generally not worth the hassle in Russia, given the arcane driving rules, greedy traffic police, and fearless Russian drivers. Car rental is still a fledgling business, with not enough competition to make rates very attractive. Much more common is renting a car with driver, either for a day, an evening, or your entire stay. This is, in fact, usually cheaper than renting a car on your own. The driver deals with the traffic police, the parking, and the gas; you just have to know where you want to go. An English-speaking driver will cost more than one who speaks Russian only. The car's make can range from an aging Volga to a gleaming new Mercedes, depending on your pocketbook.

If you do drive on your own, you need an international driving license, and you must be at least 21 years old and have at least 1 year of licensed driving experience. You also must have all the proper documents for the car and a familiarity with Russian traffic signs and rules. It is possible but not advisable to rent a car upon arrival; reserving ahead is wiser.

The following agencies rent cars with and without drivers:

AM Rent: 65 Dubininskaya Ulitsa; ① 095/952-9658; www.amrent.ru.

Budget Rent-a-Car: Sheremetevo-2 Airport; ① 095/578-7344. Also 23 1-aya Tverskaya-Yamskaya Ulitsa; ① 095/931-9700. www.budgetrentacar.com.

Hertz: Sheremetevo-2 Airport; ① 095/578-5646. Also 4 Chernyakovskogo Ulitsa; ① 095/937-3274. www.hertz.com.

Moscow Rental Service: Sheremetevo-2 Airport; ① 095/578-0919. Also 79 Krasnobogatyrskaya Ulitsa; ① 095/963-8780. www.mosrent.ru.

FAST FACTS: Moscow

Airport See "Getting There" in chapter 2, and "Arriving," earlier in this chapter.

American Express The main local office is at 21a Sadovo-Kudrinskaya Ulitsa (① **095/755-9001**). It's open from 9am to 7pm Monday through Friday; from 9am to 2pm Saturday. However, the office doesn't sell or cash Amex checks; it will only tell you at which nearby bank you can cash them. In the U.S., call ① **800/221-7282**.

Business Hours Businesses generally operate from 9am until 6pm. A few stores and businesses still take a lunch break around 1 to 2 pm. Some shops are closed Sunday, but museums and restaurants are generally open. Many restaurants and bars are open 24 hours.

Car Rentals See "Getting Around," earlier in this chapter.

Climate See "When to Go" in chapter 2.

Convention Centers Most of Moscow's big hotels are equipped to accommodate conventions and large conferences. The chief venue is the **World Trade**

Center at Mezhdunarodnaya Hotel, 12 Krasnopresnenskaya Naberezhnaya (© 095/253-1140; http://congresswtc.moscow.ru).

Currency Exchange Exchange booths *(obmen valyuty)* are found in every hotel, at many restaurants, and near all major metro stations. Many are open 24 hours, and most are well-guarded, reliable places to change cash. Rates are better than in most banks, and they're competitive, so shop around. Most don't charge a commission, and when they do, it's low—around a dollar. Make sure your bills are new and untainted; crinkled or pre-1995 bills will be rejected. Exchange booths have signs out front with four figures: the buy and sell rate for U.S. dollars, and the buy and sell rate for euros. To exchange other currencies, try the banks, the underground passage next to Arbatskaya metro station, and the booth on the corner of Pokrovka Ulitsa and Pokrovsky Bulvar. Banks can give cash advances on a credit card in rubles.

Dentist For good international-standard dentistry, including emergencies, try **US Dental Care,** 7/5 Bolshaya Dmitrovka, building 2 (© 095/933-8686; www.usdentalcare.com).

Doctor The following facilities offer Western-standard medical care and English-speaking staff who can help with everything from a broken limb to a bad flu. They are private clinics whose services are expensive and may not be covered by your insurance company, so be sure to check with your insurer before you go (see "Travel Insurance" in chapter 2).

    American Medical Center Moscow, 1 Grokholsky Pereulok (© 095/933-7700).

    European Medical Center, 10 2nd Spiridonievskiy Pereulok 5, building 1 (© 095/933-6655).

    International SOS Clinic, 31 Grokholsky Pereulok, 10th floor of Polyclinic no. 1 (© 095/937-5760 or 095/937-6477).

Driving Rules See "Getting Around," earlier in this chapter.

Drugstores See "Pharmacies," below.

Electricity Russia operates on 220-volt AC, like the rest of Europe. Bring converters if you have electrical equipment from North America, since they're harder to find in Russia. Most modern hotels use plugs with two thick prongs, as in continental Europe; some older hotels will need plugs with two thinner prongs. Small plastic adapters for these old plugs are available in Russian hardware stores, or often from the hotel staff. To guard against electricity surges for items like laptops, bring a stabilizer, too.

Embassies

All embassies are located in Moscow, the capital, with consulates for several countries in St. Petersburg as well.

    United States: 19/23 Novinsky Bulvar; © 095/256-4261

    Britain: 10 Smolenskaya Naberezhnaya; © 095/956-7301

    Canada: 23 Starokonyushenniy Pereulok; © 095/956-6666

    Australia: 13 Kropotkinskiy Pereulok; © 095/956-6070

    Ireland: 5 Grokholsky Pereulok; © 095/288-4101

Emergencies For fire, dial 01; police 02; ambulance 03. For medical emergencies, see the "Doctors" listing above. In extreme cases, the international clinics will send you to a better-equipped Russian hospital with a translator.

Eyeglass Repair Almost any eyeglass store, called *optika,* will make minor repairs, often for free. For English-speaking help, try the Karstadt store in the GUM department store on Red Square (© **095/935-7763**).

Holidays Moscow's pace slows a bit during holidays, but it doesn't come to a halt. Many museums and restaurants remain open but with limited hours. Check with your hotel concierge or call the establishment you want to visit to make sure it's open. See "When to Go" in chapter 2 for a list of Russian holidays.

Hospitals Some doctors will speak English, but most of the Russian hospital staff is unlikely to, so get a translator if you need hospitalization. Some of the biggest and (relatively) good hospitals are:

Botkin City Hospital, 5 Second Botkinsky Proyezd; © 095/242-9488

City Hospital No. 1 (Pirogovksy), 8 Leninsky Prospekt; © 095/236-6535

Morozovskaya Children's Hospital, 1 4-aya Dobryninskaya Ulitsa; © 095/958-8904

Information See "Visitor Information," earlier in this chapter.

Internet Access Though most Russians don't have computers, much less online access, Internet cafes are increasingly available in downtown Moscow. Most hotel business centers also offer Wi-Fi or online access, though at steeper rates. Try 24-hour **Time Online** on the bottom floor of the Okhotny Ryad shopping center next to the Kremlin (1 Manezhnaya Ploshchad; www.timeonline.ru). Or try **CafeMax,** a chain of cafes around town. Two convenient ones are at 25 Pyatnitskaya, building 1, near Novokuznetskaya metro station; and at 3 Novoslobodskaya Ulitsa, near Novoslobodskaya metro station. See www.cafemax.ru for other locations.

Language Russian is the principal language, a Slavic tongue that uses the Cyrillic alphabet. English is becoming more common but is not as widespread as in western Europe. In most hotels, at tourist sites, and in central Moscow, visitors should have no trouble communicating in English. Younger people are far more likely to speak it well than their elders. The main challenge is the Russian alphabet. Despite efforts to print signs in the Latin alphabet (the one used for western European languages), most streets and metro stations are labeled in Cyrillic. It is well worth it to learn the 33-letter alphabet, which is very phonetic and shares many letters with English. See appendix B for a quick alphabet lesson and list of useful words and phrases. When buying a phrasebook, make sure it has good phonetic transliterations of Russian words ("Spa-*see*-ba" is "Thank you," for example).

Liquor Laws The official drinking age in Russia is 18, but it is almost never enforced. Drinking in public is acceptable (despite a recent law against it), and seeing teenagers clutching beers on their way home from school is common. Beer, wine, and liquor—primarily vodka, but also such cocktails as gin and tonic in a can—are available at all supermarkets and most street kiosks. Beware of cheap vodka from kiosks, since it's often watered down or of stomach-wrenching quality. Bars with special licenses can serve alcohol all night, and many do. Some stores are closed on Sunday, but those that are open sell liquor then as well as every other day.

Mail   Russia's postal service is underfunded and unreliable. Postcards are a safe bet, though they may not arrive until you're back home. Postcards and letters to western Europe and North America cost about 60¢. Shipping packages through the regular post is not recommended, because there's nothing you can do if it gets lost or damaged, and because of the complex Customs rules. Several international shipping companies serve Russia, such as **FedEx** (© **095/234-3400**) and **UPS** (© **095/961-2211**), though their services are not cheap.

Maps   See "City Layout" earlier in this chapter.

Newspapers/Magazines   *The International Herald Tribune, Financial Times,* and other English-language publications are on sale at the chain hotels and some of the larger Russian hotels, but they're not available at newsstands around the city. The English-language daily *The Moscow Times* (www.themoscowtimes.com) is the most comprehensive and even-handed reference for news and entertainment listings in English. The *Russia Journal* (www.russiajournal.com) offers more politicized coverage in English, while the *eXile* (www.exile.ru) is known for its raunchy commentary and detailed bar, restaurant, and club listings. These three publications are free and available at many hotels and restaurants, though not at newsstands. For Russian speakers, *Vedomosti, Kommersant,* and *Izvestia* newspapers are the most respected; *Afisha* is the weekly magazine of note for entertainment, dining, and shopping advice.

Pharmacies   The number of pharmacies, called *apteka* and marked by a blue cross, is growing rapidly in Russia's cities. One good chain is called **36.6,** with branches all over Moscow. Check with your hotel concierge for the all-night pharmacy nearest you.

Police   Call 02.

Post Office   The main international post office is at 26 Myasnitskaya (© **095/928-6311**). It's open daily 8am to 7:45pm. Letters and postcards are mailed from the first floor in the main building; packages go through the annex, reached through the arch to the right of the main entrance.

Restrooms   Russia's public restrooms are scarce and leave much to be desired. At tourist sites they will be simple but well-maintained and usually free. Turkish-style cabins with a hole in the floor are common for both men and women, even in museums. Bring toilet paper everywhere. In a pinch, dive into any hotel or restaurant restroom.

Safety   See the "Security" section in chapter 2.

Salons   Salons are ubiquitous in Moscow, one of the most image-conscious world capitals. The simpler *parikmakherskaya* salons tucked on side streets are cheaper, while the *salon krasoty* on the chic shopping streets can cost a fortune and offer a range of beauty treatments. Most cut both men's and women's hair. For a big night out, you'll find English-speaking staff at chain **Yves Rocher,** whose main salon is at 4 Tverskaya (© **095/923-5885**); or at **Gerlen** at 15 Mokhovaya Ulitsa (© **095/258-7000**).

Smoking Russians smoke heavily, and nonsmokers are rarely catered to. Expensive hotels and an increasing number of restaurants offer nonsmoking options, so don't be afraid to ask. Bars are universally smoky. Smoking is forbidden on public transport and in museums. Crude Russian cigarettes cost about $1 a pack, while Russian-made Marlboros, available at any street kiosk, cost slightly more. Imported brands cost $2 and up.

Taxes VAT (value-added tax) of up to 18% is always included in the list price of store items and restaurant bills, though not always in hotel rates. It's a good idea to ask if you're unsure. The VAT cannot be refunded upon departure, as it is in European cities. There is no sales tax in Moscow.

Taxis See "Getting Around," earlier in this chapter.

Telephone Russia's phone service remains so basic that while many Russians have cellphones, they're still on waiting lists for land lines. Just a few years ago you had to order all international calls in advance. Today you can dial directly, but poor connections and disconnections are common on land lines. Cellphone service is quite advanced.

To call Russia: If you're calling Russia from the United States:

1. Dial the international access code 011.
2. Dial the country code 7.
3. Dial the city code (095 for Moscow, 812 for St. Petersburg) and then the 7-digit number. So the whole number you'd dial would be 011-7-095-000-0000.

Calling from Russia: To make any long-distance call from within Russia, international or domestic, you must dial 8 first, then wait for a tone.

To make international calls: To make international calls from Russia, first dial 8, then wait for a tone, then dial 10, then dial the country code (U.S. or Canada 1, U.K. 44, Ireland 353, Australia 61, New Zealand 64). Next, dial the area code and number. For example, if you want to call the Russian Embassy in Washington, D.C., you would dial 8 (tone) 10-1-202-588-7800. If you are calling from a hotel, you may have to dial 9 before dialing the 8, depending on hotel policy.

To call from city to city within Russia: First dial 8, then wait for a tone, then dial the city code and the number. For example, calling St. Petersburg from Moscow would look like this: 8 (tone) 812-777-1000.

To call within Russian cities: Just dial the 5- to 7-digit number. Local calls are free.

For directory assistance: Dial 07 if you're looking for a number inside Russia, but only if you speak Russian.

For operator assistance: If you need operator assistance in making an international call, dial 8, then wait for a tone, then dial 194. If you need help calling a number in Russia, dial 08, but few operators speak English.

Toll-free numbers: You cannot phone a 1-800 number in the States from Russia, so be sure to have standard toll numbers for all your credit card companies and travel agencies before you leave.

Pay phones: Russia is gradually phasing out its coin-operated phones for card-operated ones. The coin-run ones rarely work and should be avoided. If you get stuck with one, they accept 1-, 2-, and 5-ruble coins. Cards for the other phones can be purchased at most metro stations and at many hotel kiosks in Moscow and St. Petersburg. Not all phones accept all kinds of phone cards, and not all phone cards allow international calls. The most common is Moscow City Telephone Service, known as MGTS by its Russian initials. Most cards provide instructions in English, though the phones use only Russian and internationally recognizable symbols.

International calling cards: Direct access numbers for AT&T in Moscow are ℂ 755-5042 and 325-5042; MCI is ℂ 747-3322; BT Direct is ℂ 10-80-01-10-1044 (dial 8 first and wait for the tone); Canada Direct is ℂ 755-5045 or 747-3325.

Time Zone Moscow is 3 hours ahead of GMT from October to March, and 4 hours ahead during daylight saving time. That means it's usually 3 hours ahead of London, 8 hours ahead of New York, and 11 hours ahead of San Francisco. Russia switches to daylight saving time a week earlier than Europe and North America, and reverts to standard time a week earlier, too.

Tipping Restaurants generally include service charges in the bill, though small tips are welcome. Taxis usually set the rate before you head out, so no tip is expected. Baggage handlers and coat-check staffers should be tipped the equivalent of a dollar or so.

Useful Telephone Numbers

U.S. Dept. of State Travel Advisory: ℂ 202/647-5225 (staffed 24 hr.)

U.S. Passport Agency: ℂ 202/647-0518

U.S. Centers for Disease Control International Traveler's Hotline: ℂ 404/332-4559

5

Where to Stay in Moscow

Moscow has everything the discriminating hotel guest could dream of—for a price. The boom in Moscow hotel space since the Soviet Union's collapse has focused almost entirely on luxury or business-class accommodations. Demand is so high for the scarce mid-range hotels that they have little incentive to offer discounts or perks. Nonetheless, the major chains continue to expand into this hungry market, and lower-priced options are not far behind.

Most of the better deals on hotels are found beyond the Garden Ring Road, well away from the main sights. This can be a major factor in your Moscow experience, since traffic to and from the center can eat up a chunk of the day. However, if your hotel is near a metro station and you're comfortable on public transport, that can reduce travel time considerably and make faraway accommodations more bearable. See "Neighborhoods in Brief" in chapter 4 for a review of the districts referred to below.

The rates listed below are the "rack rates," or the highest official rate a hotel offers, but you can almost always get a discount—sometimes a deep one—by reserving through an online travel agency or even the hotel's online service. Rack rates listed here are in U.S. dollars, and do **not** include breakfast and the 18% VAT, unless noted. When you reserve online or through a travel agent, VAT **is** usually included.

Suites are quite common even in older Soviet hotels, and always mean an extra room with sofa, unless noted. A double quite often means two single beds, pushed together or across the room from each other. Make it clear when you reserve if you want a double bed. Single rooms and single rates for double rooms are widely available, so if you're traveling alone, be sure to ask.

Few hotels offer car rentals in the standard sense, but most can arrange a car with a driver for a few hours or the duration of your stay, generally at a reasonable or negotiable price. The listings below refer to this service as a "transport desk." See "Getting Around" in chapter 4 for a rundown on car rentals.

1 Around the Kremlin & Red Square

VERY EXPENSIVE

Ararat Park Hyatt 𝕲𝕲𝕲 The newest addition to Moscow's top-of-the-line hotel fleet, Ararat is worth a visit just for the view from—and of—its top-floor atrium bar. Named after the mountain where Noah's Ark is believed to have landed, the hotel aims for grandeur and succeeds. Unlike its neighbors, the Metropol and the National, the Ararat inhabits a richly modern building with no claims to historical significance. It has all the services expected of a 21st-century, five-star hotel. There's nothing quiet or subtle about this patch of Moscow, with the Bolshoi Theater, Red Square, and the

Where to Stay in Moscow

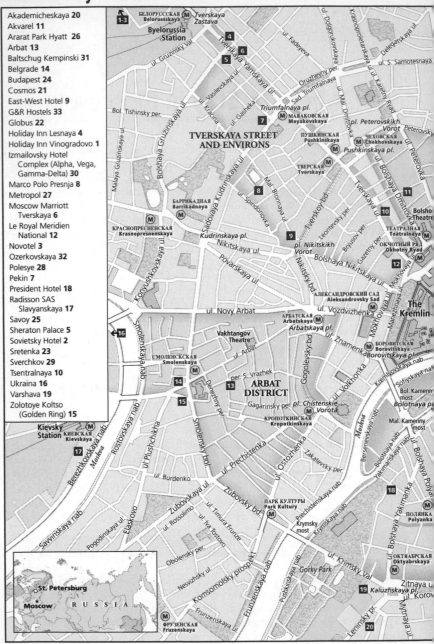

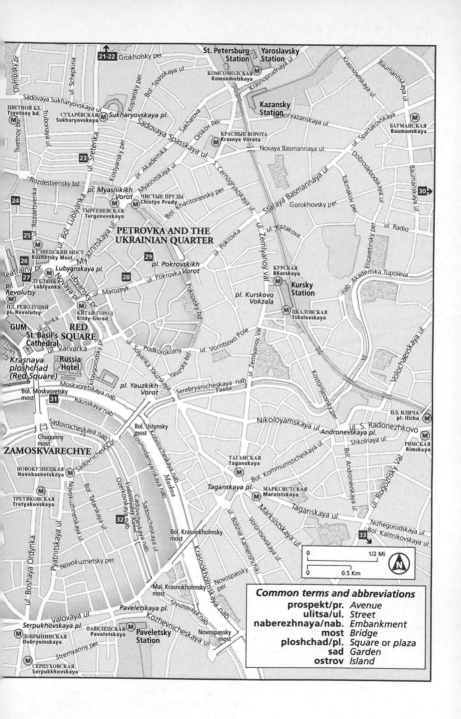

Common terms and abbreviations

prospekt/pr.	*Avenue*
ulitsa/ul.	*Street*
naberezhnaya/nab.	*Embankment*
most	*Bridge*
ploshchad/pl.	*Square* or *plaza*
sad	*Garden*
ostrov	*Island*

81

Tips Getting Back Home

Keep a hotel business card or brochure with you at all times, with the hotel's name and address written **in Russian**. You can show this to cab drivers or emergency workers to ensure you get home safely.

Kremlin just around the corner, and the *haute couture* boutiques of Tretyakovsky Proyezd across the street. The above-mentioned Conservatory lounge and bar offers snacks and cocktails, and its split-level hall is ideal for watching midnight sunsets in July from the 10th floor. True to its name, the hotel has an Armenian-themed restaurant as well, an updated version of a 1960s-era Moscow landmark. (Mt. Ararat was in Armenia until Turkey subsumed it in 1915.) An Armenian jewelry boutique offers stunning and unusual creations, at stunningly high prices.

4 Neglinnaya Ulitsa. ℂ 800/591-1234 or 095/783-1234. Fax 095/783-1235. www.moscow.park.hyatt.com. 220 units. $530 double; from $1,040 suite. AE, DC, MC, V. Metro: Kuznetsky Most or Lubyanka. **Amenities:** 3 restaurants; 2 bars; health club; spa; Jacuzzi; sauna; concierge; tour desk; car-rental desk; limo; 24-hr. business center; shopping arcade; salon; 24-hr. room service; massage; babysitting; laundry service; same-day dry cleaning; nonsmoking rooms; executive rooms. *In room:* A/C, satellite TV, dataport, minibar, fridge, coffeemaker, hair dryer, iron, safe.

EXPENSIVE

Le Royal Meridien National 𝒢𝒢   The National emerged from decades of renovation in the 1990s to become *the* place for Russia's nouveau riche to flaunt their wealth. The frenzy has since faded and the hotel is now merely a superbly located and impeccably designed spot from which to discover Moscow. Built in 1903, it housed aristocrats and their arch-enemy Vladimir Lenin, who stayed here (in room 107, according to the hotel—although the exact room number is debatable, a victim of Soviet revisionist history) as he imagined a Communist revolution. Perched on the edge of Tverskaya Street, the National looks directly at Red Square and the Kremlin and the throbbing heart of the capital. Rooms are decorated in dark lacquered woods and empire armchairs, and even the trouser presses match the decor. Hotel marketing materials admit that the single and double rooms are "not large," though they make good use of the limited space. An afternoon break in the mezzanine cafe will make you feel pampered even if you're not staying here. Clientele remains largely a mix of "new Russian" regulars who never glance at their bills, and foreign investors, though the National is increasingly reaching out to tourists through online discounts. Breakfast is included in the rates quoted below.

15/1 Mokhovaya Ulitsa. ℂ 095/258-7000, Le Meridien (toll-free in U.S.): 800/543-4300. Fax 095/258-7100. www. national.ru. 221 units. $370 double; from $470 suite. AE, DC, MC, V. Metro: Okhotny Ryad or Teatralnaya. **Amenities:** 2 restaurants; bar/lounge; mezzanine cafe; small heated indoor pool; health club; spa; Jacuzzi; sauna; concierge; tour desk; car-rental desk; limo; 24-hr. business center; salon; 24-hr. room service; massage; babysitting; laundry service; same-day dry cleaning; nonsmoking rooms; executive rooms. *In room:* A/C, TV w/satellite, dataport, minibar, fridge, coffeemaker, hair dryer, iron, safe.

Metropol 𝒢𝒢   The Art Nouveau mosaic by Mikhail Vrubel that tops the Metropol's facade sets it apart in era and in style from other hotels of its class. Some of its grandeur has faded in comparison to the newer luxury hotels in the neighborhood, but the Metropol, built in 1901 and last renovated in 1991, remains a historic and visual treasure. Even the elevators are exquisite: glass-and-wood chambers ringed with mosaics reflecting the building's exterior. The tearoom is a cozy alternative to the almost-too-opulent main dining hall. The rooms are compact for the price, but several offer antique writing tables or armchairs once belonging to aristocratic Russian families that you won't find elsewhere. The Metropol counted author Leo Tolstoy and artist Kasimir Malevich among its guests before the Soviets took it over as offices. More recent guests have included Jacques Chirac and Arnold Schwarzenegger. Although today's Moscow may be a capitalist wonderland, the hotel faces a statue of Karl Marx in Revolution Square, and the Metropol's western wall is still etched with stylistic letters reading: THE DICTATORSHIP OF THE PROLETARIAT IS READY TO FREE HUMANITY FROM THE YOKE OF CAPITAL. Across from the Marx statue is the Bolshoi Theater, making the Metropol an ideal spot for a post-theater bite. Now that the Hotel Moskva across the square has been razed, the Metropol has a view straight through to the Kremlin.

1/4 Teatralny Proyezd. (C) 095/927-6040. www.metropol-moscow.ru. 365 units. $350 double; from $500 suite. AE, DC, MC, V. Metro: Teatralnaya or Lubyanka. **Amenities:** 3 restaurants; nightclub and casino; health club; spa; Jacuzzi; sauna; concierge; tour desk; transport desk; limo; 24-hr. business center; shopping arcade; salon; 24-hr. room service; massage; laundry service; same-day dry cleaning; nonsmoking rooms; executive rooms. *In room:* A/C, TV w/satellite, dataport, minibar, fridge, coffeemaker, hair dryer, iron, safe.

Savoy 🐝🐝🐝   Tucked on an ever-livening block of cafes and boutiques behind the Bolshoi Theater, the always irreproachable Savoy is just finishing its latest face-lift. Originally built in 1912, it retains the privileged atmosphere designed to serve visiting aristocrats from St. Petersburg and abroad. It's small and almost modest by the standards of Moscow's over-the-top luxury hotels, but that's part of its appeal. It offers top-notch services, a renowned French-Russian restaurant, and a landmark lobby bar that envelops guests in rococo decor and is favored by Russia's political elite.

3 Rozhdestvenskaya Ulitsa. (C) 095/929-8500. Fax 095/230-2186. www.savoy.ru. 70 units. $215–$300 double; suites $400 and up. AE, DC, MC, V. Metro: Teatralnaya, Kuznetsky Most, or Lubyanka. **Amenities:** 2 restaurants; bar and lounge; indoor heated pool; health club; spa; Jacuzzi; sauna; concierge; tour desk; transport desk; limo; 24-hr. business center; shopping arcade; salon; 24-hr. room service; massage; laundry service; same-day dry cleaning; nonsmoking rooms; executive rooms. *In room:* A/C, TV w/satellite, dataport, minibar, fridge, hair dryer, iron, safe.

Currency Confusion

Many hotels, restaurants, and chic shops list their prices in "monetary units" (abbreviated Y.E. in Russian). The unit was essentially another way of saying "dollars" while adhering to the Russian law that forbids businesses from trading in any currency other than the ruble. This practice doesn't make much sense now that the ruble has been as stable as the dollar in recent years, but it persists nonetheless. Today the monetary unit is either pegged to the dollar, the euro, or somewhere in between. Restaurants and hotels will have a note at the front desk and on the menus or price lists indicating the current "monetary unit exchange rate" (for example: 28 rubles = 1 Y.E.). It's a good idea to have a small calculator handy for times like this. Even if the price is listed in dollar-pegged "units," however, you have to pay your bill in rubles. Whew!

Family-Friendly Hotels

Because Moscow's hotel scene still caters more to the business visitor than the school-age one, family-friendly details are not yet par for the course. That is changing gradually, led by such chains as **Marriott,** whose three Moscow hotels offer baby-friendly rooms complete with crib, toys, bottles, and sterilizers. **Sheraton Palace** boasts a children's room where clowns entertain kids during mealtimes, and hosts special holiday events for kids. The **Cosmos** has a bowling alley with croquet-sized balls great for kids' hands, as well as game rooms and a theater that often shows kid-friendly fare. Farther outside town, **Holiday Inn Vinogradovo** offers boat trips, horseback riding, and cross-country skiing in the surrounding countryside. Babysitting services are increasingly available, even if they're not listed on the hotels' official websites and brochures. It's worth a call to check in advance.

2 Tverskaya & Environs

EXPENSIVE

Marco Polo Presnja 𝒦𝒦   A rare example of style, service, and affordability when it opened in 1993, the Marco Polo now faces greater competition in its category, and its prices have risen accordingly. Yet it remains one of Moscow's most coveted places to stay. The Marco Polo's regular clients, often from foreign companies or donor organizations, are fiercely loyal and keep many of its rooms occupied year-round, so book early and check for discounts. The leafy neighborhood between the Boulevard Ring and the Garden Ring is ideal for strolling, and nearby Malaya Bronnaya Street offers several unusual shopping and dining finds you won't encounter on the city's main drags. The main attraction nearby is the park at Patriarchs' Ponds (p. 135). Despite the hotel's relatively modest size, its guest rooms, bathrooms, closets, and corridors are spacious and airy. Room designs vary, but all are modern and subtly decorated, making good use of natural light. In case of emergency, the private, international-standard European Medical Center is right next door.

4 Spiridonevsky Pereulok. © 095/244-3631. Fax 095/926-5402. www.presnja.ru. 72 units. $300 double; from $370 suite; $48 extra bed. AE, DC, MC, V. Metro: Pushkinskaya, Tverskaya, or Mayakovskaya. **Amenities:** 2 restaurants; bar and lounge; sauna; concierge; tour desk; transport desk; business center; room service; massage; laundry service; dry cleaning; executive rooms. *In room:* A/C, TV w/satellite and pay movies, minibar, fridge, hair dryer, iron.

Moscow Marriott Tverskaya 𝒦𝒦 (𝒦𝒾𝒹𝓈)   This most modest of Marriott's ever-expanding Moscow facilities is a preferred spot of business travelers seeking good location, top service, and an intimate atmosphere. Opened in 1995, the hotel blends in with the majestic, columned facades of the bustling Tverskaya-Yamskaya Ulitsa (an extension of Tverskaya St.). Its rooms are fairly well isolated from round-the-clock street noise, but a back-facing room guarantees more peace. Staff is efficient but not effusive; many services are available but you may have to ask for them. The hotel doesn't look like a family-friendly place at first, yet it offers one of the more extensive and generous baby policies in town: They'll set up your room with a crib, toys geared to the age of your child, diaper-changing equipment, high chair, and stroller. Be sure to ask about this when you reserve. The standard rooms are compact but well appointed in rich woods; the added price of the suite gets you an extra room and much more floor space. For similar standards but more luxury and higher prices, inquire about the Marriott Avrora and Marriott Grand down the street.

34 1-st Tverskaya-Yamskaya Ulitsa. ⓒ 095/258-3000; Marriott (toll-free in U.S.): 800/932-2198. Fax 095/258-3099. www.marriott.com. 199 units. $350 double; from $500 suites. AE, DC, MC, V. Metro: Mayakovskaya or Belorusskaya. **Amenities:** 2 restaurants; bar and lounge; heated outdoor pool; health club; sauna; concierge; tour desk; car-rental desk; business center; Wi-Fi; salon; 24-hr. room service; massage; babysitting and other children's services; laundry service; same-day dry cleaning; nonsmoking rooms; executive rooms. *In room:* A/C, TV w/satellite, dataport, minibar, fridge, coffeemaker, hair dryer, iron, safe.

Sheraton Palace *Kids* A sleek modern hotel perched at the top of Tverskaya, the Sheraton offers little historic value but plenty of modern convenience. Its child-friendly weekend brunches are a key draw, with multilingual clowns and an activity room that allows parents to indulge in the all-included caviar and champagne and admire the ice sculptures that decorate the dining hall. The seafood restaurant (Yakor, or "anchor") attracts visitors from around town. Despite triple-paned windows, rooms facing Tverskaya still feel its 24-hour hum; those facing the courtyard are more tranquil but have a gloomy view of apartment blocks. The hotel's glass-and-chrome style may lack character, but it offers a refreshing relief from city grime. The Sheraton was one of the first—and still one of the few—hotels in town with a real fitness center,

---

Foreigner Tax

Price lists are a dizzying affair in Russia. After you've figured out what currency is being quoted (see the box, "Currency Confusion," earlier in this chapter), the most perplexing part for visitors from capitalist economies is that most museums and some older hotels still charge foreigners more than they charge Russians. This is a leftover from Soviet days, when Soviet citizens enjoyed deep subsidies to offset low salaries. The newer hotels, and everything in the "Expensive" range and up, do not employ this practice and charge all clients the same regardless of citizenship. Some hotels, however, still offer lists that include:

• rates for Russian citizens
• rates for citizens of the "near abroad" or the Commonwealth of Independent States (basically a discount for friendly ex-Soviet states)
• rates for everyone else

It's no use protesting this system. If it's any consolation, Russians staying in such facilities often suffer worse service than international (and higher-paying) guests.

In addition, you'll find different prices depending on how upgraded the room or how recent the renovations. These rates are often euphemistically labeled, such as "tourist" rate for the newer rooms and "standard" rate for the older ones. Don't hesitate to ask to clear up any confusion.

including a small jogging track and aerobics classes. The rooms are spacious and sumptuous, and a variety of mattress styles are available upon request. Popular with the investor and luxury tourist classes, the Sheraton's attitude and prices are somewhat more upmarket than those of Sheratons in North America.

19 1st Tverskaya-Yamskaya Ulitsa. ℂ 095/931-9700. Sheraton 800/325-3535. Fax 095/931-9704. www.sheraton palace.ru. 204 units. $380 double; from $530 suite. AE, DC, MC, V. Metro: Belorusskaya. **Amenities:** 3 restaurants; cafe; bar; health club; Jacuzzi; sauna; children's playroom; concierge; tour desk; car-rental desk; limo; 24-hr. business center; salon; 24-hr. room service; massage; babysitting; laundry service; same-day dry cleaning; nonsmoking rooms; executive rooms. *In room:* A/C, TV w/satellite, dataport, minibar, fridge, coffeemaker, hair dryer, iron, safe.

MODERATE

East-West Hotel 🏨🏨   More like an embassy than a hotel, the East-West is a favorite for its central location on a leafy boulevard and its aristocratic ambience. Occupying a small former estate, it's close to the action and to a pleasant playground and paths along Tverskoi Bulvar, but it's set back enough to feel tranquil. Rooms have generous floor space and are decorated with antique or faux-antique bureaus and bathroom fixtures. Mattresses are firm and plumbing is reliable. The hotel is too small for groups, which makes it popular with tourists traveling on their own.

14 Tverskoi Bulvar, building 4. ℂ 095/290-0404. Fax 095/291-4606. www.eastwesthotel.ru. 26 units. $200 double; from $280 suite. AE, MC, V. Metro: Pushkinskaya. **Amenities:** Restaurant; bar; sauna; tour and transport desk; room service; laundry service; dry cleaning. *In room:* TV w/satellite, dataport, fridge.

Holiday Inn Lesnaya 🏨🏨   At last the hotel scene is expanding into this up-and-coming district of Moscow, at the upper end of Tverskaya just beyond the Garden Ring Road. Holiday Inn's first Moscow venture was a resort-type facility outside city limits, while the Lesnaya, opened in 2005, is a much more convenient, though much less green, option. Its meeting rooms attract business visitors, but its overall range of services make it a tourist- and family-friendly option as well. Guest rooms are rather large and more luxurious than those in many Holiday Inns in the United States. The Lesnaya is one of the few moderately priced Moscow hotels offering rooms that are fully wheelchair accessible.

15 Lesnaya Ulitsa. ℂ/fax 095/783-6500. Holiday Inn 888/355-4329. Fax 095/783-6501. www.ichotelsgroup.com. 301 units. $188–$212 double; from $255 suite. AE, DC, MC, V. Metro: Belorusskaya. **Amenities:** Restaurant; health club; concierge; tour desk; car-rental desk; limo; business center; room service; laundry service; dry cleaning; nonsmoking rooms; executive rooms; rooms for those w/limited mobility. *In room:* Satellite TV, dataport, minibar, fridge, coffeemaker, hair dryer, iron.

Pekin 🏨   This lemon-colored confection is situated at the crossing of two major arteries: Tverskaya Street and the Garden Ring Road. A plethora of dining and nightlife options, including the Tchaikovsky Concert Hall across the street, are close by. Fortunately its windows are reinforced to keep out the traffic din, though courtyard-facing rooms are still preferable to street-facing ones. Built in 1949 and named later in honor of Sino-Soviet solidarity, the Pekin fell into disrepair and Mafia hands in the 1990s. It has been undergoing gradual renovation in recent years, and about half of the rooms have been upgraded, with the upper floors converted into office space. The new rooms cost about 30% more than their older counterparts but boast wider, firmer beds and calmer, sleeker decor; some even have bidets. All rooms are spacious by Russian standards but the older rooms suffer narrow creaky beds, chipped furniture, and flowery wallpaper that seems to have absorbed 3 decades of cigarette smoke and dust. The Pekin has one Chinese restaurant, though despite the hotel's name, the food is bland and overpriced. The thugs who made the Pekin notorious a decade ago have largely gone straight or elsewhere, and now the lobby is frequented by Russian and foreign businesspeople and tourists attracted by its location and reasonable prices.

5/1 Bolshaya Sadovaya Ulitsa. © **095/209-2215**. Fax 095/200-1420. 90 units. $100 unrenovated double, $170 renovated; from $200 suite. AE, MC, V. Metro: Mayakovskaya. **Amenities:** 2 restaurants; cafes on each floor; nightclub and casino; sauna; game room; concierge; tour and transport desk; business center; salon; room service; laundry service; dry cleaning. *In room:* A/C, TV w/satellite, fridge, safe.

INEXPENSIVE

Tsentralnaya   One step inside and you understand why these are the cheapest accommodations in the heart of Moscow. The price and its central location (the hotel's name means "central" in English) are the only reasons to stay here. They just barely compensate for the dilapidated rooms, shady guests, and overtired staff. Only the two "deluxe" rooms have showers or bathtubs; the rest have hall facilities with irregular plumbing. The hotel does not arrange visas and is often full, or at least reception clerks claim it is. Securing a room takes persistence or a Russian-speaking mediator. That said, the high ceilings of the pre-revolutionary building suggest former grandeur. It once housed top foreign Communists, but its reputation soured when many Soviet *nomenklatura* staying here were arrested in nighttime raids during Stalin's purges of the 1930s. Today its guests are student travelers or struggling businesspeople from ex-Soviet republics eager for a piece of Moscow's wealth. The hotel offers almost no services of its own, but exchange booths, taxis, restaurants, and bars abound just outside its doors. The VAT is included in the rates quoted below.

10 Tverskaya St. © **095/229-8957**. 40 units. $30–$50 double (shared bathroom); from $80 deluxe with bathroom. No credit cards. Metro: Pushkinskaya or Teatralnaya. **Amenities:** Concierge, sometimes English-speaking.

3 Petrovka & the Ukrainian Quarter

EXPENSIVE

Akvarel ☆☆   This modern aquamarine building is so well hidden from the street that it feels remote, yet it's just around the corner from Moscow's top theaters and designer boutiques. The zone surrounding Akvarel was refashioned in the 1990s into a largely pedestrian district with all new buildings that vaguely echo the pastel facades of 18th-century Moscow. The hotel, built in 2003, is purely 21st century in style, with a small lobby cafe perfect for perusing Moscow's English-language press over breakfast. It attracts business groups and tourists, and offers deep discounts through online travel agencies. Reflecting the hotel's name (*akvarel* means "pastel" in Russian), rooms are decked in pale blue, green, or peach and feel light and open (though few are truly spacious). Breakfast and VAT are included in the rates quoted below.

12 Stoleshnikov Proyezd, building 3. ©/fax **095/502-9430**. www.hotelakvarel.ru. 33 units. $250 double; $320 suite. AE, DC, MC, V. Metro: Teatralnaya, Kuznetsky Most, or Lubyanka. **Amenities:** Restaurant; concierge; tour desk; transport desk; business center; 24-hr. room service; laundry and ironing service; dry cleaning; nonsmoking rooms; safe. *In room:* A/C, TV w/satellite, dataport, minibar, fridge, hair dryer.

Budapest ☆☆   A sturdy stone example of the imposing scale and solidity of Stalin-era architecture, the Budapest is slightly farther from the main streets but abuts several intriguing lanes most tourists never see. St. Peter Monastery up the hill is well worth a visit after your morning tea and *blini*. The building was erected in 1876 as an

Nighttime Companionship

This guide includes no brothels or hotels that charge by the hour, but Russia's lax attitude toward prostitution can be noticeable even in otherwise good-quality hotels. This attitude has fed the demand for prostitutes by foreign businessmen, which in turn means that many hotels, eager to cater to this demographic, double as trysting locales and quietly ignore the sexual commerce in their lobby bars. The average tourist is usually unaffected by this, but foreign men traveling alone may be surprised by a late-night phone call to their rooms offering "female company" for the night. If you make it clear you're not interested—it can't hurt to mention it to the reception desk the next morning—the solicitation will stop.

apartment building, and became a hotel at the turn of the 20th century. It was named after Hungary's capital in the days of Socialist bloc solidarity, and has been renovating for the past few years. In a neighborhood of federal and city government buildings, the Budapest still attracts official delegations as well as a lively tourist clientele. Rooms are discounted 20% Friday through Monday, and breakfast and VAT are included in the rates below. The doormen are listless but the rest of the staff are eager to help. At press time, renovations were underway to add a pool, health club, salon, and new restaurant.

2/18 Petrovskiye Linii. ℂ **095/924-8820.** Fax 095/921-5290. www.hotel-budapest.ru. 116 units. $160–$190 double; from $190 suite. AE, DC, MC, V. Metro: Teatralnaya or Kuznetsky Most. **Amenities:** Cafe; bar; concierge; tour desk; transport desk; 24-hr. business center; room service; laundry service. *In room:* A/C, TV w/satellite, dataport, minibar, fridge, hair dryer, safe.

Sretenka 🎭🎭   The lush winter garden cafe is reason enough to stay in this hotel, or at least stop in for a drink. Built recently, but in the style of the 17th-century mansions that once lined this neighborhood, the two-story hotel is somewhat overpriced for its location, though online discounts are easy to find. The Sretenka offers a more intimate Russian experience than the chains, yet has all the modern amenities, unlike its Soviet-era counterparts. Adjacent Ulitsa Sretenka has plenty of shops and restaurants less frequented by the tourist crowds, and the neighboring lanes are full of old churches and architectural finds from past centuries—though no major tourist sights. The hotel is located between two metro stations, a good 10-minute walk to either one. Rooms are tastefully arranged with a combination of modern Scandinavian design and a few antiques. Russian and foreign executives are regulars at the Sretenka; tour groups are rare because it's so small. Breakfast and VAT are included in the room rate.

15 Ulitsa Sretenka. ℂ **095/303-8647.** Fax 095/303-8648. www.hotel-sretenskaya.ru. 38 units. $198 double; from $249 suite; weekend discounts available. Extra bed $25. AE, DC, MC, V. Metro: Sukharevskaya or Turgenevskaya. **Amenities:** Restaurant; bar; small indoor pool; health club; Jacuzzi; sauna; billiards room; concierge; tour desk; transport desk; 24-hr. business center; salon; 24-hr. room service; laundry service; dry cleaning. *In room:* A/C, TV w/satellite, dataport, minibar, fridge, hair dryer, safe.

MODERATE

Polesye (Belarusian Embassy Hotel)   An unexpected treasure in this neighborhood of crooked lanes and embassies, this renovated mansion enjoys a convenient yet quiet location and reasonable prices. The building, built in 1780 by architect Matvei Kazakov, pioneer of Moscow Classicism, is among the perks the otherwise impoverished Belarusian government enjoys for its loyalty to Russia as other ex-Soviet republics have distanced themselves from Moscow. The rooms are modest and bear hints of Soviet nostalgia, with their standard-issue wallpaper and heavy dark wardrobes. Though it's connected to the embassy, the hotel is a commercial venture and most of the guests are businesspeople from neighboring countries. Despite the reputation of the Belarusian KGB, past guests insist the staff is more helpful than suspicious and that the average tourist has nothing to fear.

6 Armyansky Pereulok. © 095/928-5535. Fax 095/928-2827. hoteladmin1@embassybel.ru. 60 units. $92–$106 double. AE, DC, MC, V. Metro: Kitai-Gorod. **Amenities:** Restaurant and bar; cafes on each floor; sauna; concierge; tour desk; transport desk; business center; laundry and ironing service. *In room:* TV w/cable, fridge.

Sverchkov   The Sverchkov should serve as an example to would-be Moscow hoteliers: a two-story, 18th-century mansion converted into a small hotel, tucked in a tranquil courtyard on a historic lane, next to a folk art museum and within walking distance of Moscow's key sights. The downside of such a small place is that it's often full and its services are limited. The prices are rising faster than warranted, in response to demand and the dearth of similar options in the neighborhood. Avoid the run-down basement cafe. The restaurant upstairs is okay, but I recommend dining in the nearby Chistiye Prudy neighborhood. Guest rooms are clean, though some need remodeling—ask when you reserve whether the room has been renovated.

8 Sverchkov Pereulok, building 1. © 095/925-4978. Fax 095/925-4436. www.hotel-sverchkov.ru. 10 units. $120 double; $200 suite. AE, DC, MC, V. Metro: Turgenevskaya or Kitai Gorod. **Amenities:** Restaurant; cafe-bar; sauna; business center; laundry service. *In room:* TV w/cable, fridge.

4 Arbat

EXPENSIVE

Radisson SAS Slavyanskaya ⊛   This pioneering U.S.-Russian joint venture set the standard when it opened in 1991 and remains a gleaming oasis in an otherwise dingy neighborhood. Bill Clinton stayed here on a visit when he was president. Its reputation suffered through several management disputes and the murder of its American co-founder in 1996, but the Slavyanskaya's shadiest days appear to have passed. Rooms are large and light and are frequently updated. The hotel's gallery of designer boutiques is still a prime spot for ogling Russia's nouveau riche and the prices they pay for underwear. The hotel has a full-size movie theater that shows American and other films in English, and the hotel pool is a blissful escape from city grit. The once-seedy market and square around nearby Kievsky Station is having a long overdue face-lift that can only boost the Slavyanskaya's appeal.

2 Europe Sq. © 800/333-3333 or 095/941-8020. Fax 095/941-8000. www.radissonsas.com. 410 units. $299 double; from $399 suite. AE, DC, MC, V. Metro: Kievskaya. **Amenities:** 4 restaurants; bar; lounge; indoor pool; health club; Jacuzzi; sauna; game room; concierge; tour desk; car-rental desk; limo; 24-hr. business center; Wi-Fi; shopping arcade; salon; 24-hr. room service; massage; laundry service; same-day dry cleaning; nonsmoking rooms; executive rooms. *In room:* A/C, TV w/satellite and pay movies, dataport, minibar, fridge, coffeemaker, hair dryer, iron, safe.

Zolotoye Koltso (Golden Ring) ⊛   The entrance alone earns this hotel its "golden" epithet, with its blinding awnings and lobby fixtures (the name really refers to a ring of historic and religious cities north of Moscow). A 1998 renovation brought the Golden Ring into Moscow's executive-level hotel class, one of the few that's not part of a chain. Now the Golden Ring caters more to discriminating Russian clients and their often opulent tastes than to the average tourist. Still, it has a range of room styles and standards, and the decor grows calmer as the prices drop. The hotel towers over the Moscow River and Smolenskaya Square and is nearly adjacent to the Arbat pedestrian zone. More intriguing is the sleepier district of once-prestigious residential blocks behind the hotel, perfect for a quiet tour of "real-life" Moscow. Guest rooms and bathrooms are spacious and flawlessly equipped. Look out for online discounts or group tours that stay here. The hotel is much taller than the neighboring buildings, so many of the rooms enjoy broad views of the city and/or the river.

5 Smolenskaya Ploshchad. © 095/725-0100. Fax 095/725-0101. www.hotel-goldenring.ru. 293 units. $204–$305 double; from $300 suite. AE, DC, MC, V. Metro: Teatralnaya, Kuznetsky Most, or Lubyanka. **Amenities:** 4 restaurants; 2 bars; health club; spa; Jacuzzi; sauna; game room; concierge; tour desk; transport desk; 24-hr. business center; shopping arcade; salon; 24-hr. room service; massage; laundry service; same-day dry cleaning; nonsmoking rooms; executive rooms. *In room:* A/C, TV w/satellite, dataport, minibar, fridge, coffeemaker, hair dryer, iron, safe.

MODERATE

Arbat 🌟🌟 *Value* This 1960s hotel is a rare example of good quality, price, and location concentrated in one place. On a calm street near the commerce of the Arbat and the Garden Ring, the hotel's only downside is the renovation noise as rooms are gradually upgraded. Ask for a room away from the construction. Until the upgrade is finished, the hotel offers a range of room standards and prices, from a spare unrenovated room with a single bed to suites with new leather couches and bidets. Visiting delegations, foreign and Russian, often stay here, taking up many rooms, but it's large enough that it almost always has space available for individual visitors. Rates include breakfast and VAT.

12 Plotnikov Pereulok. © 095/244-7628. Fax 095/244-0093. hotelarbat@hotmail.com. 84 units. $140 unrenovated double, $180 renovated double; from $220 suite. AE, DC, MC, V. Parking $10 per day. Metro: Smolenskaya. **Amenities:** Restaurant; bar; concierge; tour desk; transport desk; 24-hr. business center; salon; 24-hr. room service; laundry service; same-day dry cleaning; nonsmoking rooms; executive rooms. *In room:* A/C, TV w/satellite, fridge.

Belgrade 🌟 This tower, overlooking the Moscow River, the spires of the Foreign Ministry, and enormous Smolenskaya Square, offers different levels of accommodations and good quality for the money. It's around the corner from the Arbat and all the dining and shopping that the pedestrian street has to offer. A 2003 renovation upgraded half the rooms; others are due for remodeling later. The renovated rooms (called "tourist" class) are larger; are air-conditioned; and have fresher carpeting, brighter lights, and fewer plumbing issues than the older ones (called "standard" class). Don't miss the generous breakfast. Service can be stiff, but the hotel is tourist-friendly overall. It's popular enough with business visitors to offer all the essential services that executives demand, but it doesn't feel like a conference center.

8 Smolenskaya Ulitsa. © 095/248-3125. Fax 095/248-2814. www.hotel-belgrad.ru. 232 units. $90 unrenovated double, $130–$165 renovated double; $130 unrenovated suite, $260 renovated suite. Full breakfast $12. AE, MC, V. Metro: Smolenskaya. **Amenities:** Restaurant; bar and lounge; tour desk; transport desk; business center; salon; room service; massage; laundry service; dry cleaning. *In room:* A/C, TV w/satellite and pay movies, minibar, fridge, coffeemaker, hair dryer, iron, safe.

Ukraina This monument of "Stalin Gothic" architecture—one of seven similar towers around town—offers splendid views from nearly all of its rooms, either of the Moscow River, the house of government that Russians call their White House, or some other corner of the capital. If you get a room facing the parking lot, ask to be moved to one with a better view—with nearly 1,000 rooms, there's probably one available. The feeling of grandeur overshadows the Ukraina's flaws: The dodgy characters in the lobby can be off-putting, and the casino is only worth visiting if you're looking for a prostitute. The breakfast halls are charming and the restaurant has all the pomp and shirred curtains of a Stalin-era reception. The guest rooms have high ceilings and aging furniture, though the bathrooms are renovated. The hotel is rather far from the metro and the main sights, but in good weather the walk upriver along the embankment is a memorable experience most tourists won't get. A 15-minute walk from Arbat Street, Ukraina is at the foot of the prestigious Kutuzovsky Prospekt, a broad avenue that has housed Russian dignitaries since the 1950s and now boasts designer boutiques. Keep an eye out on weekday mornings for President Putin's motorcade as it whizzes down the street toward the Kremlin.

2/1 Kutuzovsky Prospekt. ℂ 095/933-5656. Fax 095/243-3276. www.ukraina-hotel.ru. 930 units. $150 unrenovated double, $180 renovated double; from $200 suite. AE, DC, MC, V. Metro: Kievskaya. **Amenities:** 5 restaurants; cafe/bar on many floors; casino and nightclub; health club; sauna; game room; concierge; tour desk; transport desk; business center; shopping arcade; salon; room service; massage; laundry service; dry cleaning. *In room:* A/C, TV w/ satellite, fridge, safe.

5 South of Moscow River

VERY EXPENSIVE

Baltschug Kempinski 🏵🏵🏵   The Baltschug led the post-Soviet transformation of this district across the Moscow River from the Kremlin. Its pristine, buttercup-yellow facade immediately altered the neglected neighborhood of canals and abandoned churches. The Baltschug's top-floor suites have housed presidents and famous visitors, including pop stars like Michael Jackson. It's also a favorite of television crews who use its Kremlin-facing rooms for stand-ups with St. Basil's Cathedral in the background. Commerce in the immediate vicinity is limited but growing. Just over the bridge is Red Square and its attendant activity; the bohemian bustle of Pyatnitskaya Street spreads out in the other direction, to the south. The guest rooms are relatively large, modern, and subtly appointed. Don't miss the sumptuous brunch of pre-revolutionary Russian delicacies and all the caviar you could want.

1 Ulitsa Balchug. ℂ 800/426-3135 or 095/230-6500. Fax 095/230-6502. www.kempinski-moscow.com. 232 units. $360 double; from $800 suite. $65 extra bed. AE, DC, MC, V. Metro: Teatralnaya, Kuznetsky Most, or Lubyanka. **Amenities:** 3 restaurants; 2 bars; indoor heated pool; health club; spa; Jacuzzi; 2 saunas; children's center; game room; concierge; tour desk; car-rental desk; limo; 24-hr. business center; Wi-Fi; shopping arcade; salon; 24-hr. room service; massage; babysitting; laundry service; same-day dry cleaning; nonsmoking rooms; executive rooms. *In room:* A/C, TV w/satellite, dataport, minibar, fridge, coffeemaker, hair dryer, iron, safe.

EXPENSIVE

President Hotel   The elegant red brick complex looks at first like a government building, an impression fueled by the rigorous security screening at the entrance. That's no accident, since the President Hotel was designed at the Communist leadership's request in 1982 for international negotiations and party meetings. It continues to host high-profile international conferences and was frequented by Al Gore when he was the U.S. vice president. Its guests reflect whatever conference is under way: oil executives, political scientists, environmental groups. It can be hard for individual tourists to get "approved" for space, so check well in advance if you're interested. The hotel is rather removed from the top tourist sites, but it is near Gorky Park and the Central House of Artists, Moscow's chief modern art museum. Just behind the hotel, toward the Moscow River, is an unusual collection of deposed statues of Lenin and other fallen Soviet heroes (see the review of Art MUSEON on p. 130). Guest rooms lack color but are well-maintained and spacious. Breakfast and VAT are included in the rate.

24 Bolshaya Yakimanka Ulitsa. ℭ **095/239-3800.** Fax 095/239-3646. www.president-hotel.ru. 208 units. $260 double; from $350 suite. AE, DC, MC, V. Metro: Teatralnaya, Kuznetsky Most, or Lubyanka. **Amenities:** 2 restaurants; bar and lounge; health club with personal trainers; sauna; game room; concierge; tour desk; transport desk; business center; salon; 24-hr. room service; laundry service; same-day dry cleaning; presidential rooms. *In room:* A/C, TV w/ satellite, dataport, fridge, hair dryer, safe.

MODERATE

Akademicheskaya 🔆 Ⓥⁿˡᵘᵉ   A 1960s-era hotel with a modern facade, this hotel lacks grandeur but offers everything else a hotel should: efficient service, clean rooms, and low prices. Ask for an upgraded room if they're available; the price isn't that much higher than that of an older room, but the beds are larger and firmer, the bathrooms much roomier, and the windows much better at keeping out street noise. The older rooms are still a fair value for the money. All units have full bathrooms. The corridors, some of them musty, are lined with photos of renowned academics, some of whom have stayed at the Akademicheskaya. Scientific conferences still sometimes use the hotel, and an increasing number of tourists are discovering its value. The staff is often rushed, but that's a welcome alternative to the lethargic service at many Soviet-era hotels. If you need a service, be persistent. The immediate vicinity has plenty of low-budget commerce. Most major sights require a trip on the metro, which is just across the street. Gorky Park is down the hill, and the stirring statue of Lenin on nearby October Square, one of the few left standing, warrants a viewing.

1 Donskaya Ulitsa. ℭ **095/238-4682.** Fax 095/238-2539. www.maan.ru. 280 units. $55–$75 unrenovated double, $90–$120 renovated double; $200 suite. MC, V. Metro: Oktyabrskaya. **Amenities:** Restaurant; bar; sauna; concierge; tour desk; transport and airline desk; business center; salon; laundry service. *In room:* TV w/satellite, fridge.

Ozerkovskaya 🔆🔆 Ⓥⁿˡᵘᵉ   A welcome addition to the hotel scene south of the Moscow River, the Ozerkovskaya occupies a new brick building set off from the road along one of the canals in the picturesque Zamoskvarechye. Eager staff and cozy yet spacious rooms make the Ozerkovskaya one of Moscow's best hotels in this category. Run by the Central Tourism and Rest Council, whose other facilities are mostly in the countryside, this hotel feels a bit like a country inn. Attic rooms are especially appealing, with skylights in the slanted ceilings and more floor space than below. Firm, queen-size beds and new hardwood floors add to the hotel's appeal. Its location, deep in a residential neighborhood, is not exactly central, but it's certainly quiet. Tretyakov Gallery can be reached on foot; and the Paveletskaya metro station is about a 10-minute walk away. Note the curious neighborhood landscaping, with old tires used as planters and candy-colored bowling balls topping fence posts. Rates include VAT and breakfast.

50 Ozerkovskaya Naberezhnaya, building 2. ℭ **095/951-9582.** Fax 095/951-9753. ozerkovskaya@bk.ru. 25 units. $170 double; from $210 suite. AE, DC, MC, V. Metro: Paveletskaya. **Amenities:** Restaurant and bar; health club with very small pool; sauna; billiard room; tour desk; transport desk; business center; salon; room service; laundry and ironing service; dry cleaning; executive rooms. *In room:* TV w/satellite, dataport, kitchen, minibar, fridge, hair dryer.

Varshava (Warsaw)   Improved service could make the Varshava a top-value locale. It's still in a decent location, with modern rooms and reasonable rates. The main challenge is the staff's reluctance to speak English, but informational material in several languages is available in the lobby. Though the hotel's name (left over from the days when Poland was part of the Soviet bloc) and service are outdated, the guest rooms offer plain Scandinavian-style furniture in primary colors and none of the patterned wallpaper of Soviet days. Most bathrooms have showers only. International and Russian business travelers often stay here. The hotel is next to the Oktyabrskaya metro station and up the street from Gorky Park. The restaurant on the eighth floor has a rather Mafiosi feel, though the breakfast hall is pleasant. A buffet breakfast is included in the price.

2 Leninsky Prospekt. © **095/238-1970.** Fax 095/238-9639. Warsaw@sovintel.ru. 80 units. $70–$90 double; from $180 suite. AE, DC, MC, V. Metro: Oktyabrskaya. **Amenities:** Restaurant; bar; health club; sauna; tour desk; transport desk; business center; salon; laundry service. *In room:* TV, fridge.

6 Outside the Garden Ring

EXPENSIVE

Holiday Inn Vinogradovo ⚮ *Kids*   This resort-type facility is unlike anything else Moscow has to offer. Well removed from the city, it's tucked in a forest 4km (2½ miles) beyond the bypass marking the city limits, not too far from the airport. The free shuttle to and from town takes a while but makes the hotel feel less remote. The plus side of such a distant locale is the availability of outdoor amenities unheard-of at other Moscow hotels: horseback riding, sledding, and cross-country skiing in winter; watersports on a nearby lake in summer. Not surprisingly, this makes it a big draw for families traveling with children. The rooms are situated around a central courtyard, but since you're in the country, ask for a lake- or church-facing room. Guest rooms and bathrooms are generous in size, and some doubles even offer two double beds instead of two singles—a rare luxury in Russia. Kids eat free. Pets are allowed.

Dmitrovskoye Shosse, ext. 171. © **877/477-4674** (toll-free), or 095/937-0670. www.ichotels.com. 154 units. $200–$270 double, depending on when you reserve; from $300 suite. AE, DC, MC, V. 4km (2½ miles) north of Moscow Ring Rd. along Dmitrovskoye Shosse (visible from the highway). **Amenities:** 2 restaurants; 2 bars; indoor pool; health club; sauna; tour desk; transport desk; 24-hr. business center; salon; 24-hr. room service; massage; laundry room; same-day dry cleaning; nonsmoking rooms; executive rooms; bowling alley. *In room:* TV w/satellite, fridge, coffeemaker, iron.

Sovietsky Hotel ⚮   The Sovietsky was built in the 1950s on the site of a legendary restaurant, Yar (p. 116), there for more than a century. It became a residence and hotel for Soviet functionaries. After falling into disrepair as the country that it was named after collapsed, the hotel launched massive renovations in 1998. It's now increasingly popular with business and pleasure travelers, both Russian and international. Everything about the hotel is big: The 12-foot-plus ceilings, the malachite columns, the Art Nouveau chandeliers, the regal corridors built on a space-is-no-object scale. The guest rooms, too, have generous floor space and seem even bigger because of the high ceilings. The room decor remains largely stuck in the Soviet era, with clashing flowery prints on wallpaper, curtains, bedspreads, and carpets. Bathrooms are basic but modern. The restaurant is worth a tour just to glimpse the wall-to-wall-to-ceiling frescoes. The summer terrace in the courtyard is a calmer place to dine. Pets are accepted.

32/2 Leningradsky Prospekt. © 095/960-2000. www.sovietsky.ru. 100 units. $180–$220 double depending on how far in advance you book; from $220 suite. AE, DC, MC, V. Free guarded parking. Metro: Dinamo. **Amenities:** 1 restaurant (plus summer terrace dining); 2 bars; nightclub; lounge; health club; sauna; children's center; concierge; tour desk; transport desk; business center; shopping arcade; salon; 24-hr. room service; massage; laundry service; same-day dry cleaning; safe at reception. *In room:* A/C, satellite TV, dataport, fridge, hair dryer.

MODERATE

Alpha   This is one of the hotels in the **Izmailovsky Hotel Complex,** a collection of adjacent, nearly identical hotel towers that were originally under single ownership as Moscow's biggest hotel, with more than 8,000 rooms. Now they are four separate entities named after letters of the Greek alphabet. I've included three of the hotels in this section; the fourth hotel, the Beta, is in such disrepair that I don't recommend it. The complex is far from the city center but right next to a metro station—and to the biggest outdoor crafts and souvenir bazaar in town, the renowned Izmailovsky Market (see chapter 8 for shopping hints). The drab 28-story towers are linked by terraced concrete plazas with fountains in the summer, a design that seemed futuristic when they were built in the 1980s but now seems rather bleak. The Alpha is closest to the metro and the most garish of the complex's four hotels. It was renovated in 2000 and its labyrinthine lobby now clearly posts its rates on a huge board and even harbors a sushi bar. Security appears tight, although shady characters from the nearby bazaar sometimes congregate at the bars. The corridors and stairwells remain gloomy, though the rooms are fresh.

71 Izmailovskoye Shosse. © **095/721-3322.** Fax 095/166-0003. www.alfa-hotel.ru. 945 units. $100 double; from $160 suite. AE, MC, V. Metro: Izmailovsky Park. **Amenities:** 3 restaurants; 2 bars; cafe; health club; sauna; concierge; tour desk; transport desk; business center; shopping arcade; salon; room service; laundry service. *In room:* Satellite TV, fridge, iron, safe.

Cosmos 🖈🖈 *Kids*   This sweeping, semicircular structure looks down over a labyrinth of roads facing the showcase exhibition center which, like the hotel, was built to shameless Soviet scale. Size does matter at the Cosmos: 25 floors, more than 1,700 rooms, nine restaurants. Built for the 1980 Olympics, it was one of the few hotels to actively recruit Western tourists in the Soviet era, and was a magnet for American high school groups and church tours in the 1980s. Since a late 1990s renovation, the Cosmos is back in demand among foreigners of all nationalities. The style is pure late Soviet, with practicality a greater design concern than aesthetics. Endless corridors lead to basic rooms, most of which have views of large swaths of Moscow—though not its most picturesque swaths. Despite the immensity of everything else about the Cosmos, guest rooms and bathrooms are compact. Location is the major drawback here. Though the metro is nearby, it takes a good 5 minutes just to walk up the Cosmos's long driveway, and the metro ride to the center of town takes 20 minutes. Bonuses include water aerobics, a children's pool with water slides, and a bowling alley. Breakfast and VAT are included in the room rate.

150 Prospekt Mira. © **095/234-1000.** Fax 095/215-8880. www.hotelcosmos.ru. 1,700 units. $140 double; from $200 suite. AE, DC, MC, V. Metro: VDNKh. **Amenities:** 5 restaurants; 2 cafes; 2 bars; lounge; casino; nightclub; concert hall; 2 indoor pools; health club; spa; Jacuzzi; sauna; children's center; game room; bowling alley; concierge; tour desk; transport desk; 24-hr. business center; shopping arcade; salons; 24-hr. room service; massage; babysitting; laundry service; same-day dry cleaning. *In room:* A/C, TV w/ satellite, dataport, minibar, fridge, safe.

Gamma-Delta 🖈 *Value*   The sleekest, friendliest, and fairest-priced hotel in the Izmailovsky Hotel Complex (see also listings for the Alpha and the Vega), this is the closest to a Western-standard facility in this price range. Lobby computer screens tastefully and helpfully display prices and services in Russian and English. The 2002 renovation couldn't rid the hotel of its clumsy gray structure, but the soft tones of the room decor distract you from the outer ugliness. The hotel is actually two buildings, the Gamma and the Delta, connected on their lower floors. Staff is friendly and accustomed to international travelers (non-Russian speakers).

71 Izmailovskoye Shosse. © **095/737-7055.** Fax 095/166-7486. www.izmailovo.ru. More than 1,000 units. $60 unrenovated double, $80 renovated double; from $80 suite. AE, DC, MC, V. Metro: Izmailovsky Park. **Amenities:** 9 restaurants and bars; sauna; game room; concierge; tour desk; transport desk; business center; shopping arcade; salon; room service; laundry and ironing service. *In room:* TV w/cable, fridge, hair dryer.

Vega   The Vega tries to be the most elite of the Izmailovsky Hotel Complex (see also listings for the Alpha and Gamma-Delta hotels), but it succeeds more in alienating customers than in impressing them. The atmosphere is more understated than the Alpha's. The Vega is popular with low-budget businesspeople from ex-Soviet republics. Guest rooms are compact and uninventive. Avoid the nightclub, which doubles as a bordello. Cellphones are available for rent at a low price.

71 Izmailovskoye Shosse, building 3B. © **095/956-0642.** www.hotel-vega.ru. 900 units. $70 unrenovated double, $110 renovated double; from $150 suite. AE, DC, MC, V. Metro: Izmailovsky Park. **Amenities:** 5 restaurants; 2 bars; Jacuzzi; sauna; game room; concierge; tour desk; transport desk; business center; shopping arcade; salon; room service; massage; laundry service. *In room:* Cable TV in all rooms; minibar, hair dryer in some rooms.

INEXPENSIVE
Globus   Hidden behind the enormous Cosmos Hotel is the Globus, a modest hotel within an anonymous-looking apartment block. Its rooms include kitchenettes; in fact, many are renovated studio apartments. The price is reasonable, with three categories of rooms: those with Russian TV; those with satellite TV, hair dryer, iron, and air-conditioning; and those with two rooms, Jacuzzi, bidet, and coffeemaker. The big drawback here is the limited English-language service, though the staff is eager to help with taxis and theater tickets. The Globus is a 5- to 10-minute walk to the metro and the All-Russian Exhibition Center.

17 Yaroslavskaya Ulitsa. © **095/286-4189.** Fax 095/286-4616. www.hotelglobus.ru. 95 units. Category A rooms: $65–$120 double; Category B rooms: $80–$135 double; Category C rooms: $150–$180 double. AE, MC, V. Metro: VDNKh. **Amenities:** Restaurant; bar; sauna; tour desk; transport desk; business center; salon; laundry service. *In room:* See description of categories above.

G&R Hostels   Though Moscow lacks hostels of the traditional sort, several independent entrepreneurs have taken over a floor or more of existing buildings and converted them into low-budget accommodations. G&R is one of the more pleasant and reliable in this category, occupying three floors of the drab and unremarkable Hotel Asia in southeast Moscow. The hostel offers family-style units with private bathrooms and telephones, in addition to singles and doubles with shared bathrooms. All units are clean, if sparsely furnished. Run by an Indian-Russian team, staff is English-speaking and very accommodating, offering as much help as many four-star-hotel concierges. Despite its small size, the hostel can arrange for visas, a big plus in this price category. The main drawback of G&R—like all Moscow hostels—is its distance from the center of town. G&R is almost on top of a metro station (Ryazansky Prospekt), however, and the ride to the center takes about 15 minutes. They'll also arrange a ride from the airport for a reasonable price. For more immediate needs, the surrounding neighborhood has markets, shops, and a few cheap though gastronomically risky cafes. Prices include VAT and breakfast, and discounts are available.

3/2 Zelenodolskaya St. © **095/378-0001.** www.hostels.ru. 15 units. $30 single w/shared bathroom; $48 double w/shared bathroom; $70–$95 family suite. MC, V. Metro: Ryazansky Prospekt. **Amenities:** Tour and transport desk; visa support; common kitchen; business center. *In room:* Some rooms with cable TV, fridge.

7 Near the Airport

Novotel   This French-Russian venture is the only decent hotel at Sheremetevo-2 Airport, and is in fact the first thing you see as you approach the airport by car. The drab gray building matches the drab gray airport. However, the hotel's interior is much cleaner and friendlier than the terminal nearby. There's little French about its style except for its restaurant, which serves by far the best food within a several-mile radius. The hotel offers free shuttle service downtown, but be prepared for long traffic jams anytime close to rush hour.

Sheremetevo-2 Airport. ✆ **095/926-5900.** Fax 095/926-5903. www.novotel.ru. 488 units. $287 double; from $422 suite; $54 extra bed. AE, DC, MC, V. Free secure parking. **Amenities:** 2 restaurants; bar; nightclub; health club; indoor pool; sauna; game room; concierge; tour desk; transport desk; 24-hr. business center; salon; 24-hr. room service; massage; laundry service; same-day dry cleaning; nonsmoking rooms; executive rooms. *In room:* A/C, TV w/satellite, dataport, minibar, safe.

6

Where to Dine in Moscow

Russia's culinary traditions run from the daylong, table-crushing feasts of the 19th-century aristocracy to the cabbage soup and potatoes on which generations of ordinary Russians were raised. In today's Moscow you can find food to satisfy any palate, in marked contrast to the decades of Soviet shortages. The city's post-Soviet dining scene has evolved much faster than its hotel scene, fortunately, and there are now restaurants to suit any pocketbook or craving—and at any time of day or night. Moscow seems to have more 24-hour restaurants than anywhere in Europe. The farther out of the center you venture, the more limited your overall choices, though that, too, is changing fast. All restaurants listed here offer menus in English unless noted.

Restaurants generally serve continuously from lunch through dinner, and few are open before noon. Though reliable American and European restaurants proliferate, try some that specialize in Russian or fusion Russian-European cuisine. An even better idea is to sample the cuisines from other former Soviet republics, which you're much less likely to find at home: the Caucasus Mountains spices of Georgia, Azerbaijan, and Armenia; or the central Asian *plovs* (a rice pilaf dish, usually with vegetables and beef or lamb) of Uzbekistan and Tajikistan. These cuisines have worked their way into Russian cooking over the centuries, and they boast a much richer selection of fruits, vegetables, and spices than Russia's cold climate can produce.

Russians themselves, who can get traditional *pelmeny* (meat ravioli) and buttery rye *blini* (crepelike pancakes) at home, seem to prefer French or Japanese food when they eat out. Sushi in particular has experienced a boom since the late 1990s that is rather disconcerting for such a landlocked city.

Top-end hotels offer elaborate, all-you-can-eat Sunday brunches, replete with caviar and Russian delicacies as well as an abundance of standard breakfast foods, salads, meats, and mouthwatering desserts. While not cheap, they're a worthwhile splurge on a bad-weather day for the atmosphere and thoroughly satisfying food. These hotels often offer pleasant afternoon tea service, good for an elegant pick-me-up that won't cost nearly as much as a meal.

International chain restaurants, hotel restaurants, and those in the top price categories all have nonsmoking sections; elsewhere it's hit-or-miss. The trend for nonsmoking sections is catching on fast, so call in advance to check on this if smoke is a major issue for you.

Menu prices can be confusing, since they're often pegged to either the dollar or the euro. Because of this practice, prices listed here are in U.S. dollars, though when the check comes you'll have to pay in rubles at the current exchange rate. See the "Currency Confusion" box on p. 83 for a fuller explanation. Credit cards are catching on quickly but are rarely accepted in small or inexpensive cafes. For a history of Russian dining traditions and descriptions of typical dishes, see "Food & Drink" in appendix A; for a glossary of menu terms, see appendix B.

Tips Business Lunches

A great midday meal bargain is the "biznes-lanch" now offered by many Russian restaurants at all ends of the spectrum. Aimed at Russia's thriving—and busy—business clientele, the lunches are served quickly and efficiently, and generally include appetizer, main course, and dessert for $8 to $20. This is a great way to check out the cuisine or atmosphere of popular restaurants or nightclubs that are too crowded or expensive at dinnertime.

1 Restaurants by Cuisine

AMERICAN
Starlite Diner (Tverskaya & Environs, $$, p. 106)

ARCTIC
Expeditsiya ✿ (Petrovka & Ukrainian Quarter, $$$, p. 109)

BULGARIAN
Mekhana Bansko ✿ (Arbat District, $$, p. 114)

CAUCASIAN (GEORGIAN, ARMENIAN, AZERBAIJANI)
Genatsvale ✿✿ (Arbat District, $$, p. 114)
Mama Zoya ✿ (Arbat District, $, p. 115)
Noah's Ark ✿ (Petrovka & Ukrainian Quarter, $$$, p. 110)
Prisoner of the Caucasus ✿ (Beyond the Garden Ring, $$$, p. 115)
Shesh-Besh ✿ (Beyond the Moscow River, $$, p. 113)

CENTRAL ASIAN
Rakhat-Lukum (Petrovka & the Ukrainian Quarter, $$, p. 110)
White Sun of the Desert ✿ (Petrovka & the Ukrainian Quarter, $$, p. 111)
Yolki-Palki Po... ✿ (Tverskaya & Environs, $, p. 109)

FOOD COURT
Okhotny Ryad Shopping Center (Around Red Square, $, p. 104)

FRENCH
Carre Blanc ✿✿ (Beyond the Garden Ring, $$$, p. 115)

INTERNATIONAL
Bosco Cafe and Bar ✿✿ (Around Red Square, $$$, p. 102)
FAQCafe ✿ (Around Red Square, $$, p. 103)
Korrea's ✿ (Beyond the Garden Ring, $$, p. 117)
Okhotny Ryad Shopping Center (Around Red Square, $, p. 104)
Shtolnaya ✿ (Beyond the Moscow River, $$, p. 113)
Tchaikovsky Concert Hall (Tverskaya & Environs, $, p. 108)

ITALIAN
Donna Clara ✿ (Tverskaya & Environs, $$, p. 105)
Il Patio (Tverskaya & Environs, $$, p. 106)
Krem ✿ (Around Red Square, $$, p. 104)

JAPANESE
Sushi Vyosla ✿ (Around Red Square, $$$, p. 102)

JEWISH
Tsimmes (Beyond the Garden Ring, $$, p. 117)

RUSSIAN
Aristocrat ✿ (Petrovka & the Ukrainian Quarter, $$$, p. 109)
Beluga ✿✿ (Tverskaya & Environs, $$$$, p. 104)
Drova (Petrovka & Ukrainian Quarter, $, p. 111)
Kitezh ✿✿✿ (Petrovka & Ukrainian Quarter, $$$, p. 109)

Key to Abbreviations: $$$$ = Very Expensive $$$ = Expensive $$ = Moderate $ = Inexpensive

Kremlyovsky Cafe (Around Red Square, $, p. 104)

Metropol 🦀🦀 (Around Red Square, $$$$, p. 99)

Na Melnitse 🦀 (Tverskaya & Environs, $$, p. 106)

1 Red Square 🦀🦀🦀 (Around Red Square, $$$$, p. 99)

Pavilion at Patriarshy 🦀 (Tverskaya & Environs, $$$, p. 105)

Russkye Raki 🦀 (Petrovka & the Ukrainian Quarter, $, p. 112)

Shokoladnitsa 🦀 (Beyond the Moscow River, $, p. 113)

Sudar 🦀🦀 (Beyond the Garden Ring, $$$, p. 116)

Uncle Vanya 🦀🦀 (Beyond the Moscow River, $$, p. 113)

Vanil 🦀 (Arbat District, $$$, p. 114)

Yar 🦀 (Beyond the Garden Ring, $$$, p. 116)

RUSSIAN/AMERICAN

Rostik's (Tverskaya & Environs, $, p. 107) RUSSIAN/european

Easy Food (Around Red Square, $$, p. 103)

Grilyazh 🦀🦀 (Beyond the Moscow River, $$$, p. 112)

TRAM 🦀 (Tverskaya & Environs, $$, p. 107)

RUSSIAN/FRENCH

Parizhsk 🦀 (Arbat District, $$, p. 114)

RUSSIAN/GEORGIAN

Stary Gorod 🦀 (Beyond the Garden Ring, $, p. 117)

RUSSIAN/INTERNATIONAL

Cafe Pushkin 🦀🦀🦀 (Tverskaya & Environs, $$$, p. 105)

Gogol (Petrovka & Ukrainian Quarter, $, p. 111)

UKRAINIAN

Shinok 🦀 (Beyond the Garden Ring, $$$, p. 116)

Taras Bulba Korchma 🦀 (Petrovka & the Ukrainian Quarter, $$, p. 111)

VEGETARIAN/ASIAN

Tofu (Tverskaya & Environs, $$, p. 107)

YUGOSLAV

Budva (Petrovka & the Ukrainian Quarter, $$, p. 110)

---

2 Around Red Square & the Kremlin

VERY EXPENSIVE

Metropol 🦀🦀 RUSSIAN   You may not be able to take your eyes off the swimming pool–sized stained-glass ceiling of the Metropol restaurant long enough to savor the excellent cuisine. That's probably the only drawback, if you can call it that, of the chief restaurant in the top-end Hotel Metropol. Otherwise, the elegant, historic spot is a great choice if you're looking for a splurge on a meal while you're in Moscow. The Art Nouveau motifs on the ceiling are a rousing culmination of the hotel's other design features: the dreamlike mosaic on the outer wall, the colored glass elevators, and the stylized rooms. The menu is strong on seafood and Russian specialties such as boiled eggs stuffed with caviar, smoked Baltic salmon, and sterlet (sturgeon) stew. The veal with bananas, pine nuts, and cranberries is hardly traditional but is remarkably good. The hall is so large it can feel cavernous if it's empty, but evenings are usually lively with visiting executives, successful Russians, and well-to-do tourists. See the hotel listing on p. 82 for more on the Metropol's history.

1/4 Teatralny Proyezd. 🕐 095/927-6000. Reservations required for dinner. Main courses $20–$50. AE, DC, MC, V. Daily 7am–midnight (breakfast reserved for guests). Metro: Teatralnaya or Ploshchad Revolutsii.

1 Red Square (Krasnaya Ploshchad, 1) 🦀🦀🦀 RUSSIAN   The name says it all. Even if the food were dismal—which thankfully, it's not—this would be a worthwhile

Where to Dine in Moscow

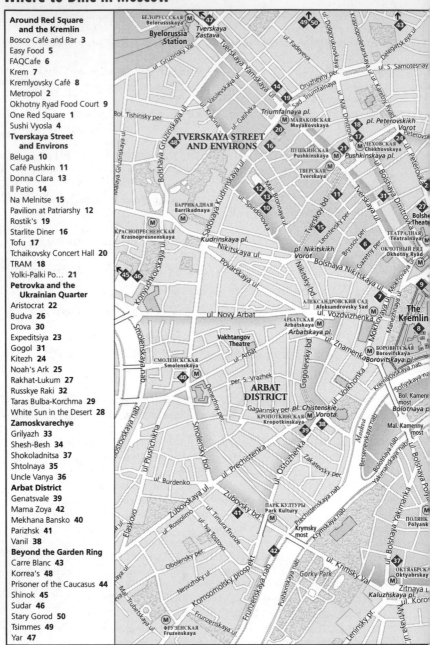

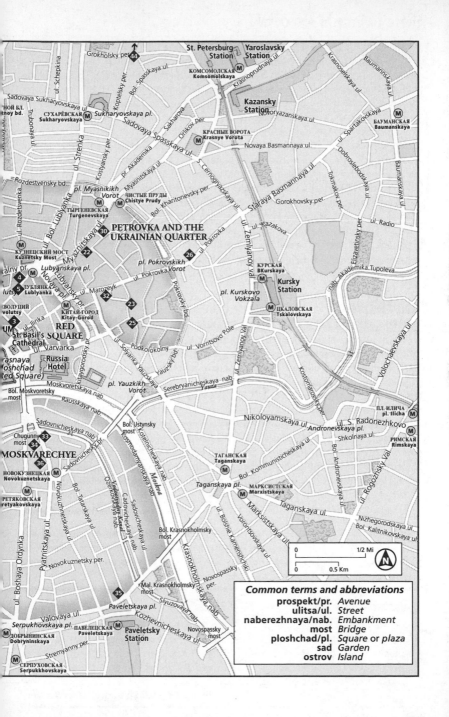

St. Petersburg Station
Yaroslavsky Station ul.

Grokholsky per.

КОМСОМОЛЬСКАЯ
Komsomolskaya

Kazansky Station

СУХАРЁВСКАЯ
Sukharyovskaya
Sukharyovskaya pl.

Sadovaya Sukharyovskaya ul

Sadovaya-Spasskaya ul.

Orlikov per.

КРАСНЫЕ ВОРОТА
Krasnye Vorota

БАУМАНСКАЯ
Baumanskaya

Novaya Basmannaya ul.

pl. Myasnikikh Vorot

ЧИСТЫЕ ПРУДЫ
Chistye Prudy

Staraya Basmannaya ul.

Rozdestvensky bd.

ТУРГЕНЕВСКАЯ
Turgenevskaya

Gorokhovsky per.

ul. Kazakova

**PETROVKA AND THE
UKRAINIAN QUARTER**

30

КУЗНЕЦКИЙ МОСТ
Kuznetsky Most

22

ul. Pokrovka

26

pl. Pokrovskikh Vorot

КУРСКАЯ
BKurskaya

Lubyanskaya pl.

Novaya L

ДУБЛЯНКА
Lublyanka

lutsy

ul. Pokrovka Vorot

32

КИТАЙ-ГОРОД
Kitay-Gorod

23

pl. Kurskovo Vokzala

Kursky Station

ВОЛУЦИЙ
volutsy

3

25

ЦКАЛОВСКАЯ
Tskalovskaya

UM
St. Basil's SQUARE
Cathedral
Varvarka

RED

Podkolokolny

ul. Vorntsovo Pole

Russia Hotel

pl. Yauzkikh Vorot

rasnaya
oshchad
(ed Square)

Moskvoretsky pr.

Serebryanicheskaya nab.

Bol. Moskvoretsky most

Rausskaya nab.

Bol. Ustynsky most

Nikoloyamskaya ul.

ПЛ. ИЛИЧА
pl. Ilicha

Andronevskaya pl.

ul. S. Radonezhkovo

РИМСКАЯ
Rimskaya

Chugunny most 33

34

Shkolnaya p.

MOSKVARECHYE

36

ТАГАНСКАЯ
Taganskaya

НОВОКУЗНЕЦКАЯ
Novokuznetskaya

Bol. Kommunisticheskaya ul.

МАРКСИСТСКАЯ
Marxistskaya

РЕТЯКОВСКАЯ
retyakovskaya

Taganskaya pl.

Taganskaya ul.

Нижегородская ул
Nizhegorodskaya ul.
Bol. Kalitnikovskaya ul

Bol. Krasnokholmsky most

| 0 | | 1/2 Mi |
| 0 | 0.5 Km | |

Mal. Krasnokholmsky most

35

Novospassky per.

Serpukhovskaya pl.

Valovaya ul.

ПАВЕЛЕЦКАЯ
Paveletskaya

Novospassky most

ДОБРЫНИНСКАЯ
Dobryninskaya

Paveletsky Station

Common terms and abbreviations

prospekt/pr.	*Avenue*
ulitsa/ul.	*Street*
naberezhnaya/nab.	*Embankment*
most	*Bridge*
ploshchad/pl.	*Square* or *plaza*
sad	*Garden*
ostrov	*Island*

СЕРПУХОВСКАЯ
Serpukkhovskaya

101

visit just for the view and the atmosphere on Moscow's main plaza. From the top floor of the National History Museum on the north side of Red Square, you can enjoy a meal as you gaze directly across the cobblestone expanse leading to St. Basil's Cathedral on the opposite end. The museum's neo-Gothic turrets and the location's historical significance imbue the restaurant staff and the Russian clientele with a sense of national importance, which foreigners are more than welcome to share. The menu is appropriately Russian and traditional, including a re-creation of the "czar's menu" of a century ago. The emphasis is on fish and appetizers, though most dishes have a lighter touch than standard Russian restaurant fare. The delicate *koulebiaka* is a culinary feat of sturgeon blended with rice, cream, and spices, carefully baked inside a flaky pastry. The venison can be tough. The appetizer *(zakuski)* menu has several versions of fish or meat in aspic, and vegetarian options such as mushrooms on toast. Sample one of the home-brewed liqueurs such as *kedrach,* made with pine nuts—it's strange but satisfying. Musicians play traditional Russian stringed instruments some evenings; other evenings a soft jazz ensemble takes over.

1 Red Square (enter through Historical Museum). ☎ 095/925-3600. http://redsquare.ru/english. Reservations recommended. Main courses $20 and up; business lunch $19. AE, MC, V. Daily noon–midnight. Metro: Ploshchad Revolutsii or Okhotny Ryad.

EXPENSIVE

Bosco Cafe and Bar 🎧🎧 INTERNATIONAL   In any other European city, a plaza like Red Square would be ringed with sidewalk cafes and other commerce. Not so in Moscow—until Bosco Cafe emerged at the turn of the millennium, at last cracking open the long facade of the GUM department store that runs nearly the length of Red Square. The cafe remains the only access to GUM from the square, which enhances its exclusivity. Started by Bosco & Ciliegi, a Russian company that markets international luxury brands to Russia's ultra-rich, the cafe is a decadent but oh-so-satisfying way to absorb the atmosphere of Moscow's epicenter, elbow-to-elbow with the people who make modern Moscow tick. Food is flawlessly prepared but often flimsy and overpriced; this is a better stop for coffee or for a sample of one of the cafe's 20 flavors of ice cream. If you're hungry, try the shrimp and arugula salad or one of the reasonably priced pastas. The entrance from within GUM is concealed behind the Bosco Sport store.

3 Red Square. ☎ 095/927-3703. Main courses $18–$30. AE, DC, MC, V. Daily 10am–10pm. Metro: Ploshchad Revolutsii.

Sushi Vyosla 🎧 JAPANESE   One of the few places to last several years on Moscow's fierce and fickle sushi bar scene, this restaurant is as hip and fresh as ever. Some of its pretension has faded with time, fortunately. Plates of ever-fresh and ever-changing

---

Impressions

Go along quickly and set all you have on the table for us. We don't want doughnuts, honey buns, poppy cakes and other dainties, bring us a whole sheep, serve a goat and forty-year-old mead! And plenty of vodka, not vodka with all sorts of fancies, not with raisins and flavorings, but pure foaming vodka, that hisses and bubbles like mad.

—Nikolai Gogol, in his novel *Taras Bulba*

> ### ⌒Tips Finding Vegetarian Food
>
> Although vegetarianism remains a rarity in Russia, vegetarian restaurant-goers are getting a boost from a surprising source: the revived observance of Russian Orthodox traditions. The Orthodox calendar requires believers to abstain from meat and dairy products during several periods throughout the year, most notably during the 40 days of Lent preceding Orthodox Easter and the 40 days preceding Orthodox Christmas (Jan 7). Many Russian restaurants offer "Lenten menus" (*post*-no-ye men-*yoo*) during these periods, with carefully conceived variations on their house specialties *sans* the meat broth and lard. During non-Lenten periods, feel free to ask the cooks for meatless suggestions.

---

sushi, sashimi, and rolls float around the bar on a continuous river. (*Vyosla* means "oars" in Russian.) The compact hall is usually full of wealthy Russians talking business or stopping in for a quick bite between shopping sprees. It's not a place for leisurely dining, but that means you never have to wait long for a seat. Choices change daily, though you can request standard rolls and sushi combinations from the chefs on the island in the middle of the "river." Anything with Baltic Sea eel or scallops is worth sampling.

25 Nikolskaya Ulitsa (entrance from Tretyakovsky Proyezd shopping center). ⓒ 095/937-0521. Rolls $5 and up. MC, V. Daily noon–midnight. Metro: Lubyanka or Teatralnaya.

MODERATE

Easy Food RUSSIAN/EUROPEAN   This energetic place on Nikolskaya Ulitsa touts itself as a "democratic restaurant," which apparently means it has something for everyone. It's a good pick-me-up option after trekking around the Kremlin or GUM. The spacious restaurant tries for a homey atmosphere, with colorful pillows piled in the wooden booths and a vegetable garden theme that involves enormous wooden carrots hanging in the window. Students, tourists, and employees from nearby government offices make up the clientele. The menu is hard to pin down: The rabbit filet wrapped in bacon sounds aristocratic and is almost too rich to be true, the salmon broccoli salad is overcooked and disappointing (Russians and broccoli don't mix), and the mushroom cream soup is just as hearty as any made by a loving Russian grandmother.

4 Nikolskaya Ulitsa. ⓒ 095/937-3469. Main courses $5–$10. MC, V. Daily 11am–midnight. Metro: Ploshchad Revolutsii.

FAQCafe ⌒ *Finds* INTERNATIONAL   This cafe/club/art gallery/performance space seems to have found the right combination of creative energy, efficient service, and good food in an excellent location, yet few tourists have discovered it. It's frequented more by designers, writers, and photographers here to bat about new ideas. Paper and pencils at each table inspire customers to create while they wait, and the often-amusing results are posted on the walls. The real action starts after 11pm, with movies, music, and performances, but during the day this is an arty, comfortable, and convenient spot for lunch or a snack. Try the grilled pork with basil, or the curried chicken. They also offer a decent Caesar salad, pastas, and club sandwiches—and an extensive list of coffees and teas.

9 Gazetny Pereulok. ⓒ 095/229-0827. Main courses $5–$14. AE, MC, V. Daily noon–6am. Metro: Okhotny Ryad.

Krem ✿ ITALIAN   A good lunch option across from the Kremlin's north wall, Krem attracts young Russian businesspeople with discriminating palates. Dining options on this street are remarkably sparse given the prime location, making Krem all the more appealing. The quick, unobtrusive, and stylish waitstaff blend in with the neat lines of the silver and black decor, accommodating the rushed lives of Russia's business class. The lunch buffet offers salads and meats with an Italian bent, plus a few Russian touches like beet-and-herring salad and rich rye bread (not to be missed). Dinner is largely Northern Italian, with specialties such as delicately prepared Venetian calves' liver and fresh pastas.

7 Mokhovaya Ulitsa. ℂ 095/961-2193. Main courses $10–$20. MC, V. Mon–Sat 11am–midnight. Metro: Biblioteka Imeni Lenina.

INEXPENSIVE

Kremlyovsky Cafe RUSSIAN   The only public food available inside the Kremlin walls is found in this bright but bland cafe in one of the gray Soviet-era buildings in the complex. Its shelter from competition has given it no incentive to lure tourists, but the management has surprisingly refrained from jacking up the prices. It's good for small, open-faced salmon or cheese sandwiches, cabbage pies, and mayonnaise-heavy salads. While not worth paying the Kremlin entrance fee just to eat here, the cafe is a welcome spot for a cool or hot drink after a tiring tour. The basement hall serves a fuller lunch from noon to 2pm, with mediocre Russian soups and thin steaks.

Kremlin, between Patriarch's Palace and Palace of Congresses. Lunch $4–$10. Fri–Wed 11am–5pm. Metro: Okhotny Ryad.

Okhotny Ryad Shopping Center ✿Kids FOOD COURT/INTERNATIONAL   It may not be fine dining, but the kid-friendly food court on the bottom floor of this shopping center just off Red Square offers familiar and unfamiliar fare, all at budget-pleasing prices. For a treat you won't find at home, try the apricot-stuffed or cabbage-filled pies at Russkoye Bistro. If you're looking for pizza, however, stick with Sbarro's and skip the inferior Russian imitation. The hall gets busy and ear-splitting in the evening; lunchtime on a school day is a much mellower time to visit. On the upper floors are a TGI Friday's and a few pub-cafes that offer pleasant outdoor dining the summer months, with views of the fountains and playful statues from Russian fairy tales that ring the mall, and the Kremlin as the ultimate backdrop. Try the Phlegmatic Dog Internet Café for a quick and original bite.

Manezh Sq. Food court prices $1–$5 main course. Credit cards not accepted in food court but MC, V accepted at cafes on top floor. Daily 10am–10pm. Metro: Okhotny Ryad.

3 Tverskaya & Environs

VERY EXPENSIVE

Beluga ✿✿ RUSSIAN   The *haute couture* attitudes, decor, and clientele of this caviar bar fit perfectly with the luxuriousness of its specialty, pearly sturgeon eggs. The caviar is excellent and expensive, though not necessarily better than what you find in other top Russian restaurants. The bar's appeal includes the variety (which you normally find only in specialty shops) and the atmosphere's exclusivity. They're purists here, not adventurers, so there are no experimental caviar sauces or salads. Caviar is served straight, in set quantities by the gram, and accompanied by a generous array of rich dark breads, pasta, and grilled vegetables. For a traditional Russian-style caviar experience, try it in tartlets or on mini-pancakes called *olady.* Their shrimp and chilled dorade are flown in daily from France, but the real reasons to come are the *beluga, sevruga,* and *osetra.*

12/9 Spiridonevsky Pereulok. ⓒ 095/411-4444. Reservations recommended. Main courses $20–$100. AE, DC, MC, V. Daily noon–midnight. Metro: Pushkinskaya.

EXPENSIVE

Cafe Pushkin 👾👾👾 RUSSIAN   Perhaps Moscow's most sophisticated 24-hour restaurant, the three-story Cafe Pushkin has the feel of an 18th-century mansion but dates from the late 1990s. Each of the floors has a different thrust, with a cherrywood bar and well-lit cafe on the first floor, a more formal dining room on the second, and a decadent and breezy summer cafe on the top. The menu weighs a ton—both the Russian and English versions—and the script is so flowery as to be unreadable at times. Pretty much anything listed is bound to be successful, though standouts are *ukha,* a creamy, spiced fish soup that manages to be both light and filling; and grilled sterlet with forest mushrooms. Prices are high—you're paying for the faux-pre-revolutionary atmosphere and top-quality service as well as the food. The vodka selection is impressive and impressively priced, and the hot chocolate and dessert selections offer good, low-budget options.

26a Tverskoi Bulvar. ⓒ 095/229-5590. Reservations required for restaurant and summer terrace. Main courses $15–$40. AE, DC, MC, V. 1st floor open daily 24 hr., top floors daily noon–midnight. Metro: Pushkinskaya.

Pavilion at Patriarshy 👾 RUSSIAN/INTERNATIONAL   This picturesque pavilion overlooking Patriarch's Ponds has gone through several lives in recent years, but the latest incarnation looks to be its most successful. Its spacious, beige-themed main hall is ringed by a balcony hung with pop-art portraits and filled with greenery to make it feel summery and outdoors-y year-round. The restaurant has made it on the circuit of Moscow's young, hip professionals, who seem to expect sushi on any menu. The pavilion complies, but the rest of its repertoire is more intriguing. Try the white mushroom soup served with a quarter-loaf of rich, brown caraway-flavored bread; the cottage cheese tartlets *(syrniki);* or the borscht with duck breast. Skip the sushi.

7 Bolshoi Patriarshy Pereulok (on the grounds of Patriarch's Ponds park). ⓒ 095/203-5110. Main courses $10–$20. AE, DC, MC, V. Daily 24 hr. Metro: Mayakovskaya.

MODERATE

Donna Clara 👾 ITALIAN/RUSSIAN   Chic and cozy, this cafe is a great place to stop during a stroll through the similarly chic and cozy Patriarch's Ponds neighborhood. The cafe is on Malaya Bronnaya, a street that figures in literary masterpieces

---

Impressions

Already Olga's hand was gripping
the urn of perfumed tea, and tipping
Into the cups its darkling stream;
Meanwhile a hallboy handed cream.

—Alexander Pushkin describing a delicate romantic
moment in his epic poem *Eugene Onegin*

such as Bulgakov's *Master and Margarita,* and that's now lined with original boutiques. Donna Clara is good for a quick coffee or a long, drawn-out one, and for lunch as well. Highlights include their pasta, veal in cream sauce, and green salads (as opposed to the marinated ones). A three-course prix-fixe lunch runs less than $10. They serve a breakfast for late risers (they don't open until 10am). The desserts are the cafe's strong point; try the cherry strudel or the yogurt cheesecake. There's even a nonsmoking section, a welcome option in the evenings when the main hall fills up with the cigarette-loving, after-work crowd.

21/13 Malaya Bronnaya Ulitsa. © 095/290-6974. Main courses $5–$10. No credit cards. Mon–Sat 10am–midnight; Sun noon–midnight. Metro: Pushkinskaya.

Il Patio *Kids* ITALIAN/RUSSIAN   This chain's management was the first in Moscow to recognize the city's need for reasonably priced restaurants with edible food and decent service, a concept that didn't exist 15 years ago. The market was huge and untapped, and after some trial and error the Russian company hit on the successful Il Patio formula. Thin-crust pizzas, generously spiced pastas, a salad bar, and a children's menu may be standard fare in your home town, but in Moscow they remain scarce. Il Patio is a safe choice for kids or the unadventurous, or if you're sick of Russian fare. It opens early for breakfast, too—another rarity in Russia. The salad bar includes Russian mayonnaise-based salads and garlic-marinated vegetables, in addition to fresh raw greens. The selection of vegetarian pizzas is broader than those at most other Russia pizza joints.

2 Pervaya Tverskaya-Yamskaya Ulitsa. © 095/251-0884. Main courses $7–$15. AE, MC, V. Weekdays 8am–midnight; weekends noon–6am. Metro: Mayakovskaya.

Na Melnitse (On the Windmill) ⚜ RUSSIAN   Another themed restaurant, Na Melnitse transports you from the clogged traffic of the Boulevard Ring outdoors to a bucolic farmyard centered around a windmill. The three halls are decked out as a farmyard with a stream and live pheasants; a country attic; and a blacksmith's workshop. From a culinary standpoint, the best thing about the restaurant is the half-portions offered for many of their dishes, allowing you to eat lightly or sample several of their traditional Russian specialties. Fish features prominently, but the veal dishes are just as successful. Try one of the homemade liqueurs—a small 50-gram glass is enough to sample the flavor without losing your lucidity.

7 Tverskoi Bulvar. © 095/290-3737. Main courses $10–$18. AE, MC, V. Daily noon–midnight. Metro: Pushkinskaya.

Starlite Diner *Kids* AMERICAN   If you're desperate for a 4am burger, you'll be forgiven for heading to this silver trailer parked incongruously in a Moscow square. This all-night diner has become something of an institution in its decade on the Moscow dining scene, thanks largely to expats who flock here with their families on weekend mornings, or with their Russian clubbing partners after a night of partying. It inhabits a leafy square well-hidden from the Garden Ring Road, and offers one of the city's few summer terraces free of exhaust fumes. Check out the informal lending library in the back near the bathrooms. Burgers are generous and juicy, and fries are crisp. Most of the fare is authentic American, though the bagels are frozen. Prices are higher than at any diner you'll find back home, but they may be worth it to say you ate a banana split in Moscow.

16 Bolshaya Sadovaya Ulitsa. © 095/290-9638. Main courses $8–$20. AE, DC, MC, V. Daily 24 hr. Metro: Mayakovskaya.

Tips Sushi

Just because a restaurant brags about its sushi menu doesn't mean Japanese food is exclusively served. An inordinate number of not-at-all Japanese restaurants now include some sushi and sashimi on the menu, just to keep up with the Moscow obsession with raw fish on rice. My advice is to skip the sushi page and order whatever the restaurant does best. If you're a sushi fan, go to a real Japanese restaurant instead.

Tofu VEGETARIAN/ASIAN   At last, an unapologetic, centrally located spot for vegetarians in Russia's biggest city. The emphasis is on Asian recipes, from Japanese noodles to Indonesian rice plates, and there's the inevitable sushi bar. The sushi is more organic than elsewhere in town but otherwise can be dismissed. The salads and soups are creative and lighter than those in most Russian restaurants, and the fruit-based desserts are well worth sampling. Tofu, while it does feature on the menu, is not the only nonmeat sustenance. The restaurant's design is rather austere, with bare solid wood tables and minimal wall-coverings. International travelers have made this their favorite spot, as have plenty of young, adventurous Russians.

2/4 Malaya Dmitrovka, building 2. © **095/299-3073.** Main courses $6–$12. MC, V. Daily noon–midnight. Metro: Pushkinskaya.

TRAM ℛ RUSSIAN/EUROPEAN   This all-night cafe and restaurant housed in the renowned Lenkom theater is a longtime favorite of Russian actors, screenwriters, and clubgoers. It's a convenient, intimate rest stop for anyone touring Moscow, too, though few tourists venture in. At night the halls get thick with smoke and pretension, but during the day the leather armchairs and footstools are often empty and the service is more attentive. Silent films flicker across an enormous screen day and night. Menu items are named after film and theater stars from Russia and abroad, producing sometimes-puzzling combinations. For example, the Belmondo salad is heavier on mayonnaise than anything you'll find in France, and the "Sumo Wrestler" dumplings taste more Russian than Japanese, but are succulent nonetheless. The salad bar is a good bet, and the desserts are enjoyable, reliable stomach-fillers any time of day. The $3 business lunch can't be beat.

6 Malaya Dmitrovka (in the Lenkom theater). © **095/299-0770.** Main courses $10–$20. AE, MC, V. Daily 24 hr. Metro: Pushkinskaya or Tverskaya.

INEXPENSIVE

Rostik's _Kids_ RUSSIAN/AMERICAN   This is basically a fried-chicken joint run by the same Russian company that manages **Il Patio** (see above). Cheap, fast, and kid-friendly, Rostik's offers standard chicken combos plus nuggets and chicken wraps. The slightly more Russian options include lamb shish kebab and smoked salmon wrapped in Armenian lavash bread. There's not much in terms of light dining. The urban setting means the kids' play area is indoors. The Mayakovskaya branch is the most convenient, but keep an eye out for other branches around town.

2/1 Pervaya Tverskaya-Yamskaya Ulitsa. © **095/251-4950.** Meal packs $3–$5. No credit cards. Weekdays 9am–midnight; weekends 10am–midnight. Metro: Mayakovskaya.

Tchaikovsky Concert Hall INTERNATIONAL   The lobby of the concert hall has turned into a slightly more elegant version of the food court, with a cluster of inexpensive restaurants. It's a good place to fuel up and freshen up before a concert or at any time of day. **Delifrance** has croissants and French patisserie and boulangerie treats; **Tandoor** has good, predictable Indian fare; the coffee bar boasts multiple blends including decaf (a rarity here); and there's even a **Pizza Hut.**

4/31 Triumfalnaya Sq. ⓒ 095/299-0378. Snacks from $1; meals from $5. No credit cards. Daily noon–8pm. Metro: Mayakovskaya.

Family-Friendly Restaurants

Russians rarely take their children to restaurants, largely because for decades there was nothing remotely child-friendly about them. The international chains are starting to change that, and a few homegrown restaurants are adopting high chairs and children's menus, too, but they're still relatively rare, so don't expect them everywhere you go. Among top-end establishments, the best family venues are the Sunday brunches at the big hotels. **Sheraton Palace** is especially child-centered, with a well-equipped playroom, clown performances, and free balloons. The all-you-can-eat buffet has enough options for the pickiest of eaters. Mid-range suggestions include **Il Patio,** whose three restaurants offer children's seats and menus, as well as servers who are patient with scampering little ones (a rarity here). It serves plenty of familiar pizzas and pastas. The budget chain **Yolki-Palki** (which translates into something like "Good grief!") offers simple Russian cuisine and is one of the few places where you'll see Russian kids eating out. The mini-pancakes *(olady)* and jam-filled dumplings *(vareniki)* are good finger foods. The American-style **Starlite Diner** has milkshakes and cereal and attracts expat families on weekend mornings. The Russian fried-chicken chain, **Rostik's,** has familiar fare and a play area in most of its restaurants, but the equipment is often crowded and shabby. The most child-friendly places in town are still the U.S. chain **TGI Friday's** (main branches at the Okhotny Ryad shopping center and at 18/2 Tverskaya St.); and, of course, the ubiquitous **McDonald's.** (Check out their flagship restaurant on Pushkin Sq., the world's biggest when it opened in 1989.)

Some Yolki-Palki branches follow. All are open daily 11am to 11pm, except the one listed above, which is open around the clock. None takes credit cards.

- 23 Bolshaya Dmitrovskaya Ulitsa. ⓒ 095/200-0965. Metro: Tverskaya.
- 14 Klimentovsky Pereulok, building 1. ⓒ 095/953-9130. Metro: Tretyakovskaya.
- 18 Sadovo-Triumfalnaya Ulitsa. ⓒ 095/299-2936. Metro: Mayakovskaya.
- 12 Bolshaya Dorogomilovskaya Ulitsa. ⓒ 095/243-2019. Metro: Kievskaya.
- 8/10 Neglinnaya Ulitsa. ⓒ 095/928-5525. Metro: Kuznetsky Most.
- 11 Novy Arbat. ⓒ 095/291-6888. Metro: Arbatskaya.

Yolki-Palki Po . . . *Value* CENTRAL ASIAN   As soon as you shed your coat, you'll be greeted by a row of fresh ingredients that you heap into a bowl according to your mood and hand to the chef at the center of an enormous circular grill. He sizzles up your selection within minutes, and you take it to your table. The Mongolian barbecue–style concept is adapted with central Asian ingredients and Russian side dishes, and it has found huge success in Moscow. Most other branches of the Yolki-Palki chain only offer basic Russian fare; its three barbecue-style branches, including this glass-enclosed pavilion on bustling Pushkin Square, are its most popular and tasty, as well as a great choice for anyone on a budget. Ingredients include sliced chicken, pork, beef, sole, eggs, assorted vegetables, several sauces, and a large selection of fresh spices, including unique offerings from central Asia and the Caucasus Mountains. Vegetarians will find plenty of options here.

18a Tverskaya Ulitsa. ℂ 095/200-3920. Main courses $7. No credit cards. Daily 11am–5am. Metro: Pushkinskaya or Tverskaya.

4 Petrovka & the Ukrainian Quarter

EXPENSIVE

Aristocrat *Value* RUSSIAN   This wing of an 18th-century mansion isn't shy about its place in the social order, as its name implies. More cafe than dinner destination, Aristocrat makes a big deal of its teas, coffees, and desserts, both in their preparation and presentation. Fresh mint, fresh lemon, and homemade honey arc on hand to add to any of your beverages for a few rubles more. For a light lunch, try the foie gras with forest berries or the mushrooms on toast. The service is usually refined and reserved, as befits the setting, but the clientele is not as snobbish as the cafe's name implies; diners range from local office workers to women stopping in after a day at the salon. The mansion is on bustling Myasnitskaya Street, but the cafe is set back from the road; enter through the courtyard.

37 Myasnitskaya Ulitsa, building 3. 9/1 Smolenskaya Ploshchad. ℂ 095/207-4212. Main courses $13–$20. MC, V. Daily 10am–midnight. Metro: Chistiye Prudy.

Expeditsiya *Value* ARCTIC   One of Moscow's stranger culinary experiences, this restaurant offers recipes collected from Arctic tribes during expeditions to Russia's Far North. The food is hit-or-miss, but the decor and inventiveness of the restaurant's creators make it an unforgettable stop on any Moscow tour. A helicopter used in Arctic expeditions hangs in the central hall, and a river runs under the glass floor. Clientele and staff are awfully haughty for a place with such a rugged theme. Reindeer and trout feature prominently on the menu, though it's unclear whether the shipment from northern shores is the meat or the recipes.

6 Pevchevsky Pereulok. ℂ 095/917-9510. Main courses $20–$40; business lunch $11. MC, V. Daily noon until the last guest leaves. Metro: Kitai-Gorod.

Kitezh *Value* RUSSIAN   From the pre-revolutionary Russian alphabet used on the menu to the restaurant's name (a mythical city that would disappear when enemies approached), Kitezh sees its purpose as upholding tradition and legend. If you have just one real Russian meal in Moscow, make it here. The restaurant is poised in a stone basement that re-creates a 17th-century farmhouse atmosphere, across from a 14th-century monastery on a quiet stretch of historic Petrovka Street, a great district for a post-meal stroll. Allow a couple of hours to savor the large portions and to let the various courses digest. Sauces are rich, divine, and heavy. This is one of the few Russian restaurants that does justice to beef Stroganoff, which despite its Russian roots is more common outside Russia. The pikeperch is expertly seasoned and sauced. Desserts include thick, jello-like *kisel,* and light and buttery *bliny* with homemade jam.

23/10 Ulitsa Petrovka. ℂ 095/209-6685. Reservations recommended. Main courses $12–$25. AE, MC, V. Daily noon–midnight. Metro: Kuznetsky Most.

Noah's Ark (Noyev Kovcheg) 𝒢 ARMENIAN
The staff at Noah's Ark take responsibility for your pleasure during the several hours required for a meal here. Each course is discussed with the waiter before the order is made; and each must be accompanied by the appropriate spirit—preferably Armenian brandy (which they call *konyak*). Nestled in one of the steep, zigzag lanes of the Ukrainian Quarter, the restaurant can be hard to find; however, it's worth the exploration of this quiet and oft-ignored neighborhood in Moscow's historic center. The atmosphere gets pretentious on weekend nights, as rich Armenian and Russian executives try to outdo each other by ordering the most expensive items on the menu. The *meza,* or appetizers, incorporate the spices and fruits of the Caucasus Mountain region, with an emphasis on cilantro, apricots, and pomegranates. The *dolma,* grape leaves stuffed with lamb and rice, are succulent. The plain roast lamb is better than the cubed version.

9 Maly Ivanovsky Pereulok. ℂ 095/921-5885. Reservations recommended for dinner. Main courses $20–$30. AE, DC, MC, V. Daily noon until the last customer leaves; 15% discount before 3pm. Metro: Kitai-Gorod.

MODERATE

Budva YUGOSLAV
Its name comes from a town in what's now Montenegro, but many of the dishes are Serbian or Bosnian; the owners are sick of politics, so just call the place Yugoslav. The cheerful atmosphere and generous portions make Budva appealing for lunch or dinner, and offer few reminders of the turmoil that has ripped the Balkans. Many of the dishes have a Russian or Mediterranean thrust, reflecting Yugoslavia's geography between the eastern Slavs and the southern seas. The *rpshut,* or dry cured ham, features in several dishes, as does *kaimak,* a kind of buttermilk. The sausages and stuffed peppers are top choices.

23 Pokrovka Ulitsa. ℂ 095/923-3364. Main courses $8–$15. MC, V. Daily 11am–midnight. Metro: Kitai-Gorod.

Rakhat-Lukum CENTRAL ASIAN
This is an accessible way to sample central Asian cuisine without risking the desert heat or the digestive indignities that often accompany travel in that part of the world. The name translates as "rest for the throat" in the Turkic tongues spoken in most of the "-stans" of former Soviet Central Asia. The grilled meats live up to the region's reputation, especially the pork loin, as does the *plov,* lamb chunks cooked in seasoned rice. The *samsas,* the Uzbek version of samosas, are an excellent starter choice. Even better, try the all-you-can-eat buffet bar (called *Vostochny Bazar*) and sample the food you're curious about, such as dried horsemeat. The buffet runs $7 at lunch, twice that at dinner. "Rakhat-Lukum" often refers to a pistachio-based dessert common in central Asia. It's an acquired taste, but if you're feeling brave, it's a pleasant way to round off your meal. Otherwise, try some Bukharan tea or a hookah with flavored water as an after-dinner treat.

9 Bolshaya Dmitrovka, building 1. ℂ 095/514-6478. Main courses $5–$12. MC, V. Daily noon–midnight. Metro: Teatralnaya.

Taras Bulba-Korchma ☞ UKRAINIAN   When it opened in the late 1990s, this chain of Ukrainian restaurants quickly became a citywide hit among busy, middle-class Russians looking for a taste of the countryside. The decorators went a bit over-board on the Ukrainian country kitsch, but the food is hearty and reliable and free of pretension, and the atmosphere is cheery. You can recognize the restaurant by the doormen, who are extravagantly decked out as Cossacks all seasons of the year. The name comes from a story by Nikolai Gogol, a tragic and epic tale of an aging 18th-century warrior (Bulba) who sets off with his sons to join a Cossack band fighting for Ukrainian independence. The menu has plenty of meat and potatoes, but also several soups based on beets, cabbage, or forest greens. Ukrainian cooking makes heavy use of garlic, so if you're not a fan, let your server know. If you do like garlic, try the *pampushki,* garlic-infused buttery rolls.

Main restaurant at 30/7 Petrovka; a dozen others around town. ☎ 095/200-6082. Main courses $10–$15. MC, V. Sun–Thurs noon–11pm; Fri–Sat noon–2am. Metro: Smolenskaya.

White Sun of the Desert (Beloye Solntse Pustyni) ☞ CENTRAL ASIAN   A series of kitschy yet elite themed restaurants opened in Moscow in the late 1990s, feeding rich Russians' demands for simultaneous novelty and nostalgia. White Sun in the Desert, named after a cult Soviet film about central Asia, features cuisine from Uzbekistan and its neighbors, including a few dishes with an Arabian or Chinese fla-vor. The lunch buffet is a staggering smorgasbord of fresh, marinated, and dried fruits and vegetables; grilled lamb; delicately spiced ground-meat kebabs; and flaky pies. The menu offers several versions of the central Asian favorite *plov,* a lamb-based rice pilaf. The staff is costumed in technicolored turbans and wide-legged pants, a theatricalized version of traditional Uzbek desert garb. Hookahs and belly dancing are offered after 8pm.

29/14 Neglinnaya St. ☎ 095/209-7525. Reservations recommended for dinner. Main courses $8–$20. AE, DC, MC, V. Mon–Sat 11am–midnight. Metro: Chekhovskaya or Tsvetnoi Bulvar.

INEXPENSIVE

Drova (Logs) *Value* RUSSIAN   This chain of all-you-can-eat Russian eateries has helped bury the 2-hour lunch tradition. Moscow's workers dive into Drova at 1pm; load up on Russian coleslaw *(kvashennaya kapusta),* spicy red bean stew *(lobio),* and ground-beef kebabs; gulp down some tea; and are out the door by 1:30. With plenty of convenient locations around town, Drova is a good place for tourists to sample sev-eral Russian dishes risk-free. If you don't like something, go back and get something else. It's all included in the 350-ruble ($12) price. The wood (fake and real) decor reflects its name, which means "logs" in Russian.

24 Myasnitskaya. ☎ 095/925-2725. All you can eat, $12. AE, DC, MC, V at both locations. Daily 24 hr. Metro: Lubyanka or Chistiye Prudy. There's a 2nd location at 7 Bolshaya Dmitrovka. ☎ 095/229-3227. Metro: Kuznetsky Most or Teatralnaya.

Gogol RUSSIAN/INTERNATIONAL   Lurking behind an arch on a posh pedes-trian street, this restaurant/bar/concert space is anything but chic. Grungy performers slump against the arch, and students inside grab post-party bites, making the atmos-phere laid-back and cutting-edge simultaneously. The outdoor courtyard is a great summer breathing space and party spot. Food is basic and cheap. The *pelmeny* (small meat dumplings) are lightly spiced, juicy, and filling. There are plenty of vegetarian

---

Tips Planning a Picnic

Russians are not casual picnickers; when they eat outdoors it's usually a feast of meat grilled over a makeshift fire, plus homemade salads and generous servings of wine or vodka followed by tea boiled over the embers. If you're staying in a hotel, this is hardly feasible. Your picnic options are limited, since sandwich shops are rare and not many restaurants offer meals to go. Your best bet is to go to a big supermarket and pick up ready-made salads, smoked meats, Russian cheeses, and loaf of rich brown or white bread. A bottle of *kefir* or *ryazhenka* (a yogurtlike drink), *mors* (a delicious forest berry nectar), or *kvas* (a strange yet refreshing drink made from fermented bread) adds to the Russian experience. You might have to ask for utensils from your hotel or buy something disposable. Some good picnic spots include Kolomenskoye, Victory Park, or any of the aristocratic estates outside central Moscow such as Kuskovo, Tsaritsino, or Ostankino (see listings for all of these, see chapter 7).

---

options, primarily on the appetizer menu. Gogol is rarely crowded in the daytime, and if the terrace is open, there's plenty of space to relax.

11/1 Stoleshnikov Pereulok. © **095/514-0944.** Main courses $3–$10. No credit cards. Daily 24 hr. Metro: Chekhovskaya or Kuznetsky Most.

Russkye Raki (Russian Crayfish) ☞ RUSSIAN   To a Russian, the crayfish is a summertime staple as crucial to the national cuisine as caviar, and much more accessible. If you're a fan, make it a point to visit this restaurant, since it's a glimpse of what for many Russian men is the ultimate dining experience. Bright red, just-boiled crayfish are the main draw, with variations such as boiled in beer, spiced, or doused in cream sauce. Grilled fish is also on offer, as well as seafood-based appetizers and salads. The only appropriate beverage for a crayfish lunch is Russian beer. The constant crunch of the shells provides a surreal soundtrack for the sight of young and middle-aged Russian businessmen on their lunch break, trying not to drip sauce on their suits.

11/4 Maroseika, building 1. © **095/921-8545.** Main courses $3–$8. No credit cards. Daily 11am–11pm. Metro: Kitai-Gorod.

5 Beyond the Moscow River (Zamoskvarechye)

EXPENSIVE

Grilyazh ☞☞ RUSSIAN/EUROPEAN   The stylized grillwork at the entrance and the discriminating maitre d' tell you right away to expect the best from this restaurant. Specializing in Italian- and French-inspired Russian cuisine, the food is sometimes as pretentious as the service, but overall it's a pleasing experience in fine dining. At the top of the otherwise bohemian Pyatnitskaya Street, it occupies a two-story mansion decked in Art Nouveau light fixtures and antique furniture. Russian executives like to hold banquets here, but it's also a good spot for a romantic interlude, with its soft lighting and exclusive atmosphere. The wine list is impressive. The tuna and salmon carpaccio with ginger and greens is a winning appetizer, and the duck breast with "poacher's" sauce makes a hearty main course. The borscht with garlic rolls is surprisingly better than the lobster bisque.

1/2 Pyatnitskaya Ulitsa, building 1. ℂ 095/953-9333. Reservations recommended. Main courses $18–$40. AE, MC, V. Daily noon–midnight. Metro: Novokuznetskaya.

MODERATE

Shesh-Besh ⚘ AZERBAIJANI   This is a cheerful and tasty introduction to Azerbaijani cuisine, a combination of Turkish, Greek, and Russian flavors with a distinctly Caucasian (as in the Caucasus Mountains) accent. It goes overboard with its multicolored decor and faux-traditional costumery, but the pillows are comfy and the service friendly. The *souffra*, or salad bar, is heaped with fresh and marinated vegetables, along with stalks of cilantro, parsley, and dill that you're supposed to munch raw to cleanse the palate. Grilled meats are the pride of the Caucasus, but also worth trying is the *cutaby*, a thin, crepelike dough stuffed with fresh greens, sheep's cheese, or ground lamb. Their chief gimmick is a game called *shesh-besh* (it means "six-five"), in which you toss two dice, and if you get a six and a five you get a free pitcher of (barely drinkable) wine or other beverage. Shesh-Besh's two most convenient locations are listed below.

24 Pyatnitskaya. ℂ 095/959-5862. Main courses $4–$10. MC, V. Daily noon–midnight. Metro: Novokuznetskaya. Also at 6a Smolenskaya Ploshchad. ℂ 095/241-6542. Metro: Smolenskaya.

Shtolnaya ⚘ INTERNATIONAL   The main draw here is the table-top beer taps, with meters that keep track of how many milliliters you pour. Each table has a different combination of beer choices, so if your favorite isn't here, you'll have to order it from the bar. Vladimir Putin took Tony Blair here for a friendly pint, though its usual clientele is more modest. The fried appetizers are too greasy to enjoy, but the steaks and baked trout in mushroom sauce are quite good. Shtolnaya is across from Paveletsky Train Station near a few bars and clubs, right on the Garden Ring Road.

6/13 Zatsepsky Val. ℂ 095/953-4268. Reservations recommended on weekend nights. Ask for a table with a tap when you reserve. Main courses $8–$18. AE, DC, DISC, MC, V. Daily noon–2am. Metro: Paveletskaya.

Uncle Vanya ⚘⚘ RUSSIAN   This cozy, artsy treasure left its original location in a theater basement to relocate to another basement in this even more cozy, artsy section of town. The restaurant takes its name from one of Anton Chekhov's plays. It has no real link to the playwright, but maintains a literary atmosphere and decor reminiscent of early 20th-century Russia, when Chekhov reached his zenith. The menu of Russian favorites is accessible and safe, with highlights including cold sorrel soup *(zelyoniye shchi)*, wild mushrooms, and buckwheat kasha. The restaurant serves a hearty breakfast, too. The whimsical placemats are a good way to learn the Russian alphabet. A talented, understated jazz trio plays most evenings.

16 Pyatnitskaya (entrance in courtyard). ℂ 095/951-0586. Main courses $5–$15. MC, V. Daily 8:30am–midnight. Metro: Novokuznetskaya.

INEXPENSIVE

Shokoladnitsa ⚘ RUSSIAN   This unassuming cafe is often full of young Russian women discussing their jobs and boyfriends over tea or chocolate *bliny* (crepes). A good rest stop any time of day, it offers cheap soups and mediocre salads. Its name translates as "a pot of hot chocolate." The chocolate items on the menu are probably your best bet here.

58 Bolshaya Yakimanka. ℂ 095/203-4958. Desserts and snacks from $1.50. No credit cards. Daily 24 hr. Metro: Novokuznetskaya.

6 The Arbat District

EXPENSIVE

Vanil ☞ RUSSIAN   This may be Moscow restaurateur Arkady Novikov's most successful creation, a masterful blend of Russian ingredients, European cooking techniques, and smattering of Asian cuisine aimed at the increasingly demanding Muscovite *nouveau riche* palate. The sparkling chandeliers face little other decorative competition in the airy interior, leaving diners to concentrate on the restaurant's subtleties—especially its food. Hits include the barabulka fish filet with asparagus and orange sauce, and the rich and ever-changing soups. A Szechuan duck liver soup might unexpectedly include oysters when they're in season. The restaurant is not as imposing as the massive Christ the Savior Cathedral across the street, but it's not a casual experience, either. Save this for a special night.

1 Ostozhenka. ☎ **095/202-3341.** Reservations required on weekends, recommended on weekdays. Main courses $25–$40. AE, DC, MC, V. Daily noon–midnight. Metro: Kropotkinskaya.

MODERATE

Genatsvale ☞☞ GEORGIAN   This family-run restaurant—whose name means "comrade" in Georgian—is Moscow's best introduction to the colorful and flavorful cuisine of Georgia. Other restaurants may have finer decor or subtler chefs, but at Genatsvale you get accessible prices, an inclusive atmosphere, and copious choices. The country-style dining hall is a welcome dose of earthiness on this street of chic restaurants and posh residences. The only drawback is the cabaret show, a performance of overly loud Georgian love songs accompanied by tinny synthesizers. Come here for lunch or early dinner to avoid it. Try the three-cheese *khachapuri,* a kind of sauceless pizza; the finely ground lamb kebab; or the garlic-walnut paste rolled in thinly sliced eggplant. It's a good choice for vegetarians, who can easily fill up on a selection of appetizers (which is what most Georgians seem to do). The restaurant has another location on the Arbat, which is more convenient but is gaudier and less pleasant and cozy.

12/1 Ostozhenka. ☎ **095/202-0445.** Main courses $8–$20. MC, V. Daily noon–midnight. Metro: Kropotkinskaya.

Mekhana Bansko ☞ BULGARIAN   This friendly basement restaurant may be your only chance to try Bulgarian cuisine, so why not? It's similar to Russian cooking, but with copious feta cheese, olives, and a few other southern European touches. Folk musicians dance through the hall and waitstaff sometimes join in, keeping things festive even on the gloomiest of winter nights. Embroidered wall hangings and traditional pottery enhance the Slavic atmosphere. Any dish with Bulgarian cheese is worth sampling, as are the hearty soups. Salads are rather heavy, as are the wines—make sure you clarify whether you want dry or sweet, since the house wine is somewhat sugary.

9/1 Smolenskaya Ploshchad. ☎ **095/244-7387.** Main courses $5–$10. MC, V. Sun–Thurs noon–11pm; Fri–Sat noon–2am. Metro: Smolenskaya.

Parizhsk ☞ *Finds* RUSSIAN/FRENCH   Its name is a Russified version of the word "Paris," and its cuisine is a Russified version of familiar and nourishing French fare. The dark woods of the furniture contrast with the playful light fixtures, and the atmosphere is artsy and laid-back. It attracts local journalists and graduate students, as well as anyone looking for a good meal around the clock, though tourists rarely venture in. The *confit de canard* in cherry sauce is a good choice, and the crème-brûlee is divine. Russian beer competes with French wines on the menu, both reasonably priced. Parizhsk is open around the clock, which attracts some of the post-party crowd in the wee hours, and makes it a safe and friendly place to head if jet lag has you discombobulated.

13 Zubovsky Bulvar, building 2. © 095/247-0912. Main courses $10–$15. AE, MC, V. Daily 24 hr. Metro: Park Kultury.

INEXPENSIVE

Mama Zoya 𝒢 GEORGIAN   The family of Mama Zoya started with a rudimentary cafe, than expanded to an out-of-the-way cellar restaurant, and now boasts a multistory boat-restaurant moored along the Moscow River across from Gorky Park. The latest location is less intimate but more accessible and successful. The food is just as homey even if the service is not quite so familial. This is an atmospheric and decently priced way to sample the rich and underappreciated pleasures of Georgian cuisine. The grilled lamb—cubed and skewered, ground and skewered, or grilled by the leg— is a specialty, and it's divine. Also try *adzhapsandal,* an eggplant-and-tomato based ragout; or *pkhali,* spinach, garlic, and walnuts ground to a rich paste. Ignore the weird decor of gnomes, palms, and mannequins, and look out at the river instead.

Mama Zoya on the Water at 16d Frunzenskaya Naberezhnya. © 095/242-8450. Main courses $5–$12. No credit cards. Daily noon–11pm. Metro: Frunzenskaya. Cellar restaurant at 8 Sechenovsky Pereulok. © 095/201-7743. Main courses $3–$8. Mon–Sat 11am–midnight. Metro: Kropotkinskaya or Park Kultury.

7 Beyond the Garden Ring

EXPENSIVE

Carre Blanc 𝒢𝒢 FRENCH   Chic and delicious, this restaurant is a perfect marriage of French cuisine and a Russian setting. Rather off the beaten track, it's an excellent choice for an evening splurge or a languorous summer brunch. The French chef earned his credentials at *haute cuisine* establishments elsewhere in town before branching out on his own and settling in this 18th-century mansion. The main dining hall is sparsely elegant, the adjoining piano/jazz bar has a sleek design, and the brasserie in back is an upscale version of laid-back, offering a menu similar to the one in the main hall but at discounted prices. Opt for the summer terrace when the weather is fine. The oysters and other seafood, flown in daily, are a house specialty, though if you come from a seaside hometown it might seem silly to order seafood in landlocked Moscow. Instead, try the foie gras with fennel or the traditional but excellent veal. The wine list is predictably good, as is the sommelier. Vladimir Putin did wonders for French-Russian relations when he stopped by here unannounced.

19/2 Semyonovskaya. © 095/258-4403. Reservations recommended. Main courses $14–$42. AE, DC, MC, V. Daily 11am–11pm. Metro: Novoslobodskaya.

Prisoner of the Caucasus 𝒢 CAUCASIAN   Another restaurant named after a popular Soviet film (like White Sun in the Desert, reviewed earlier in this chapter), this one plumbs the cuisines and stereotypes of the ex-Soviet lands of the Caucasus Mountains: Georgia, Armenia, and Azerbaijan. People don't come here just for the food but for the wild mountain ambience, which includes caged livestock and waiters decked in capes and daggers. This atmosphere makes it cost more than other restaurants in the same genre. It can be over the top but is fun for large groups or a weekend night out. The extensive appetizer bar is the best way to sample the unfamiliar fare; choose from piles of marinated and fresh vegetables, smoked meats, and spicy salads. The grilled meats (especially lamb) are a specialty. Caucasus wines tend to be sweeter and cruder than most tourists prefer, but if you feel daring, try a *Saperavi* or *Mukuzani,* two rich, dry Georgian reds.

36 Prospekt Mira. ℂ 095/280-5111. Main courses $18–$35. AE, MC, V. Daily noon–midnight. Metro: Prospekt Mira.

Shinok ✿ UKRAINIAN   Among the most exclusive of Moscow's themed restaurants, Shinok is a tangle of juxtapositions. Its genre is Ukrainian farmhouse, with a multilayered dining hall decorated with haystacks, chicken cages, and the occasional goat, and waitstaff adorned as milkmaids and cowhands. Yet its prices are purely urban, and its clientele is decked out in Armani and Dior. Service is efficient, if somewhat haughty. The chefs present elegant, satisfying versions of countryside standards such as borscht with garlic rolls, potato-stuffed dumplings *(vareniki),* and suckling pig. The cold sorrel soup *(zelyoniye shchi)* is both tangy and filling, and the egg-and-spice–stuffed carp is mouthwatering. The wines are overpriced; stick to beer or a simple dry Georgian wine. This is a good splurge option, though count on taking a taxi home since it's a long way from the metro—or even better, order a taxi in advance to avoid the overcharging cabbies lying in wait outside.

2 Ulitsa 1905 Goda. ℂ 095/255-0888. Reservations recommended. Main courses $20–$50. AE, MC, V. Daily 24 hr. Metro: Ulitsa 1905 Goda.

Sudar ✿✿ RUSSIAN   Expansive and proudly Russian, this restaurant is best appreciated over a long dinner after you've had some time to explore the rest of Moscow. It's located in a district full of reminders of Russia's military victories: the Triumphal Arch, designed to mimic Napoleon's Arc de Triomphe; Victory Park, marking the defeat of the Nazis; and the Battle of Borodino Museum, depicting the brutal battle with Napoleon's Grande Armée. Inside, the restaurant's fireplace is inviting on a cool night, and its bookshelves are lined with Russian tomes. The cuisine is Russian tinged by the French influences so popular in 18th- and 19th-century court circles. Top choices include braised rabbit with forest mushrooms, crab salad, and the dessert of baked apple with honey, cranberries, and almonds.

36A Kutuzovsky Prospekt. ℂ 095/249-6965. Main courses $10–$30. AE, DC, MC, V. Daily noon–midnight. Metro: Kutuzovskaya.

Yar ✿ RUSSIAN   This 19th-century landmark on the ground floor of the Sovietskaya Hotel earned popularity for its festive Gypsy music and decadent menus. After recovering from the stale Soviet years, it's again as opulent as ever, if a bit overpriced. The stunning and spacious Red Hall is named not for the Communists, but for the favored color of the partying nobility. Russia's new rich and visiting executives make business deals here, and though there's no dress code you'll feel uncomfortable in jeans. Neither staff nor diners are in much of a hurry, which gives you plenty of time to savor the *Dobry Molodets* ("Good Fellow") meat stew. Russians consider soups like this a first course, though it's hearty enough for a meal. The dishes are frivolously named, so don't be afraid to ask what the "Lady's Caprice" dessert contains. The baked grouse with figs and chestnuts is excellent.

32/2 Leningradsky Prospekt. ℂ 095/250-7449. Reservations recommended weekends. Main courses $13–$28. AE, MC, V. Mon–Sat 11am until the last guest leaves. Metro: Dinamo.

My, what an inefficient way to fish.

Ring toss, good. Horseshoes, bad.

Faster! Faster! Faster!

We take care of the fiddly bits, from providing over 43,000 customer reviews of hotels, to helping you find our best fares, to giving you 24/7 customer service. So you can focus on the only thing that matters. Goofing off.

✳ travelocity®
You'll never roam alone.™

MODERATE

Korrea's *INTERNATIONAL*   If you need fresh fruits and vegetables or familiar flavors after one too many Russian marinated salads, try Korrea's. Named after the New York chef who runs it, the restaurant caters to expats and adventurous Russians. The food is generally grilled or braised instead of fried or boiled as in Russian cuisine, but heavier dishes also make an appearance (for example, the house-made foie gras). Highlights include Caesar salad, eggplant-and-mushroom pizza, and carrot cake. The simple stone-and-wood hall is small and the kitchen is partly visible, giving the place an intimacy and casualness many Russian restaurants lack. Since reservations are not taken, avoid rush hours (noon–2pm and 7–9pm) if you don't want to wait. Korrea's opens early for breakfast, too—a rarity here. There's not much to see nearby, but Tverskaya Street and the zoo are not too far away.

32 Bolshaya Gruzinskaya. (C) **095/933-4684**. Main courses $9–$15. AE, DC, MC, V. Mon–Fri 8am–10pm; Sat–Sun 9am–10pm. Metro: Belorusskaya or Mayakovskaya.

Tsimmes JEWISH   This fun restaurant with tasty food calls itself Jewish, though only some of the dishes are kosher. Many of the menu's dishes have incorporated themselves into Russian cuisine, such as pickled fish. With an emphasis on Odessa cuisine, specialties include plenty of seafood, including gefilte fish, of course. Some call the decor the Disney version of "Fiddler on the Roof," but the service is tasteful.

3 Novoslobodskaya Ulitsa. (C) **095/973-0873**. Main courses $11–$20. MC, V. Daily noon–midnight. Metro: Novoslobodskaya.

INEXPENSIVE

Stary Gorod *RUSSIAN/GEORGIAN*   A wood-beamed wine-tasting loft and a cozy biergarten are the last things you expect on this corner, next to a busy bazaar and a somewhat seedy suburban train station. Stop in for a glass of wine from a small French vintner; spicy, hefty *khinkali* meat dumplings; or a hot cappuccino. Photos of old European cities complement the wall mural of a mythical "Old Town," which is what Stary Gorod means in English. The place is a slightly confusing mélange of Russian, European, and Georgian tastes, which is an accurate reflection of Muscovite tastes in recent years. It's away from the main tourist sights but is right outside a metro station and is a great place for an authentic, non-touristy meal. There's no English menu, but the manager and owner can help translate.

3 Sushchyovsky Val. (C) **095/973-1431**. Main courses $4–$15. No credit cards. Daily 11am–midnight. Metro: Savyolovskaya.

7

Exploring Moscow

Moscow is less a beautiful city than a collection of beautiful sights, many of them hidden beyond the expansive modern boulevards that successive Soviet governments bulldozed through town. The key to delighting in Moscow is to not let it overwhelm you. Keep your eye out for twisted gold cupolas peeking from residential courtyards, turn your gaze upward to admire the caryatids and atlantes supporting the balconies of otherwise unremarkable apartment buildings, and stay cool when challenges come your way. You'll be rewarded by the discovery of a new world, one that daily news reports from Red Square can't possibly convey. Taking in even a few main sights can give you an idea of the hardships that made Ivan the Terrible so terrible, introduce you to the nuances of icon painting, and help you appreciate the motivations and misjudgments of the Soviet regime. All this is essential to understanding why Russia and the Russians are the way they are today.

The things to see in Moscow fall roughly into four categories: church-related, art-related, Soviet-related, and everything else. Try to get a taste of each, regardless of your interests. The Kremlin is a category unto itself, representing every era of Russian history for the past 700 years and continuing to emanate an aura of mystery and authority as the seat of modern Russian politics. It is the most logical starting point for any glimpse of Moscow, providing a historical and contextual frame for viewing the rest of the city.

Moscow's art museums are often unfairly overlooked and overshadowed by the magnificent Hermitage Museum in St. Petersburg, but squeeze in at least one of Moscow's. Closing days for museums vary, and many close one day a month for maintenance in addition to their weekly days off. Many museums adhere to the Soviet policy of charging foreigners significantly more for admission than Russians (see the box, "Foreigner Tax," on p. 85). The foreigner's fee is usually equivalent to what you would pay at a similar site in western Europe. In addition, admission fees, though posted and paid for in rubles, are usually pegged to the U.S. dollar and therefore change frequently. For that reason, fees in this chapter are listed in dollars. Children 7 and under are always admitted free, unless noted.

Half of Moscow's buildings date from the Soviet era, which spawned a range of architectural styles and governing attitudes despite its overall authoritarian bent. Much of the Soviet legacy has been (rightly) discredited in recent years, but ignoring Russia's Soviet history gives you a half-picture of what the country is about. Brilliant artists, writers, and architects managed to produce masterpieces in the Soviet era despite the pressure and whims of the state.

Moscow may not boast the literary traditions that St. Petersburg does, but many of Russia's most famous writers lived and worked here, and Muscovites are proud enough of the country's literary heritage to erect museums in their honor. Most museums label their exhibits in Russian only, though we've listed some below that offer printouts in English describing room contents. Among other Moscow highlights are the aristocratic estates around the city's edges, which often host festivals in the summer.

Many of the cathedrals listed here are functioning churches as well as museums, and services can be held almost any time of day. That doesn't bar visitors; however, you should follow local custom during your visit (see the box, "Visiting Churches," later in this chapter).

1 The Kremlin ⟨★⟨★⟨★

This 28-hectare (130-acre) fortress, called *kreml* in Russian, emerged in the 12th century as a wooden encampment, and survived many an invader to become synonymous with modern totalitarianism in the 20th century. Physically it's still a citadel, surrounded by unscalable red brick walls and tightly guarded gates, though the river and moat that once protected its north and east sides were filled in nearly 200 years ago. These defenses make it all the more magical once you get inside, a world away from the din and modernity beyond. Its oak and birch walls were replaced with white stone ones in the 1360s, which were replaced again by 2.2km (1½ miles) of red brick ramparts in the 1490s. Much of that brick remains standing today. Most of the buildings inside were wooden, however, and suffered several devastating fires. Despite its forbidding location and reputation, Mongol Tatars sacked the fortress in 1382, and revolt and bloodshed were familiar plagues throughout the centuries. Ivan the Terrible, Ivan the Great, Boris Godunov, and the first century of Romanov czars ruled from the Kremlin palaces. The Kremlin suffered some neglect after Peter the Great moved his capital to the swampland of what would become St. Petersburg, but it flourished again in a very different way when the Soviets made it the seat of Communist power.

Architecturally, the complex centers around its churches, as did Russian life and politics until the 20th century. The administrative and residential buildings and the tranquil, car-free plazas complement the cathedrals and reflect centuries of development and design. The Russian president no longer lives here, but his motorcade whisks him to work here every morning. Several buildings used for state functions are off limits to tourists, with violators strictly reprimanded.

The ticket desk is a confusing affair, with different fees for different buildings and lower fees for Russians. The ideal itinerary would include everything: entrance to the Kremlin itself, Cathedral Square, the Armory, and the Diamond Fund. However, the latter two are open at limited times, not always on the same day. You can purchase tickets separately for each attraction. At the very least, choose the entrance-plus-Cathedral Square ticket, which allows you access to the chief buildings and will fill up

---

Impressions

Fortress, sanctuary, seraglio, harem, necropolis, and prison . . . this violent contrast of the crudest materialism and the most lofty spirituality—are they not the whole history of Russia, the whole epic of the Russian nation, the whole inward drama of the Russian soul?
　　　　　　　　　　　　　　　　　　—Maurice Paléologue, *An Ambassador's Memoirs*, 1925

Crown of Monomakh (Shapka Monomakha)

A key reason to visit the Kremlin early in your trip is to view the Crown of Monomakh *(Shapka Monomakha)*. Once you've seen this unusual crown, you'll recognize its likeness on many of your other stops: in the shape of church cupolas, in paintings of medieval Russia in Tretyakov Gallery, in frescoes in any Orthodox cathedral, even in modern fur hats on display at Russian designer boutiques. The crown was made of eight triangles of gold joined to form a cone; studded with red, blue, and green gems; topped with a cross; and trimmed with a brim of sable. The shape recalls the hats worn by central Asian khans, and reflects Russia's cross-continental geography. According to legend, the crown was presented to Prince Vladimir Monomakh of Kiev (1053–1125) by his grandfather, Byzantine Emperor Constantine IX. Though most historians say the existing crown wasn't made until much later (around the 14th c.), it still came to symbolize Russia's claim to the heritage of Byzantium. It was used in coronations at least as far back as the 1400s, until Peter the Great introduced more Western-style crowns in the 1700s. The Crown of Monomakh remained a key Kremlin treasure, and Peter and his successors continued to use the orb and scepter symbolizing the czar's dominion over the earth. All three are on display at the Armory Museum in the Kremlin.

a good hour or two. Visiting the cathedrals plus the Armory Museum will take you an entire afternoon.

Cathedral Square (Sobornaya Ploshchad) 🟊🟊🟊 forms a monument to Russian architecture of the 15th and 16th centuries, and its cathedrals deserve a thorough tour inside and out. It's easiest to start at **Ivan the Great Bell Tower,** which shows selected pieces from the Armory Museum. The tower was built in three stages over 3 centuries, starting in 1505, giving it a rather inconsistent appearance. Its heaviest and lowest bell is a staggering 64 tons (compared to Big Ben's 13.5 tons), but it is still dwarfed by the Czar Bell (see below). Continue to the **Cathedral of the Archangel Michael,** also built in 1505. Italian architect Alevisio Novi introduced the Corinthian capitals and Venetian shell scallops in the gables. The cathedral holds the tombs of Russia's rulers from Ivan I (1328–41) to Tsar Ivan V (1682–96), Peter the Great's predecessor. The interior of the church is fittingly somber, its hall of coffins surrounded by small shrines. The **Cathedral of the Annunciation** was built in 1482, and was where the czars were christened and married. Its tiers of tented gables and *kokoshniki* (pointed arches) are reflective of early Moscow architecture. Faded frescoes line the stone walls and columns from marbled floor to painted ceiling, their enormous faces and curved figures gazing over the central chamber. Renowned icon painter Andrei Rublev is buried here. Next door is the reconstructed **Red Staircase** mounted by centuries of czars after coronation. Also from these stairs, a young Peter the Great watched relatives impaled during an uprising that prompted him to flee Moscow to found his own capital. Tucked in the corner is the small **Church of the Deposition of the Robe,** built in a more traditional style of the late 15th century, with narrow windows and

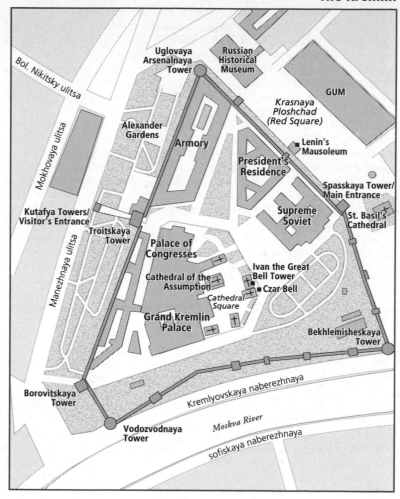

stained glass, a rarity in Russian churches. It's now a museum of wooden figures and church relics. Behind it you see the layered cluster of 11 domes that top **Terem Palace,** the oldest structure in today's Kremlin and the quarters of Russia's rulers until Peter the Great.

The most prominent building on the square is the **Cathedral of the Assumption** 🖈🖈, a white limestone building with scalloped arches topped by almost chunky golden domes. Started in 1475 by Italian architect Aristotle Fiorovanti, this church is the most tourist-friendly of the cathedrals on the square, with detailed English labels on icons and architectural details, and plenty of room for groups. The church is light and spacious, unlike any of the other churches on the square—or indeed of this period. Czars were crowned here, and patriarchs of the Russian Orthodox Church were inaugurated and buried here—the Patriarch's Seat is built into one of the pillars.

Napoleon's cavalry stabled horses here during their brief occupation of Moscow in 1812. Most of the frescoes date from a later restoration, in the 1660s. The **Patriarch's Palace and the Cathedral of the Twelve Apostles** are next door, both part of one structure that is now a museum of 17th-century Russian life and art. The exhibit includes a goblet with no base, requiring drinkers to toss back a full cup of wine in one gulp. The huge stove was used for making holy oil (involving more than 50 ingredients) once every 2 or 3 years. Other personal effects include a 17th-century chess set with knights mounted on elephants.

The **Armory Museum** 🕱🕱 (ⓒ 095/302-3776), despite its name, holds much more than guns. The Russo-Byzantine building, dating from the 19th century, occupies the spot where royal treasures were housed since the 14th century and offers a sweeping introduction to Russian history. Exhibits include the Fabergé eggs exchanged by Russia's last royal couple, Czar Nicholas II and Empress Alexandra, on Orthodox Easter for 3 decades; the silver goblet used by the man considered Moscow's founder, 12th-century Prince Yuri Dolgoruky; the velvet caftan Peter the Great wore while training in Holland's shipyards; and the gold brocade robes he wore at his coronation. The throne display, a Goldilocks-style delight, includes a compact throne for the diminutive Czar Paul and a double throne for Peter the Great and his co-ruler, his feeble half-brother Ivan. The imperial carriages will simultaneously satisfy fashion fans and car buffs. The weaponry through the ages is also impressive. Admission is limited to four sessions per day of 1 hour and 45 minutes each, at 10am, noon, 2:30pm, and 4:30pm. Audioguides in English are available and worth the $4 price tag if you're not with a group.

The **Diamond Fund** holds the crown jewels, including Catherine the Great's coronation crown, the 89-carat Shah diamond presented to Nicholas I by the Shah of Persia in the early 1800s, and the 190-carat Orlov diamond that one of Catherine the Great's lovers gave her in an (unsuccessful) effort to keep her attentions. The fund can be visited only with a tour made by previous arrangement; the fee costs upwards of $20. If you're short on time or money, skip it. The entrance is through the Borovitsky Gate of the Kremlin (ⓒ **095/229-2036**).

The **Grand Kremlin Palace,** not open to tourists, is used to receive foreign dignitaries. Watch television footage of a Kremlin reception and you may glimpse luxurious St. George's Hall, encircled with statues representing Russia's military victories throughout the centuries. The building, originally erected in the 1840s, underwent a costly renovation in the 1990s that uncovered a massive corruption scandal involving the Kremlin property department and questionable Swiss construction companies.

The staggeringly huge **Czar Cannon** and **Czar Bell** are two striking and bizarre features of the Kremlin and indeed of Russian history. The cannon, with a 40-ton barrel, was designed in 1586 to defend the Kremlin's Savior Gate, but it has never been fired. The chassis and the cannonballs alongside were built 3 centuries later and give a sense of the enormity of the weapon (though it was designed to fire stones and not cannonballs). The bell is by far the largest in the world, at 200 tons, 6.1m (20 ft.) high, and nearly 6.6m (22 ft.) in diameter. It was built in the 1730s but was abandoned and cracked before it could be rung. Both remain monuments to Russian ambition and royal excess.

Kremlin entrepreneurs recently reintroduced the centuries-old changing of the guard on Cathedral Square—but for a fee. The elaborate and carefully choreographed ceremony, which involves 12 horses, 45 soldiers in czarist-era uniforms, and the presidential orchestra, is held every Saturday at noon for visitors who pay $35 for a special ticket. In addition to the guard-changing ceremony, the ticket includes tours of the churches on Cathedral Square (but not the Armory or Diamond Fund).

Note: The Kremlin is sometimes closed to the public during state visits and other important ceremonies. Check with your hotel concierge or tour guide before you go.

You can buy Kremlin tickets at Kutafya Tower in Alexander Gardens (© **095/203-0349**). Access to the grounds costs $3 for adults, $1.50 for students with ID and for children 7 and up. Admission to the grounds and the Cathedral Square complex costs $12 for adults, $6 for students with ID and for children 7 and up. Admission to the Armory costs $14 for adults, $7 for students and for children 7 and up. An audioguide costs $8. If you'd like to take photos, you must pay an additional $2. Bag check (downstairs beneath the ticket offices) costs $1 if you leave a backpack, $2 if you leave a camera or video camera. *Tip:* If you plan to visit Lenin's Mausoleum (see below), do so before reclaiming your bags. The Kremlin is open to visitors Friday through Wednesday from 10am to 5pm unless there's a special event, as noted above. Armory admission times are limited; see above for details. The closest metro stops are Okhotny Ryad and Biblioteka Imeni Lenina.

2 Around Red Square

Red Square (Krasnaya Ploshchad) ✿✿✿   One of the world's most recognizable public spaces, Red Square is as impressive in reality as it is on screen. Its uneven surface leads to a rounded peak at the center, from which Moscow unfurls beneath you on all sides. The square was already famous by 1434, when it was dubbed "Trading Square." Its current name appeared in the 1660s, when the word *krasnaya* meant "beautiful" or "important" as well as "red." The name took on different connotations in the 20th century, when the red flag–bearing Communists staged massive parades and demonstrations on the aptly titled square. Tanks no longer roll over its cobblestones on Soviet holidays, but the square still hosts big parades and the occasional rock concert. The best way to enter is through Resurrection Gates, next to the History Museum. Before heading to St. Basil's Cathedral, note the other two churches on the square, Kazan Cathedral in the northeast corner (a 1990s reproduction of a 17th-c. church), and the new and rather kitschy Gate Church of the Iberian Virgin beneath Resurrection Gates. Watching the sun rise or set over the landmark square is unforgettable, especially during the long days of summer.

Red Square (Krasnaya Ploshchad). No phone. Free admission. Metro: Ploshchad Revolutsii or Okhotny Ryad.

St. Basil's Cathedral (Khram Vasiliya Blazhennogo or Pokrovsky Sobor) ✿✿   The geometric domes and vivid tones of this 16th-century cathedral are almost garish up close, but they perfectly complement the solid red brick of the Kremlin wall and the gray cobblestones of Red Square. The church was built to honor the victory over

---

Impressions

The streets teemed with spectators, some coming out of their houses to watch the extraordinary spectacle, others moved to indignation or even pity.

—Jacob Reitenfelts, nephew of the czar's doctor, describing the execution of revolutionary Stepan Razin in front of St. Basil's in 1671

Exploring Moscow

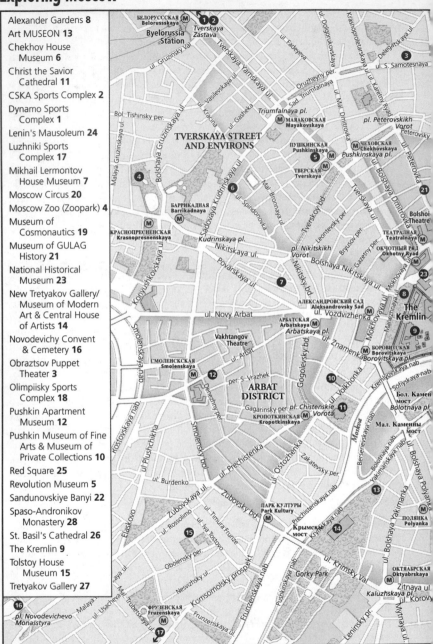

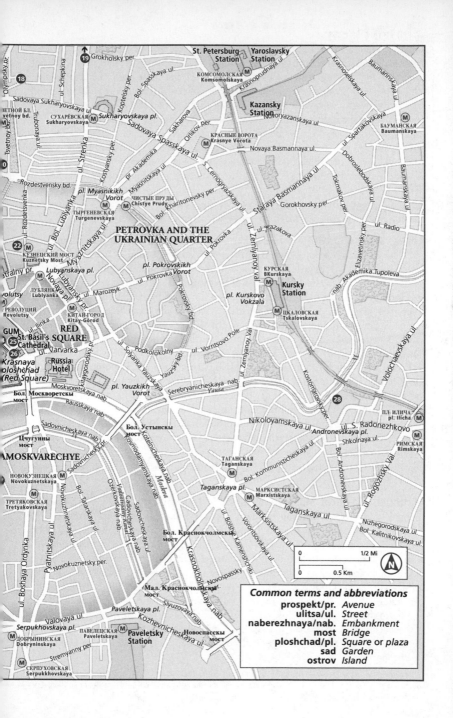

Common terms and abbreviations

prospekt/pr.	*Avenue*
ulitsa/ul.	*Street*
naberezhnaya/nab.	*Embankment*
most	*Bridge*
ploshchad/pl.	*Square* or *plaza*
sad	*Garden*
ostrov	*Island*

Mongol Tatars in 1555, and legend has it that Ivan the Terrible had its architect's eyes poked out to keep him from making anything to rival Moscow's "stone flower." Inside, the cathedral is more reminiscent of the Middle Ages. The church lacks one large chapel, instead housing several dim and chilly sanctuaries reached by climbing deep and treacherously worn stairs and wandering through narrow, winding passages. Literature about the different chapels and niches is surprisingly limited, though vendors offer icons and souvenirs. St. Basil's is essentially a union of nine different churches and styles, and nine different chapels, beneath nine domes, each unique in size, form, and color. From the upper-floor windows you get a close-up view of the pilasters and a broad view of the Moscow River. You should be able to see everything in an hour or less.

Red Square. ✆ 095/298-3304. Admission $3.50 adults, $1.75 students and children over 7. Joint ticket with Historical Museum $8 adults, $4 students and children. Wed–Mon 11am–5pm. Metro: Ploshchad Revolutsii.

Lenin's Mausoleum (Mavzolei Lenina)   Yes, the embalmed body of the founder of the Soviet state is still on display in a mausoleum on Red Square. The stark Constructivist pyramid of red granite and gray and black labradorite was built in 1930, 6 years after Vladimir Lenin's death. The lines of pilgrims and solemn changing of the guard are long gone, and threats to bury him—as he wished for himself—have surfaced every few years since his USSR collapsed in 1991. In the meantime, the curious and a few faithful are shepherded through the cool, dim chamber by guards who make sure no one stands still long enough to ask any questions. The whole visit takes barely a few minutes. Equally fascinating are the gravestones of other Soviet icons along the Kremlin wall, which can be accessed only by visiting the mausoleum. Admirers still heap flowers on Stalin's grave daily. Because Nikita Khrushchev left office in disgrace, he is the only dead Soviet leader not buried here. Other remains here include those of Yuri Gagarin, the first man in space; and American journalist John Reed. Cameras and bulky backpacks are forbidden; they must be left at the bag check by the Borovitsky gate to the Kremlin, a good 5-minute walk away. It's easiest to visit here right after seeing the Kremlin, and then go get your bags.

Red Square. No phone. Free admission. Tues, Thurs, Sat, and Sun 10am–1pm. Metro: Ploshchad Revolutsii, Teatralnaya, or Okhotny Ryad.

National Historical Museum (Nationalny Istorichesky Muzei)   The intricately paneled and turreted crimson building on Red Square is the official repository of Russian historic artifacts, though Tretyakov Gallery (reviewed in the "Major Museums" section later in this chapter) and the Kremlin provide richer pictures of the country's 1,200-year-old history. The Historical Museum reopened in the 1990s after renovation, and hawkers lure tourists in from the throngs on Red Square, but the exhibits are labeled in Russian only, and maps and tours in other languages are scarce. An audioguide in English is promised to arrive soon. Several exhibit halls remain closed to the public. The whole museum takes about an hour to tour. It's an impressive collection of garments, manuscripts, and weaponry from centuries past. The restaurant 1 Red Square (p. 99), on the second floor, is a deluxe dining choice in a prime location.

1 Red Square. ✆ 095/292-4019. Admission $5.25 adults, $2.60 students and children. Photo permission $3, video $3.50. Ticket including St. Basil's $8 adults, $4 students and children. Mon and Wed–Sat 11am–8pm; Sun 10am–6pm. Metro: Okhotny Ryad, Ploshchad Revolutsii, or Teatralnaya.

Alexander Gardens (Alexandrovsky Sad) This green strip beneath the Kremlin's north wall was once a river that further isolated the fortress from its enemies. Now it's perfect for a peaceful stroll and perhaps a taste of ice cream or the savory pies sold along the path (avoid the hot dogs). At the gardens' entrance is an elegant marble monument of a helmet abandoned next to a flame. This **Tomb of the Unknown Soldier** was erected to honor those killed in World War II, and is surrounded by plaques to Soviet cities honored for their valiance and suffering at Nazi hands. The tomb, and the surrounding gardens, are often graced by newlyweds making a tour of Moscow sights after exchanging rings. The gardens run parallel to Mokhovaya Ulitsa, between the street and the Kremlin wall.

Metro: Ploshchad Revolutsii, Teatralnaya, or Okhotny Ryad.

3 Cathedrals, Monasteries & Convents

Christ the Savior Cathedral (Khram Khrista Spasitelya) ℛ This is not the oldest church in town, nor is it historically revered, but it is the largest and the most expensive, and it has become an unmistakable part of the skyline. It occupies such a key geographical and political spot in today's Moscow that it warrants a visit. Originally built over 5 decades in the 19th century, the cathedral was a monument to Russia's victory over Napoleon, and to the gilded yet modernizing architecture of the day. Stalin ordered it razed in the 1930s and made plans for an immense Palace of Soviets in its place. Those plans never materialized, and the site became a large and popular indoor/outdoor swimming pool. In 1994, Moscow Mayor Yury Luzhkov drained the pool and ordered a speedy reconstruction of the cathedral. The finished product boasts staggering domes plated with gold alloy and clifflike white walls rising above the Moscow River—and it remains a controversial construction 10 years later. It houses huge Orthodox church conferences and many official ceremonies. Lighter and airier than most Orthodox churches, it attracts some believers but turns away more traditional ones. A chronicle of Russian military victories is engraved on the marble panels leading to the main hall. Set aside about an hour to see the cathedral.

15 Volkhonka. ℭ **095/202-8024.** Free admission. Tours $22 at ticket booth on Soimonovsky Proyezd. Daily 11am–7pm. Metro: Kropotkinskaya.

Novodevichy Convent & Cemetery (Novodevichy Monastyr i Kladbishche) ℛℛ If you visit only one holy site in Moscow, make it this one. The convent, founded in 1524, became over ensuing eras a carefully arranged complex of churches in a variety of architectural styles. The stark white walls and gold-trimmed green domes of the **Cathedral of Our Lady of Smolensk** complement the deep red of the **Gate Church of the Intercession,** the two main churches in the complex. The fortresslike walls surrounding the convent reflect one of its key early purposes: to sequester daughters, sisters, and wayward wives of the nobility. Ivan the Terrible and Peter the Great sent their female foes here, which meant the convent enjoyed generous funding from the Kremlin. Today that disturbing page in the convent's history is largely forgotten. It is a haven of tranquillity, its adjoining pond and shaded paths a world away from the crowded rush of the rest of town. Don't miss the **cemetery** down the hill behind the convent. Considered Moscow's most prestigious burial site since the 18th century, it bears the unique and artful gravestones of many of Russia's literary, musical, and scientific heroes. Pick up a map at the entrance to locate the graves of writers Anton

Old Believers

Russian Orthodoxy is among the world's most ritual-oriented religions, yet almost since its birth more than 1,000 years ago, believers have differed over which rituals are more spiritually "correct." In the 1600s, a century after the Protestant Reformation began sweeping western Europe, the powerful and popular leader of the Russian Orthodox Church, Patriarch Nikon, introduced major reforms to church ritual. Ironically, many of the changes were intended to bring the church back to its earlier traditions, but he set off a furor among many believers who accused him of tampering with their faith. The period of reforms later became known as the Schism. Even today, pockets of Old Believers who refuse to accept the "new" rules can be found in remote Russian forests and even in a few big-city congregations.

Nikon's reforms eventually gained sway, so that believers now cross themselves with two fingers instead of three, and church architecture abandoned the tent-roofed tower (or *shatyor*) used in St. Basil's Cathedral and other pre-Nikonian cathedrals. A few decades later, Peter the Great further modernized and westernized the church by ordering Orthodox men to shave their beards—previously considered a sin. Peter also introduced the Julian calendar, which dated from the birth of Christ instead of from creation as the earlier Russian calendar had. Implementation of the new rules was unforgiving, and thousands of Old Believers fled into the forests to escape forced conversions. Those who were caught often burned themselves to death, singing hymns as they went up in flames. The Old Believers eventually won the freedom to worship under Catherine the Great in 1771, and some families returned to the big cities, though they were often marginalized.

The Old Believers (*staroobryadtsy* in Russian), also known as the Dissenters *(raskolniki)*, eventually split into sub-sects, including the relatively liberal *popovtsy*, who were willing to deal with Orthodox priests; the *bezpopovtsy*, who totally rejected the official church and the state; the *skoptsy*, who castrated themselves to demonstrate their faith; and the *khlisty*, who believed in salvation through sin. Grigory Rasputin, controversial advisor to Czar Nicholas II, and his wife, Alexandra, were rumored to belong to this last group.

For a glimpse at the Old Believers' world, visit **Nikolsky Old Believers' Commune (Nikolskoye Staroobryadtsoye Kladbishche)** in eastern Moscow. The striking Gothic-style church was commissioned in 1790, and its aristocratic sponsors included the respected Ryabushkinsky and Morozov families. They spent fortunes acquiring the religious art—dating from before the Schism—displayed in the church. Its unusual architectural features include sunburst windows, obelisks, and elaborate reliefs. The commune, at 29 Rogozhkaya Ulitsa, holds services at 8am and 6pm Monday through Saturday, and at 7am and 10am Sunday (✆ **095/161-3110;** metro: Taganskaya).

Tips **Visiting Churches**

Moscow and its environs boast hundreds of beautiful Orthodox churches, many of which only reopened recently after decades as storehouses, offices, or abandoned lots. Don't hesitate to wander into any church that appeals to you, as long as you do so respectfully. Dress codes are rarely enforced, but men are expected to remove their hats, and women should keep their heads covered (a hood or small scarf is enough to deflect critical glances). Both genders should wear clothing covering legs and shoulders. You will be rewarded by a hushed hall covered in frescoes and illuminated largely by candles. If you enter during a service, you're likely to hear the pure, hypnotic melodies of the priest or a choir, always *a capella*. Services are held frequently throughout the day but attendance is generally low; believers often prefer to come and pray individually.

Chekhov, Nikolai Gogol, and Mikhail Bulgakov; composer Dmitry Shostakovich; filmmaker Sergei Eisenstein; and Nikita Khrushchev, the only Soviet leader not buried at the Kremlin wall (because he died in disgrace instead of in office). Mikhail Gorbachev will likely choose Novodevichy as his resting place; his wife Raisa was buried here in 1999. Note also the curious grave-top monuments, such as a tank (for a World War II commander), a telephone (for a communications minister), and the tragicomic statue of circus clown Yuri Nikulin. The cemetery is a bit of a walk from the nearest metro station through an otherwise unremarkable neighborhood. Reserve this trip for a good-weather day, and allow 2 or 3 hours.

Novodevichy Proyezd. (095/246-8526. Admission to the grounds $2; a combined ticket including churches and exhibits $7. Cemetery admission $2. Cathedrals may be closed to tourists on Easter and feast days. Wed–Sun 10am–5pm. Metro: Sportivnaya.

Spaso-Andronikov Monastery *®*   Founded in 1360, this monastery on the east bank of the Yauza River was slated for demolition in the Soviet era. Instead, it became a museum of early Russian art. Today the museum shares the site with monks who are again using the monastery for its original purpose. While simpler and less well-preserved than the Kremlin's cathedrals or Novodevichy, this monastery feels more authentic. Tour groups usually ignore it, making it calmer and less souvenir-heavy. Andrei Rublev, perhaps Russia's greatest icon painter, spent his last years in this monastery and died here in 1430. You can see many of his works here—if you have any interest in Orthodox icons, this is *the* place to visit. Andrei Tarkovsky's film *Andrei Rublev* is a chilling and gripping journey through medieval Russia that took years to make it past Soviet censors, and provides a great context for visiting this monastery. It's rather out-of-the-way, so give yourself at least an hour once you get here.

10 Ploshchad Pryamikova. (095/278-1489. Admission to grounds free, icon exhibit $3, applied art museum $2.50. Thurs–Tues 11am–5pm; closed last Fri of the month. Metro: Ploshchad Ilicha, then a 10-min. walk toward the Yauza River.

4 Soviet Sights

Although many monuments of Socialist realism around town have been deposed, a few remaining examples are worth viewing if you're in the neighborhood. **The Worker and Collective Farmer** is an oversized statue of a man and woman reaching boldly toward the sky; he's holding a hammer, and she, a sickle. Their determined expressions aren't exactly cheerful, but you can feel their strength and commitment to overcoming hardship. (At the entrance to the All-Russian Exhibition Center; metro: VDNKh). **The Gagarin Monument** is a sweep of steel rocketing toward the cosmos, topped with a sculpture of the first man in space, Yuri Gagarin. Gagarin remains a cult figure in Russia, seen as the man who made the world finally take Russians seriously. (Gagarinskaya Ploshchad; metro: Leninsky Prospekt). **The Lenin monument** on Oktyabrskaya Square shows the Soviet founder with a crowd of enthusiastic followers preparing to build a nation at his feet. (Oktyabrskaya Ploshchad; metro: Oktyabrskaya).

The Moscow Metro *Value*   Most cities' public transit systems are eyesores. Moscow's is a masterpiece. Central planning meant that Stalin was free to pour funds and artistic energy into creating the metro. Today it's the world's busiest subway system. However, it's starting to show some strain, as even trains that run every 90 seconds aren't enough to diffuse crowding. The system is still cleaner than most other big-city subways. Its oldest stations, dating from the 1930s and 1940s, are its grandest, particularly those on the Circle Line. The newer stations at the edges of town are corridors of bland but well-polished white tile. Even if you don't use the metro to get around, take a peek at one of the following stations: Ploshchad Revolutsii, with its bronze sculptures of Soviet swimmers, mothers, and sailors holding up the marble columns; Kievskaya (Circle Line stop), with its cheerful mosaics portraying Ukrainian-Russian friendship; Novokuznetskaya, with its cast-iron streetlights; and Novoslobodskaya, with its Art Nouveau stained glass.

For an even closer view of the metro, with models and an avalanche of statistics, visit the tiny **Metro Museum** atop the Sportivnaya station (© **095/222-7309;** free admission; open to individuals Thurs 9am–4pm; open for groups only Tues, Wed, Fri 9am–4pm). The friendly director is a former metro driver who has a lifetime of stories to share (though in Russian only). Most stations are quite deep, and all have head-spinningly long escalators; some of the stations were even built as bomb shelters during World War II. See "Getting Around" in chapter 4 for metro ticket prices.

Revolution Museum (State Museum of Contemporary Russian History)   This museum officially changed its name in the 1990s but is still commonly referred to as the Revolution Museum. The thrust of the exhibits is the same, though the moral weight has been lifted and now much of it appears more kitschy than political. Beyond the excess of red (banners, carpets, lighting), the museum is a piece of Russian history saved from the hands of those who would have erased the Soviet era from memory the way the Soviets tried to erase czarist-era memories. Newer exhibits include labor camp grave posts and glasnost-era efforts at a more honest look at history. The museum is housed in an elegant building on Tverskaya Street that once hosted Masonic meetings. Allow an hour or so.

21 Tverskaya St. © 095/299-6724. Admission $4. Tues–Sat 10–6pm; Sun 10am–5pm; closed last Fri of each month. Metro: Pushkinskaya, Tverskaya, or Chekhovskaya.

Art MUSEON *   Another example of Russia's confused allegiances in the post-Communist era, this park gathers together scores of busts and full-size statues of Lenin and other now-disgraced Soviet icons. The pieces were torn down in the democratic fervor of the early 1990s, but not destroyed. Many ended up in a graceless heap in an alley in nearby Gorky Park before a group of independent artists righted them and gave them a new home behind the modern art museum. Despite its political overtones, the park is a peaceful and pleasant place, with wooden bench swings, bird feeders, and a garden of exotic and Russian pines. The statues of Soviet leaders are interspersed with other icons such as pianist Van Cliburn, and surrounded by lanes of avant-garde sculptures. It's easy to combine this with a visit to the modern art museum (see review below). Allow a half-hour or so for exploring and resting in the park.

10 Krymsky Val (behind the Central House of Artists). © 095/291-6248. Admission $1.75. Daily 9am–9 pm. Metro: Oktyabrskaya or Park Kultury.

Museum of Cosmonautics (Muzei Kosmonavtiki) 𝓚 *Kids* *Value*   Housed beneath a giant aluminum monument of a rocket soaring into space, this museum is a tribute to the minds and might that put the Soviet Union head to head with the United States in the Space Race. This is the team that sent the first man and woman into space, among the Soviet space machine's other accomplishments. The museum itself could use some innovation, and occasionally feels more nostalgic for former grandeur than celebratory of progress, but its overall message and appeal are still universal. Exhibits include spacesuits, moon rocks, pieces of rockets and satellites, and film of early space flights. Though most items are labeled in Russian only, a good English-language audioguide is now available and worth the additional fee. Although space travel and a career as an astronaut have lost their appeal for many children, travel-obsessed kids and sci-fi fans will have a great time here. Allow an hour, plus travel time to get here since it's far from the center (but right on top of a metro station).

Prospekt Mira 111. © 095/283-7914. Admission $1.50 adults, 75¢ children over age 7. Audioguide in English $3.50. Tues–Sun 10am–6pm; closed last Fri of each month. Metro: VDNKh.

Museum of GULAG History (Muzei Istorii GULAG)   This stop is not for the faint of heart. Tucked on a street of posh boutiques, a gloomy archway leads into a courtyard strung with barbed wire and hung with huge portraits of victims of the GULAG, or Soviet labor camp. The sign beneath the portraits reads: these are 12 of many million . . . , referring to the millions of Soviet citizens who passed through labor camps. Most were punished for political crimes, often only imagined by a paranoid Communist leadership. Many were killed or tortured. Those who survived usually faced repression and discrimination for the rest of their lives, as did their families. The Moscow city government runs this museum, one of the city's newest. The federal government has a more complex attitude toward its Soviet predecessors; rehabilitating GULAG victims is far from the current agenda.

16 Petrovka. © 095/209-6609. www.museum-gulag.narod.ru. Admission: $1.75. Wed–Sun 11am–5pm. Metro: Kuznetsky Most.

5 Major Museums

Tretyakov Gallery (Tretyakovskaya Galereya) 𝓚𝓚𝓚   Newcomers to Russian art and connoisseurs alike leave awed by this collection of masterpieces. Started by the Tretyakov brothers, merchant philanthropists in the 1800s, the gallery was Russia's first public art museum. The brothers' collections are a big part of it, but many works were nationalized from private collections by the Soviets. The museum is the premier repository of Russian art, starting with the earliest Orthodox icons, which date from Russia's conversion in the 9th century. It then traces the country's history through the

Conquering the Cosmos

The big, bad Soviet Union, America's rival in the race to space and nuclear superiority, was as surprised at its superpower status as the outside world. An unwieldy mass of illiterate peasants before Lenin came along, Russia took just a few decades to reach the scientific heights needed to conquer the cosmos.

The Soviet government poured funding and pressure on its rocket scientists, who stunned the world when they beat the Americans in sending the first satellite into space in 1957. **Sputnik,** the name of the vessel and the Russian word for "satellite," instantly entered the international vocabulary. A month later a Soviet mutt named **Laika** orbited the earth. She was merely setting the stage, however, for the Soviets' next breakthrough: **Yuri Gagarin's first manned flight** in 1961—a month before U.S. astronaut Alan Shepard made the journey. Gagarin came to represent Russia's victory over its own backward and repressive past, with a literal and figurative blast into the future. The anniversary of his flight, April 12, is informally celebrated as a national holiday, and his smiling image is one of the few Soviet-era faces that evokes universal pride. Just 2 years later, textile worker-turned-cosmonaut Valentina Tereshkhova became the **first woman in space,** a full 20 years before the United States sent Sally Ride into orbit in 1983.

The Soviet space program suffered plenty of defeats, including the deaths of four cosmonauts in accidents on the Soyuz-1 in 1967 and the Soyuz-11 in 1971, but propagandists largely concealed them from the public. Pilots from dozens of countries flew to space on Soviet rockets, and it wasn't until the late 1980s that the bankruptcy of the Soviet Union started crippling its once-mighty space machine. **Mir space station** became a remarkable symbol and victim of Russia's post-Soviet plight. Launched in 1986, just weeks after the U.S. shuttle *Challenger* exploded in tragedy, the Mir orbiting lab was built to last 3 or 4 years. But when the country that launched it crumbled in 1991, the Mir's crew was told to stay aloft for another 6 months while the government found money to bring them home. The station and Russia's space program scraped by, helped out by a once-unthinkable partnership with NASA, which had no space station of its own. After a string of accidents in the late 1990s, the Mir was finally sent to a choreographed demise in the Pacific Ocean in 2000.

Russia's space program has since dedicated most of its energies to the International Space Station—and to sending the world's first **"space tourists"** into orbit. The once-secretive compounds at Star City and Korolev outside Moscow now occasionally open their doors for well-paying tourists, who can test their stamina on centrifugal machines even if they don't plan any space journeys.

For a cheaper and less stomach-churning way to learn more about the Russian space program, visit the **Museum of Cosmonautics** (reviewed above) or climb aboard a real **Buran space shuttle** in Gorky Park (reviewed later in this chapter). One, two, three, blastoff . . .

naturalism of the 19th century, the Art Nouveau works of Mikhail Vrubel, and the 20th-century avant-garde works of Malevich and Kandinsky. Seek out Ilya Repin's heart-wrenching portrait of Ivan the Terrible ripped by remorse after slaying his son in a rage, and underrated talents such as the eerie Impressionist Arkhip Kuindzhi. Several artists represented had only a casual relation to Russia, but that doesn't diminish their artistic value. Much improved by a lengthy renovation, the Tretyakov reopened in 1995 with a visitor-friendly layout and increased services for non-Russian speakers. Viewing the museum chronologically makes the most sense, though it requires one clumsy detour to view the earliest icons on the second floor. The English audioguide is good if you're on your own. Allow a full morning or afternoon for this one. The pedestrian street in front is ideal for strolling, and the adjacent restaurant is a treasure of Russian cuisine, though it's often full.

10 Lavrushinsky Pereulok. ℂ 095/230-7788. Admission $8 adults, $4.50 students and children over 7. Audioguide $10. No credit cards, but there's an ATM. Small group tours in English $35 plus admission. Tues–Sun 10am–7:30pm. Metro: Tretyakovskaya or Novokuznetskaya.

Pushkin Museum of Fine Arts (Muzei Izobratitelnykh Isskustv imeni Pushkina) 𝕽𝕽 This rich and worthwhile museum is often overlooked in favor of St. Petersburg's Hermitage Museum. In fact, the two complement each other, and both deserve a look. Most visitors head straight for the impressive collection of French Impressionist works, though the museum also boasts ancient Greek sculptures and Egyptian bronzes, as well as works by Rembrandt, Rubens, and the Italian masters of the Renaissance. There is also a small but worthwhile collection of post-Impressionist and modernist art. Be sure to view the ever-expanding exhibition of controversial paintings stolen from European Jews by the Nazis and later seized by looting Soviet troops (Russians call them "rescued" artworks), including pieces by Renoir, Daumier, and van Gogh. Note that this Pushkin Museum is merely named after Russians' favorite author Alexander Pushkin; if you want to see a museum about him, skip ahead to the "Literary Moscow" section later in this chapter.

12 Volkhonka. ℂ 095/203-7998. Admission $11 adults, $5.25 students and children 7 and up. Exhibits $3.50. Audioguides $7; available at the coat check downstairs. Tues–Sun 10am–7pm. Metro: Kropotkinskaya.

Museum of Private Collections Adjacent to the Pushkin is this three-story mansion-turned-exhibition hall, which hosts rotating exhibits from private Russian collections, often of very high caliber. Recent shows have included a collection of antique glass, engravings from the collection of the Norwegian ambassador, and still lifes by Russian "Wanderer" artists (*peredvizhniki*).

14 Volkhonka. ℂ 095/203-1546. Admission varies with exhibit. Wed–Sun noon–7 pm.

Funny Feet

Don't be alarmed if a Russian museum employee stops you at the entrance and makes you put on plastic or felt slippers. Many Russian museums, especially "house museums" or those installed in former palaces, require visitors to cover their shoes to protect wood floors from soggy street shoes. The free slippers (called *bakhili*) are stored in bins near the coat check, and evoke giggles from most first-time wearers. Tread carefully at first, since some are slippery. Russian visitors don't blink at this practice, since they all keep shoes-free homes, shedding footwear (especially slush-coated winter boots) at the door in favor of house slippers.

Cult of the Coat Check

Regardless of what time of year you travel, you are sure to face this peculiarly Russian form of hospitality. All museums and theaters (and even most restaurants) will not let you past the foyer unless you take off your outer layers and leave them at the coat check. In the depth of winter this is a welcome way to shed heavy and soggy coats and hats. On a chilly summer day, however, be prepared for a fight if you want to keep your cardigan with you as you wander drafty museum spaces. When you fetch your coats, tips are not expected but are greatly appreciated, even small amounts. You may find that the woman who so sternly disrobed you upon arrival has mended your dangling button.

New Tretyakov Gallery/Museum of Modern Art (Novaya Tretyakovka) ☝ A gargantuan concrete slab of a building across from Gorky Park houses Moscow's main modern art museum (the New Tretyakov) and the Central House of Artists, a cluster of galleries, concert spaces, and art shops (see next review). The New Tretyakov follows Tretyakov Gallery's trajectory into the modern era, starting with Russian art from the 1920s and heading to the present. The building's scale and style are well-suited for the Constructivist canvases of Vasily Kandinsky and Kasimir Malevich, and for its impressive collection of Soviet avant-garde art. The museum has suffered in recent years from competition by more cutting-edge galleries, but it still mounts big-name exhibits. Entrance to the museum is on the south side of the building, not the side facing the street.

10 Krymsky Val. ☎ 095/238-1254. Admission $7.75 adults, $4.75 students and children over 7. Tues–Sun 10am–7:30pm. Metro: Oktyabrskaya or Park Kultury.

Central House of Artists (Tsentralny Dom Khudozhnika) *Value* These four floors of galleries and art shops are great for getting a look at what Russia's artists are currently up to, but most people come to buy gifts. The unusual and creative souvenirs include art books in Russian and English, embroidered felt boots, Art Nouveau tea sets, Constructivist vases, tongue-in-cheek T-shirts, and Soviet post cards. Inexpensive evening concerts and other experimental performances draw Moscow's creative crowd. Many visitors come for the informal art market that wends along the adjacent embankment, though beware of rules for exporting works of art (see "Entry Requirements & Customs" in chapter 2).

10 Krymsky Val. ☎ 095/238-9634. Admission $1.75. Tues–Sun 11am–8pm. Metro: Oktyabrskaya or Park Kultury.

6 Parks & Gardens

Gorky Park ☝ The official name of this famed, sprawling green space is Central Park of Culture and Rest, named after Maxim Gorky, but Russians refer to it as Park Gorkovo (Gorky Park) or Park Kultury (the name of the nearby metro station). The most visited—and least restful—part of the park is near the entrance, where an amusement park, ponds, and a dizzying array of game booths, trinket stands, and street performers compete for attention. In fact, the park extends several acres beyond that, tracing a swath of green between the southwest loop of the Moscow River and the sharp slope of Sparrow Hills. The park amusements are standard fare for most Western visitors (especially savvy young ones), with one notable exception: A real Buran space shuttle, designed for space flight but scrapped for lack of funding, is now parked along the river and open to visitors. It doesn't emulate weightlessness, though it will shake you up a bit in a blastoff simulation. Some of the other rides are in dodgy condition. Note the Lenin carving over the park's columned entrance.

Krymsky Val. Admission $1.75. Daily 9am–9pm. Metro: Oktyabrskaya or Park Kultury.

Victory Park (Park Pobedy)   The Great Patriotic War, as Russians refer to World War II, is a crucial part of Russia's collective memory, and this park seeks to pay tribute to those who brought the Soviet Union victory over the Nazis. The crushing cost of the war—27 million Soviet lives, more than those suffered by any other country—remains a painful and defining memory even today. Children frolic on tanks parked along the park's lush lanes, and newlyweds pose in front of its various monuments. In a decidedly post-Soviet gesture of religious tolerance, the park now houses a synagogue, mosque, and Orthodox chapel. The stirring images of the museum are worth viewing, though be prepared for a jolt when you exit into crowds of carefree in-line skaters. Don't miss the collection of World War II aircraft along the back road.

Kutuzovsky Prospekt. Daily sunrise to sundown. Metro: Park Pobedy.

Izmailovsky Park 𝒦   Most tourists only make it as far as the enormous souvenir market in the park's corner, but the park itself is well worth deeper investigation. Take the metro to the next stop (simply called Izmailovskaya) past the market, and stumble off the train into a maze of trails that wind among dense forest, hidden ponds, and gurgling streams. Wooden pavilions scattered through the park house picnickers or clusters of chess players in heated play. It's a superb spot for cross-country skiing half the year if you have your own equipment, or for biking or hiking in summer.

Izmailovskoye Shosse. Daily until sundown. Metro: Izmailovskaya (not Izmailovsky Park).

Patriarch's Ponds (Patriarshiye Prudy) 𝒦𝒦 *Kids*   This patch of green in central Moscow is a great getaway from the buzz of nearby Tverskaya Street and the Garden

---

The Silvery Islet (Serebryanny Bor)

This unusual island in northwest Moscow is a surprising refuge of oak-lined paths, silky dunes, and even beaches. It's well upstream from the factories and other pollutants that make the Moscow River so murky in the center of town. The island's relatively clean air and parkland, and its proximity to the Kremlin, made it a prime spot for *dachas* (country cottages and gardens) for the Soviet elite, and its well-protected cottages are still prized real estate. Several small beaches line the two shores, some more secluded than others, including sections preferred by nudists and gays. Water equipment such as pedal boats and canoes are available for rent, beach volleyball games are common, and a few rides have been set up for children. On hot summer weekends the island gets crowded, but summer weekdays, or pleasant weekends in spring or autumn, are great times to enjoy a break from traffic-clogged streets and watch Muscovites unwind.

To get to the island, take the metro to Polezhayevskaya; then take trolley-bus no. 20, 21, or 65 to the last stop, on the island. A taxi ride from downtown Moscow takes about 15 minutes, except during rush hour.

Ring, and an unmatchable spot for lazy people-watching. Mikhail Bulgakov made the neighborhood famous and gave it a permanently bohemian reputation with his novel *Master and Margarita,* in which the devil meets the protagonists next to the ponds. There's actually just one pond now, which serves as an ice rink in winter and shelters a few swans in summer. Kids appreciate the playground, surrounded by bronze screens depicting the fables of another favorite Russian author, Ivan Krylov. The benches fill up in late afternoon, as young people congregate with guitars and beer. Nearby Café Margarita carries on the Bulgakov tradition, and offers funky fare along with Gypsy or jazz music.

Malaya Bronnaya Ulitsa. 24 hr. Metro: Mayakovskaya or Tverskaya.

Botanical Gardens (Botanichesky Sad)   This vast, overgrown park is quite far from the center of town, and is fairly lifeless for much of the year given Moscow's climate. In season, however, the flowers are often unusual and breathtaking. Outside the chief displays, the park is rather overgrown and labyrinthine, but it's still a lovely place for a stroll, bike ride, or picnic. Since they're so far off the main track, the gardens are only worth visiting if the weather's clear, or if you're visiting the adjacent All-Russian Exhibition Center (see next review). Wear good shoes.

Daily until sundown. Metro: Botanichesky Sad.

All-Russian Exhibition Center (formerly VDNKh) *Kids*   It used to be called the Exhibit of the Achievements of the People's Economy, and the park's design certainly has a propagandistic feel, with its "friendship of peoples" fountains and pavilions once used to show off the fruits of Soviet factories, the nuclear energy industry, and collective farms. The stunning centerpiece is a fountain with gilded statues of women representing each of the 15 former Soviet republics. Its current contents reflect the hard-core capitalism of today's Moscow. Some halls are packed with vendors selling the latest DVD players, cellphones, and PDAs; others hawk in-line skates and high-speed bikes; still others have stalls packed with stuffed animals and Chinese-made plastic toys. Some pavilions still house international expos, from high-tech fairs to sugar refinery exhibits. Amusement park rides are scattered throughout the grounds, with the fast and enormous Ferris wheel a major draw. The park is far from the center of town, but if you're staying nearby or have kids, it can make for a fun afternoon. Muscovites call it by its Soviet acronym, VDNKh.

Free admission; exhibits sometimes charge entrance fee. Daily 9am–9pm. Metro: VDNKh.

7 Aristocratic Estates

Several former private estates seized by the Soviets have been turned into museums or concert spaces, with their extensive grounds now used for picnics, jogging, and cross-country skiing. The **Kuskovo** estate boasts a porcelain exhibit and a luxurious orangerie. On the Fourth of July it's taken over by the American Chamber of Commerce for a bash that Muscovites have come to love (© **095/370-0150;** palace Wed–Sun 10am–5pm; metro: Ryazansky Prospekt). The neoclassical **Ostankino** mansion, like Kuskovo, belonged to the prominent noble family the Sheremetevs. It has a small exhibit of 18th-century art and artifacts, and hosts chamber music concerts throughout the summer (Ostankino Park; © **095/283-4645;** May–Sept only, Wed–Sun 10am–5pm; metro: VDNKh.). The **Tsaritsino** estate is Catherine the

Great's never-finished masterpiece, meant to be her residence on Moscow's outskirts before she lost interest in and money for the project. The lush grounds, now within city limits, are easy to lose yourself in on a lazy summer day (1 Dolskaya Ulitsa; ⓒ 095/321-0743; park daily, museum Wed–Sun 11am–6pm; metro: Tsaritsino).

Kolomenskoye 🎬🎬🎬 _Kids_   This park, museum, festival site, and religious history tour is the jewel of Moscow's estate museums. Extending several acres along the Moscow River well south of the city center, Kolomenskoye gathers churches and historic buildings from the 15th to the 20th centuries in a huge green space perfect for picnicking, sledding, or lounging in the grass. It holds several festivals throughout the year themed around Russian holidays, with different period dress and performances (in Russian only). The breathtaking white facade of the 16th-century Church of the Ascension is closed to the public due to disrepair, but it's a perfect backdrop for a roll down the grassy slope. Apple orchards, a honey farm, and tea huts provide fun and nourishment for kids. A boat dock launches leisurely trips up and down this section of the river, though the view opposite Kolomenskoye is industrial and colorless. The site is a good 10-minute walk from the metro.

39 Prospekt Andropova. ⓒ 095/112-5217. Admission to the park $1.75. Daily 9am–9pm; museums Tues–Sun 10am–5:30pm. Metro: Kolomenskaya.

8 Literary Moscow

Tolstoy House Museum 🎬🎬   This is the most authentic and atmospheric of Moscow's "house museums," laden with original belongings and details that help you reenact the long winters that Leo Tolstoy, his wife, and their 13 kids spent here from 1882 to 1901. The museum includes the stable yard, Tolstoy's treasured garden, and a souvenir shop in the room where he stored his printing press. The dining table is laid out with the family's English china, and the walls are still covered with some of the original oil-cloth wallpaper. The children's toys and etchings give the whole house an intimate feel. For literature buffs, the most powerful room is Tolstoy's study, where he penned _The Death of Ivan Ilyich,_ among other works.

21 Ulitsa Lva Tolstogo. ⓒ 095/246-9444. Admission: $3. Tues–Sun 10am–6pm. Closed last Fri of the month. Metro: Park Kultury.

Chekhov House Museum 🎬   This is the house where the doctor-turned-playwright first found literary success, as an author of short stories and one-act plays. He lived in the pink two-story house with his family between the autumn of 1886 and the spring of 1890.

6 Sadovaya Kudrinskaya. ⓒ 095/291-6154. Admission: $3. Thurs and Sat–Sun 11am–6pm; Wed and Fri 2–8pm. Closed last day of the month. Metro: Barrikadnaya.

Impressions

You, greedy mob standing by the throne,
Executioners of Freedom, Genius and Glory!
Hidden under the protection of laws
Before you justice and truth are silent
                    —Mikhail Lermontov, blaming the frivolity of court
                                circles for Pushkin's death in a duel

Pushkin Apartment Museum   Russia's favorite poet, Pushkin, lived here right after his marriage. The building was made into communal apartments in the Soviet era. Tchaikovsky also lived in the building.

53 Arbat St. ℂ 095/241-9295. Tues–Thurs noon–8pm; Fri–Sun 10am–6pm. Metro: Arbatskaya or Smolenskaya.

Mikhail Lermontov House Museum   Chronicler of Russia's Caucasus campaigns, poet and painter Lermontov lived in this cheerful yet studious pink house during his formative student years.

2 Malaya Molchanovka. ℂ 095/291-5298. Admission $2. Thurs and Sat–Sun 11am–6pm; Wed and Fri 2–6pm. Metro: Arbatskaya.

9 Especially for Kids

Moscow doesn't appear at all child-friendly on the surface, and Russia's plunging birth rates only exacerbate Moscow's image as a city for grown-ups. That said, Russians revere their kids, and Moscow has plenty for children to do if you're a bit creative. The **circus** is a world-famous draw, the **zoo** is impressive, and several **puppet theaters** around town offer top-quality performances. The shows are in Russian only, but younger children are often content to enjoy the visuals. Be aware that animal rights activism remains totally alien to Russia, so sensitive parents would be advised to stay away from the circus and zoo if this is an issue. Seasonal festivals, such as those at **Kolomenskoye** (see review earlier in this chapter), are a sure winner for kids, as are the attractions at **Gorky Park** (see review earlier in this chapter). Another kid-pleaser is the **Police Relay Race** that whips around the Garden Ring the first Sunday after Police Day on October 24. The highlights are the motorcycle and patrol car races; see local newspapers for details of the best vantage spots.

Moscow Circus Named after Y. Nikulin (Tsentralny Tsirk) 𝕮𝕮   The acrobatics are what set this circus apart from its counterparts outside Russia, though many come to see the musical cats, gymnastic elephants, and clowns that know tragedy as only a Russian can. On weekends there are three shows a day. The performances are long: 2 hours, with an intermission.

13 Tsvetnoi Bulvar. ℂ 095/200-6889. Tickets $3–$25, depending on seats, time of day, and who's performing. Free for kids under 7 accompanied by an adult. Metro: Tsvetnoi Bulvar.

New Moscow Circus (Novy Tsirk) 𝕮   This venue offers more varied performances and a bigger hall, meaning it's cheaper and easier to get tickets if the central circus is full. Despite its distance from the center of town, it's right across from a metro station.

7 Prospekt Vernadskogo. ℂ 095/930-2815. Tickets $1.75–$7. Metro: Universitet.

Moscow Zoo (Zoopark)   This zoo in the center of town is divided into two parts connected by a whimsical footbridge. The dolphinarium is packed in summer, and the petting zoo is a scramble of groping hands on weekends. Try a Tuesday or Wednesday morning for leaner crowds.

1 Bolshaya Gruzinskaya. ℂ 095/255-5375. Admission adults $3.50, children under 18 accompanied by adult are free. Tues–Sun 10am–8pm May–Oct; 10am–5pm Nov–April. Metro: Barrikadnaya or Krasnopresnenskaya.

Obrazstov Puppet Theater (Kukolny Teatr)   Half the fun of this performance space is the enormous cuckoo clock on the facade that puts on a show of its own every hour. The performances are in Russian but the repertoire includes well-known tales such as "Puss in Boots," "Pinocchio," and "Jack and the Beanstalk." The quality of the puppets and the actors is superb. The performances run from 1 to 2 hours, which may be long for the youngest guests.

3 Sadovo-Samotechnya St. (C) 095/299-3310. Tickets $2.50–$11. Metro: Tsvetnoi Bulvar.

10 Organized Tours

Most organized Moscow tours in English are unadventurous and overpriced, an unfortunate remnant of Soviet days when only certain sites were open to tourists and only the state tourist agency Intourist was authorized to escort them. One welcome exception is **Patriarshy Dom Tours** (C) **095/795-0927;** http://russiatravel-pdtours. netfirms.com), which offers informative and unusual tours of the Moscow that most tourists don't see. Selections include metro tours, tours of Jewish Moscow, antiques tours, Easter tours in medieval Orthodox towns, and tours of Bulgakov in Moscow. The tours run from an hour to a weekend in length.

For general city tours and Kremlin tours, **Capital Tours** (4 Ilinka Ulitsa, inside Gostiny Dvor; (C) **095/232-2442;** www.capitaltours.ru) is the best-equipped and most friendly. Its Kremlin tours include the Armory and run 6 days a week at 10:30am and at 3pm, for $20 plus admission. City bus tours run daily at 11am and 2:30pm for $20.

Intourist (11 Stoleshnikov Pereulok; (C) **095/923-8575**) is still around and improving its service slowly to keep up with competition. It offers Kremlin and city tours, cruises along the Moscow River, and weekend trips to Sergiev Posad and Vladimir and Suzdal (all described in chapter 10). Most tours must be booked 2 days in advance. Intourist also has offices in the Ukraina (p. 90) and Cosmos (p. 94).

11 Outdoor Pursuits

Moscow's climate means its chief outdoor pursuits involve snow and ice. Most Russians, however, aren't particularly into sports; rarely will you see anyone out for a casual jog. City streets are unwelcoming to bikers and in-line skaters, though the vastness of Moscow's parks makes them great places for just about any physical activity. Check out the "Parks & Gardens" section earlier in this chapter for more specific suggestions.

BOATING

There are very few places where you can row your own boat in Moscow, other than the small ponds at Chistiye Prudy (see the "Walking Tour" at the end of this chapter) and Patriarch's Ponds (p. 135). Several companies offer trips up and down the Moscow River on small ferries from May to September. Most leave across from the Kremlin or across from Kievsky Station. The **Moscow Shipping Company** ((C) **095/242-0407**) is the chief operator, with a boat that takes a 90-minute trip from Kievshy Station to the Novopassky Monastery and makes several stops along the way. It costs $3 one-way on weekdays, $6 weekends (half-price for children under 7).

SKIING

Moscow has two downhill ski slopes, one in Krylatskoye and one in Bitsevsky Park, but both are small, with rickety lifts and endless lines. Cross-country skiing options, however, are endless. Izmailovsky Park (p. 135), Bitsevsky Park (directly south of the city center, accessible by metro station Bitsevo), Losiny Ostrov (a tranquil, wooded mass that covers the northeast corner of the city map; best reached by taxi), and Sokolniki (near the metro station Sokolniki) are just some of the spots within city limits where you can get in a few hours of skiing without spotting a vehicle. Basic ski rentals are available at Sokolniki and Bitsevsky. A package of cross-country skis, boots, and poles rents for 400 to 500 rubles ($14–$18)

FISHING

In deepest winter, you'll often glimpse men in fur hats perched on the frozen-over Moscow River waiting for something to bite. This is not recommended because of the risk of the ice cracking and the questionable quality of the catch.

GYMS

Gym culture has only recently hit Moscow, and is still limited to a few chains. If your hotel doesn't have a health club, try **Planeta Fitness**'s several branches for a day pass (© 095/933-7100; www.fitness.ru/en).

HIKING

The city's bigger parks are good for a few hours of hiking, as are several forested areas outside town. **Bitsevsky Park** is a long rectangle of green space south of the center, criss-crossed with streams and ravines, hilly enough to hold one of the city's two downhill ski slopes, and dense enough to muffle the sounds and smells of this enormous city. **Losiny Ostrov** occupies a huge swath of evergreen forest in the northeast corner of the city, and is a few minutes by taxi from metro Shcholkovskaya, or a good 15-minute walk. Beyond the Moscow city limits, organized trails are rare, but forests and streams are ubiquitous. To avoid getting lost, you should go with a group or a reliable Russian guide. The most popular and pristine spots are along the Moscow River upstream (northwest) of the city, such as around Usovo, Tryokhgorka, and Zvenigorod. All three can be reached by commuter train (*elektrichka*) from Belorussky Station. Patriarshy Dom tours (see listing under "Organized Tours," above) occasionally offers English-language weekend hikes in the warmer months. The **Central Moscow Tourist Club** also arranges hikes, usually in Russian, but the club will arrange English guides for a fee (4 Ulitsa Sadova-Kudrinskaya; © 095/203-5133 or 095/291-6367; metro: Barrikadnaya).

ICE SKATING

Gorky Park (p. 134) floods its main lanes in the winter, turning them into a rough but exhilarating open-air skating zone. You can rent skates here. The ponds at Patriarch's Ponds (p. 135) and Chistiye Prudy (see the "Walking Tour" at the end of this chapter) also are transformed into free skating rinks in winter, though you need your own skates and, if the winter has been mild, be sure the ice is thick before you try.

IN-LINE SKATING

Victory Park (p. 135) has the smoothest paths for in-line skating and several good slopes for an afternoon workout. Skating on city sidewalks is not advised, as they're usually too crowded and Muscovites have little experience with dodging skaters.

JOGGING

Moscow's air quality and sidewalk disrepair is such that jogging through your hotel neighborhood would be crueler to your body than it would be kind. Any parks mentioned in this book can offer good running routes. There's also a great path along the river beneath Sparrow Hills (Vorobyoviye Gory), which run along the south side of the Moscow River where it forms a loop beneath Moscow State University; and another along the Moscow River behind the Ukraina hotel (p. 90). Running during daylight hours is recommended. Casual joggers may get a few stares, since the only Russians who run for fun are generally current or former athletes.

Moments Banya Bliss

It's not on most tourist itineraries, but if you can squeeze it in, there's no better way to shed city grime and immerse yourself in Russian culture than to visit a banya. Something between a steam bath and a sauna, the banya has been an important cleansing and resting ritual for centuries. Traditional banyas are huts built alongside rural houses, where families take turns steaming themselves clean, then plunge into a tub of cool water or a nearby stream, or roll in the snow to cool off. In Moscow, banya culture ranges from elite spa-type facilities with expensive body masks and luxurious pedicures (for both sexes) to more proletarian facilities used by residents of communal apartments tired of waiting in line for the shower at home. Thought to cure many ills, the banya is a great rainy-day activity for tourists, too, if you pick one with a bit of history. In the women's halls, bathers treat the steam water with eucalyptus oil and coat their skin with honey, coffee grounds, or whatever other remedy they learned from grandma. In the men's halls, business deals are often made over copious beer and snacks. In both halls you're likely to see bathers beating each other (gently) with birch branches; the practice is believed to accelerate and enhance the cleansing process. The steam is great for warming up in winter; the icy pools cool you off in summer.

Sandunovskiye Banyi, an ornate and cheerful 19th-century bathhouse, is a favorite with "new Russians" and Moscow-based expatriates. They have two levels of service for each gender. A 2-hour deluxe-level session costs $22; a 2-hour standard-level session costs $14. The differences between the deluxe and standard sessions are minimal; a "deluxe" session basically translates into more elegant furnishings and a larger steam room. Sheets, towels, and slippers can be rented for $1 to $4, or you can bring your own. The deluxe level is offered Tuesday through Sunday from 8am to 10pm; the standard level is offered Wednesday through Monday from 8am to 10pm. You'll find the baths at 14 Neglinnaya St., buildings 3 to 7; the entrance is on Zvonarsky Pereulok (② 095/925-4631; www.sanduny.ru).

Seleznyovskiye Banyi is a more modest and out-of-the-way option. This bathhouse has been serving customers since 1854 and is the one Russian connoisseurs prefer, especially the men's hall with its "professional steamers" running the show. A standard 2-hour session costs $11 for men and women; entrance to the deluxe halls (men only) costs $16. The baths are open Tuesday through Sunday from 8am to 10pm, and are located at 15 Seleznyovskaya Ulitsa, building 2 (② 095/978-9430).

S lyokhim parom, as the Russians say, or "Good steam to you."

12 Spectator Sports

FIGURE SKATING

Russia is still a breeding ground for world-class skaters, though the top Russian names now train in North America or Europe. The local, regional, and international championships held here showcase some stars-in-waiting, and you might even glimpse a future Olympic medalist. Most tournaments are in January or February in the **Olimpiisky Stadium** (see below for complete address and contact information); check the Russian Figure Skating Federation website (www.goldskate.ru) or the International Skating Union (www.isu.com) for schedules.

HOCKEY

Russians are among the world's best practitioners of hockey, which is no surprise given their nation's icy latitude. Many NHL stars have come back to play with their home teams—or coach them—which has boosted the level of play after the rough and cash-poor 1990s. Sponsorship from Russia's flush oil majors has also helped. Check *The Moscow Times* (www.themoscowtimes.com) or the Russian Hockey Federation (www.russianhockey.net) for Russian or European championship matches, or for season matches involving CSKA (Red Army) or Dinamo, Moscow's premier clubs. Crowds at the **CSKA Sports Complex** can be rowdy, especially for evening matches or highly sensitive standoffs, like Russia and Ukraine. Join in the fun and keep a low profile, and you should have no trouble. Tickets are sold at theater kiosks around town. Chances of getting tickets for a big championship match at the stadium are slim, unless you resort to scalpers. For smaller matches it's easy to show up and purchase tickets; prices can be as low as $3. Advance tickets are also available at theater kiosks around town. See below for complete address and contact information for the CSKA arena.

SOCCER

Soccer actually beats out hockey as Russians' favorite sport. Any Muscovite you meet can fill you in on the standings of their home teams, CSKA, Dinamo, Spartak, and of course the national team. Hotel employees can often help you get tickets. The season for local matches runs March to November. Tickets for major international matches are bought up by speculators and not available at the stadium the day of the game, but any other match is easy to get into on the spur of the moment for just a few dollars. Theater kiosks around town also sell advance tickets to the bigger events. The main stadiums are **Luzhniki Sports Complex** (avoid sections B and D, where the roughest fans gather) and **Dinamo Stadium** (hard-core fans here prefer the stands on the south side of the stadium). See below for complete address and contact information for the stadiums. See www.uefa.com for upcoming European League matches in Moscow.

TENNIS TOURNAMENTS

Russian names have packed the rosters of the world's top tennis tournaments in recent years, with the women especially dominating the sport. Moscow's Kremlin Cup, held every October at Olimpiisky Stadium, has become a big international tournament, and Moscow frequently hosts the Davis Cup as well. Tickets for these events are available online at www.kremlincup.ru or www.daviscup.com. Theater kiosks around town also sell tickets, though you must purchase them well in advance. Matches are held at the following venues:

- **Luzhniki Sports Complex,** 24 Luzhniki Ulitsa. © 095/245-3611. Metro: Sportivnaya
- **Dynamo Sports Complex,** 36 Leningradsky Prospekt. © 095/212-7092. Metro: Dinamo
- **CSKA (Red Army) Sports Complex,** 39a Leningradsky Prospekt. © 095/213-7812. Metro: Aeroport
- **Olimpiisky Sports Complex,** 16 Olimpiisky Prospekt. © 095/288-1533. Metro: Prospekt Mira

---

WALKING TOUR   HISTORIC MOSCOW

Start:	Red Square.
Finish:	Chistiye Prudy (Clean Ponds).
Time:	2½ to 3 hours.
Best times:	Wednesday through Sunday mornings, when exhibits are open and crowds are thinner than in the afternoon.

This tour covers several centuries of Moscow's history, taking in some major sights and some lesser-known ones. It starts with the obvious, becomes more subtle, and ends with a peek into the Ukrainian Quarter, a neighborhood few tourists explore. The city's design has been too haphazard for the tour to be chronological, but it provides a sense of how the eras blend to make modern Moscow. The walk turns sharply uphill about halfway through, so save some energy, and be well-shod. The first five stops along the tour take you through the neighborhood of **Kitai-Gorod**, with its showcase of Russian architecture from the 15th to 17th centuries.

Start at Red Square, taking a moment to get your bearings from the peak of this sloped plaza. Then head down toward the beckoning cupolas of:

❶ St. Basil's Cathedral

The oldest building on this tour, this 16th-century cathedral has come to symbolize Russia to the rest of the world, but it was almost torn down by Stalin as an anachronistic eyesore. Legend has it that a favorite architect rescued the cathedral by threatening to take his own life on its stairs. Climbing its labyrinthine stairwells and corridors, note how cramped and cool it feels inside, compared to its vivid, abundantly designed exterior.

When leaving the cathedral, turn right, away from the Kremlin, down Varvarka Street. Ignore, if you can, the street's most prominent feature, stadium-size Hotel Rossiya (if it hasn't yet been razed, as the mayor threatens). Take the stairs on the right-hand side of the street down to the path that runs alongside a string of churches and mansions. This is one of the few sections of Moscow preserved as it was in centuries past, a sort of accidental architectural museum. The first building, the pink-and-white Church of St. Barbara, is closed. Continue to no. 4:

❷ English Courtyard (Angliisky Podvorye)

This wooden-roofed building is one of the oldest civilian structures in Moscow, a 16th-century merchant's center granted to English traders by Ivan the Terrible to boost trade between the countries. It's now dwarfed by the hotel next door. The small exhibit inside is worth a visit in order to see the building's interior and artifacts (and everything is labeled in English as well as Russian). The building also hosts concerts of medieval music. It's open Tuesday through Sunday from 10am to 6pm (© **095/298-3952**).

Continue up the path, noting the yellow-and-white (and no longer functioning) Church of St. Maxim the Blessed. The next few buildings were once part of the Znamensky Monastery. The strange four-story building at no. 10 houses:

❸ The Museum of the Romanov Boyars

The Romanov Boyars (nobles) lived here before Mikhail Romanov was crowned czar in 1613, launching the Romanov imperial dynasty. The only original part of this building is the basement; the rest was added later to re-create conditions of 16th-century Moscow. The building was once part of a vast mini-city that stretched down to the Moscow River. The thick walls, small windows, and rugged conditions were typical of the day, even for aristocratic families such as this one. The museum is open Wednesday from 11am to 7pm, and Thursday through Sunday from 10am to 6pm (℃ **095/298-3706**). It's closed the first Monday of each month.

Head to the building next door, the last one along the row, just beneath the hotel driveway:

❹ St. George's Church

This church was built in two different eras, the 16th and 18th centuries, and its two parts remain different colors as if to draw attention to the church's split personality. It's the only one of Varvarka Street's churches to hold regular services; you may see an Orthodox wedding if you're here on a weekend.

Head up the stairs to Varvarka proper, and continue down the hill. The street opens onto a busy intersection that can only be crossed by underground walkway. The sole remaining part of the 16th-century Varvarka gate tower is the white stone base, still visible in the underground passage. Once you're underground, continue straight along your trajectory from Varvarka. Take the first stairwell on your left aboveground. You should emerge in front of:

❺ Cyril and Methodius Monument

Perched in the middle of Slavic Square, this monument portrays the two 9th-century monks credited with inventing the Cyrillic alphabet, used in Russia and many Slavic countries to this day.

Up the hill behind the monument stretch the leafy slopes of Novaya Ploshchad (New Square), crisscrossed by shaded paths lined with benches.

TAKE A BREAK
There are several mid-range cafes along the east side of **Novaya Ploshchad,** but if the weather's fine, a better alternative is an ice cream or snack from the street vendors nearby. You can perch on a bench or flat stone in the square for a rest and a mini-picnic.

At the top of Novaya Ploshchad, the square opens onto a neo-Gothic, mustard-colored building:

❻ The Polytechnical Museum

Built in the 1870s to promote science and technology during Russia's industrial boom, the museum now houses (rather outdated) collections of clocks, rockets, early movie cameras, typewriters, and other technological innovations over the past century. It's open Tuesday through Sunday from 10am to 6pm (℃ **095/223-0756**). Model robots and electronic instruments are switched on briefly every 2 hours starting at 11am.

Head to the plaza on the opposite side of the museum from Novaya Ploshchad, and look across it at the building that no Russian feels indifferent towards:

❼ Lubyanka

The Bolshevik secret police seized this granite and sandstone building from an insurance company in 1918, and its residents have spied on Russians ever since. Its six-story stone facade takes on a sinister feel when you imagine the persecutions and interrogations that have gone on here. Now it's the headquarters of the Federal Security Service, once led by President Putin.

The bare patch in the grass across from Lubyanka is the site where a monument

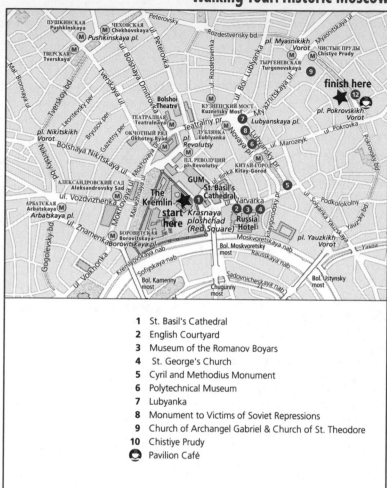

1 St. Basil's Cathedral
2 English Courtyard
3 Museum of the Romanov Boyars
4 St. George's Church
5 Cyril and Methodius Monument
6 Polytechnical Museum
7 Lubyanka
8 Monument to Victims of Soviet Repressions
9 Church of Archangel Gabriel & Church of St. Theodore
10 Chistiye Prudy
🛈 Pavilion Café

to Soviet secret police founder Felix Dzerzhinsky stood for decades before democracy protesters tore it down in 1991.

In the little green space between Lubyanka and the Polytechnical Museum, note the small stone and plaque:

❽ Monument to Victims of Soviet Repressions

A lonely slab of stone from the Solovetsky Islands, an Arctic prison camp for enemies of the Soviet regime, honors the millions of people repressed by the Soviet government. The stone was brought here and placed across from Lubyanka during the soul-searching days after the Soviet collapse, but gatherings here have dwindled in recent years as new concerns occupy Russian minds. A nearby plaque written in English and Russian tells visitors to contact the Memorial, Russia's leading human rights organization and the group responsible for the monument, for more information.

Head back into the capitalist rush of modern Moscow by crossing over to Myasnitskaya Ulitsa, to the right of Lubyanka. Follow the street past a string of bookshops and cafes until you see Krivokolyonny Pereulok off to the right. Take this street (which translates as "Crooked Knee Lane") past the 18th- and 19th-century mansions now housing offices and apartments, until you reach two churches clustered together:

➒ Church of the Archangel Gabriel & Church of St. Theodore Stratilites

The twisting gold dome of the Church of the Archangel Gabriel is the most noticeable of its nontraditional architectural features. Commissioned in 1705 by Peter the Great's advisor, Alexander Menshikov, the church is a clear example of the period when European classicism overrode Russian architecture, with grand buttresses and cornices not seen on most Orthodox churches. The 19th-century, quasi-Gothic Church of St. Theodore Stratilites is next door.

Continue a few yards to the end of Krivokolyonny Pereulok. You'll emerge onto Chistoprudny Bulvar, a boulevard with a stretch of green space running down its center. Enter the park and head right, until you reach:

➓ Chistiye Prudy

This area was referred to as "Dirty Ponds" in the days when it housed a meat market, whose refuse ran into the murky pools. The 19th-century city government cleaned it up and rechristened it "Clean Ponds," or Chistiye Prudy. Only one pond remains; it's a mecca for skaters and toddlers on sleds in winter, and for rental boats in summer.

 WINDING DOWN Pavilion (✆ 095/203-5110), perched on the ponds, is packed most evenings with a haughty, hipper-than-thou crowd, but it's a lovely spot for a midday bite. The wooden deck makes it feel homey amid the pretentious clientele. The food is a mélange of Russian, European, and central Asian cuisines.

8

Shopping in Moscow

Most visitors limit their Moscow shopping to a few *matryoshka* nesting dolls and some Soviet memorabilia, but a bit of perseverance can uncover unusual crafts and striking gifts. Hand-embroidered table linens from the textile-producing towns along the Volga are a good buy, as are scarlet-and-gold Khokloma wooden spoons, intricate wooden Easter eggs, or jewelry cut from richly colored Siberian stones you won't find at home, such as lilac-colored charoite and deep pink radonite.

Moscow has also become one of the world's fastest-growing luxury shopping destinations, with a bigger Prada store than Milan, and Russian designers' top-of-the-line creations that sell for jaw-dropping prices. There are also plenty of mid-market clothing chains such as Benetton and Mexx, but overall, Moscow remains less touched by this kind of globalization than other European capitals.

Moscow's vendors have become much more market-savvy after a decade of capitalism. That means the shocking bargains of black market days are long gone, but it also means that quality is more reliable and competition has livened up the selection of products available. Beware, as in any big city, of con artists on the street trying to sell a "real" silver fox hat or czarist medal hat for a suspiciously low price. Several typical Russian souvenirs are described below. For more on amber and lacquer boxes, see chapter 16.

1 The Shopping Scene

When you buy anything in Russia, keep in mind that you'll want to take it home—and Customs officers can bar the export of anything antique, any book printed before 1960, or any painting or other work of art considered of cultural value to Russia. You'll have no problem with the majority of souvenirs, and even the antique or valuable ones can usually be cleared for export by the Ministry of Culture. This process takes a few days, involves getting the item appraised and then approved, and can cost anywhere from 10% to 100% of the item's value. If you're in doubt about a purchase, check with the vendor about its exportability, and also with a tour guide or other third party, if possible. Many hotel concierges can help you get Culture Ministry clearance. Otherwise, you can try contacting the ministry's Moscow appraisal and certification agency (8 Neglinnaya Ulitsa, 3rd floor, room 29; © 095/921-3258). The rules change frequently, but items like samovars and old icons are always on the iffy list (see the box "Russian Orthodox Icons" below).

Hotel gift shops are the most expensive places in town for souvenirs, and heavily touristed areas such as Red Square are a close second. Better bets are the small crafts shops or outdoor markets farther from the center of town. For Orthodox icons and other church-related paraphernalia, the monasteries have the most authentic and attractive selection.

Moscow Shopping

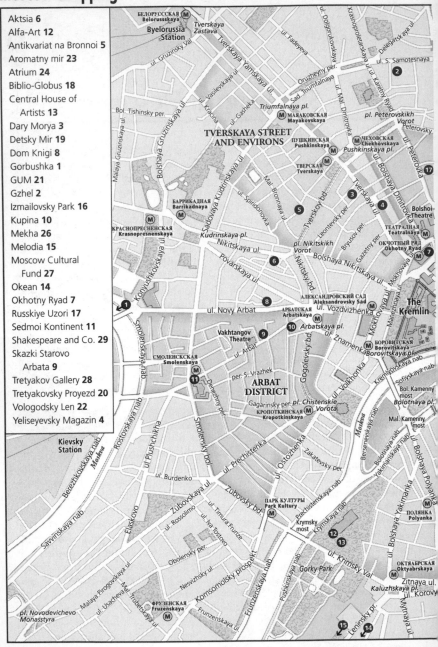

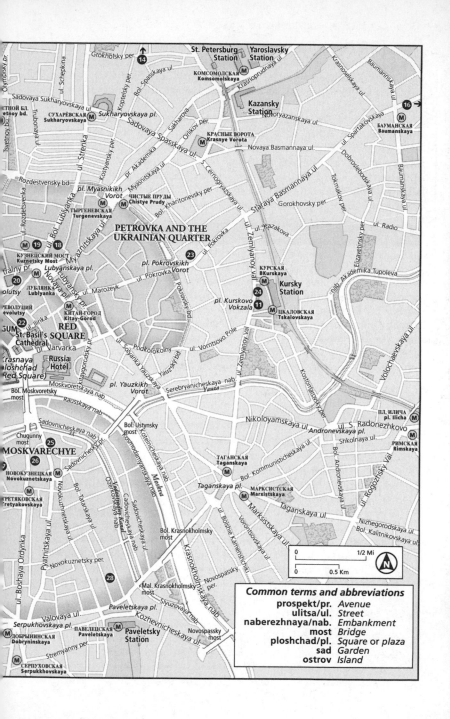

Moscow has no sales tax, so the price printed on an item is the price you'll pay, as long as you know what currency is being cited (see the "Currency Confusion" box on p. 83). Prices include VAT (value-added tax), which adds from 5% to 18% to the item's original price. The Russian VAT is not refundable at the border as it is in some European countries.

Shops and shopping centers are generally open daily from around 10am to 8pm. Food stores open earlier, and kiosks around town are often open round-the-clock. Most stores are closed on Russian holidays, and smaller stores are closed Sunday or Monday. A very few shops still close for an hour at lunch, usually from 1 to 2pm.

Companies such as **DHL** (11 Pervaya Tverskaya-Yamskaya; ℂ **095/956-1000**) and **UPS** (8 Bolshoi Tishinsky, building 2; ℂ **095/961-2211**) can ship paintings, rugs, or other large items to your home and take care of any clearances you need.

2 Great Shopping Areas

Just about any souvenir, bauble, or item of clothing can be found just off Red Square, at the two major shopping centers: **GUM** and **Okhotny Ryad.** Heading up **Tverskaya Street,** you'll find more variety, and you can enjoy the long stroll and historic plaques interspersed with shoe stores and specialty food shops. One to look out for is **Eliseyevsky Magazin,** a refurbished version of an elite 19th-century food emporium that now offers Russia's most expensive chocolates, premium vodkas, and smaller and more affordable treats such as tasty Russian tea cookies and salted herring. For a dazzling glimpse at the Russian new rich, wander through the boutiques of the world's top fashion and jewelry designers in gleaming **Tretyakovsky Proyezd,** designed to

Russian Orthodox Icons

The haunting, gold-flaked biblical images on Orthodox icons hold a magnetic appeal for many visitors to Russia, regardless of their faith. The angular, distorted faces and figures may seem jarring if compared to western Renaissance art, but that's because Russian icon painters were not aiming at three-dimensional realism. Russian Orthodox icons are rich in symbolism but lacking in light or shadow; they do not aim to render beauty but to honor and inspire spirituality. Modern icons strictly follow the traditions and images established centuries ago, and all must be blessed by an Orthodox priest. The design is carved into a wood panel, then hand-painted. Gold leaf and silver crowns can make the icon more valuable, but they don't make it any more authentic. The vendor should be able to explain what era of iconpainting is represented or what artist is being emulated. Most of the icons for sale today are safe for export, but any made before the Soviet era require permission. Be sure to get a receipt even for the new ones, preferably with the date of production (data izgotovleniya) printed on it. The larger icons are more likely to arouse the suspicion of Customs officers.

Icons are best purchased at Orthodox monasteries or cathedrals. Novodevichy Convent (p. 127) is known for an extensive collection.

replicate a 19th-century gallery. It's not far from Red Square, between Teatralny Proyezd and Nikolskaya Ulitsa.

The Arbat has fashioned itself as Moscow's premier shopping district, though most of the souvenir booths lining the center of the pedestrian street are overpriced and seem to offer the same merchandise as their neighbors. The Arbat's better shopping deals can be found in its few remaining crafts shops, which sell boxes made of carved birch wood in traditional Russian patterns, hand-embroidered bed and table linens, and traditional Russian caftans and gowns. Look for children's sizes, too—some make good choices for holiday or Halloween outfits. The New Russian Store is worth a peek inside; the tongue-in-cheek boutique of traditional Russian handiwork caters to—and makes fun of—Russia's extravagant nouveau riche. On a recent visit I saw a delicate ceramic cellphone and a lacquer box painted with a scene of thuglike businessmen being fed grapes by scantily clad nymphs.

A less abundant but more original shopping area is **Pyatniskaya Street** in Zamoskvarechye, south of the Kremlin. Several independent artists sell their paintings and sculptures in galleries and small shops here, along with traditional Russian crafts. This is also where Moscow's few vintage clothing stores reside, plus a few shops offering secondhand designer wear.

Moscow's shopping mecca for foreign and Russian visitors alike is the huge open-air bazaar at **Izmailovsky Park,** in eastern Moscow outside the Garden Ring. The rough-and-tumble stalls and garage-sale feel of a few years back have been replaced by organized rows of vendors behind a cheerful, towering facade of carved wood. On weekends an entrance fee of 50 rubles ($1.75) is charged. Inside, you'll find 10 times the selection of *matryoshka* nesting dolls than the Arbat displays, plus Russian space-program memorabilia, malachite chess sets, intricate and original jewelry, blue-hued Uzbek plates, surprisingly patterned quilts, Soviet propaganda posters, booths and booths of lacquer boxes, wooden toys, and much more. Most prices are negotiable, and all vendors speak some English. Get off at the Izmailovsky Park metro stop and follow the crowd.

Muscovites often spend their weekends at the open-air food and clothing markets scattered around town, where they buy produce, meat, diapers, winter boots, cleaning supplies, and any number of things at prices much lower than those in department stores or supermarkets. The quality ranges from cheap Chinese toy trucks to fine Russian-made parkas. If you're curious, check out the food and clothing markets at Izmailovsky (to the left of the souvenir bazaar) or Fili (between the Bagrationovskaya metro station and the Gorbushka electronics market).

3 The Shopping Centers

The concept of the shopping mall as North America knows it remains foreign to Russian shoppers, though they have their own version of shopping centers that serve the same purpose. Moscow's premier shopping gallery is **GUM** (pronounced *goom*), which stands for State Department Store. This magnificent, oblong building extends nearly the full eastern side of Red Square, and is organized into three open arcades of three floors connected by curved bridges and anchored by a fountain at the center. The shops bear little resemblance to the 19th-century stalls of GUM's early days or to the rows of drab, identical stores that inhabited it in Soviet times. Today, designers such as Christian Dior, Max Mara, and their Russian counterparts fill the most prestigious Red

Nesting Dolls

Matryoshka nesting dolls are so ubiquitous in today's Russia that they're almost banal, but a quality doll can be a symbol of Russian art and history. The first dolls, believed to be based on a Japanese tradition, were created in the 19th century in the Orthodox Church center of Sergiev Posad. The richest versions depict scenes from Russian fairy tales opening up to reveal the next stage in the story. The most common version is a rosy-cheeked woman in a vibrant head-scarf, holding a series of sisters or daughters inside. The dolls are usually made from birch wood, and a proper set of dolls will be made from the same tree so that the wood responds uniformly to temperature and humidity changes.

Matryoshka dolls are a great, inexpensive gift for girls and boys from infancy up to school-age. The basic versions can sell for as little as $2 at open-air markets. Older kids and adults may appreciate those with more intricate designs—or those with a theme such as all of Russia's leaders over the last century stacked inside each other (or U.S. presidents, or international pop stars . . .). Most vendors will claim the dolls are hand-painted, but a better gauge of quality is your own eye. If the colors are delicate and distinct, it's worth more than a *matryoshka* with crude and over-bright pictures. Sergiev Posad's Toy Museum has a small display on the history of the dolls (see the side trip to Sergiev Posad in chapter 10).

Square–facing storefronts, and shoe and clothing stores fill the upper floors. The food selection is disappointing; the several bland cafes seem designed for people-watching rather than for culinary enjoyment. (The exception is the Bosco Cafe and Bar, reviewed on p. 102.)

GUM's chief competition is the partially underground **Okhotny Ryad** mall, a grandiose project by Moscow Mayor Yuri Luzhkov that attracted the ire of conservationists for digging into treasured archaeological sites just outside the Kremlin walls. Russia's 1998 financial crisis hit soon after the mall opened, threatening its survival, but it's now a thriving, three-story shopping haven densely packed with stores for nearly all pocketbooks. Souvenirs here are pricey, but the food court on the bottom floor is a cheap and reliable bet for children, with international standards and their Russian fast-food rivals. The mall's design is eclectic, with a shallow dome on top shaped like the Northern Hemisphere, and terraces below overlooking fountains decorated with sculptures from Russian fairy tales.

Russia's other shopping centers are architecturally bland and largely aimed at the new rich, since most Russians cannot afford and haven't developed a taste for mall shopping. One such spot is the **Atrium** in front of Kursky Train Station (10 Zemlyanoi Val; metro: Kurskaya), with several top- and mid-range clothing shops, a well-stocked supermarket, and lots of clean toilets.

4 Shopping A to Z

This is a short list of personal recommendations, though a little exploring can uncover much more.

ANTIQUES & COLLECTIBLES

See the discussion of export rules at the beginning of this chapter before you purchase any antique.

Aktsia   A specialist in antique books and unusual inventions, this store also sells paintings and sculptures. 21/18 Bolshaya Nikitskaya St. ℂ **095/291-7509.** Metro: Arbatskaya.

Antikvariat na Bronnoi   Atmospheric and packed with stuff, this store is getting more upscale as rich Russian clients discover it. 27/4 Bolshaya Bronnaya Ulitsa, building 1 (in courtyard). Metro: Pushkinskaya.

Kupina   This company's two stores on the Arbat offer Russian and European art and antiques. 6/2 Arbat and 18 Arbat. ℂ **095/202-4100.** Metro: Arbatskaya.

ART

Alfa-Art   This established gallery inside the New Tretyakov Modern Art Museum holds regular auctions for its most valuable works as well as regular sales of its icons, paintings, and other items. They will take care of any export issues for you. 10/14 Krymsky Val. ℂ **095/230-0091.** Metro: Oktyabrskaya or Park Kultury.

Central House of Artists   (New Tretyakov Gallery)   The ground floor of Moscow's Modern Art Museum serves as a showcase for new painters and sculptors, whose works are for sale at the dozens of stalls and halls. 10 Krymsky Val. ℂ **095/238-9634.** Metro: Oktyabrskaya or Park Kultury.

BOOKS

Dom Knigi   (House of Books)   This landmark store is a great source of art books in Russian and English, travel guidebooks, maps, and old lithographs. Books in English are on the second floor facing the back. 8 Novy Arbat. ℂ **095/290-3580.** Metro: Arbatskaya.

Biblio-Globus   You'll find this Russian book emporium just beneath the computer center of the successor to the KGB. Its selection includes books in English, children's picture books, and antique books. 6 Ulitsa Myasnitskaya. ℂ **095/924-4680.** Metro: Lubyanka or Kuznetsky Most.

Shakespeare and Co.   Way off the beaten track in the basement of a residential building, this laid-back shop has an eclectic selection of English-language novels and guidebooks. 5/7 Pervy Novokuznetsky Pereulok. ℂ **095/231-9360.** Metro: Paveletskaya.

CAVIAR

Dary Morya   This seafood specialty store has a large selection of caviar, as well as other "gifts of the sea," as its name translates. 17 Tverskaya St. ℂ **095/229-5562.** Metro: Tverskaya or Pushkinskaya.

ⓕ*Tips* **An Outdoor Art Market**

For a less official selection of modern art, visit the outdoor market along the embankment of the Moscow River next to the Central House of Artists. Year-round, regardless of weather, vendors display works ranging from naturalist landscapes to charming images of modern and not-so-modern Russia. Prices are negotiable, and you'll get a better deal if you speak Russian or have a Russian-speaking helper. There's even a stall run by a framer who can mount the work for you. Though these works are all new and shouldn't pose a problem at Customs, be sure to get a receipt with the artist's name and the year the work was created. The underground walkway between the Central House of Artists and Gorky Park is also packed with art vendors, but prices here are higher and the choices less inspiring.

Gzhel

This blue-and-white ceramic style carries hints of the Dutch Delft Blue, but with an outcome that's more homey and distinctly Russian. Named after the town southeast of Moscow where the style originated, Gzhel appears most often in thick ceramic teacups, figurines, or furniture tiles (especially on old palace fireplaces). Each piece is hand-painted and individually molded, finished, glazed, and fired. The more valuable ones have subtle hints of gold woven into the patterns.

Okean   Similar to Dary Morya but with even larger selections, both locations are listed here. 69 Leninsky Prospekt. ✆ 095/132-1411. Metro: Leninsky Prospekt. Also at 91 Prospekt Mira. ✆ 095/287-7796. Metro: Prospekt Mira.

CHINA & PORCELAIN

Gzhel   This store is a great introduction to the Russian ceramic style known as Gzhel, with delicate blue designs painted on white porcelain and occasionally trimmed in gold. Cheaper versions are available at some souvenir shops, but in this store you are assured of the quality. Tea sets in other styles are also available. 2/12 Sadovaya-Samotechnaya. ✆ 095/299-2953 or -1892. Metro: Mayakovskaya or Novoslobodskaya.

CRAFTS

See also Izmailovsky Market under "Great Shopping Areas," above.

Moscow Cultural Fund   Hand-painted ceramics in Russian folk themes, original painted dolls, wind chimes—gifts for every budget can be had here. The fund has two cramped but highly satisfying shops. 41 Prospekt Mira. ✆ 095/280-5366. Metro: Prospekt Mira. Also at 16 Pyatnitskaya Ulitsa. ✆ 095/280-5366. Metro: Novokuznetskaya.

Russkiye Uzori (Russian Patterns)   Here you'll find a broad selection of hand-embroidered linens, painted plates, lacquer boxes, and more. Most prices are higher than they should be, but the quality is good and, with some perseverance, you can uncover great deals even here. 16 Petrovka. ✆ 095/923-1883. Metro: Kuznetsky Most.

DISCOUNT SHOPPING

Izmailovsky Market (Vernisazh)   The souvenir and gift bazaar is the main draw, but trinkets and some quality clothing can be found at the adjacent open-air market. See the description under "Great Shopping Areas," above. The market is open daily from around 8am to 5pm. Metro: Izmailovsky Park.

FASHION & SHOES

CHILDREN'S

Detsky Mir   This was the primary children's department store in the Soviet era, and though now it has plenty of competition, it also has the largest selection of toys and children's clothing under one roof. 5 Teatralny Proyezd. ✆ 095/926-2152. Metro: Lubyanka or Kuznetsky Most.

WOMEN'S & MEN'S

GUM   This arcade features mostly international brands, but in a distinctly Russian atmosphere. 3 Red Square. ✆ 095/926-3458. Metro: Ploshchad Revolutsii or Okhotny Ryad.

Okhotny Ryad   The shops in this mall get cheaper as you descend further underground, so that the bottom floor offers the best buys. Mostly international brands are offered. Manege Sq. © 095/737-8449. Metro: Okhotny Ryad, Ploshchad Revolutsii, or Teatralnaya.

FOOD

Eliseyevsky Gastronome   An abundant collection of teas, sweets, and other Russian goods is on display beneath the soaring ceilings of this flowery, ornate shop, which has a 100-year history of serving Russia's discriminating palates. 14 Tverskaya St. © 095/209-0760. Metro: Teatralnaya or Chekhovskaya.

Couture a la Russe

For most of the 1980s and 1990s, Russian fashion was best characterized by a TV ad for the Wendy's fast-food chain. At a Soviet fashion show, an emcee shouted "Eveningwear!" and a stern, shapeless woman stomped down a runway in a burlap sack, carrying a flashlight. "Beachwear!" the emcee cried, and the same woman in the same sack appeared, holding a beach ball. Wendy's, the ad claimed, offered the dizzying choices so unavailable behind the Iron Curtain. Indeed, for decades Russians wore variations on the same gray suits and uncomfortable shoes made in Soviet-bloc textile factories, and the brave ones offered visiting tourists money for their Levi's jeans and leather jackets.

All that changed after 1991. The birth of Russia's nouveau riche, a class of people dripping with money made in privatizations and hungry for once-inaccessible luxuries, affected marketing departments at fashion houses around the world. Boutiques along the tony Rue de Faubourg St-Honore in Paris now keep Russian-speaking staff to handle the steady stream of Russian customers ready to drop several thousand dollars in cash at one go. Miami's Versace boutique counts Russians as its most reliable customers. Sales at the Prada boutique in Moscow rival those at its flagship store in Milan. Russian models, too, are a hot commodity on runways in Paris and Milan.

Meanwhile, Russian designers have matured fast, and are increasingly collaborating with American, Italian, and French colleagues. Perhaps as a backlash against years of dull uniformity, Russian fashion tends to be brightly colored, sparkly, sexy, and daring, something you're sure to notice on the streets of Moscow or St. Petersburg. Russians' love for showing off labels is starting to fade, but you still may see people dressed head to toe in gear covered in the names CHANEL and DIOR. To see work by Russian designers, try the following boutiques:

Valentin Yudashkin Trading House (Moscow). 19 Kutuzovsky Prospekt. © 095/785-1051. Metro: Kievskaya or Kutuzovskaya.

Igor Chapurin Boutique (Moscow). Women's clothing and accessories. 38 Ulitsa Myasnitskaya, building 1. © 095/928-9947 or 095/921-3278. Metro: Chistiye Prudy.

Tatyana Parfionova (St. Petersburg). 51 Nevsky Prospekt. © 812/113-1415. Metro: Gostiny Dvor.

Sedmoi Kontinent   This Russian supermarket chain is a good source of unusual tea cookies and meringues, pickled herring and eel, and herbal liqueurs—as well as most standard grocery-store staples. Two prominent locations, both open 24 hours, are listed here. 54 Arbat St. (C) 095/241-0761. Metro: Smolenskaya. Also at Atrium shopping center (on Zemlyanoi Val). (C) 095/241-2881. Metro: Kurskaya.

FUR

Mekha   Russia's climate and centuries-old traditions mean fur coats and hats are a winter staple. If you're comfortable with the idea, browse the unique collections at Mekha. 13 Pyatnitskaya. (C) 095/231-9880. Metro: Lubyanka or Kuznetsky Most.

GIFTS/SOUVENIRS

In addition to the store listed below, Moscow Cultural Fund (under the "Crafts" section above) and Izmailovsky Market (under "Great Shopping Areas" earlier in this chapter) are both good places to shop for souvenirs and gifts for family and friends back home.

Skazki Starovo Arbata   A good selection of souvenirs both basic and elaborate, from carved birchwood knickknacks to amber brooches and porcelain tea sets. 29 Arbat St. (C) 095/241-6135. Metro: Arbatskaya.

JEWELRY

Izmailovsky Market, described under "Great Shopping Areas" earlier in this chapter, is a good place to look for jewelry bargains. For more upscale jewelry shopping, try:

Bulgari   The sleekest of Moscow's jewelry boutiqes, on the city's sleekest street. Where Russia's nouveau riche seek the latest in jewelry design. 1 Tretyakovsky Proyezd. (C) 095/933-3390. Metro: Lubyanka.

Cartier   The Moscow boutique of the renowned jeweler has an extensive selection of both fresh and classic models. 19 Kuznetsky Most. (C) 095/921-0172. Metro: Kuznetsky Most.

LINENS

Linen tablecloths, curtains, bed coverings, and clothing from the textile towns along the Volga River bear distinctly Russian patterns. Because few people have heard of Russian linen, these items make for great and unexpected gifts. Even the handmade items are much cheaper than goods of pure linen you find in the West. Most crafts stores, as well as the Izmailovsky Market (see "Great Shopping Areas" earlier in this chapter), are good sources.

Vologodsky Len   This small shop near Red Square features linen from the Volga-area producers. Included are clothing for children and adults. 4 Ilinka. (C) 095/232-9463. Metro: Ploshchad Revolutsii or Kitai-Gorod.

MUSEUM STORES

In addition to Tretyakov Gallery, Central House of Artists (listed under "Art," above) is worth a stop.

Tretyakov Gallery   The gallery has no single store, but several stands in its lobby sell reproductions from postcard to poster size, along with a large selection of books, many in English. 10 Lavrushinsky Pereulok. (C) 095/230-7788. Metro: Tretyakovskaya or Novokuznetskaya.

Gorbushka Electronics Market

For a mind-boggling selection of software, music, DVDs, videos, and computer games, head to Gorbushka, Moscow's biggest "underground" market for legal and illegal electronic goods. In the 1990s, it was upgraded from a chaotic outdoor venue at Gorbunov Park to a spacious, clean warehouse up the street, on Ulitsa Barklaya (it's visible from the Bagrationovskaya metro station). Despite years of industry pressure, Russia remains a major producer of pirated software, music, and movies. The good news is that efforts to fight piracy have brought the prices of licensed goods down to levels well below what you'll pay at home—for example, the latest *Star Wars* DVD was available in an official Russian version the same time it was available in the United States, but at half the price. At Gorbushka, the selection includes more and more licensed products, and a fair share of obscure Russian recordings from decades past. The enormous hall for vendors of CDs, DVDs, videos, cassettes, and software is surrounded by a larger network of minishops selling electronics of every kind, often quality brand names at prices below the department stores'. It's a good place to pick up camera accessories or cheap batteries. If you want to buy movies, keep in mind that not all DVDs can be viewed on your player at home, and that not all offer English versions, so check with the vendor just in case. Russian videos are in PAL format (not compatible with most North American VCRs), and even American films are voiced over in Russian unless indicated. Be prepared for crowds, especially on weekends.

Gorbushka offers a mix of legal products and pirated goods, but beware of the stands you'll see in metro stations and at street corners around town: Their only trade is the illegal stuff, from the latest Hollywood blockbuster to CD-ROMs packed with Microsoft programs. Taking pirated goods out of Russia is illegal, and Customs officers can (though rarely do) seize them when you leave and levy a small fine.

MUSIC

Moscow's biggest bookstore, Dom Knigi (listed under "Books," above), has an extensive selection of Russian and international sheet music, and a decent selection of CDs as well.

Gorbushka   The vast and bustling market offers the broadest selection of Russian and foreign artists, though you'll have to ask around if you're looking for anything obscure. See the "Gorbushka Electronics Market" sidebar below for more information. 8–10 Ulitsa Barklaya. Metro: Bagrationovskaya.

Melodia   This shop has a good selection of Russian and international music. 22 Novy Arbat. ✆ 095/291-1421. Metro: Yugo-Zapadnaya.

TOYS

See Detsky Mir under "Fashion & Shoes," above. Also check out the Izmailovsky Market (described under "Great Shopping Areas," earlier in this chapter) for original wooden toys and chess sets.

VODKA & WINE

See also Sedmoi Kontinent, listed under "Food," above.

Aromatny Mir   You'll find a broad selection of vodkas you won't find at home, including several flavored with Russian wildflowers and herbs. Note also the wines from the former Soviet republics of Georgia and Moldova, and the rich Armenian brandies. The most central location is listed here. 29 Ulitsa Pokrovka. (C) 095/917-1160. Metro: Kitai-Gorod.

9

Moscow After Dark

A large proportion of Moscow's tourists come primarily for its performing arts or, increasingly, its nightlife. Its reputation in both departments is well-deserved. The Bolshoi Theater is merely the most famous of the city's top-quality ballet and opera houses, which survived the cash and identity crisis of the 1990s to emerge livelier and just as talent-packed as before. Prices are no longer the rock-bottom bargains of the tumultuous early 1990s, but most performances will still cost less than in the West, especially classical music concerts.

The club scene, meanwhile, raced out of the restrictive Soviet era to make Moscow one of the most cutting-edge party spots in Europe, complete with sex, drugs, and enough over-the-top behavior to impress even the most jaded clubbers. Until the 1990s, Russia's bar scene was limited to hotel lobbies and seedy, standing-only beer halls frequented largely by construction workers. Today's gamut of bars is as broad as that of any European capital, with cool cocktail bars, kitschy Soviet theme bars, billiard bars, cigar bars, sports bars, and more. The booming Russian beer industry has helped, with several brewery-run bars around town.

Less obvious but no less impressive is Moscow's jazz scene, the legacy of devoted musicians who coveted banned LPs in the Soviet era and have taken Russian jazz to a nuanced, world-weary level.

The most thorough English-language listings for theater, music, and movies are found in the Friday edition of *The Moscow Times* (www.themoscowtimes.com), the *Russia Journal* (www.russiajournal.ru), and the monthly magazine *Passport* (www.passportmagazine.ru). The intentionally offensive weekly *eXile* newspaper (www.exile.ru) is a guide to hedonistic Moscow as well as the premier English-language source of bar and club advice.

1 The Performing Arts

Russians take their arts very seriously, and even the smallest of dance companies and music schools demands perfection from performers to a degree that no other nation seems to match. This leaves less room for amateur and experimental performance, but means that any show you see in Russia will feature rigorously trained artists. Despite this rigidity, Russian dancers, singers, and musicians manage to infuse their art with a powerful, often tragic, passion. Even if it sounds trite, you'll never forget watching a Russian ballerina interpret the dying swan in *Swan Lake* in her (and Tchaikovsky's) homeland, or hearing a Russian pianist resurrect Rachmaninoff in the conservatory where the great composer played. For a historical overview of Russian ballet, theater, classical music, and opera, see "The Performing Arts" in appendix A.

Performances generally start at 7pm. Moscow's major theaters close down in July and August. Some, such as the Bolshoi Theater, stay open but send their regular troupes on vacation (or on tour) in the summer and host visiting companies instead.

> **Tips** **Buying Tickets**
>
> Russian theaters rarely run one show at a time. Instead, they have a constantly rotating repertoire; for example, the Bolshoi Theater runs *Giselle* once or twice a month all season long. Tickets for top venues are available through most hotels, though they often include a hefty service charge, and the choice is limited. If you're looking for something cheaper or more unusual, you can try the independent theater kiosks throughout the city and in several metro stations. These can offer same-day tickets for conservatory concerts or daring new operas. Lists of available performances are often written out on index cards in Russian, making for chaotic reading. If you're looking for something specific, just ask—there's a good chance either the vendor or another customer will speak English. These sources are generally reliable, but be sure to check your ticket (sometimes just a flimsy paper with the theater's name and the show's name stamped on it) for the proper date and time. Dates are written European-style, with the day before the month, and times are usually written using the 24-hour clock. So "19:00, 01.07.06" means 7pm on July 1.

Festivals to watch for include the **Cherry Orchard Arts Festival** in early May, with symphony concerts, plays, and dance parties; the **Easter Arts Festival** in spring, with classical music concerts, church concerts, and dance performances; and the **Russian Winter Festival** around Christmas and New Year's, featuring top Russian dancers and musicians. The **Tchaikovsky Competition,** one of the world's premier classical music contests, is held every 4 years at the Moscow Conservatory. For more information on these and other festivals, refer to the newspapers and magazines discussed in the chapter introduction, above.

DANCE

Bolshoi Theater   Moscow's top dance venue remains the Bolshoi, the showcase for several generations of internationally adored ballet stars. The company has at last begun loosening up its long-stale repertoire, though the results are mixed so far, and Tchaikovsky's classics still form its backbone. Besides the impeccable dancing, another major reason to visit the Bolshoi is the sumptuous setting. The 18th-century theater is fronted by a triumphant sculpture of Apollo's chariot topping the eight-columned portico. A blinding abundance of red and gold decorates the interior, inspiring viewers even before the curtain (still embossed with the Soviet hammer and sickle) opens. Its four balconies rise steeply over the orchestra seats and above the velvet-lined czar's box (long referred to as "Stalin's box"). The seats are separate, movable chairs, and the balconies are divided into separate cabins of a few seats each. Most hotels can arrange tickets, but at a hefty markup. The official ticket office is in an adjacent building, with computer screens listing available seats and their prices—but in Russian only. Lines are not long. Tickets must be purchased at least a week in advance. For the main stage, prices range from $30 to $200, with big draws such as the ever-popular *Swan Lake* more expensive than others. A smaller, newer stage hosts performances of the same caliber as those on the main stage, but at about half the price. Tickets can also be purchased online before your trip.

Note: The Bolshoi is currently undergoing extensive, much-needed renovations. The main stage shut down for the summer of 2005, and full renovations are expected to take a few years (2008 is the target year for completion of renovations), but the company promises to reopen on a part-time basis in 2006.. The second stage is still open, hosting the main company and all the same performances. 1 Teatralnaya Sq. © 095/ 292-9986 or 095/250-7317. www.bolshoi.ru. Metro: Teatralnaya.

Moiseyev Ballet   Founded in 1937 by Bolshoi Theater choreographer Igor Moiseyev, this company sought to break free from the restraints of classical dance and has been putting on brilliant performances of their mixture of ballet and folk dance ever since. Folk dances emphasize rhythms from Russia and other former Soviet republics. The company performs at different theaters around town (and around the world), so keep an eye out for their posters at theater kiosks (called *teatralniye kassy*) or for ads in the English-language press. 31 Tverskaya St. © 095/299-5372. www.moiseyev.org.Metro: Pushkinskaya.

Stanislavsky Nemirovich-Danchenko Theater   This opera and ballet theater is a more modest but well-respected younger sister of the Bolshoi, with an impressive interior and talented company. The repertoire is unadventurous, though a current renovation of the building may result in upgraded shows, too. Reliable choices include *Le Corsaire, Don Quixote,* and of course anything Tchaikovsky. It's a good option if the Bolshoi is sold out or beyond your budget. 17 Bolshaya Dmitrovka. © 095/229-2835. Metro: Pushkinskaya.

State Kremlin Palace   The spectacular performances by the Kremlin Ballet Company suffer from this unfortunate venue, an enormous hall built to house Communist Party congresses. The sleek but bleak 1970s-era design kills most of the beauty and wonder projected by the performers. Still, the performances are strong and this is a fine place to come if you can't afford tickets anywhere else. Many organized tours include shows here. If you're on your own, tickets cost as little as $2, but it's worth paying a bit more to get centrally located seats instead of seats on the very-far-away balcony or at the fringes. Concentrate on the dancing, not the surroundings, which include 6,000 seats equipped with electronic voting buttons and earphones for simultaneous interpretation of political congresses. State Kremlin Palace (also known as the Kremlin Palace of Congresses), on the Kremlin grounds; entrance through Borovitsky Gates. © 095/928-5232. Metro: Borovitskaya or Biblioteka Imeni Lenina.

Moscow Operetta Theater   This charming theater staged ideologically correct musicals, mocking the aristocracy and the consumer class, for decades after its founding in 1927, but over the years it gradually shed most of them from its repertoire. Today, the theater mostly sticks to classics and accessible musicals, such as *The Merry*

⟨Tips⟩ Up All Night

Moscow is a city that doesn't sleep, so if you can't sleep either because of a switch in time zones, don't despair. Whether it's a midnight burger, a 3am tanning session, 5am sushi, or home electronics at 6am that you crave, Moscow's many all-day, all-night establishments are ready to accommodate you. Venturing out alone in the dark is unwise, but if you have a traveling companion you should be fine. If there's nothing near your hotel, call a cab—all major taxi companies work 24 hours. (See "Getting Around" in chapter 4 for phone numbers of reputable taxi companies.) Look for signs on establishments saying 24 or KRUGLOSUTOCHNO (round-the-clock).

Moscow After Dark

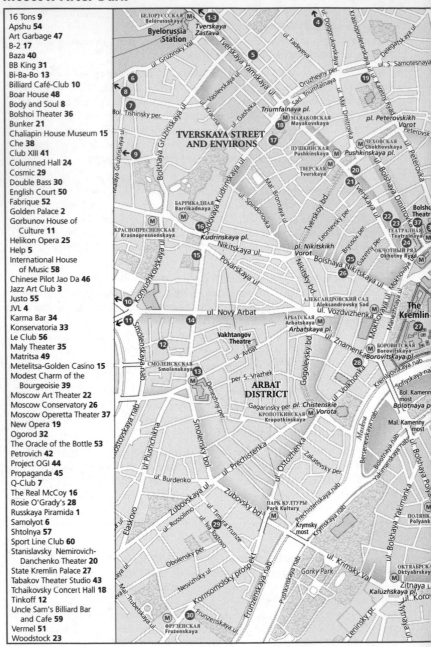

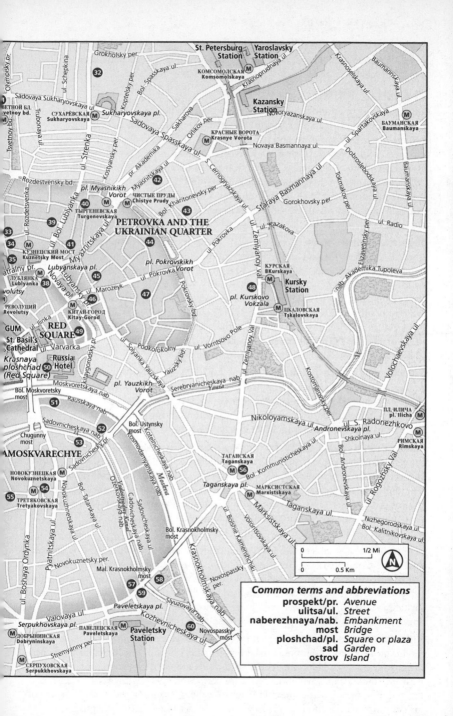

Common terms and abbreviations

prospekt/pr.	*Avenue*
ulitsa/ul.	*Street*
naberezhnaya/nab.	*Embankment*
most	*Bridge*
ploshchad/pl.	*Square* or *plaza*
sad	*Garden*
ostrov	*Island*

Widow and *My Fair Lady*, but also features new Russian operettas. Performances are in Russian, but if the fare is familiar it's well worth a visit—the performers are quite strong . 6 Bolshaya Dmitrovka Ulitsa. © 095/916-5555. Metro: Teatralnaya.

CLASSICAL MUSIC

Classical music performances in Russia are perhaps the country's most underrated pleasure. The performers are rigorously trained, the concert halls are rich with history and architecturally inspiring, and you can enjoy it all for just a few dollars. For the full experience, select a performance of a Russian composer in a hall where he once played, even if the music is unfamiliar. In addition to the listings below, several estate museums around town host chamber music concerts in the warm-weather months. Combine the performance with a walk around aristocratic gardens and a tour of the museum exhibit for an idyllic summer evening. See "Aristocratic Estates" in chapter 7 for addresses.

Moscow Conservatory (Konservatoria) This is the most popular and most historic place to hear Russian and international compositions performed by some of the country's top orchestras and soloists. The conservatory, housed in an 18th-century mansion now fronted by a statue of Tchaikovsky, who taught here for 12 years, is still the premier training ground for Russian musicians. The bigger shows with visiting symphony orchestras are in the Grand Hall (Bolshoi Zal). The smaller Rachmaninoff Hall and the Small Hall (Maly Zal) offer more intimate atmospheres, often featuring performances by rising student stars. Tickets for the Grand Hall can be as low as $5. 13 Bolshaya Nikitskaya St. © 095/299-8183. Metro: Arbatskaya.

Tchaikovsky Concert Hall (Kontsertny Zal Im. Tchaikovskogo) This 19th-century concert space has an impressive columned facade and a more modern outlook than the conservatory. It presents a range of musical styles, from the classics to performances for children, folk music, piano jazz, and avant-garde shows. Tickets run from $2 to $30. 4/31 Triumfalnaya Sq. © 095/299-0378. Metro: Mayakovskaya.

International House of Music (Mezhdunarodny Dom Muzyki) This vast, ultramodern venue is now the primary one for international music stars. It's reserved for major events, which are priced like similar venues in Europe. The acoustics are excellent, and nearly any seat provides great sound. Take a walk around the island before the concert, among futuristic office towers and picturesque bridges. 52 Kosmodamianskaya Naberezhnaya, building 8. © 095/730-4350. Metro: Paveletskaya.

Columned Hall (Kolonny Zal) This early 18th-century mansion became the "House of Unions" under the Soviets, who made its magnificent gold-and-white ballroom (the Columned Hall) into the elite concert space it remains today. Lenin and Stalin both lay in state here, as millions of Russians filed past to pay their respects. English author George Bernard Shaw celebrated his 75th birthday here. Now its repertoire includes visiting international symphony orchestras and choirs, children's performances, and even fashion shows. 1 Bolshaya Dmitrovka. © 095/292-0956. Metro: Teatralnaya.

Chaliapin House Museum You'll really feel transported to pre-revolutionary Russia during a concert in this house, where opera singer Fyodor Chaliapin lived and performed for friends and family. A cluster of chairs around the piano ensures intimacy with the soloists and small ensembles who perform here a few nights a week. Take a few minutes to explore the museum before the show, including the display of some of his costumes. It's hard to imagine that during Soviet times, the Chaliapin home held communal apartments for up to 60 people. 25 Novinsky Bulvar (next to the U.S. Embassy). ✆ 095/205-6236. Metro: Barrikadnaya.

English Court (Angliiskoye Podvorye)   This 16th-century boardinghouse for English merchants has been turned into a museum that hosts chamber music concerts one or two evenings a week. See the "Walking Tour" at the end of chapter 7 for more on the history of this building and neighborhood. 4 Varvarka Ulitsa. ✆ 095/298-3952. Metro: Ploshchad Revolutsii.

OPERA

Russian opera is less renowned abroad than its ballet, but opera fans will appreciate hearing gems by Rimsky-Korsakov, Mussorgsky, and, of course, Tchaikovsky in their home country, performed by top-notch singers. Opera tickets at the **Bolshoi Theater** cost less than ballet tickets and sell out less often, but that's more a reflection of ballet's popularity than the opera's quality.

Bolshoi Theater   Operas at the Bolshoi stick to the classics, such as *The Marriage of Figaro, The Barber of Seville,* and *Carmen,* but they may include pleasant Russian works such as Tchaikovsky's *Iolanta.* Mussorgsky's *Boris Godunov* is a major draw for Russian audiences, delving into the 16th and 17th centuries, when Russian history was fraught with battles for succession and much shifting of alliances—but the opera reflects more of the romantic nationalism of the 19th century when Mussorgsky wrote it than the murky turmoil of Godunov's era. Hearing opera at the Bolshoi is just part of the exprcience; viewing the grandiose theater is the other, no less important half. See the listing under "Dance" above for details on the theater and how to get tickets. Tickets must be purchased at least a week in advance unless you get them through your hotel. Operas are staged at least once or twice a week. 1 Teatralnaya Sq. ✆ 095/292-9986 or 095/250-7317. www.bolshoi.ru. Metro: Teatralnaya.

Helikon Opera   This theater, a rounded space of graduated platforms that feels almost intimate, presents more innovative and controversial performances than the Bolshoi, such as updated renditions of Wagner's *Ring* Cycle. The theater's popularity among Russians means tickets are often scarce. 19 Bolshaya Nikitskaya St. ✆ 095/290-0971. Metro: Arbatskaya.

New Opera (Novaya Opera)   Stylistically somewhere between the Bolshoi and the Helikon, the New Opera has a strong repertoire of standards and a few more anthology-style shows. Highlights include *La Traviata* and other Verdi works, Tchaikovsky's *Eugene Onegin,* and Rimsky-Korsakov's *Snow Maiden.* 3 Karetny Ryad. ✆ 095/200-0868. Metro: Pushkinskaya.

Stanislavsky Nemirovich-Danchenko Theater   As with its ballet company, the Stanislavsky's opera company is strong and respected, though it is often over-shadowed by colleagues at the Bolshoi. The theater itself is similarly shaped and decorated, and a current renovation is expected to renew the shine on the banisters and refresh the repertoire. Operas are staged about once a week, and tickets are cheaper and easier to obtain here than those for the Bolshoi or the other opera houses. 17 Bolshaya Dmitrovka. ✆ 095/229-2835. Metro: Pushkinskaya.

THEATER

English-language theater troupes often visit Moscow and perform Russian classics, and occasionally Russian theater companies stage a few performances in English. See

Theater Dining

Because Moscow's theaters are spread out throughout town, there's no real theater district dining. Many Russian restaurants don't start dinner service until 7pm, which is when most performances begin, so you may have to wait until after the show to eat. If you're in the area of the Bolshoi Theater in summer, treat yourself to an after-theater confection at the Metropol tearoom followed by a stroll through Red Square to watch the midnight sunset.

the English-language newspaper *The Moscow Times* for listings of English-language theater (www.themoscowtimes.com).

Maly Theater   The theater is called "Maly" (small) only because it's across from the Bolshoi (which means "big" or "grand"), but the Maly's hall is full-sized and its performances top-quality. Most shows are in Russian, with an emphasis on classics from Chekhov, Ostrovsky, and Griboyedov, but international companies occasionally perform both Russian and foreign works in English. 1/6 Teatralnaya Sq. (across from the Bolshoi). ☎ 095/923-2521. Metro: Teatralnaya.

Moscow Art Theater (MKhAT imeni Chekhova)   This was where playwright Anton Chekhov and the Stanislavsky method of acting made it big, and actors and writers from around the world have been making pilgrimages here for a century. It's worth stopping by even if you don't attend a performance; you can view the strange and scrawny statue of Chekhov in front and wander the pleasant pedestrian street while you're at it. Inaugurated in 1898, the theater and the company that bore its name brought together Stanislavsky's innovative acting school, Nemirovich-Danchenko's more established name and theater studio, and Chekhov's new brand of psychological drama. Today the theater puts on some of Moscow's most popular plays, from revivals of Russian classics to premiers of plays dealing with Chechnya and other up-to-date themes. The second stage hosts more experimental works for a slightly lower ticket price (though ticket prices for both stages are well below those in London or New York). English-language performances are rare. Don't confuse this theater with the Moscow Art Theater named after Maxim Gorky, a more modern venue with a less lofty reputation. 3 Kamergersky Pereulok. ☎ 095/229-5370. Metro: Teatralnaya.

Tabakov Theater Studio   Oleg Tabakov is perhaps Moscow's most famous and energetic theater director, with several studios around town and fresh performances constantly enlivening his repertoire. His chief performance space is a stuffy basement hall in the picturesque Chistiye Prudy neighborhood, always full of enthusiastic, friendly theater-goers. If you're learning Russian, attending a show here is a great way to get some practice—the hall is so small you can watch the actors enunciate, and the visuals aid comprehension. 1A Ulitsa Chaplygina (through the arch and to the right). ☎ 095/923-6125. Metro: Chistiye Prudy.

2 The Club & Music Scene
DANCE CLUBS & DISCOS

Moscow's club scene has been called the hottest, wildest, most expensive, and most offensive in Europe. It attracts top DJs from London and New York, top models, and plenty of uncontrolled substances. Although the industry has been driven by the excesses of Russia's new rich, it offers plenty of options for less affluent onlookers as well. Even if you're not a clubber, you'll find it worthwhile to get a glimpse into the world where modern Moscow absorbs and expends its energy. Be prepared for strict "face control" at the most popular spots, with jeans and athletic shoes inadmissible and men's attire appraised as carefully—or more so—than women's. The earlier you go, the shorter the lines and the more relaxed the door policy, but you're in for a long and possibly dull wait before the real partying starts, well after midnight.

The hippest places rarely remain so for more than a few months, so listings get stale fast. Check *eXile* newspaper (www.exile.ru) or *The Moscow Times* (www.themoscow times.com) for the latest hot spots. Here are a few places that have stood the test of time.

Che   As in Guevara, of course. This self-proclaimed egalitarian nightspot has a relaxed door policy and cheap drinks flowing all night to the beat of fairly mainstream club music. Open daily 24 hours. 10/2 Nikolskaya Ulitsa. © 095/921-7477. Metro: Lubyanka.

Propaganda   The cafe tables quietly vanish around 11pm and the dance floor starts throbbing within minutes to the beats of house, trance, and techno. The lines get long on weekend nights, and the doormen seem fierce, but they don't care about how you're dressed—they're just trying to control crowds. The place is popular with students, expats, straights, gays, artists, and young capitalists. Try to get a table upstairs for a little more space and a perfect people-watching angle. Open daily from noon to 6am. 7 Bolshoi Zlatoustinsky Pereulok. © 095/924-5732. Cover Saturday only, $3. Metro: Lubyanka or Kitai-Gorod.

Modest Charm of the Bourgeoisie (Skromnoye Oboyaniye Burzhuazi)   This compact hall is the favored "pre-party" spot of Moscow clubbers. It features lounge music in a mellow atmosphere to get you in the mood before the real party-hopping begins. It's open daily 24 hours. 24 Bolshaya Lubyanka. © 095/923-0848. Metro: Lubyanka.

Karma Bar   The basement attracts just about everyone, but its ever-fresh rotation of DJs keeps it from being too mass-market. Salsa dancing takes place on Sunday nights. Open Thursday through Sunday from 7pm to 6am. Pushechnaya Ulitsa. © 095/924-5633. Cover $3–$10. Metro: Kuznetsky Most.

Justo   This club has outgrown its extravagant, *nouveau riche* image and is now merely an exclusive, elegant club for the young, rich, and restless. It's still a challenge to get in, but if you're dressed just right it's a great place to glimpse the cynical decadence of Moscow's most excessive generation. 9 Bolshoi Tolmachevsky Pereulok. © 095/953-6595. Cover $10–$20. Metro: Novokuznetskaya.

Fabrique   This former workshop of Design University hosts fashion shows of Russian designers and plenty of fashion-oriented parties. It's set up like an enormous loft with concrete walls and good acoustics. 33 Sadovnicheskaya Embankment. © 095/953-6576. Cover $10–$20. Metro: Novokuznetskaya.

Club XIII   It was the hottest spot in late-1990s Moscow before scandal closed it down. Now it's open again and is as elegant and over-the-top as ever. Housed in an 18th-century mansion (the name comes from its street address), it begs you to pose on the upper landing above the carved staircase or on the columned balcony. There's a strict door policy after midnight. Open Friday through Sunday from 11pm to 6am. 13 Myasnitskaya Ulitsa. © 095-925-3550. Cover $5–$20. Metro: Chistiye Prudy.

Ogorod Thursday night is the only worthwhile time to visit, when a 1980s theme brings an enthusiastic crowd of college students and plenty of professionals. The music is international hits from the era, most remixed for modern sound. 28 Prospekt Mira. ℂ 095/280-8947. Cover $3. Metro: Prospekt Mira.

The Oracle of the Bottle (Orakul Bozhestvenny Butylki) The name refers to the treasure sought by heroes of medieval French author Rabelais, though the "bottle" referred to has a clear double meaning. The Divine Bottle cocktail is among many alcoholic specialties here. Friday and Saturday nights it goes dance party, with live bands and DJs and a frivolous atmosphere. 1/13 Sredny Ovchinnikovsky Pereulok. ℂ 095/953-0556. Metro: Novokuznetskaya.

ROCK & POP

Russian rock sprang from a semi-dissident scene of trading bootleg Beatles and Rolling Stones LPs, and has had a rough time evolving with today's freer-than-free Russian youth culture. A blend of ironic pop and Russian hip-hop has largely eclipsed rock as the soundtrack for the post-Soviet generation. The biggest Russian stars today masterfully blend the traditions of their pioneering rock predecessors—lyrics tinged with Russian fatalism and melodies in minor keys—with the latest mixing technology and a dose of humor. Beneath all this usually lies a musician with classical training.

B–2 The city's chief new music venue, this multi-level club showcases popular and more obscure bands and is always hopping. Open daily 24 hours. 8 Bolshaya Sadovaya Ulitsa. ℂ 095/209-9909. Cover $3–$10 depending on band. Metro: Mayakovskaya.

Bunker Rock, pop, and things in between take the stages here, where dinner turns seamlessly into dancing in the ever-crowded hall. Open daily from 8pm to 6am. 28 Tverskaya St. ℂ 095/508-4019. Metro: Pushkinskaya.

Gorbunov House of Culture (Dom Kultury im. Gorbunova) This theater-style venue is a required stop for Russian rock giants, as well as international stars like David Byrne and local and European alternative bands. The balcony offers a calmer alternative to the sweaty main floor. This is the club that helped spawn Moscow's thriving bootleg music market, which has since moved down the street (see listing for Gorbushka on p. 157). 27 Novozavodskaya Ulitsa (just south of Filyovsky Park). ℂ 095/145-8974 or 095/145-8305. Metro: Bagrationovskaya.

Art Garbage This is a reliable venue for up-and-coming Russian and European rock and some mainstream bands. Open Friday to Sunday from 11am to 6am. 5 Starosadsky Pereulok, building 6 (deep in the courtyard; follow the graffiti). ℂ 095/928-8745. Cover for concerts $3–$10. Metro: Kitai-Gorod.

Tips Getting a Taste of Russian Nightlife

If you'd rather not stay up late or stand in line, try having a midday "business lunch" in one of the top clubs, which often have their own restaurants. It's a chance to glimpse the sleek interiors and a few of the glitzy regulars while you eat lunch, usually for a quite reasonable price. **Studio,** at 10 Tverskaya Ulitsa, building 1 (entrance from the side street; ℂ 095/744-5566; metro: Pushkinskaya), is a glamorous spot that's not worth the lines and attitude at night but serves excellent lunches.

Matritsa This is a good old, down-and-dirty rock club, with some of the cheapest beer in town and shows by dedicated rock artists. The crowd—college students and old-time rockers—gets rowdy on weekends. It's open Thursday and Sunday from 6pm to midnight; Friday and Saturday from 6pm to 6am. 14 Varvarka Ulitsa. ℂ 095/298-3317. Metro: Kitai-Gorod.

JAZZ & BLUES

It sounds strange to look for jazz and blues in a land of Arctic frost and Slavs, but the search is worthwhile. Russia's version of jazz and blues is certainly its own, with its melancholy coming from a different kind of slavery and isolation. See the website www.jazz.ru/eng for a more detailed rundown.

Jazz Art Club For avant-garde shows and cuisine, try this club with its graduated dining platforms and somewhat 1970s decor. 20 Leningradsky Prospekt. ℂ 095/191-8320. Metro: Begovaya.

JVL One of the most inventive jazz clubs in town, JVL has its own recording studio and equipment. It's open Monday through Saturday from noon until the last guest leaves. Enter from 21 Sushyovskaya Ulitsa, then go through the arch. 14 Novoslobod-skaya. ℂ 095/928-1030. Cover $5–$10. Metro: Novoslobodskaya.

Le Club This laid-back, friendly venue was one of the first music clubs in Moscow. Open daily noon to 2am. 21 Verkhnaya Radishchevskaya Ulitsa. ℂ 095/915-1042. Metro: Taganskaya.

BB King Moscow's only real blues bar showcases the legendary Russian band Cross-roads and top blues artists, as well as several crossover and mediocre musicians. Their seafood okra gumbo is out of this world. Open daily from noon to 2am. 4/2 Sadovaya-Samotechnaya Ulitsa. ℂ 095/299-8206. Metro: Tsvetnoi Bulvar.

FOLK & ALTERNATIVE

Traditional Russian folk music is best heard at seasonal festivals or at the Tchaikovsky Concert Hall. Less formal, more rock-tinged versions can be heard at the following clubs around town.

Chinese Pilot Jao Da The two halls here often offer starkly contrasting music to keep you sharp, from Tuvan throat singers to British folk artists to techno salsa played by a DJ. Open daily 24 hours. 25 Lubyansky Proyezd. ℂ 095/924-5611. Cover for some shows $5–$10. Metro: Kitai-Gorod.

Project OGI You could visit here just to read the concert listings or flyers on the wall. More fun is to come on a night featuring Finnish percussionists or other music you might not find at home. Open daily 24 hours. 8/12 Potapovsky Lane, building 2. ℂ 095/927-5609. Metro: Chistiye Prudy.

Vermel No longer as cutting-edge as it once was, Vermel is still a cozy spot for Celtic duets, Russian bards, and other non-pop offerings. Open Monday to Friday from noon to 5am, Saturday and Sunday from 6pm to 6am. 4/5 Raushkaya Naberezhnya. ℂ 095/959-3303. Metro: Novokuznetskaya.

Apshu This is another good choice for seeing the exploration of new genres by Russia's non-mainstream musicians and some well-known international visitors. Check out the bathtub in the middle of the hall lined with a mattress and blanket for anyone who wants to climb in. 10 Klimentovsky Lane, building 1. ℂ 095/953-9944. Metro: Tretyakovskaya.

NIGHTCLUBS & CABARET

Several hotels have their own nightclubs, though quality varies widely. Many, especially the older Soviet hotels, offer cabaret shows of stale pop music, a few *chansons,* and inevitably a topless or near topless kick-line finale. These shows are overpriced and of dubious cultural value. Nightclubs (as distinct from dance clubs) are plentiful but often double as bordellos, and even the places that look chic or elite all include a strip show. A favorite spot among many (male) expats is Night Flight, which you'll see vigorously advertised.

3 The Bar Scene

Moscow is full of places that call themselves bars but that can be anything from a fine dining establishment or repository of rare Armenian brandy to a funky book-lined cafe or a grungy pub where the neighborhood gathers to watch soccer matches. The only thing they have in common is their willingness to serve you alcohol.

Conservatory   This atrium bar on the top floor of the Ararat Park Hyatt Hotel is one of the few elegant and accessible places to watch Red Square at night. The ergonomic design and gorgeous customers are as eye-catching as the view from the wraparound windows. Cocktails and expensive French wines are the specialties, but the beer is fine, too. 4 Neglinnaya Ulitsa. ℭ 095/783-1234. Metro: Teatralnaya or Kuznetsky Most.

Boar House   The wee hours get rather raunchy, but the rest of the time this is a reliable, relaxed spot for decent beer, international sports matches, and multilingual conversation. 26 Zemlyanoi Val. ℭ 095/917-9986. Metro: Kurskaya

Tinkoff   This St. Petersburg–based brewery has a hip, large, and lively Moscow bar with an extensive beer and liquor selection, along with a restaurant. It's a popular after-work spot among Russian and expat professionals. 11 Protochny Pereulok. ℭ 095/777-0300. Metro: Smolenskaya.

Petrovich   The schtick here is Soviet nostalgia, aimed at Moscow's worldly, post-Soviet creative set. Much of the humor on the menu and in the decor will be lost on anyone who didn't grow up under Brezhnev, but don't let that worry you. Its creative drinks menu is well worth a visit, as is its lunch buffet. Unfortunately, Petrovich is ostensibly a private club at night, so unless you tell the guards you're meeting someone or otherwise finesse your way in, it may be hard to get in after 6pm. The entrance in the courtyard is on the left through an unmarked gray door. 24/1 Myasnitskaya. ℭ 095/923-0082. Metro: Chistiye Prudy.

Woodstock   The after-theater crowd populates this place following performances in the adjacent Moscow Art Theater, where Chekhov made his name. The cozy bar and restaurant hosts weekend music performances with a grown-up, laid-back atmosphere. 3 Kamergersky Pereulok. ℭ 095/292-0934. Metro: Teatralnaya.

Shtolnaya   With beer taps at nearly every table, this is a fun but dangerous drinking hole. The taps are metered, but you always end up drinking more than you intended. Indecisive types or light drinkers can pour just a few sips at a time. Each table has its own selection of three or so beers, so if it's crowded you might have to order your favorite from the bar. 6 Zatsepsky Val. ℭ 095/953-4268. Metro: Paveletskaya.

Help   This cocktail bar has about 200 selections undergoing constant revision. Reasonably priced and chic but unpretentious. 27 Pervaya Tverskaya-Yamskaya, building 1. ℭ 095/973-8000. Metro: Belorusskaya.

16 Tons   This pub is a spacious two-story venue for an eclectic mix of Russian and visiting bands, with a shaded terrace for relaxed summer evenings and warm booths for cozy winter ones. Open daily noon to 1am. 6 Presnensky Val. $\textcircled{C}$ 095/253-5300. Metro: Ulitsa 1905 Goda.

The Real McCoy   Its atmosphere aims for American hillbilly bar, but it turns into a raucous urban dance club after midnight. In early evening the popular after-work drink spot offers jazz, swing, and occasional bluegrass bands. It's located in the basement of an enormous apartment tower. 1 Kudrinskaya Sq. $\textcircled{C}$ 095/255-4144. Metro: Barrikadnaya.

Rosie O'Grady's   Irish bars are a standard in any city around the world by now; Moscow's Rosie O'Grady's went from being the only place in town with imported beer on tap to becoming an institution that's always friendly and a good source of Guinness for students and seniors alike. Live music on weekend nights. 9/12 Ulitsa Znamenka. $\textcircled{C}$ 095/508-0752. Metro: Arbatskaya.

4 The Gay & Lesbian Nightlife Scene

Whatever stigmas surround homosexuality in Russia, they fade as soon as night falls. Russia's clubs are among its most gay-friendly venues, and many hold special gay nights once a week. In addition, the gay club scene is thriving and evolving, though the hottest spots tend to be accessible only by word-of-mouth—not out of fear of persecution, a likely and terrifying possibility in the Soviet era, but out of fear that the masses will find out about them and dilute their chic. Clubs change orientation and open and close frequently. The website Gay.ru has an English-language page (www.gay.ru/english) with up-to-date listings. See chapter 2 for more gay-friendly resources in Russia.

Body and Soul (Dusha I Telo)   This is a huge and men-centric party spot, rather far from the center of town. Open daily 11pm to 6am. 19a Kuusinena. $\textcircled{C}$ 095/943-3606. Metro: Polezhayevskaya.

Q-Club   A hot spot for drag shows, Wednesday night's "Military Party," and more. Open daily from 9pm to 6am; shows are at 11pm and 2am. 52 Malaya Gruzinskaya. $\textcircled{C}$ 095/253-5513. Metro: Belorusskaya.

Baza   A mixed club with a friendly and feisty atmosphere, Baza is tucked in a seedy courtyard. 6 Milyutinsky Pereulok. $\textcircled{C}$ 095/927-3193. Metro: Lubyanka.

Propaganda   This eternally popular club has a mixed crowd throughout the week but throws the city's best-known gay parties Sunday night. Open daily noon to 6am. 7 Bolshoi Zlatoustinsky Pereulok. $\textcircled{C}$ 095/924-5732. Cover Sat $3. Metro: Lubyanka or Kitai-Gorod.

5 More Entertainment

MOVIES

The language barrier makes movie-going a challenge for most visitors, though the **Moscow International Film Festival,** which takes place every even-numbered year in June and July, offers an often surprising repertoire of international films in their original languages. Also, the **International Film Center** (15 Druzhinnikovskaya Ulitsa; $\textcircled{C}$ 095/255-9292; metro: Barrikadnaya or Krasnopresnenskaya) has a rich and varied schedule of movies from across borders and eras; you might luck into a silent film treasure from Sergei Eisenstein or a big-screen showing of *West Side Story* in English.

Make sure that any English-language film you're interested in is subtitled, not voiced-over, which is common in Russia. If you're itching for a new Hollywood blockbuster in English, try **Dome Cinema** at Penta Olympic Renaissance Hotel (18 Olimpiisky Prospekt; (C) 095/931-9873; metro: Prospekt Mira); or the **American House of Cinema** at the Radisson Slavyanskaya Hotel (2 Berezhkovskaya Naberezhnaya; (C) 095/941-8747; metro: Kievskaya). See *The Moscow Times* weekend edition or other English-language publications for weekly listings.

CASINOS

Forget Las Vegas. Moscow sometimes looks like the gambling capital of the world, with slot machines available even in the airport for a quick pre-departure or post-arrival fix. The road into town is lined with casinos' flashing lights and neon facades, and most big hotels have a casino or at least a slots room. A post-Soviet phenomenon, and the phenomenon seems targeted at foreigners and elite Russians with time and money to blow. A glimpse at this over-the-top world can be fun, though minimum stakes are often quite high, and dress codes are enforced. Two well-established venues, which are safe and glitzy bets (though not cheap), are **Metelitsa-Cherry Casino,** 21 Novy Arbat ((C) 095/291-1170; noon–8am daily; metro: Smolenskaya); and **Golden Palace,** 15 3rd Yamskovo Polya ((C) 095/212 3909; daily 24 hr.; metro: Dinamo or Belorusskaya).

BILLIARDS

If you have any interest at all in billiards or pool, it's worth discovering the Russian version while you're here. Called *russky billiard* or *russkaya piramida,* the game is played on a table much larger and thicker than a pool table, and with enormous cues. The balls, all one color, are nearly twice as big as pool balls, but the pockets are quite small, making it much harder to score the requisite 71 points. Up to four people can play at once. The game dates back to Peter the Great's time, when he brought back the billiard-table concept after his voyages to the West, and Russians adapted the game to their tastes. Long a game reserved for the elite, today it enjoys a much wider following, and the billiards bars around Moscow cater to all pocketbooks. Tables run between $3 to $15 an hour depending on the establishment, and few but the most elite spots take reservations for tables. In addition to Russian billiards, most places offer tables and equipment for "American pool," English snooker, and French carambole.

Russkaya Piramida   Tables for Russian billiards, snooker, pool, and carambole are available in two adjacent halls on the grounds of the renowned CSKA (Red Army) sports complex. Daily 24 hours; tables $4 per hour. 39a Leningradsky Prospekt (in the sports complex set back from the main road). (C) 095/157-8040. Metro: Nevsky Prospekt.

Billiard Cafe-Club   Housed in the Expocenter, a sprawling complex for international conferences and events, this club offers tables for all tastes and a multilingual clientele. Daily 24 hours; tables $10 per hour. Expocenter, 12 Krasnogvardeisky Proyezd. (C) 095/256-0691. Metro: Ulitsa 1905 Goda (take a taxi from the metro).

Double Bass   They offer courses in Russian billiards here, but only for those quite serious about the sport. Otherwise, this is a fine, inexpensive place to shove a few balls around a table and drink draft beer. Russian billiards only. Tables $3/hour. Daily 24 hours. 21 Komsomolsky Prospekt (adjacent to the Gorizont movie theater). (C) 095/246-0615. Metro: Frunzenskaya.

Uncle Sam's Billiard Bar and Cafe   This is a popular and laid-back spot among expats and tourists, with 15 tables for American pool and Russian billiards. Tables $5/hour before 6pm; $10/hour evenings. Daily noon to 6am. 5 Zatsepsky Val. ℂ 095/235-6530. Metro: Paveletskaya.

BOWLING

Russians discovered bowling over the past decade, partly in thanks to the Coen brothers' film *The Big Lebowski*, a cult hit among Russian audiences. The country's first bowling alleys aimed at a decidedly different clientele from the pot-bellied, working-class crowd in the film. Bowling started in Moscow as a sort of polo for the new rich, with the impeccably buffed lanes costing upwards of $100 an hour, and bowlers decked out in Prada and Versace. Today bowling has trickled down to a broader player base, with some serious bowlers mixed in with the after-work crowd and family parties. All alleys provide "disco bowling" at night, switching to black light and cranking up the music after 10pm or so. The following alleys are good choices:

Bi-Ba-Bo: 9 Karmanitsky Pereulok (in courtyard across from John Bull Pub); ℂ 095/937-4337; from $18 per hour per lane; metro: Smolenskaya.

Cosmic: 18 Ulitsa Lva Tolstogo; ℂ 095/258-3131; $21–$25 per hour per lane weekends, $13–$16 per hour per lane weekdays; metro: Park Kultury.

Samolyot (Airplane): 14/1 Presnensky Val; ℂ 095/234-1818; from $12 per hour per lane; metro: Krasnopresnenskaya.

Sport Line Club: 21 Kozhevnicheskaya Ulitsa; ℂ 095/959-7875; from $20 per hour per lane; metro: Paveletskaya.

10

Side Trips from Moscow

Venturing outside Moscow demonstrates how deeply the capital differs from the rest of the sprawling country it represents. Beyond the clogged beltway that marks the city limits, you'll see the casinos, chain stores, and English signage quickly vanish, revealing an ungroomed landscape of rivers, oak groves, and clusters of wooden houses. Moscow's outskirts look nothing like the suburban sprawl so familiar to North Americans and Europeans. Here, the "inner city" is the most elite place to live, the urban fringes are depressed districts of dreary apartment blocks for those not rich enough to afford a Moscow address, and beyond that is endless countryside.

The most-visited and most historically revealing destinations around Moscow are along the Golden Ring (Zolotoye Koltso), a circle of eight cities dating back to the 11th century, that served as a nucleus of Russian culture and politics. Their splendid Orthodox cathedrals and monasteries and their medieval fortresses form their key attractions. We've included three of them here: Sergiev Posad, considered Russia's holiest Orthodox site; plus Vladimir and Suzdal, two towns usually visited together. Sergiev Posad is a feasible day trip and can be reached relatively easily on your own. Vladimir and Suzdal are farther afield, so we recommend an overnight trip. The other stops are closer to Moscow and focus on the secular: the landscaping marvels of the estate at Arkhangelskoye, and the simple charms of the writers' village at Peredelkino.

To get the most out of these trips, go with a tour group or get an individual tour guide. Unless you've done extensive background reading, you'll miss much of the context and significance of these towns if you tackle them alone.

Be warned that roads outside the big cities (and sometimes within them) are rough and pot-holed, so if you take a bus, be prepared for some bouncing. Watch how quickly traffic thins as you leave town, as urban turns to rural and high-rises abruptly give way to rickety outhouses.

1 Sergiev Posad

75km (47 miles) NE of Moscow

This town's magnificent 14th-century monastery and its history as the holiest of Russia's Orthodox shrines draws pilgrims from around the country, and plenty of tourists from beyond. The trip serves as a course in Russian architecture and sociology, as well as an immersion into Orthodox traditions. Music enthusiasts can delight in informal choral concerts—even a small midday church service produces hypnotizing harmonies. The town also claims to be the birthplace of the *matryoshka*, the ubiquitous nesting doll. Visiting the monastery, *matryoshka* shopping, and wandering the run-down but charming streets are enough to make this Moscow's most satisfying out-of-town day

Moving to the Suburbs

The character of *Podmoskovye* ("the region surrounding Moscow") is evolving as the city's ever-expanding upper classes set up camp—in other words, build multimillion-dollar homes—in the exclusive villages once reserved for *dachas* (country cottages) of the Communist Party elite. Meant to complement their luxurious Moscow apartments, these nouveau riche homes often reach absurd levels of extravagance and incongruity. Keep your eyes peeled as you take your side trips and you're sure to spot some of them. Look for castlelike modern constructions surrounded by massive security gates or fences, often fronted by armed guards. Turrets, buttresses, and Japanese gardens are common architectural features. These new homes are the only places in Russia you're likely to see a closely mowed lawn.

trip. It's also the only city on the historic Golden Ring that's a comfortable 1-day trip from the capital.

ESSENTIALS

Sergiev Posad, called Zagorsk in the Soviet era, can be reached by bus, commuter train, or taxi. Many hotels and tour companies arrange bus trips here. **Patriarshy Dom** tours has an informative and intimate English-language tour (✆ 095/795-0927; http://russiatravel-pdtours.netfirms.com). **Intourist** offers a more standard trip, which includes more religious history and less propaganda than in Soviet times (11 Stoleshnikov Pereulok; ✆ 095/923-8575). Intourist also has offices in the Ukraina (p. 90) and Cosmos hotels (p. 94).

If you're traveling on your own, consider taking a bus from the main Shcholkovsky Bus Terminal. The cheap, direct trip takes about 2 hours (though tour buses manage to make the trip a bit quicker). The bus you need is labeled MOSCOW-SERGIEV POSAD-YAROSLAVL, meaning you get off mid-journey. The driver may know only a few words of English. You'll be dropped off at the bus station near the monastery.

The commuter train, called *elektrichka,* leaves from Yaroslavsky Train Station (go to the suburban ticket desk, called *prigorodniye kassy*). The ride is cheaper and smoother than the bus, but it's slightly less convenient. It makes a few stops on the 1½-hour journey, and you have to be able to read SERGIEV POSAD in Russian to make sure you don't miss your stop. When you get off, it's a 10-minute walk through town to the cathedrals. Train cars are fitted with hard wooden benches that can be crowded on weekend days, especially in summer. Weekdays during off season they're calm and pleasant, as long as you don't get stuck with a curious or alcoholic seat mate. Tickets on the bus or train cost less than $10.

An excellent but pricier option if you're on your own is hiring a car and driver for the day. That way you can depart and return at your leisure, and perhaps take some side roads to better view the countryside. The price of the trip is negotiable, and costs more if you get an English-speaking driver or guide. Try your hotel tour desk, or contact Moscow Taxi (www.moscow-taxi.com).

WHAT TO SEE & DO

Trinity Monastery of St. Sergius (Troitse-Sergiyevo Lavra) is the place to start. Sergius of Radonezh founded the monastery in 1345, and it gained a reputation as the source of Russian military and spiritual strength after his blessing was believed to inspire victory in one of Russian history's most crucial battles, against the Mongol Tatars at Kulikovo Pole in 1380. For centuries, Russian czars and commoners trekked here in pilgrimage, traveling in gilded carriages or on foot for days or weeks, many fasting throughout the journey. The site was so charged with history that even Stalin couldn't bring himself to raze it, though its monks were sent to labor camps after the Bolshevik Revolution. Stalin even allowed the monastery to reopen after World War II as the spiritual center of the emasculated, state-monitored Orthodox Church of the Soviet era.

Sergius was canonized after his death, and his remains lie in the monastery's **Cathedral of the Trinity.** This cathedral boasts several works by Andrei Rublev, Russia's most famous icon painter. Many pilgrims come to Sergiev Posad just to see his iconostasis masterpiece, *Old Testament Trinity.* The monastery's version is a copy; the original now hangs in Moscow's Tretyakov Gallery. The cathedral started a trend with its use of *kokoshniki,* the pointed arches that became a defining feature of Moscow church architecture in ensuing centuries.

The monastery's current walls were built in the mid–16th century, as was the **Cathedral of the Assumption** that rises in the center of the complex. Its four blue onion domes around a larger gold one may look familiar—they were inspired by the Cathedral of the Assumption in the Kremlin. The Chapel Over the Well is a dizzying structure carved with flowers and vines and blue arabesques, built over a spring discovered in 1644. Pilgrims still come with empty bottles, jugs, and buckets to fill with its holy water.

Among the prominent people buried at the monastery is **Boris Godunov,** Russia's ruler from 1598 to 1605, the only czar not buried in Moscow or St. Petersburg. He ascended to the throne in controversy and his death plunged Russia into the Time of Troubles, a decade of war and jockeying for power. Godunov's court enemies are also here, in more elegant tombs inside the Cathedral of the Assumption.

A century later, Peter the Great took refuge here from the *streltsy* royal guards and later from the Regent Sofia, who was conspiring to keep him from power. He later showered funding on the monastery, and his daughter Elizabeth bestowed it with the title of *lavra,* the highest religious rank for an Orthodox monastery.

The monastery's **Museum of History and Art** houses an impressive collection of jewel-encrusted robes, gems, and icons from centuries past. The more unusual garments and exhibits are on the second floor. Entrance to the monastery is free, but the museum charges a fee of $3. Permission to take photos also costs a fee. Anyone wearing shorts will not be let on the grounds. The monastery, the main resident of Ulitsa Krasnaya Armii, is open daily from 8am to 6pm. The churches are open to the public Monday through Friday, and the museum is open Tuesday through Sunday from 10am to 6pm.

The monastery produced wooden toys as far back as Sergius's time, for children of local residents and visiting royalty. In the 19th century the town became a center of *matryoshka* workmanship, and now many rare nesting dolls and other wooden toys and dolls are on display and for sale at the town's **Toy Museum** (123 Ulitsa Krasnoi Armii; Wed–Sun 10am–5pm). For tips on *matryoshka* purchasing, see chapter 8. If you have time and energy, wander south of the monastery around Kelarsky Pond, a popular spot for amateur artists in summer.

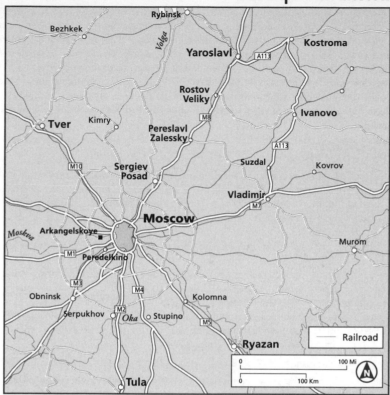

Side Trips from Moscow

WHERE TO DINE

For such a touristed town, Sergiev Posad has minimal dining options. Russians outside the big cities don't generally eat out, and residents here are no exception. For years the only restaurants in Sergiev Posad were colorless dining halls offering flavorless food, designed to house official Russian tour groups. Today one of the nicer spots is **Russky Dvorik**, a wooden cottage between the train station and the monastery, with traditional Russian fare for about $20 per person per meal. **Café Posadskoye** is a cheaper, simpler version, opposite the monastery at 22 Prospekt Krasnoi Armii. Large groups prefer the neighboring **Russkaya Skazka**, with overpriced Russian standards and a spacious dining hall. There's even a McDonald's if nothing else suits you.

2 Suzdal & Vladimir

Suzdal is 215km (130 miles) NE of Moscow; Vladimir is 175km (110 miles) NE of Moscow

Suzdal's conservative, tranquil beauty complements Vladimir's grand heritage, and together they form an ideal weekend trip away from Moscow's madness. Vladimir was a major political, religious, and cultural center when Moscow was still an unremarkable provincial capital. Suzdal houses a fortress and a collection of riverside convents and monasteries that date back to the town's heyday in the 11th to 13th centuries. Its populace and architecture stay loyal to tradition despite the steady of flow of tourists. Vladimir, once a provincial capital more prosperous and holy than Moscow, centers around its incomparable Cathedral of the Assumption, whose architectural features caused a sensation when it was completed in 1158 and inspired cathedral designers for centuries to come. The town has grown and modernized more than Suzdal and has more tourist services but less charm. Both towns are lush and breezy in summer. They are inviting in winter, when snowflakes glisten off the cathedral spires and bilberry bushes along the road, and when the thick walls of the cathedrals lure you in from the cold.

ESSENTIALS
PLANNING YOUR TRIP
The distance, Moscow traffic, and lack of direct train routes make it nearly impossible to visit both these towns in 1 day. If you're short on time, you could take a day trip to Vladimir alone. Visiting Suzdal as a day trip from Moscow is only worthwhile if you have a car, preferably with a driver or guide who knows the roads and the town. I strongly recommend spending the night to savor both these towns.

Tours that arrange transportation and accommodations will save you time and energy and are probably your best bet. The main drawback is that they favor the drab hotels of Vladimir over the romantic overnight offerings in Suzdal. Of the English-language tour companies, **Patriarshy Dom** (© 095/795-0927; http://russiatravel-pdtours.netfirms.com) offers occasional trips here, but check before you leave home since the dates might not be convenient. **Intourist** (11 Stoleshnikov Pereulok; © 095/923-8575) offers more frequent but very standard trips. Intourist also has offices in the Ukraina (p. 90) and Cosmos hotels (p. 94)

GETTING THERE
Tour buses are the most convenient way to see both towns. Otherwise, intercity buses run direct to Vladimir from Moscow's main Shcholkovsky bus station a few times a day on weekends, and just once or twice a day during the week. To get to Suzdal, you need to transfer at Vladimir's run-down bus station and find the bus labeled SUZDAL in Russian. The trip to Vladimir takes 2 hours, with another 40 minutes to get to Suzdal. There's one train a day to and from Vladimir, leaving from Moscow's Kursky Train Station and taking 2½ hours, for about $3. You can also arrange for a car and driver from Moscow, either at your hotel or by calling a taxi company (see "Getting Around" in chapter 4 for taxi listings).

GETTING AROUND
There are no official tourist offices for either town, so if you can't read the Russian alphabet, you'll have a hard time getting around on your own. Taking a walk along the Kamenka River in Suzdal gives you a great perspective of the city, and it's hard to get lost since the domes of the monastery cathedrals are visible from almost anywhere in town.

Vladimir, on the other hand, is too large and spread out to be able to enjoy much on foot, though Bolshaya Sadovaya Street and Bolshaya Moskovskaya Street have some concentrated dining and shopping. If you stay at a Vladimir hotel, you can hire a taxi for an hour to show you the city sights. Prices are negotiable and should be much lower than in Moscow—no more than $10 an hour.

WHAT TO SEE & DO
VLADIMIR

The **Golden Gates** mark what was the western entrance to Vladimir when they were built in 1164, and are a logical place to start viewing the town. The massive arch supports a church and is flanked by two castlelike structures added later. The enormous wooden doors that once kept outsiders away are long gone, and the city has grown up all around the gates. You'll find the gates at the intersection of Dvoryyanskaya Ulitsa and Bolshaya Moskovskaya streets.

Next, head to the **Cathedral of the Assumption** (on Sobornaya Ploshchad, or Cathedral Sq.; ✆ 0922/224-263) overlooking the Klyazma River. The key Russian building of its era, it was founded in 1158 by Vladimir prince Andrei Bogolubsky (whose name means "god-loving"). The cathedral suffered massive looting and violence during Tatar invasions, but was restored in the 18th century. The heavy tiered bell tower and unadorned white walls dominate the adjacent square. English-language brochures are available for a small fee. It's open Saturday through Thursday from 1:30 to 5pm. Admission is $1.

The **Cathedral of Dmitry** (✆ 0922/224-263), across the square from the Cathedral of the Assumption, is unlike any other Russian church in the region, and its exterior is more fascinating than its interior. Detailed carvings climb the cathedral's steep stone walls on all sides. The images are surprisingly secular, depicting princes of the period at their various activities. The carvings at the base are more precise and two-dimensional, while farther up the facade the carvings are cruder but set in deeper relief so as to be visible from street level. The interior is almost austere in comparison, light and free of excess. The cathedral is open Tuesday through Sunday from noon to 5pm.

SUZDAL

Suzdal thrived between its founding in 1024 and its sacking by Mongols in 1238, and has remained peripheral ever since. Its residents have retained a quiet dignity and sometimes the town feels untouched by Russia's past century of upheaval. The town centers around Trading Square (Torgovaya Ploshchad) and nearby Red Square (Krasnaya Ploshchad), which hosts the town hall and post office. The 11th-century **Kremlin**—the word means "fortress" in Russian—retains some of its original walls and houses a museum and restaurant. The Kremlin's rather run-down state reminds you how old it really is.

Suzdal's highlights are its convents and monasteries. The oldest and the first on most tours is **Rizopolozhensky Monastery** (20 Kremlyovskaya Ulitsa; ✆ 09231/21624), founded in 1207. Most structures inside date from 300 years later, including the three-domed Rizopolozhensky Cathedral at the center of the complex. Monks again wander the grounds, seemingly unperturbed by tourists. It's open Wednesday through Monday from 10am to 4pm (closed the last Fri of every month).

Your next priority should be **Pokrovsky Convent** (Ulitsa Lenina; ✆ 09231/20908), which came to be used as a storehouse for the first wives of Russian czars seeking younger companionship, including Peter the Great's wife Evdokia Lopukhina. The solemn grounds are again a functioning convent, and include an unusual inn of wooden cottages open for tourists. In summer, the nuns graze cows at dawn in the surrounding fields. The convent is open Thursday through Monday from 9:30am to 4:45pm.

Across from the convent is **Euthimiev Monastery-Fortress** (Ulitsa Lenina; ✆ 09231/20746), which earned political popularity in the 16th and 17th centuries and substantial donations from czars and nobility. Its high, thick stone walls reveal its dual purpose as a fortress as well as a monastic refuge, and served it well when Catherine the Great founded a prison here for political opponents. The central Spaso-Preobrazhensky Cathedral combines several styles of Vladimir-Suzdal architecture from the 11th to 16th centuries. It's open Tuesday through Sunday from 10am to 5pm.

One of the few Soviet contributions to Suzdal was the **Museum of Wooden Architecture and Peasant Life** (Pushkarskaya Ulitsa; ✆ 09231/20937), across the Kamenka River from the Kremlin. It includes *izbas* (small wooden homes), mills, and wooden churches brought here from surrounding Vladimir Province. The museum is open May through October, Wednesday to Monday from 9:30am to 4:30pm. In June the town hosts a lively **crafts festival.**

A wander around Suzdal gives you good glimpses of the decorative wooden frames of typical Russian houses, and a peek at the compact but rich vegetable gardens that feed many rural families.

WHERE TO STAY
VLADIMIR

Accommodations here are much cheaper and generally more intimate than in Moscow, but the selection and services are limited. Because Suzdal lacks any large hotels, most organized tours put groups in Vladimir, often at the **Golden Ring Hotel** (27 Chaikovsky St.; ✆ 0922/600-028). It's a bland, Soviet-style tower 4km (2½ miles) from the center of town, meaning you rely on buses or taxis to get around. The advantage is that it has plenty of space (170 units) and that a basic double costs only $40 to $60.

SUZDAL

Small groups and individuals prefer to stay in Suzdal's more romantic inns and lodges. A top choice is **Likhoninsky House** (34 Slobodskaya Ulitsa; ✆ 09231/21901; aksenova-museum@mt.vladimir.ru), a wooden home with a small museum of local history and seven cozy guest rooms, located just behind Rizopolozhensky Monastery. One single has a fireplace with a mattress over it, so you can sleep on top as Russian families did for centuries. (There's also a regular bed.) Most rooms have traditional country furniture. The house is a 5-minute walk from the center and costs just $15 to $40 per night. Reserve a few weeks in advance.

If you've ever fancied monastic life, try a night at **Pokrovskaya Hotel** (Ulitsa Pokrovskaya; ✆ 09231/20889) on the grounds of Pokrovsky Convent. The wooden cottages are basic but quite roomy and comfortable. It's run by Intourist so the service is less than effusive. Rates are about $50 per night for two people.

A higher-end option is the bright and inviting **Hotel Sokol** (2a Torgovaya Ploshchad; ✆ 09231/20088), a sunny yellow building next to the Kremlin with recently renovated rooms for $100 per night.

WHERE TO DINE
VLADIMIR

Restaurant options are expanding more quickly than hotels, though they remain limited. The best restaurants are along Bolshaya Moskovskaya Street. Most bars (several of them quite seedy) are on Bolshaya Sadovaya Street. **Stary Gorod,** opposite the Cathedral of Dmitry, is a pleasant restaurant with European-influenced Russian cuisine at reasonable prices, and unusually competent service for a provincial town. Main courses run $3 to $5. **Sobornaya Ploshchad,** the restaurant next door, is almost as good and just as cheap.

SUZDAL

Though its name means "monastic dining hall," the **Trapeznaya** in the Kremlin is one of the most cheery, colorful restaurants in Suzdal. It's housed inside the fortress, up a set of steep stone stairs. Try their *zhulyen,* wild mushrooms baked in sour cream and cheese; or the juicy meats cooked in clay ovens. Main courses run $3 to $8 (Kremlin; ℂ 09231/21639). A dining hall at **Pokrovsky Convent**, also called **Trapeznaya** (Ulitsa Pokrovskaya; ℂ **09231/20889**), serves hearty food in a more austere setting, with hard wooden benches and narrow windows in the stone walls. Try the fresh cranberry juice or home-brewed mead. Local residents prefer the raucous atmosphere of the **Kharchevnya** (73 Ulitsa Lenina; ℂ 09231/20722) restaurant and bar. The pancakes with honey and cream are divine.

3 Arkhangelskoye

20km (12 miles) W of Moscow

This accessible estate offers an excellent opportunity to appreciate aristocratic architecture and breathe pine-scented air at the same time, without traveling too far from your hotel. Owned by a series of wealthy princes from the 17th to the 20th centuries, the estate once housed one of Russia's richest private art collections. Its design still bears testimony to the whims of its owners, with its frivolous pavilions, a Grecian-style mausoleum, and a Gothic bridge. Plenty of Russians come here just to wander the grounds, hide amid the tunnels of rose-covered trellises, look over granite balconies at children frolicking in the Moscow River on a summer day, or picnic on a bench in the oak groves.

ESSENTIALS

Surprisingly few organized tour groups visit here, preferring to take visitors to the more famous towns along the Garden Ring. That's part of Arkhangelskoye's appeal, making it feel more like a discovery. Most Moscow tour guides and many Moscow hotels can arrange an individual trip, with or without an English-speaking guide. You should be able to negotiate such a tour for around $40 to $50 per car for the day, plus the cost of the guide ($40–$100). In the calmer days of July and August, the ride from central Moscow shouldn't take more than 40 minutes one-way, meaning you can make the whole trip in an afternoon. The rest of the year, Moscow traffic can make the trip take an hour or even two.

If you go on your own, ride the metro to Tushinskaya, then bus no. 549 to Arkhangelskoye; the bus ride takes about half an hour, runs three times an hour, and costs less than $2. Drivers are unlikely to speak much English but the estate is the last stop so you can't miss it. Patriarshy Dom occasionally offers a summer English-language tour (ℂ **095/795-0927;** http://russiatravel-pdtours.netfirms.com).

WHAT TO SEE & DO

The architectural epicenter of the estate is **Yusupov Palace,** which is set back from the Moscow River in an overgrown grove. Many visitors don't notice the palace at first, instead heading for the long facade of the more exposed, Stalin-era Military Convalescent Home overlooking the river. The palace originally dated from the 1670s, when it belonged to the family of Prince Cherkassky. Little remains from that era, however, since in the 1730s it became the pet project of Nikolai Golitsyn, who later became a favorite of Catherine the Great. The building's classical form and Ionic pillars date from Golitsyn's time, but much of the interior—including the art collection—was designed under the direction of Prince Nikolai Yusupov, who bought the estate in 1810 and whose name the palace retains.

Yusupov was a devoted art patron, amateur scientist, and philosopher, as well as one of Russia's richest property owners. A renowned *bon vivant,* he called Arkhangelskoye "a corner of paradise." He brought many of his treasures to Arkhangelskoye when he moved in, and in 1825 he turned the palace into one of Russia's first public museums. More than 500 paintings by European masters, including Tiepolo, Van Dyck, and Boucher, graced its walls. The library held 16,000 volumes and was often visited by famous writers of Yusupov's day, including Alexander Pushkin. Sculptures, antique furniture, tapestries, and rare china completed the collection. The palace itself has been undergoing renovations for years, and only parts of it are open to visitors. The estate stayed in Yusupov's family for more than 100 years, until the revolution saw it fall to Bolshevik hands. Its last owner, Felix Yusupov, went down in history as the prince who shot Grigory Rasputin, the controversial spiritual adviser to Czar Nicholas II and his family. The Soviets turned the estate into a museum in 1919.

Leading down from the palace toward the river are the geometrical, Italian-style **gardens,** which were long neglected but are again being planted with roses and grape vines. The surrounding pavilions are in various states of disrepair, making them seem older than they are—almost like the ancient Greek temples they emulate. The **military convalescent home** was built in the 1940s for the Red Army elite. Still in operation today, it is closed to visitors. Its terraces overlooking the river are accessible, and its staircases are the best way to reach the riverbank.

Before or after visiting the river, head left to see the rest of the grounds. Highlights include the **Gothic bridge** over the ravine and the rose-colored granite-and-limestone temple built as a **mausoleum** for the Yusupov family in the late 19th century. The Corinthian columned **Holy Gates** lead up to the **Church of the Archangel Michael,** which dates from 1667 and is the oldest building on the grounds. It's also the source of the estate's name. Note the remains of the theater across the main road from the palace, which Yusupov had built for his troupe of serf actors and musicians. The estate is open Wednesday through Sunday from 11am to 6pm (© **095/560-2231**).

WHERE TO DINE

There's nothing to eat on the grounds of the estate itself except ice cream and cold drinks from stands in the warmer months. Just outside the grounds, across the main road, is the charming wooden **Arkhangelskoye Restaurant** (Ilyinskoye Shosse; © **095/562-0328**). It's rather touristy since it's the only place to eat here, but the satisfying Russian food and drinks are served in a more relaxed setting than you'll find in Moscow. The walls are decorated with panels made to resemble lacquer boxes from the town of Palekh, and the long windows look out on the surrounding woods. Anything with wild mushrooms is worth trying, including the mushroom soups or veal with mushrooms. Salads are heavy on mayonnaise or sour cream in the traditional Russian style. A full meal will run $10 to $20. The restaurant is open daily from 11am to 11pm.

4 Peredelkino

15km (9 miles) SE of Moscow

This tranquil "writers' colony" contrasts with the religious ornamentation of the Golden Ring towns and the romantic pomp of the aristocratic estates in and around Moscow. Peredelkino is the place to go for a glimpse at more human-sized architecture, and for a lesson in 20th-century Russian literature. Before the Revolution, the village was part of the Kolychev family estate, but it was taken over by the Soviet government in the 1930s to house members of the influential Writers' Union. Its residents—including Alexander Solzhenitsyn and Boris Pasternak—often fell victim to shifts in Communist Party policy and ideology. The village still feels artsy despite its official beginnings and its carefully planned layout (and the bankers who have since moved into several of the homes). In Soviet times, officially sanctioned writers got the best *dachas,* but censors were such fickle beasts that the fear of arrest or exile hung over many who wrote here. Peredelkino has lost some of its intellectual verve but is still a sacred spot for many Russian and visiting foreign writers.

ESSENTIALS

Some tour packages offer trips here, but they're not all that common. **Patriarshy Dom Tours** arranges a worthwhile trip (© **095/795-0927;** http://russiatravel-pdtours. netfirms.com). Many Moscow hotels can arrange an individual car with driver and/or English-speaking guide. A guide is highly recommended, since unless you've done extensive background reading, you'll miss much of the village's history. The cost of an individual tour will vary depending on how upscale your hotel is. You'll find it worthwhile to shop around at other hotels to see if they can arrange something cheaper. Expect to spend at least $40 per car for the day plus $10 per hour for a guide. The trip should take about an hour one-way from central Moscow if you avoid rush hours (8–10am and 5–8pm).

Otherwise, the trip is a fairly easy 30 minutes on the *elektrichka,* or commuter train, from Kievsky Station in Moscow. After you exit, you either must walk 15 to 20 minutes along a wooded path by the train tracks until you reach the *dachas* (country homes) of Peredelkino, or take bus no. 47 and go three stops to the end of Ulitsa Pavlenko. This street is the best place to start your tour.

WHAT TO SEE & DO

The best place to start is at the **Pasternak House Museum** (Ulitsa Pavlenko; © **095/ 934-5175**), a tribute to Boris Pasternak's life and work and the saga surrounding *Doctor Zhivago.* Museum employees (there are only a few) are a good source of tips on what else to see in town. Pasternak's life reflected those of many Russian writers struggling to publish and stay in their homeland without offending the fickle Soviet censors. The fate of his novel *Doctor Zhivago* was almost as tumultuous as the story itself. Pasternak wrote the novel (which is about the Russian Revolution and ensuing civil war) during Stalin's rule but kept it under wraps. Encouraged by signs of thaw under Nikita Khrushchev, Pasternak brought the novel out into the open—only to be expelled from the Writers' Union and to see the book banned by Soviet authorities. The book was eventually published abroad and earned a Nobel Prize, but Pasternak was forced by Soviet leaders to turn down the honor. The writer died of lung cancer in this house in 1960. The book was only published in Russia a generation later, in 1986. The modest *dacha* includes some paintings by Pasternak's father and fragments from the writer's other works. Pasternak is best known to most Russians as a prolific poet, and many of his poems are on display here, though in Russian only, as are his translations of Shakespeare (translations were a safer path for writers of Stalin's era than original works). Note also the painting of Leo Tolstoy, a longtime Pasternak family friend. The museum is open Thursday through Sunday from 10am to 6pm (closed the last day of the month); admission is $7.

The **Church of the Transfiguration** and the **cemetery** behind it are also worth visiting, if only to see Pasternak's grave. Once a sacred site of pilgrimage for members of Moscow's intelligentsia and dissident community, it is still often heaped with fresh flowers. The church itself, located near the train station, originally dated from the 15th century, and was closed for much of the Soviet era. Today it's worth a visit to see how much more modest and intimate rural Russian churches are when compared with the magnificent cathedrals of Moscow and the Golden Ring.

The best way to appreciate Peredelkino is to wander the streets of wooden homes and imagine the intellectual activity and often surreptitious creativity the village engendered. If you're lucky, one of the residents tending a garden may point out a particular writer's house or unusual sight. Solzhenitsyn, who won a Nobel Prize for his brutal account of Soviet labor camps in the *Gulag Archipelago,* stayed in Peredelkino before his exile in 1974, diligently continuing to chronicle Soviet abuses in tiny, easy-to-hide notebooks. In a sign of changing times, the head of the Russian Orthodox Church, Patriarch Alexy II, has a *dacha* here.

WHERE TO STAY & DINE

There's only one official place in town to eat or sleep, unless you have friends in Peredelkino. **Villa Peredelkino** (2a Pervaya Chobotovskaya Alleya; ✆ **095/435-1478** or 095/435-8184; call for current rates), near the train station, was the official resort of the Young Communists' League (Komsomol) in its younger days. It has since been taken over by an Italian family, who renovated the pleasant rooms, added a sauna, and rent cross-country skis in winter. The English-speaking staff is usually quite helpful. The restaurant offers good Italian cooking, including melon with prosciutto and excellent veal, but at prices closer to Moscow standards than rural ones.

Another pleasant option is to rent a room or house for the weekend from one of the residents, who often post ads on the website www.expat.ru. These accommodations are reasonably priced and can offer such bonuses as a steam in a wooden bathhouse, a home-cooked meal, or the inside scoop on Peredelkino history from a longtime resident.

11

Suggested St. Petersburg Itineraries

St. Petersburg, for all its size and grandeur, is best viewed in small glimpses, by first studying the columns and crannies of each square at a time, and only then looking at the genius of the city plan. You could spend a full day walking up and down Nevsky Prospekt, its main thoroughfare, or tracing the banks of the Neva River. Either itinerary would exhaust and overwhelm you, and probably do little to enhance your understanding of the city's brilliance and beauty. The tours below are designed to help you appreciate both the minutiae and the scale that comprise St. Petersburg. Though they are as compact as possible, the tours still include long quayside walks, so bring good shoes.

1 The Best of St. Petersburg in 1 Day

This blitz tour begins at Palace Square and the Hermitage, for an intense morning of history and art that provides context for the rest of the St. Petersburg experience. The semicircle of sights surrounding this nucleus provides a sense of the careful vision the city's designers infused into their masterpiece. A walk along the embankment and across the Neva to the Peter and Paul Fortress rounds out the day. An optional stroll along Nevsky Prospekt is reserved for evening, when the avenue lacks its midday intensity. *Note:* Don't do this tour on Monday, when the Hermitage is closed. *Start:* Metro Nevsky Prospekt. Then follow Nevsky west to Bolshaya Morskaya Ulitsa and turn right, entering Palace Square through the arch.

❶ Palace Square (Dvortsovaya Ploshchad) ⬅⬅⬅

Site of czarist processions, raucous imperial revelry, revolutionary riots, Soviet displays of worker unity, and anti-Communist demonstrations, Palace Square encapsulates St. Petersburg's rich and troubled 300-year history. The best way to enter it is through the Triumphal Arch from Nevsky Prospekt. If you get here by 9:30am or so, you'll have it mostly to yourself and have plenty of time to explore its facets before the Hermitage opens at 10:30. See "Around Palace Square" in chapter 15 for more information.

❷ State Hermitage Museum ⬅⬅⬅

With a collection second in size only to that of the Louvre, the Hermitage would be an international treasure even if it were housed in a concrete warehouse. But its packaging, the resplendent Winter Palace, enhances the experience of viewing world art from the ancient Egyptians to the French Impressionists. Entering through the tranquil courtyard, you forget that the mighty Neva River splashes against the palace's other face. Get a map at the entrance—or even better, print one out from the museum website before you leave home—and plan your visit in order to avoid exhaustion. See p. 234 for a complete review.

See p. 234

> **⒊ LITERATURNOYE CAFÉ** ⭐
>
> A city landmark perched on the corner of Moika Canal and Nevsky Prospekt, this cafe plays up its past as a haunt of Alexander Pushkin and other 19th- and 20th-century poets and writers. The first floor has been taken over by a KFC, but the second floor is great for a cup of tea or a midday meal overlooking the city in a cozy setting. The terrace is nice on a summer day, but awfully tiny. The cafe is located at 18 Nevsky Prospekt (☎ 812/312-6057). See p. 225 for a full review.

❹ Moika

For a reminder of the city's swampy past, wander the embankment of Moika Canal as it heads south from Nevsky Prospekt. You'll pass little commerce and few tourists, but you'll see quaint arched bridges closer in scale and style to those of western Europe than to Moscow. An exception is the Blue Bridge between St. Isaac's Cathedral and City Hall, a cast-iron bridge so wide that you don't notice the water under it. Note the Stroganov Palace on the opposite bank. The Moika's more remote banks inspired philosophical and suicidal strolls by Dostoyevsky's heroes. Many of the historic buildings you pass are rather dilapidated and look better from a distance or at dusk.

❺ St. Isaac's Cathedral (Isaakevsky Sobor) ⭐⭐

The Moika opens onto Isaac's Square just south of the staggering gold dome of St. Isaac's Cathedral. Unadorned by the peripheral cupolas that characterize other Russian churches, St. Isaac's is a monolith inside and out. To 20th-century Russians it stood less as a religious symbol than a wartime bastion, having survived shelling by Nazi forces during the 900-day blockade of the city then known as Leningrad. The balcony surrounding the dome,

sometimes open to visitors, offers a stunning vista. See p. 242 for more information.

See p. 242

❻ Bronze Horseman (Medny Vsadnik) ⭐⭐

St. Petersburg's most famous rider, the Bronze Horseman rears fearlessly over the Neva River at the opposite end of Decembrists' Square from St. Isaac's. It depicts Peter the Great commanding his city in a rather fierce and autocratic interpretation favored in the era of Catherine the Great, who commissioned the monument. Alexander Pushkin made the statue come alive to generations of Russians with his brooding, stormy poem of the same name. See "Monuments, Memorials & Squares" in chapter 15 for more information.

❼ Admiralty ⭐⭐⭐

Following the shore of the Neva eastward from the Bronze Horseman, you come to the carefully classical Admiralty building. Its spire is the building's *raison d'etre*, providing a compass point visible from the city's chief avenues. Once used as a fortified shipyard, the Admiralty is now a naval academy, and though it's closed to the public, its grounds are worth a wander. Its 400m-long (¼-mile) facade blends in with the Senate building next door, and both provide a counterweight to the Winter Palace up ahead, framing the Palace Bridge (Dvortsovy Most) across to Vasilevsky Island. See "Around Palace Square" in chapter 15.

> **⒏ SIT ON STRELKA** ⭐⭐
>
> There's not much in terms of snacks along this walk, but if you have a bottled drink or something to munch on in your bag, this spit of land pointing into the Neva is a great place to stop and enjoy it. It's adorned by the two Rostral Columns representing four great rivers, which were Russian at the time the columns were built: Neva, Volga, Dnieper, and Don. It gets windy here, but the view can't be beat. The spit is on Vasilevsky Island, at the north end of Palace Bridge (Dvortsovy Most).

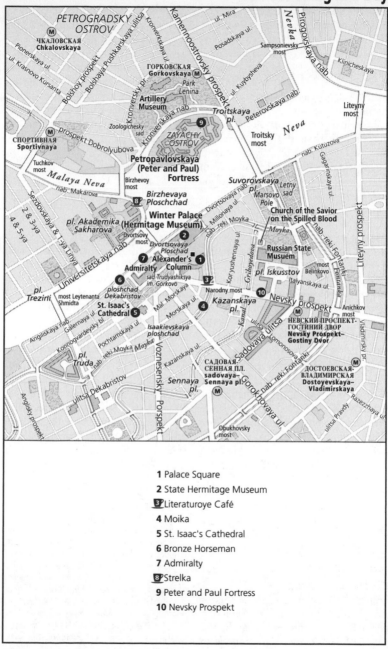

1 Palace Square
2 State Hermitage Museum
3 Literaturoye Café
4 Moika
5 St. Isaac's Cathedral
6 Bronze Horseman
7 Admiralty
8 Strelka
9 Peter and Paul Fortress
10 Nevsky Prospekt

❾ Peter and Paul Fortress (Petropavlovskaya Krepost) 𝒢𝒢𝒢

This next stop demands either a good 15-minute walk or a taxi ride. Rabbit Island, the sandbar upon which Peter chose to base himself while his city arose from the marsh, later became the Peter and Paul Fortress. You can wander the grounds for free but must pay to visit the cathedrals and galleries. It's worth the fee to see the Peter and Paul Cathedral, which holds the tombs of Russia's royal families from Peter's until that of the last Romanov czar, Nicholas II. See the "Peter & Paul Fortress" sidebar in chapter 15.

❿ Nevsky Prospekt

Evening is the ideal time to discover St. Petersburg's main thoroughfare, as the daytime traffic thins (a bit) and dusk, or the long summer sunset, softens its harsher edges. The street's architectural precision can still be appreciated by streetlight. Passersby are less rushed, and the dining and bar scenes buzz with Russian and just about every other language. See chapters 14 and 16 for restaurant and nightlife suggestions.

2 The Best of St. Petersburg in 2 Days

A second day in St. Petersburg is best spent discovering why the city still considers itself Russia's cultural capital. Starting at the Square of the Arts, this tour takes in the masterpieces of the Russian Museum and the ensemble of theaters joining it on the square. The eye-catching Church on the Spilled Blood, the sculpted Summer Gardens, the prestigious banks of the Fontanka River, and the architectural nuances of Ostrovsky Square follow. Rest up and shop in Gostiny Dvor, then use this evening for a visit to the renowned Mariinsky Theater. *Start: Metro to Gostiny Dvor, then take Mikhailovskaya Ulitsa north of Nevsky to the Square of the Arts.*

❶ Square of the Arts (Ploshchad Isskustv) 𝒢𝒢

A masterpiece of classical symmetry, this square includes the Mikhailovsky Palace, which now houses the Russian Museum, the St. Petersburg Philharmonic, the Mussorgsky Opera and Ballet Theater, and a statue of Pushkin that pulls it all together (even though it wasn't added until 1957). Take your time to circle it and note the vistas from every side street. See "Monuments, Memorials & Squares" in chapter 15.

❷ Russian Museum 𝒢𝒢𝒢

Even if you can't name a single Russian artist, this museum is a superb introduction to Russian art through the ages. Its display of Orthodox icons shows more clearly than any book the evolution of their styles. The Constructivist and post-Impressionist

images by Kandinsky, Chagall, and Malevich take on different meaning in their original, Russian setting. Though exhibits are labeled in English, the audioguide is very worthwhile. See p. 244 for a full review.

---

❸ STRAY DOG CELLAR (PODVAL BRODYACHY SOBAKI) 𝒢𝒢

Ensconced in a basement just off the Square of the Arts is this friendly cafe that flourished in the early 1900s as an artists' den. Poet Anna Akhmatova and her contemporaries once held readings and staged raucous and daring performances here. The cafe is again enjoying a revival, hosting musical shows and one-act plays. Grab a coffee, lunch, or some jam-filled pancakes. The cafe is at 5/4 Square of the Arts (Ploshchad Isskustv); ☏ 812/315-7764. See p. 227 for a full review.

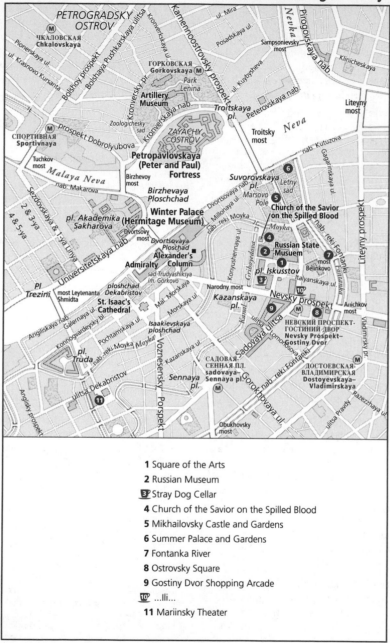

1 Square of the Arts

2 Russian Museum

3 Stray Dog Cellar

4 Church of the Savior on the Spilled Blood

5 Mikhailovsky Castle and Gardens

6 Summer Palace and Gardens

7 Fontanka River

8 Ostrovsky Square

9 Gostiny Dvor Shopping Arcade

10 ...lli...

11 Mariinsky Theater

❹ Church of the Savior on the Spilled Blood (Tserkov Spasitelya Na Krovi) ⌖

The festive facade of this church is almost gaudy and frivolous, despite its morbid name. The real name is the Church of the Resurrection, but it earned its common moniker because it was erected on the site where Czar Alexander II was assassinated in 1881. Brilliantly restored, the church's interior is almost as vivid as its exterior. Look for the tiles marking the exact spot of the murder. The adjacent embankment is full of souvenir vendors; the better deals and quality are on the opposite side of the canal. See p. 242 for a full listing.

❺ Mikhailovsky Castle and Gardens (Mikhailovsky Zamok)

The castle itself was built by the paranoid Czar Paul I, who felt too exposed in the Winter Palace. The interior, now an Engineering Museum, reflects his more austere tastes and is only worth visiting if the weather is lousy. Otherwise, use this time to wander the lush grounds, which make the bustle of Nevsky seem worlds away. See the walking tour in chapter 15 for more information.

❻ Summer Palace and Gardens (Letny Dvorets, Letny Sad) ⌖⌖

Farther on is the compact Summer Palace that Peter built, a cheery (though unheated) contrast to the somber citadel of Mikhailovsky Palace. The surrounding gardens hosted decadent imperial balls, and include Renaissance-era statues Peter had imported from Italy to perfect his meticulously planned parks. See p. 246 for more information.

❼ Fontanka River

The river was so named because it once fed the luxurious fountains of the Summer Gardens. Today its embankments house some of the city's architectural masterpieces; note Sheremetev Palace on the east side, where Anna Akhmatova once lived. It now houses a musical instrument museum (p. 245). The circular building on the west bank houses the well-known city circus (see "Especially for Kids" in chapter 15). Study the horse sculptures anchoring the four posts of Anichkov Bridge, which carries Nevsky Prospekt across the Fontanka.

❽ Ostrovsky Square ⌖

Head back west on Nevsky Prospekt to Ostrovsky Square, recognizable by its monument to Catherine the Great (see "Monuments, Memorials & Squares" in chapter 15). The statue incorporates images of the empresses' favorites in various moods and poses, and usually gets giggles out of kids. Behind her is the Pushkin Theater (p. 269), which puts on ballets, operas, and plays, and is a superb alternative to the Mariinsky Theater if tickets aren't available. In summer you can enjoy intermission on the columned balcony and feel like royalty.

❾ Gostiny Dvor Shopping Arcade

This spot has been a raucous outdoor market, an upmarket arcade supplying delicacies to the aristocracy, and a Soviet department store with rows of identical shops. Today it's a tightly packed modern shopping mall. You can get fresh cabbage or apricot pies for a few cents in its cafes, or a fur coat for a few thousand dollars. Both a landmark and a convenience, it also has public toilets and 1-hour film developing.

☕ ❿ ...ILI...

This busy corner cafe across from Gostiny Dvor attracts young Russians and tourists alike. Its name means "either . . . or" and is good for the indecisive: It has a bistro, a restaurant, and Internet tables, and is open around the clock. There's nothing elite about it, but it represents more of what Petersburg is today, at a low price—and it's nicer than any of the cafes inside Gostiny Dvor. Ice cream, salads, and soups are safe and satisfying choices. The cafe is at 54 Nevsky Prospekt (✆ 812/331-9090).

⓫ Mariinsky Theater (formerly Kirov Theater) ✿✿✿

The aquamarine walls hint at the city's naval ambitions, but everything else about the Mariinsky celebrates St. Petersburg's cultural heritage. Its exterior symmetry and interior opulence are worth the price of a ballet ticket themselves. If orchestra seats are sold out or beyond your price range, don't be afraid of the upper balconies. They offer a better view of the magnificent ceiling fresco and a more relaxed viewing experience. See p. 272 for a full listing.

3 The Best of St. Petersburg in 3 Days

Although St. Petersburg itself has plenty more to explore, a third day offers an ideal opportunity to whiz up the Baltic Coast to Peterhof, the palace Peter modeled partly on Versailles. The ride itself—either on hydrofoil, ferry, or the private boats roaming the shore—is part of the adventure, offering a seafarers' view of the city and surrounding forest. In the winter, you can take a bus or commuter train and enjoy the countryside that way. You can easily return in time for a dinnertime cruise through the city's canals in the months when they're not frozen over (May–Oct). *Start: The piers on Dvortsovaya Naberezhnaya in front of the Winter Palace, or the bus stop outside Nevsky Prospekt metro station. Nearest metro: Nevsky Prospekt.*

❶ Peterhof (Petrodvorets) ✿✿✿

Gliding to the pier of this opulent "country house" is the most impressive way to greet it. The dense forest is suddenly cleaved by a hill of fountains cascading from the palace toward the sea. The palace holds so much gold it's almost headache-inducing. The long and rather narrow structure gives every room a view, but this means that visitors are herded in one direction with little room to maneuver. Explore the caves beneath the fountains for an inside view of this 18th-century engineering feat. See chapter 18 for more on visiting Peterhof.

❸ Evening Canal Cruise

Once you're back in town, continue the waterway theme with a canal tour. Boats holding up to 15 people start from Griboyedov Canal just north of Nevsky Prospekt. They offer English-speaking tours or tour guides. Private boats also roam the area offering rides for up to five people for an always negotiable price, which is often less than the group-tour price. During the White Nights of summer, the private boats run much of the night. However, they often lack security features, so they're not a good option if you're traveling with kids.

> **❷ IMPERATORSKY STOL** ✿
>
> Dining options on the palace grounds are mediocre, but Imperatorsky Stol (✆ 812/427-9106) is the most pleasant. Housed in the orangerie close to the river, it's a good spot for a hot drink or a full, Russo-European meal. See "Peterhof" in chapter 18 for more information.

12

Getting to Know St. Petersburg

St. Petersburg was a planned city from day one, and therefore makes sense to most visitors right away. The center of town is relatively compact, and the increasing use of English on street signs and billboards breaks up the puzzling array of Russian lettering and helps visitors get their bearings. But globalization has only encroached so far, and even though the city was Peter the Great's window to the Western world, there's no mistaking St. Petersburg's Russianness. Here are some tips on how to get oriented and get on with your Petersburg adventure.

1 Orientation

ARRIVING
BY PLANE
All international flights into St. Petersburg land at **Pulkovo-2 Airport** (© 812/ 104-3444; http://eng.pulkovo.ru), which is friendlier and more manageable than Moscow's Sheremetevo-2 Airport. Pulkovo also has the advantage of a 2003 renovation that opened up the halls and lightened up the atmosphere, making the long lines for security and passport control much more tolerable.

Use of luggage carts is free. The airport money-exchange booths offer poorer rates than downtown; a better bet are the airport ATMs, which give rubles at the official Central Bank exchange rate. Internet access is available. The arrivals hall has an information desk with English-speaking personnel, car rental desks, and airline ticket offices.

Tour groups won't have to worry about transfers to and from the airport, which is 16km (10 miles) south of the city limits or about a 30-minute ride to the center of town. If you're an individual traveler, arrange a taxi in advance from Pulkovo-2 by calling the **official airport cab company** at © 812/312-0022. Otherwise, you can negotiate a ride upon arrival. Official cabs are often scarce, and charge about $20 to Nevsky Prospekt. The ubiquitous independent cabbies rarely go below $40 for the same trip. Public bus no. 13 takes you to the Moskovskaya metro station, south of the city center, for a few rubles. No trains serve the airport.

Domestic flights into St. Petersburg, from Moscow for example, come into the neighboring **Pulkovo-1 Airport** (© 812/104-3822; http://eng.pulkovo.ru). The facilities are similar to those of Pulkovo-2, though more basic. Taxi service is the same as at Pulkovo-1, and public bus no. 39 takes you to the Moskovskaya metro station.

BY TRAIN
Entering St. Petersburg by overnight train from Moscow is one of the most romantic things you can do in Russia. The Moscow-based trains arrive at, appropriately, **Moskovsky (Moscow) Station,** right on Nevsky Prospekt, within walking distance of several major hotels and adjacent to the Ploshchad Vostanniya and Mayakovskaya

metro stations. The official taxis in front of the station set their own prices, which are invariably higher at the train station than elsewhere in town.

Another easy train connection is from Helsinki, 5½ hours away (plus a 1-hour time difference). The trip ends at St. Petersburg's **Finland Station** (Finlandsky Vokzal; 6 Ploshchad Lenina). Taxis from there to Nevsky Prospekt cost about $15, and there is a metro station (Ploshchad Lenina) as well. Two daily trains run to and from the Finnish capital, both stopping in Vyborg to clear Customs.

From Poland, Germany, and the Baltic states, trains arrive at **Warsaw Station** (Varshavsky Vokzal; 118 Naberezhnaya Obvodnogo Kanala). Taxis cost about $15 to Nevsky Prospekt, and the metro station is Baltiiskaya. If you are entering Russia from a European Union member country, you will need only a Russian visa. But if you enter through Belarus or Ukraine, you will need transit visas for those countries. Be aware, too, that rail passes that serve the rest of Europe do not include Russia.

BY BUS

A few tour companies offer bus tours to St. Petersburg from Scandinavia on top-class Finnish coaches. From Helsinki the ride takes about 6 hours, including the long stop to clear Customs. Ordinary, non-tour buses, which are cheaper than the train, are also available to and from Helsinki. If you travel alone you must take care of your visa yourself. The road from Helsinki is relatively well maintained, unlike many others in the region. Buses arrive at **St. Petersburg Bus Station** (Avtobusny Vokzal; 36 Naberezhnaya Obvodonovo Kanala; 𝄐 812/166-5777).

BY BOAT

Many Scandinavian cruises include a stop in St. Petersburg, the major commercial port 20 minutes south of the center. Most cruises include an organized bus trip to the center. If not, the only way to get from the piers into town is by special taxi, since regular taxis are not allowed into the port itself and the main road is a long walk from the ships. The fare is generally $20 each way, though sometimes bargaining works. You can arrange a ride back to the pier from Kazansky Cathedral on Nevsky Prospekt. No metros serve the area.

BY CAR

A few intrepid travelers come to St. Petersburg by car from Finland. Not including the long lines for Customs and document check at the border, the 370km (230-mile) drive from Helsinki is about 6 hours. Once in St. Petersburg, head straight to your hotel and settle the parking question. It's easy to park in St. Petersburg, since any sidewalk or embankment is fair game, though underground garages are extremely scarce in this city built on swampland. It's harder to guarantee secure parking, however. Existing maps in English do not indicate one-way streets or other crucial driving details, though the Russian-language pocket-size *Atlas of St. Petersburg Roads (Atlas Dorog Peterburga)* is quite useful. Traffic in St. Petersburg has gone from a trickle to a substantial rush-hour event over the past decade. Be sure to have all of the car's documentation in perfect order, as the ever-hungry traffic police will quickly spot and fine any infraction. Renting a car with a driver is easier and often cheaper than driving your own.

VISITOR INFORMATION

The **St. Petersburg City Tourist Office** is quite modest for such a significant city, with not much more to offer than most hotels. Still, it's worth a visit to find out about festivals or special events that you might otherwise miss. The main offices are at 54 Sadovaya Ulitsa (𝄐 812/453-2121).

Drawbridge Dilemma

The drawbridges that span the Neva are both a charming attraction and a logistical consideration for St. Petersburg's tourists. They remain down during the day for automobile and foot traffic, but lift in the middle of the night in a carefully synchronized performance to allow shipping traffic from the Baltic Sea into Russia's inland rivers. That means you want to be sure to be on the same side of the river as your hotel when night falls, or else you may be stuck for a few hours.

The main bridges are up at the following times:

Volodarskiy: 2 to 3:45am and 4:15 to 5:45am
Alexandra Nevskogo: 1:30 to 5:05am
Liteiny: 1:50 to 4:40am
Troitskiy: 1:50 to 4:50am
Dvortsovy: 1:35 to 2:55am and 3:15 to 4:50am
Leytenanta Shmidta: 1:40 to 4:55am
Birzhevoy: 2:10 to 4:40am
Tuchkov: 2:10 to 3:05am and 3:35 to 4:45am

Maps are available free in most hotels, and for a low price at bookstores and newspaper stands, though sometimes they're only in the Cyrillic alphabet. An easy-to-read and richly detailed map to look out for is the bilingual "St. Petersburg Guide to the City." Avail yourself of the numerous free listings magazines at nearly all hotels and many restaurants. Most are in English and Russian and are heavy with ads but are full of information. Pick up a copy of *The St. Petersburg Times,* a twice-weekly English-language newspaper, for local and international news.

CITY LAYOUT

Peter the Great built his dream city on a cluster of islands in the marshland of the Gulf of Finland. To make sense of this boggy site, he designed a network of canals and bridges whose grueling construction cost the lives of many of the city's builders. The gift they left later generations is a city of remarkable logic and beauty despite the irregularity of its land.

The Neva River folds around the city center in a rounded number "7," taking in water from the city's dozens of canals before flowing out to the Baltic Sea. The city's main land artery is Nevsky Prospekt, a 4km-long (2½-mile) avenue that slices across the city center roughly northwest to southeast. The city retains a coherent center even as it has expanded north, east, and south in recent decades. (The sea stops it from expanding westward.) Museums, hotels, and shopping are conveniently concentrated in and around Nevsky and the historical downtown. Train and bus stations are all attached to the subway system, which is fast and efficient even though the city has outgrown its overcrowded four lines.

Today's St. Petersburg houses five million residents and, like Moscow, is both dense and territorially large. That means a lot of walking even within the city center, but St. Petersburg is not nearly as unwieldy or overwhelming as its southern sister.

Addresses in Russia are often perplexing, so don't be afraid to ask for detailed directions. (See "Address Advice" in chapter 4.)

THE NEIGHBORHOODS IN BRIEF

The city's historical and royal heart beats around **Palace Square (Dvortsovaya Ploshchad),** presided over by the resplendent, sea-green Winter Palace, home of the Hermitage Art Museum. This small district houses few hotels and restaurants, but it's a crucial starting point for experiencing St. Petersburg. The curved facade of the General Staff headquarters faces the Winter Palace from across the square, its three-layered arch leading to Nevsky Prospekt while shielding the square from the street noise and bustle. The square opens westward toward the Admiralty Building, whose ever-glistening spire acts as a compass point for the city, the nexus of three main avenues. Farther west lies the Decembrists' Square, anchored on one end by the enormous single-domed St. Isaac's Cathedral, and on the other by the fearsome Bronze Horseman statue rearing up over the stone banks of the Neva River.

New Holland

It's covered in cobwebs and is not on most tourists' itineraries, but this island is unlike anything you'll find elsewhere, and provides a fascinating way to immerse yourself in St. Petersburg's history. Peter the Great named it after his sojourn in Holland, where he learned shipbuilding and was inspired to found Russia's navy. Formed by the creation of two canals on the city's western edge, the island became a key naval training and testing ground, and has housed a submarine testing pool, a prison, an arsenal, timber storehouses, and a printing press.

New Holland (Novaya Gollandiya in Russian) was closed to the public for most of its history, until the military abandoned it in 2003 and ceded its real estate to the city. Its banks are long overgrown, and its stately brick warehouses stand largely empty amid a network of artificial pools and canals, giving it a mystical, "lost city" feel. Many of the buildings are protected architectural monuments, but the city has done little to renovate or maintain them amid heated debate about what to do with the island. Some want to make it a tourist complex, with hotels, restaurants, and entertainment spaces; others want to make a cultural center with theaters and galleries; others propose a commercial center, or conference center, or elite residential zone. So far, only a few businesses have moved in, and it has staged exhibits by Russian and foreign artists intrigued by the space and its history. The easiest way to enter now is via Konnogvardeisky Bulvar. Guards may ask where you're headed, so just explain that you're a tourist (tu-*reest* in Russian). Even if you don't go in, walk or drive around the island and take a moment to look through the strikingly elegant New Holland Arch, designed by French architect Vallin de la Mothe in 1779.

The triangular island is between the Moika Canal, Kryukov Canal, and Admiral Canal. The nearest metro stations are Nevsky Prospekt and Sadovaya Ploshchad.

St. Petersburg Neighborhoods

Around Palace Square **1**

Square of the Arts/
  Summer Gardens **2**

Upper Nevsky **3**

Lower Nevsky/
  Smolny Convent **4**

South of Nevsky **5**

Vasilevsky Island/
  Petrograd Side **6**

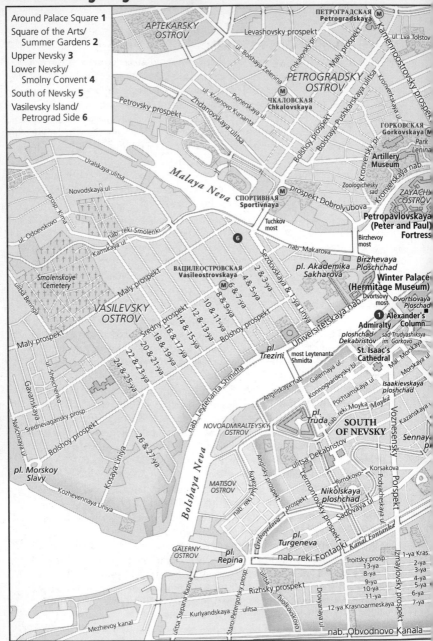

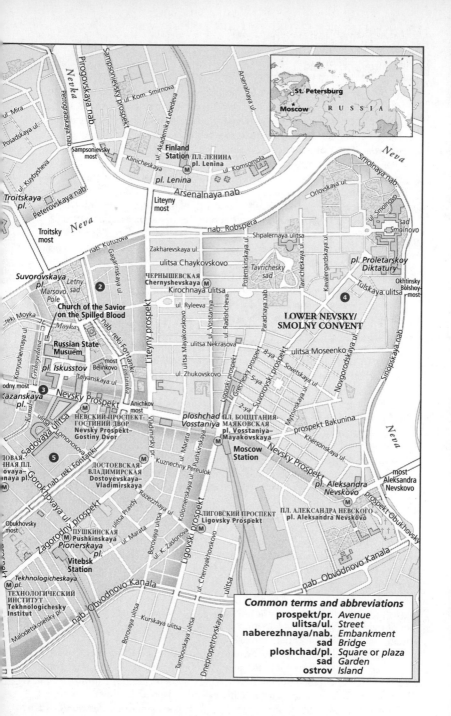

St. Petersburg

★ Moscow   R U S S I A

Neva

Neuka

Pirogovskaya nab.

Sampsonievsky prospekt

Petrogradskaya nab.

ul. Kom. Smirnova

ul. Akademika Lebedeva

Arsenalnaya ul.

ul. Mira

Posadskaya ul.

Sampsonievsky most

Klinicheskaya

Finland Station ПЛ. ЛЕНИНА
Ⓜ pl. Lenina

ul. Komsomola

Kuybysheva ul.

ul. Kuybysheva

Sampsonievsky nab.

pl. Lenina

Troitskaya pl.

Peterovskaya nab.

Arsenalnaya nab.

Orlovskaya ul.

Smolnaya nab.

Liteyny most

ul. Smolnovo

sad Smolnovo

Neva

Troitsky most

nab. Kutuzova

nab. Robspera

Shpalernaya ulitsa

Zakharevskaya ul.

Potemkinskaya ul.

Tavrichesky sad

Tavricheskaya ul.

Kavalergardskaya ul.

pl. Proletarskoy Diktatury

Suvorovskaya pl.

Letny sad

Marsovo Pole

Gagarinskaya ul.

⓶

ulitsa Chaykovskovo

ЧЕРНЫШЕВСКАЯ
Chernyshevskaya Ⓜ

Kirochnaya ulitsa

Paradnaya nab.

Okhtinsky Bolshoy most

Tulskaya ulitsa

⓸

Church of the Savior on the Spilled Blood

reki Moyka

Moyka

Liteyny prospekt

ul. Ryleeva

ulitsa Mayakovskovo

ul. Radishcheva

ulitsa Nekrasova

LOWER NEVSKY/ SMOLNY CONVENT

nab. reki Fontanki

Russian State Museum

most Belinkovo

pl. Iskusstov

Italyanskaya ul.

reki Fontanki

ul. Zhukovskovo

ulitsa Moseenko

8-ya

Grechesky prospekt

Suvorovsky prospekt

Sovetskaya ul.

Novgorodskaya ul.

Konyushennaya ul.

Griboyedova

odny most

⓷

Kazanskaya pl.

Kanal

Nevsky Prospekt

Anichkov most

Vladimirsky pr.

Ligovski prospekt

5-ya

2-ya

Mytninskaya ul.

Neva

НЕВСКИЙ ПРОСПЕКТ-ГОСТИНИЙ ДВОР
Nevsky Prospekt– Gostiny Dvor Ⓜ

ploshchad Vosstaniya

ПЛ. БОШСТАНИЯ
МАЯКОВСКАЯ
pl. Vosstaniya– Mayakovskaya Ⓜ

prospekt Bakunina

Khersonskaya ul.

most Aleksandra Nevskovo

Sadovaya ulitsa

Lomonosova

⓹

ДОСТОЕВСКАЯ-ВЛАДИМИРСКАЯ
Dostoyevskaya– Vladimirskaya Ⓜ

Kuznechny Pereulok

Pushkinskaya ul.

Moscow Station

Nevsky Prospekt

pl. Aleksandra Nevskovo

prospekt Obukhovsky

ДОВАЯ ПЛ.
ovaya– naya pl. Ⓜ

Gorokhovaya ul.

nab. reki Fontanki

Razezzhaya ul.

ul. Marata

Obukhovsky most

Zagorodny prospekt

ulitsa Pravdy

Kolomenskaya ul.

ПУШКИНСКАЯ
Pushkinskaya Ⓜ
Pionerskaya pl.

Borovaya ulitsa

ul. K. Zaslonova

ЛИГОВСКИЙ ПРОСПЕКТ
Ligovsky Prospekt Ⓜ

ПЛ. АЛЕКСАНДРА НЕВСКОГО
pl. Aleksandra Nevskovo

nab. Obvodnovo Kanala

Vitebsk Station

Tekhnologicheskaya Ⓜ
pl.

ТЕХНОЛОГИЧЕСКИЙ
ИНСТИТУТ
Tekhnologichesky Institut Ⓜ

nab. Obvodnovo Kanala

Borovaya ulitsa

ul. Marata

ul. Chernyakhovskovo

Ligovski prospekt

ulitsa

Malodetskoselsky pr.

Kurskaya ulitsa

Tamboskaya ulitsa

Dnepropetrovskaya

Obukhovsky most

Common terms and abbreviations

prospekt/pr.	*Avenue*
ulitsa/ul.	*Street*
naberezhnaya/nab.	*Embankment*
sad	*Bridge*
ploshchad/pl.	*Square* or *plaza*
sad	*Garden*
ostrov	*Island*

Vasilevsky Island

It's been called St. Petersburg's Bloomsbury or Peter the Great's precursor to Manhattan, but Vasilevsky Island (Vasilevsky Ostrov) is something all its own. It's just across the Neva River from the Hermitage, but far enough from the bustle of Nevsky Prospekt that many visitors never make it here. A growing cluster of mini-hotels, restaurants, and shops is starting to change the island's rather remote, removed reputation.

Peter the Great considered basing his capital on Vasilevsky Island, but its location made it too vulnerable to storms and flooding. Its western shore is buffeted by winds from the Gulf of Finland year-round, and the spit (called the *Strelka*) at its eastern tip bears the brunt of the Neva as it splits off into two branches right before reaching the sea. The first bridge built from the island to the "mainland" across the Neva had to be taken down every autumn until the spring thaw because of the rough winters. Despite these challenges, the island quickly became the city's learning center, housing St. Petersburg's first museum, observatory, and university.

St. Petersburg State University still dominates the eastern side of the islands, with several of its buildings dating from the 18th century. In the 19th century, factories grew up on the western reaches of the island, and its mix of students and workers made it a hotbed of revolutionary activity. Today, the west side of the island remains a rather bleak landscape of neglected harbors and warehouses, while the east side boasts vibrant student life and commerce, with a pedestrian street and some restored churches. Finding addresses on Vasilevsky is highly logical, yet confusing at first. The island is laid out on a numbered orthogonal grid, but the north-south streets have different names for each side of the street, so that the first street is called "1st Line" (1-aya Liniya) on the east side and "2nd Line" (2-aya Liniya) on the west side. Highlights of the island include **Menshikov Palace, Kunstkamera** and the **university complex,** and or **Lieutenant Shmidt Embankment,** good for a walk. The nearest metro station is Vasileostrovskaya.

Nevsky Prospekt is St. Petersburg's geographical anchor, an elegant avenue named after medieval Russian warrior prince Alexander Nevsky. When touring the city, it helps to bear in mind where you are in relation to Nevsky at any given time. The hotels on upper Nevsky, near Palace Square, are mostly top-notch and top-price. Lower Nevsky has a few mid-range Soviet-era options and an increasing number of inexpensive bed-and-breakfasts. Restaurants on the avenue range from Russian fast food for a few rubles to members-only *nouveau riche* hideouts. More creative dining options can be found on the side streets just off Nevsky.

North of central Nevsky are the **Square of the Arts** and the **Summer Gardens,** an area that includes the underrated Russian Museum, the St. Petersburg Philharmonic, several theaters and galleries, and the dizzying domes of the Church on the Spilled Blood. Hotels here are scarce but bars and cafes dot the neighborhood.

Heading east toward the bend in the Neva River takes you to the **Taurida Gardens** and **Smolny Cathedral and Convent.** This quiet neighborhood, generally termed

North of Nevsky, is ideal for casual strolling and admiring the city's lesser-known architectural wonders. It has a strong selection of private hotels, with reasonable prices and eager service, though some are rather far from the metro and Nevsky. Continuing south brings you to the Alexander Nevsky Monastery and Nevsky Prospekt's eastern end.

South of Nevsky, the neighborhoods become defined by a series of canals, the chief ones being the Moika Canal, Griboyedov Canal, and Fontanka River. The area includes such landmarks as the Mariinsky (formerly Kirov) Theater, the St. Petersburg Conservatory, Dostoyevsky's House Museum, and several picturesque bridges and embankments perfect for a romantic or introspective evening. Less chic and touristy than the area north of Nevsky, this area is more innovative in dining and entertainment, with several restaurants and bars competing for largely local business. The hotel industry is starting to catch up, with "mini-hotels" popping up along the lanes and quays.

On the north side of the Neva, the Peter and Paul Fortress forms a beacon overlooking the rest of the city. This often overlooked part of town, including **Vasilevsky Island** and the **Petrograd Side,** is spiffing up more slowly than the area around Nevsky but has produced several chic and inviting restaurants and a few small, inexpensive hotels. Several ship-restaurants line the shore on this side of the Neva, playing up the city's marine traditions. You must take the metro or a taxi to get here from Nevsky and the main museums and shopping.

2 Getting Around

See "Getting Around" in chapter 4 for a rundown of Russian transport options. St. Petersburg–specific suggestions are listed below.

BY PUBLIC TRANSPORTATION

The **St. Petersburg Metro** is a fast, cheap, and extraordinarily deep subway system that every visitor should try out at least once. Station entrances are marked with a big blue letter "M." The four-line system is easy to follow, with each line color-coded and transfers clearly marked—though usually in Russian only. This is where it's highly useful to learn the Cyrillic alphabet (see alphabet lesson and glossary in appendix B). Trains run from 5:45am to 12:15am. Each train car has a metro map inside to consult, though it's a good idea to carry one with you (they're available free at all ticket counters). The trains run quite frequently but the system is insufficient for the size of the city and doesn't serve many of the key tourist attractions. It can also be crowded at any time of day, and you can find yourself in a waddling mass squeezing onto the fast, steep escalators. Most platforms are enclosed and resemble a long hall full of elevator-like doors. You can't see the train as it approaches, but you hear a tone and suddenly the doors open—and there's a train on the other side.

Tips Don't Drink the Water

Most hotels have their own clean water supply, or use filtered water, because of St. Petersburg's often bacteria-infected groundwater. It's a good idea to ask before brushing your teeth with tap water. Numerous brands of locally bottled spring water are good cheap sources of clean water. Some safe brands are Saint Springs (Svyatoi Istochnik) and Natalia. Make sure you ask for *voda bez gaza*—literally, water without gas—unless you want the carbonated kind.

St. Petersburg Metro

One ride costs the same no matter how far you're going. The city is phasing out metro tokens, replacing them with paper cards using a magnetic strip. For the time being, every metro station sells tokens, which cost 5 rubles (about 18¢), or they sell cards for 1, 2, 5, or 10 trips that get cheaper the more you buy.

The blue plastic tokens are dropped into machines with marked slots. The cards are slid into machines with slots on the side and pulled out on the other end before you can cross.

Trams are a pleasant way to see the city, but few lines are convenient for hotels and tourist sights. Two lines worth trying are the #14, which runs from the Mariinsky Theater up through the center of town and across the Neva; another is the #1, which runs through Vasilevsky Island, including a stop just outside the Vasileostrovskaya metro station. **Trolleybuses** run along Nevsky Prospekt and some other large avenues.

Tickets for trams and trolleybuses cost 11 rubles (40¢) and are available from the driver or sometimes from a conductor who roams the vehicle selling them. **Passengers must punch their own tickets** in the little red contraptions posted throughout the vehicle (watch other passengers and imitate). Failure to do so makes your ticket worthless, and you risk earning a fine. Maps are posted inside the vehicles, and routes are often listed at the stops, but in Russian only.

BY TAXI

Reliable companies to try are the official **Petersburg Taxi** (© **068**—that's right, just 3 digits) or **Taxi Park** (© **812/265-1333**).

BY CAR

See "Getting Around" in chapter 4 for driving advice. Some rental companies to try are:

Hertz/Travel Rent: Pulkovo Airport-1 and -2, arrivals halls. © **812/324-3242.** www.hertz.com. Rents cars with or without drivers.

Biracs: Pulkovo Airport-1 and -2, arrivals halls, or 8 Boytsova Pereulok. © **812/310-5356.** www.biracs.ru. Cars without drivers.

Europecar: Pulkovo Airport-1 and -2, arrivals halls. © **812/380-1662.** www.europcar.com. Rents with or without drivers.

Rolf-Neva: 17/10 Vitebsky Prospekt. © **812/327-0660.** www.rolfrent.ru. Rents with or without drivers.

FAST FACTS: St. Petersburg

Airport See "Getting There" in chapter 2; and "Arriving," earlier in this chapter.

American Express The main local office is in the Grand Hotel Europe (1 Mikhailovskaya Ulitsa; © 812/326-4500). It's open from 9am to 6pm and will cash traveler's checks. In the U.S., call © 800/221-7282.

Business Hours Businesses generally operate from 9am to 6pm. A few stores and businesses still take a lunch break between 1 and 2 pm. Some shops are closed Sunday, but museums and restaurants are generally open. Several restaurants and bars are open 24 hours.

Car Rentals See "Getting Around," above.

Climate See "When to Go" in chapter 2.

Currency Exchange Every St. Petersburg hotel, many restaurants, and all major streets have exchange booths *(obmen valyuty)*, many of which are open 24 hours. They're well-guarded, reliable places to change cash. Rates are better than in most banks, and they're competitive, so shop around. Most don't charge a commission. Make sure your bills are new and untainted, since crinkled or pre-1995 bills will be rejected. Exchange booths have a sign out front with four figures: The buy and sell rate for U.S. dollars, and the buy and sell rate for euros. To exchange other currencies, try the bigger banks, or the exchange booths in the underground walkway at Gostiny Dvor.

Dentist For international-standard service, try **Dental Palace**, 10 Millionaya Ulitsa; © 812/325-7100.

Doctor For Western-standard medical care and English-speaking staff, try these private clinics. They'll help you deal with emergencies, allergy attacks, or general health problems. Their services are expensive and may not be covered by your insurance company, so be sure to check with your insurer before you go. See "Travel Insurance" in chapter 2 for more information.

- **American Medical Center St. Petersburg,** 10 Serpukhovskaya Ulitsa (© 812/326-1730)
- **British-American Family Practice and Urgent Care,** 7 Grafsky Pereulok (© 812/327-6030).
- **Euromed,** 60 Suvorovsky Prospekt (© 812/327-0301)

Driving Rules See "Getting Around," above.

Drugstores See "Pharmacies" below.

Electricity Russia operates on 220-volt AC, as does the rest of Europe. Bring converters if you have electrical equipment from North America, since they're harder to find in Russia. Most modern hotels use plugs with two thick prongs as in continental Europe; some older hotels will need plugs with two thinner prongs. Small plastic adapters for these old plugs are available in Russian hardware stores, or often from the hotel staff. To guard against electricity surges for items like laptops, bring a stabilizer, too.

Embassies St. Petersburg has consulates for many countries, though the embassies are in Moscow (see "Fast Facts: Moscow" in chapter 4 for embassy addresses in Moscow).

United States: 15 Furshtadskaya Ulitsa (© 812/275-1701)

Britain: 5 Ploshchad Proletarskoi Diktatury (© 812/320-3200)

Canada: 32 Malodetskoselsky Prospekt (© 812/325-8448)

Emergencies For fire, dial 01; police 02; ambulance 03. For medical emergencies, see the "Doctor" listing above. In extreme cases, the international clinics will send you to a better-equipped Russian hospital with a translator.

Holidays During holidays, St. Petersburg's commerce slows down but doesn't shut down. Many museums and restaurants remain open. Check with your hotel concierge or call the establishment to make sure it's open. See "When to Go" in chapter 2.

Hospitals Most Russian hospital employees speak little or no English, except for the top doctors. Some of the bigger and relatively reliable hospitals are:

Regional Medical Unit no. 20, 21 Gastello Ulitsa (© 812/108-4808)

City Children's Hospital no. 1, Avangardnaya Ulitsa (© 812/135-1207)

Mariinsky Hospital no. 16, 56 Liteyny Prospekt (© 812/275-7433)

Information See "Visitor Information" earlier in this chapter.

Internet Access Most hotel business centers offer online access, though at steeper rates than the Internet cafes popping up around the center of town. Try **Quo Vadis,** at 24 Nevsky Prospekt; or **Café Max** at 90/92 Nevsky Prospekt. Both are open 24 hours. Café Max also has a branch inside the Hermitage Museum.

Language Russian is the principal language, a Slavic tongue that uses the Cyrillic alphabet. English is becoming more common but is not so widespread as in western Europe. In most hotels, at tourist sites, and in central St. Petersburg, visitors should have no trouble communicating in English. Younger people are far more likely to speak it well than their elders. The main challenge is the Russian alphabet. Despite efforts to print signs in the Latin alphabet, most streets and metro stations are labeled in Cyrillic. It is well worthwhile to learn the 33-letter alphabet, which is very phonetic and shares many letters with English. Use the glossary in appendix B to help, or take any good phrasebook with phonetic transliterations of Russian words (spa-SEE-ba is "thank you," for example).

Liquor Laws The official drinking age in Russia is 18 but it is almost never enforced. Drinking in public is acceptable (despite a recent law against it), and seeing teenagers clutching beers on their way home from school is common. Beer, wine, and liquor—primarily vodka, but also such cocktails as gin and tonic in a can—are available in all supermarkets and at most street kiosks. Beware of cheap vodka from kiosks, since it's often watered down or of stomach-wrenching quality. Bars with special licenses can serve alcohol all night, and many do. Some stores are closed on Sundays, but those that are open sell liquor then as they do every day.

Mail Russia's postal service is underfunded and usually unreliable. Postcards are a safe bet, though they may not arrive until you're back home. Postcards and letters to western Europe and North America cost about 10 rubles (35¢); leters cost 16 rubles (60¢). Both should be addressed Russian-style; see examples posted up in the post office. Shipping packages through the regular post is not recommended because of the risk, the delay, and the complex Customs rules. Several international shipping companies serve Russia, such as **FedEx** (© 812/379-9040) and **DHL** (© 812/318-4472). See "Post Office" below.

Maps See "City Layout" earlier in this chapter.

Newspapers & Magazines The twice-weekly English-language newspaper *The St. Petersburg Times* (www.sptimes.ru) is the best and pretty much only worthwhile source of local news and entertainment listings in English. *The International Herald Tribune, Financial Times,* and other international publications are sold at the chain hotels and some of the Russian hotels, but not at city newsstands. The many bilingual guidebooks offered free at hotels and tourist offices are good for listings and museum reviews. For Russian speakers, *Vedomosti, Kommersant,* and *Izvestia* newspapers are the most respected; *Afisha Petersburg* is the best weekly magazine for entertainment, dining, and shopping advice.

Pharmacies St. Petersburg has an ever-growing number of pharmacies, called *apteka,* many of which are 24 hours. Look for a blue or green cross. Check with your hotel concierge for the all-night pharmacy nearest you.

Police Call © 02.

Post Office The main city post office (Glavny Pochtamt) is at 9 Pochtamtskaya Ulitsa (© 812/312-8302).

Restrooms St. Petersburg has far too few public restrooms for its size, and the ones it has are odorous and often no more than a hole in the floor. A recent phenomenon is the vans parked at tourist sites such as Palace Square with portable toilets inside; these charge a small fee. Bring toilet paper everywhere. In a pinch, dive into any hotel or restaurant restroom.

Safety See "Security Concerns" in chapter 2.

Salons St. Petersburg residents make salons a part of their routine, and you can find the simpler *parikmakherskaya* (barber shop/hair salon) or the more elaborate *salon krasoty* (beauty salon) just about anywhere. Quality and prices are higher in the center. If you've got a night on the town, two central places to try (for both men and women) are **Prestige,** 25 Bolshaya Morskaya Ulitsa (© 812/314-7521); and the fancier **Adamant-Caprice** at 90/92 Nevsky Prospekt (© 812/272-7514).

Smoking Russians smoke heavily, and nonsmokers are rarely catered to. Expensive hotels and an increasing number of restaurants offer nonsmoking options, so don't be afraid to ask. Bars are universally smoky. Smoking is forbidden on public transport and in museums.

Taxes Stores and restaurants include VAT (value-added tax) of up to 18% on the list prices of store and menu items, though many hotels do not include it in their listed rates. Ask if you're unsure. VAT is not refundable upon departure as it is in some European cities. St. Petersburg has no sales tax.

Taxis See "Getting Around," above.

Telephone Russia's phone service remains so basic that many Russians have cellphones but are still on waiting lists for land lines. Just a few years ago you had to order all international calls in advance. Today you can dial direct, but poor connections and disconnections are common on land lines. Cellphone service is quite advanced.

To call Russia: If you're calling Russia from another country:

1. Dial the international access code (011 in the U.S. and Canada, 00 from the U.K. and New Zealand, 0011 from Australia).
2. Dial the country code, which is 7.
3. Dial the city code (095 for Moscow, 812 for St. Petersburg) and then the 7-digit number. For example, if you are making a call from North America to Moscow, the whole number you'd dial would be 011-7-095-000-0000.

Note: To make any long-distance call from within Russia, international or domestic, you must dial 8 first, then wait for a tone. Note that some Russian cellphone numbers also require you to dial 8 first.

To make international calls: To make international calls from Russia, first dial 8, then wait for a tone, then dial 10, then the country code (U.S. or Canada 1, U.K. 44, Ireland 353, Australia 61, New Zealand 64). Next you dial the area code and number. For example, if you want to call the Russian Embassy in Washington, D.C., you would dial 8 (tone) 10-1-202-588-7800. If you are calling from a hotel, you may have to dial 9 before dialing the 8.

To call from city to city within Russia: First dial 8, then wait for a tone, then dial the city code and the 7-digit number. For example, calling St. Petersburg from Moscow would look like this: 8 (tone) 812-777-1000.

To call within Russian cities: Just dial the 7-digit number. Local calls are free.

For directory assistance: Dial 07 if you're looking for a number inside Russia, but be prepared to hear no English.

For operator assistance: If you need operator assistance in making an international call, dial 8, then wait for a tone, then dial 194. If you want to call a number in Russia, dial 08, but few operators speak English.

Toll-free numbers: You cannot phone a 1-800 number in the States from Russia, so be sure to have standard toll numbers for all your credit card companies and travel agencies before you leave.

Pay phones: St. Petersburg is phasing out its token-operated phones for card-operated ones. The token-run ones rarely work and should be avoided. Cards for the other phones can be purchased at any metro station and many hotel kiosks in Moscow or St. Petersburg. Not all phones accept all kinds of phone cards, and not all phone cards allow international calls. The most common is Petersburg City Telephone Service, or MGTS by its Russian initials. Most cards and card phones provide instructions in English.

International calling cards: Direct access numbers in St. Petersburg are AT&T 325-5042; MCI 747-3322; BT Direct 8 (tone) 10-80-01-10-1044; Canada Direct 755-5045 or 747-3325.

Time Zone St. Petersburg is on the same time zone as Moscow, 3 hours ahead of GMT from October to March, and 4 hours ahead during daylight saving time. That means it's usually 3 hours ahead of London, 8 hours ahead of New York, and 11 hours ahead of San Francisco. Russia switches to daylight saving time a week earlier than Europe and North America, and reverts to standard time a week earlier, too.

Tipping Restaurants generally include service charges in the price, though small tips are welcome. Taxis usually set the rate before you head out, so no tip is expected. Baggage handlers and coat check staffers should be tipped the equivalent of a dollar or so.

Useful Telephone Numbers

U.S. Dept. of State Travel Advisory: ☎ 202/647-5225 (staffed 24 hr.)

U.S. Passport Agency: ☎ 202/647-0518

U.S. Centers for Disease Control International Traveler's Hotline: ☎ 404/332-4559

13

Where to Stay
in St. Petersburg

Variation and innovation characterize St. Petersburg's hotel scene, in contrast to the overburdened and uneven offerings in Moscow. St. Petersburg's nicest and priciest hotels, and nearly all of the international chains, are clustered on upper Nevsky Prospekt. The huge Soviet-era hotel towers are farther from the center, and sometimes quite far from the metro. They offer better prices, and their quality ranges from luxurious leather armchairs to saggy, stained mattresses. The best price-to-quality ratio is found in the numerous "mini-hotels" springing up around town.

The tourist season in St. Petersburg is much more pronounced than in Moscow, centering around the White Nights festivals in late June. Accommodations are at a premium beginning the several weeks leading up to this time of year, and reservations are essential. The rest of the year, particularly the sleepy winter months, offer more options and deep discounts.

When choosing accommodations in St. Petersburg, bear in mind that it's a city of bridges that are drawn up in the wee hours to allow shipping traffic through. This means that if your late-night plans involve something on the other side of the Neva River from your hotel, you may be in for a long wait or a detour to get back. See chapter 12 for drawbridge schedules, and for a description of the neighborhoods listed below.

Rates listed here are rack rates, the highest official prices charged by hotels. Hotel websites often offer discounts or package deals, as do many traditional and online travel agencies. Prices below are listed in U.S. dollars (see the "Currency Confusion" box on p. 83 and do *not* include breakfast or 18% VAT unless noted; most travel agencies (online and traditional) *do* include VAT in their quotes. For more hotel hints, see "Tips on Accommodations" in chapter 2.

Few Russian hotels offer car rentals, but most can arrange a car with a driver for a few hours or for the duration of your stay at a reasonable, sometimes negotiable price. The hotel's "transport desk" offers something between a taxi and a limo service.

Suites in Russia (called *luxe* or *demi-luxe*) nearly always have two rooms, though size varies broadly. In older hotels a double will usually mean two single beds, while newer hotels offer the choice of one double bed for two people, or two single beds. Single rooms and single rates are nearly always available, so be sure to ask about them if you're traveling alone.

1 Around the Hermitage

VERY EXPENSIVE

Astoria 🎭🎭🎭   An example of Art Nouveau at its apex, the five-star Astoria offers 21st-century decadence in a pre-revolutionary setting, overlooking St. Isaac's Cathedral with the Neva River in the background. It's St. Petersburg's only hotel in its class to have preserved its historic design and ambience, though new management has modernized room furnishings. The Astoria and adjacent Angleterre (see next listing) opened in 1912 on the site of a 19th-century English/Russian hotel venture. They were appropriated by the Soviets, and the Astoria was later used as a field hospital during the Nazi blockade of Leningrad in World War II, before it made it back into private hands in the 1990s. A favorite of well-to-do tourists and executives alike, the Astoria underwent its latest renovation in 2002. Designers retained the crystal chandeliers and tapestries but relegated the antique chairs to the corridors. It was one of the first St. Petersburg hotels with a pool, heated and indoors for year-round enjoyment. Unfortunately, the mirrored, Art Nouveau Winter Garden is open only for special events—peek inside and imagine the balls held here a century ago. Harpists play in the lobby bar at teatime, at the base of the marble staircase, and a jazz pianist takes over in the evening. The Astoria is an excellent stop for tea even if you're not staying overnight.

39 Ulitsa Bolshaya Morskaya. ⓒ 812/313-5757. Fax 812/313-5059. www.astoria.spb.ru. 220 units. From $380 double; from $700 suite. Rates 10% higher May–July. AE, DC, MC, V. Metro: Nevsky Prospekt. **Amenities:** 2 restaurants; bar and lounge; pool; health club; spa; Jacuzzi; sauna; billiard room; concierge; tour desk; car-rental desk; limo; 24-hr. business center; shopping arcade; salon; 24-hr. room service; laundry service; same-day dry cleaning; nonsmoking rooms; executive rooms. *In room:* A/C, TV w/satellite, dataport, minibar, fridge, hair dryer, iron, safe.

EXPENSIVE

Angleterre 🎭🎭   Initially a wing of the Astoria, the four-star Angleterre shares a designer and a kitchen with its "sister hotel," though they're now under separate management. See the above review for details on the building's history. Today the Angleterre is a slightly less expensive, less well-preserved neighbor of the Astoria, but it is still a luxurious place to stay. Corridors are plainer, and the lobby, while glistening in white marble, lacks any period style. The spacious guest rooms, many boasting wide windows, are decorated in warm woods that differ little in quality and style from the Astoria's. The view of St. Isaac's makes a street-facing room worthwhile; triple-paned windows keep the traffic roar to a light hum.

39 Bolshaya Morskaya Ulitsa. ⓒ 812/313-5787. Fax 812/313-5118. www.angleterrehotel.com. 193 units. $260 double; from $400 suite. Mid-May to mid-July $330 double. AE, DC, MC, V. Metro: Nevsky Prospekt. **Amenities:** Restaurant with live jazz pianist every evening; small indoor pool; health club; spa; sauna; concierge; tour desk; car-rental desk; limo; 24-hr. business center; salon; 24-hr. room service; laundry service; same-day dry cleaning; nonsmoking rooms; executive rooms. *In room:* A/C, TV w/pay movies and satellite, dataport, minibar, fridge, coffeemaker, hair dryer, iron, safe.

MODERATE

Pulford Apartments 🎭   This British-Russian company offers apartments all over town, but its prime spots are along the lanes between Palace Square and Nevsky Prospekt metro station. These are also its more expensive apartments, though they still cost less than most hotel options in the neighborhood. All apartments are renovated to Western standards, with fully equipped kitchens and bathrooms, and from one to several bedrooms. Maid service can be arranged as often as you like, as can any number of

Where to Stay in St. Petersburg

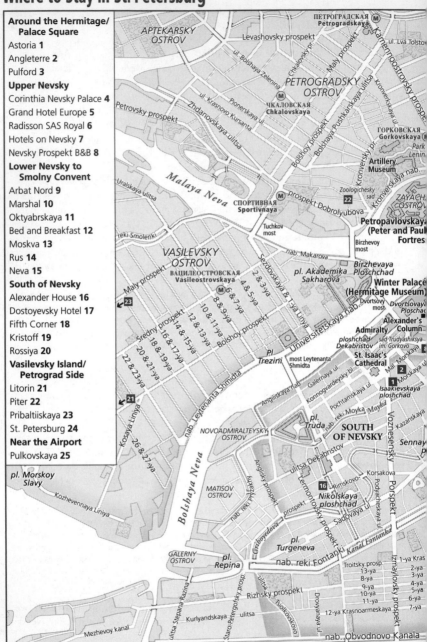

Around the Hermitage/ Palace Square
Astoria **1**
Angleterre **2**
Pulford **3**

Upper Nevsky
Corinthia Nevsky Palace **4**
Grand Hotel Europe **5**
Radisson SAS Royal **6**
Hotels on Nevsky **7**
Nevsky Prospekt B&B **8**

Lower Nevsky to Smolny Convent
Arbat Nord **9**
Marshal **10**
Oktyabrskaya **11**
Bed and Breakfast **12**
Moskva **13**
Rus **14**
Neva **15**

South of Nevsky
Alexander House **16**
Dostoyevsky Hotel **17**
Fifth Corner **18**
Kristoff **19**
Rossiya **20**

Vasilevsky Island/ Petrograd Side
Litorin **21**
Piter **22**
Pribaltiiskaya **23**
St. Petersburg **24**

Near the Airport
Pulkovskaya **25**

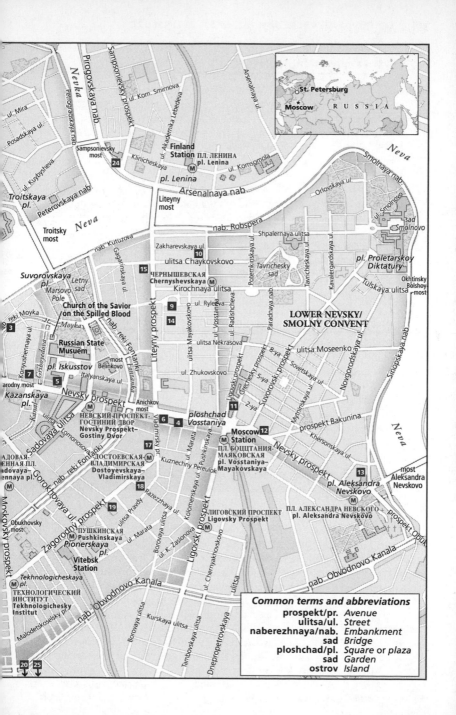

St. Petersburg

Moscow   R U S S I A

ul. Mira

Posadskaya ul.

Troitskaya pl.

ul. Kuybysheva

Suvorovskaya pl.

Church of the Savior on the Spilled Blood

Russian State Musuem

pl. Iskusstov

Kazanskaya pl.

Nevsky prospekt

Sadovaya ulitsa

САДОВАЯ СЕННАЯ ПЛ. Sadovaya-Sennaya pl.

Moskovsky prospekt

Obukhovsky most

Tekhnologicheskaya pl.

ТЕХНОЛОГИЧЕСКИЙ ИНСТИТУТ Tekhnologichesky Institut

Pirogovskaya nab.

Nevka

Petrogradskaya nab.

Sampsonievsky prospekt

ul. Kom. Smirnova

Akademika Lebedeva

Sampsonievsky most

Klinicheskaya

Finland Station ПЛ. ЛЕНИНА pl. Lenina

pl. Lenina

ul. Komsomola

Arsenalnaya ul.

Arsenalnaya nab.

Liteyny most

Troitsky most

Peterovskaya nab.

Neva

nab. Kutuzova

Gagarinskaya ul.

Letny sad

Marsovo Pole

Moyka

nab. reki Moyki

Konyushennaya ul.

Griboyedova

Italyanskaya ul.

Anichkov most

nab. reki Fontanki

most Belinkovo

Fontanka

Nevsky prospekt

НЕВСКИЙ ПРОСПЕКТ-ГОСТИНИЙ ДВОР Nevsky Prospekt-Gostiny Dvor

Lomonosova

Gorokhovaya ul.

Zagorodny prospekt

ulitsa Pravdy

ul. Marata

ПУШКИНСКАЯ Pushkinskaya Pionerskaya pl.

Vitebsk Station

Razezzhaya ul.

Kuznechny Pereulok

ДОСТОЕВСКАЯ-ВЛАДИМИРСКАЯ Dostoyevskaya-Vladimirskaya

Vladimirsky pr.

Liteyny prospekt

ulitsa Mayakovskovo

ul. Ryleeva

Kirochnaya ulitsa

ЧЕРНЫШЕВСКАЯ Chernyshevskaya

ulitsa Chaykovskovo

Zakharevskaya ulitsa

nab. Robspera

Liteyny most

ul. Radishcheva

ulitsa Nekrasova

ul. Zhukovskovo

ploshchad Vosstaniya

Moscow Station

ПЛ. ВОССТАНИЯ МАЯКОВСКАЯ pl. Vosstaniya-Mayakovskaya

Ligovsky prospekt

Grechesky prospekt

8-ya

5-ya

2-ya

Suvorovsky prospekt

Mytninskaya ulitsa

Sovetskaya ul.

ulitsa Moseenko

Novgorodskaya ul.

prospekt Bakunina

Khersonskaya ul.

Nevsky prospekt

Shpalernaya ulitsa

Potemkinskaya ul.

Tavrichesky sad

Tavricheskaya ul.

Paradnaya nab.

Kavalergardskaya ul.

Orlovskaya ul.

Sinopskaya nab.

Neva

Smolnaya nab.

ul. Smolnovo

sad Smolnovo

pl. Proletarskoy Diktatury

Okhtinsky Bolshoy most

Tulskaya ulitsa

LOWER NEVSKY/ SMOLNY CONVENT

most Aleksandra Nevskovo

pl. Aleksandra Nevskovo

ПЛ. АЛЕКСАНДРА НЕВСКОГО pl. Aleksandra Nevskovo

prospekt Obuk

Kolomenskaya ulitsa

Pushkinskaya ulitsa

ЛИГОВСКИЙ ПРОСПЕКТ Ligovsky Prospekt

Ligovsky prospekt

Borovaya ulitsa

ul. K. Zaslonova

ul. Chernyakhovskovo

nab. Obvodnovo Kanala

Kurskaya ulitsa

Tambovskaya ulitsa

Dnepropetrovskaya ulitsa

Malodetskoselsky pr.

Troitskaya pl.

Common terms and abbreviations

prospekt/pr.	*Avenue*
ulitsa/ul.	*Street*
naberezhnaya/nab.	*Embankment*
sad	*Bridge*
ploshchad/pl.	*Square* or *plaza*
sad	*Garden*
ostrov	*Island*

Family-Friendly Hotels

Russians dote on their kids but don't generally take them to city hotels, preferring to take them to a family *dacha* (country cottage) or *dom otdykha* (country resort) for vacations. Because Russia's newer hotels are aimed more at lucrative business clients than at families, child-friendly services remain rare. The international chains have the most amenities for families. **Corinthia Nevsky Palace** stands out in this category, offering a children's playroom and babysitting, as well as a fantastic Sunday brunch with children's entertainment. The **Pribaltiiskaya** hotel offers an expanse of beachfront good for running around (though the Baltic is too cold for swimming any time of year), as well as a video game room. In addition, its forthcoming Aquapark should make it a big family draw. Two smaller hotels with child-friendly attitudes are the **Fifth Corner,** whose young staff is happy to babysit; and **Alexander House,** run by a couple ready with help and advice on how to share St. Petersburg with your children.

hotel-like services such as extra towels, theater tickets, cellphone rental, and visa help. It's a bit more isolated than hotel living, but English-speaking help is just a phone call away. Security is assured, but some apartments are in unguarded buildings, so if you come home alone late at night, get someone to accompany you to the door (even a cab driver). The top locations offer perks such as a personal grocery-shopping service and delivery of videos or DVDs.

Main office: 6 Moika Embankment. (C) **812/325-6277.** Fax 812/320-7561. www.pulford.com. From $130 double for 1-bedroom apt. AE, DC, MC, V. **Amenities:** Tour arrangements and personal guides; transport services; laundry service; dry cleaning; nonsmoking rooms; executive rooms. *In room:* A/C, TV w/satellite, dataport, kitchen, fridge, coffeemaker, hair dryer, iron, safe.

2 Upper Nevsky Prospekt

VERY EXPENSIVE

Corinthia Nevsky Palace 𝒦𝒦 *Kids*   Hidden behind a 19th-century facade on Nevsky is a glass-enclosed lobby and atrium lush with greenery that feels more like Sydney or Los Angeles than subarctic St. Petersburg. The five-star Nevsky Palace opened in 1993 in two renovated neoclassical mansions, and completed another upgrade in 2005. Geared more towards executives than tourists, the hotel offers a range of suites and thoroughly modern (if somewhat colorless) rooms. Even the smallest room has a bidet along with the standard bathroom facilities. Staff is businesslike but not particularly effusive, though every imaginable service is available if you're bold enough to ask. In a nod to the building's history, the hotel houses a small theater museum, in honor of the Samoilov family of actors who lived on the property in the 1800s. Its prime location almost justifies its high prices. Though street-facing windows are well-fortified, Nevsky's constant buzz makes a courtyard-facing room more appealing. Even if you don't stay here, their Sunday brunch, a smorgasbord of international cuisines, is worth a splurge. On-site are child-friendly entertainment, a playroom, and a babysitter.

57 Nevsky Prospekt. ℂ **812/380-2001.** Fax 812/301-1937. www.corinthia.ru. 155 units. Double $300 mid-Oct to mid-May, $390 mid-May to mid-Oct; suite from $400 mid-Oct to mid-May, from $500 mid-May to mid-Oct. AE, DC, MC, V. Metro: Gostiny Dvor. **Amenities:** 4 restaurants; bar; cafe; health club; spa; Jacuzzi; sauna; concierge; tour desk; car-rental desk; limo; 24-hr. business center; Wi-Fi; shopping arcade; salon; 24-hr. room service; massage; babysitting; laundry service; same-day dry cleaning; nonsmoking rooms; executive rooms. *In room:* A/C, satellite TV, dataport, minibar, fridge, coffeemaker, hair dryer, safe.

EXPENSIVE

Grand Hotel Europe 🏰🏰🏰   This hotel has every right to call itself grand. Grandeur seeps from its ceiling friezes to its carpeting. Originally opened in 1875, it served as a children's quarantine center during the Russian Revolution and as an evacuation center during World War II. It was completely rehauled for a 1991 reopening, and much of what seems pre-revolutionary is recent re-creation, from the baroque facade to the Art Nouveau interiors. That detracts little from the overall experience of this Kempinski-run hotel. Its five floors surround a luscious winter garden and mezzanine cafe visible from inward-facing rooms. Even if you don't stay here, spend a lazy morning or rainy afternoon savoring tea from a silver samovar and listening to the harpist on the mezzanine. Previous guests included Tchaikovsky, Dostoyevsky, and Bill Clinton when he was U.S. president; its current clientele seems to be European tourists and international executives. Guest rooms are elegant, modern, and (except for the presidential suite) mid-size.

1 Mikhailovskaya Ulitsa. ℂ **800/426-3135** or 812/329-6000. Fax 812/329-6001. www.grandhoteleurope.com. 300 units. From $310 double; from $790 suite. Rates 20% higher May–July. $40 extra bed. AE, DC, MC, V. Metro: Gostiny Dvor or Nevsky Prospekt. **Amenities:** 5 restaurants; 2 bars; health club; Jacuzzi; sauna; concierge; tour desk; car-rental desk; limos; 24-hr. business center; shopping arcade; salon; 24-hr. room service; massage; babysitting; laundry service; same-day dry cleaning; nonsmoking rooms; executive rooms. *In room:* A/C, TV w/satellite and pay movies, dataport, minibar, fridge, hair dryer, iron, safe.

Radisson SAS Royal 🏰🏰   The stylish corner bar sets the mood for this five-star hotel, with its curved wooden bar and cozy window seats. The suites retain this elegance; the standard rooms offer all the same amenities and spaciousness without the character. Young, friendly staff is helpful in finding you the best room—except during the busiest season, or when large groups of business visitors fill up its floors. Opened in 2002, the Royal is the newcomer in town as a top-end hotel, but the building's history dates back to the 1730s. Courtyard-facing rooms are considerably quieter than street-facing ones, though they cost the same, and the view of Nevsky, while romantic at night, is just as well experienced from the above-mentioned Cannelle bar on the ground floor as from your room.

49/2 Nevsky Prospekt. ℂ **800/333-3333** or 812/322-5000. Fax 812/322-5002. www.radissonsas.com. 164 units. $280 double; from $420 suite; May–July $380 double, from $560 suite. Children 18 and under stay free. AE, DC, MC, V. Metro: Gostiny Dvor. **Amenities:** Restaurant; bar and lounge; health club; sauna; concierge; tour desk; car-rental desk; limo; 24-hr. business center; salon; room service; laundry service; same-day dry cleaning; nonsmoking rooms; executive rooms. *In room:* A/C, TV w/satellite, Wi-Fi, dataport, minibar, fridge, coffeemaker, hair dryer, iron, safe.

MODERATE

Hotels on Nevsky 🏰🏰 *(Value)*   This company has three mini-hotels along Nevsky, offering modern hotel rooms and fully furnished apartments that are a big hit with American and European travelers, both first-time and repeat visitors. Staff is cheerful and always open to suggestions. Of the three, Nevsky 91 opened first and has the most basic services and the least appealing locale, just across from the exit to Moskovsky Train Station and its attendant grime. Nevsky 90 is across busy Insurrection Square

(Ploshchad Vosstaniya), on a posher section of the avenue. Nevsky 22 boasts the best location, one building away from Nevsky Prospekt on a slightly quieter boulevard, with half the rooms facing the peaceful courtyard around the Armenian Cathedral. It's the only one with air-conditioning. All charge the same rates for basic wood decor, plenty of greenery, and natural light. The apartments have fully equipped kitchens and a range of business services for long-term guests, and can be rented per night or per month. The company can arrange visas and translators, too. All-in-all, an excellent mid-range choice.

22 Nevsky Prospekt, 90 Nevsky Prospekt, 91 Nevsky Prospekt. ⓒ 812/103-3860. www.hon.ru. 115 units total. Double $90 Oct–Apr, $130 May and July–Sept, $150 June; from $150 suite. $30 extra bed. AE, MC, V. Metro: Nevsky Prospekt or Ploshchad Vosstaniya. **Amenities:** Cafe in each hotel; Jacuzzi in suites; sauna; tour desk; transport desk; business center; 24-hr. room service; laundry and ironing service; dry cleaning; executive rooms. *In room:* A/C (some units), TV w/satellite, kitchen available in apts, hair dryer, safe.

Nevsky Prospekt Bed and Breakfast 𝒢   The unbeatable location means this rather modest bed-and-breakfast charges a bit more than it should, but overall it's an appealing place and a welcome addition to the hotel scene in this neighborhood. The five-room apartment building was appropriated by the Soviets and made into communal housing, but it is again privately owned. Guests share two semi-renovated bathrooms. Though the lodging is in the heart of the city, the decor is reminiscent of Russian *dachas*, or country houses: basic wooden furniture, embroidered bedspreads, and white walls, instead of the busy wallpaper favored by apartment-dwellers. The high ceilings and hardwood floors give it a sense of faded grandeur, as does a 5pm tea service in the small dining room. The owners make Russian, European, and American breakfasts, which can be a choice between coffee and a roll, ham and eggs, or steaming porridge, depending on who's cooking. Internet access and visa arrangements are available. VAT is included.

11 Nevsky Prospekt. ⓒ 812/325-9398. www.bnbrussia.com. 5 units. Double Nov–Mar $80, Mar–Apr and Aug–Oct $99, summer $120. AE, DC, MC, V. **Amenities:** Cafe; business center; tour desk; transport desk; laundry. *In room:* TV.

3 Lower Nevsky to Smolny Cathedral

MODERATE

Arbat Nord 𝒢𝒢   An inviting, peach-colored building on a quiet side street, the Arbat Nord is an elegant mix of antique desks and top-of-the-line laptop reservation terminals. Opened in 2004, it blends more carefully with St. Petersburg's 18th-century classicism than the hotels of the Soviet era. Staff is always ready to include personal touches, such as guidebooks in your native language or wine from your country left at the bedside. Its five stories hold mid- to large-size rooms of polished dark woods and sumptuous, firm bedding. The top-floor rooms have skylights that offer stunning views of the long summer sunsets and sunrises—though be sure the blinds close securely if you want to get any sleep during the White Nights. The neighborhood feels almost isolated, but it's just around the corner from Chernyshevskaya metro station and plenty of usual and unusual commerce.

4 Ulitsa Artillereiskaya. ⓒ 812/103-1899. Fax 812/103-1898. www.arbat-nord.ru. 33 units. $180 double. AE, DC, MC, V. Metro: Chernyshevskaya or Mayakovskaya. **Amenities:** Restaurant and bar; tour and transport desk; business center; room service; laundry service; same-day dry cleaning; nonsmoking rooms. *In room:* A/C, satellite TV, dataport, fridge, hair dryer, iron, safe.

Marshal &&   This one-story, 18th-century mansion is well suited to hotel life, with corridors circling a courtyard that once sheltered the household cavalry of nearby nobility. The building was turned into a hotel in 2001, and houses a one-room museum to the first president of Finland, one-time cavalryman Duke Mannerheim. Guest rooms are spacious, and even the smallest singles have sunny furniture and spotless modern bathrooms (most with shower only). The rooms facing the army barracks feel so far from the rest of the hotel that they're almost isolated. One room offers a waterbed. The small glass and chrome cafe offers a simple but satisfying breakfast, and coffee and snacks throughout the day. The Marshal's winning combination of charm and conveniences means it's increasingly popular among independent European tourists, which in turn means space is often limited. The nearby streets hold several unsung architectural and historical treasures.

41 Ulitsa Shpalernaya. ⓒ 812/279-9955 or 812/279-7500. www.marshal-hotel.spb.ru. 26 units. $145 double; from $175 suite. Extra bed $35. Breakfast included. AE, DC, MC, V. Parking. Metro: Chernyshevskaya. **Amenities:** 24-hr. restaurant; Jacuzzi; sauna; tour desk; transport desk; business center; 24-hr. room service; laundry service; nonsmoking rooms; ironing rooms. *In room:* A/C, TV w/cable, dataport, fridge, hair dryer.

Oktyabrskaya &   Right across from Moskovsky Train Station and on Nevsky's bustling Insurrection Square (Ploshchad Vosstaniya), the Oktyabrskaya is another example of Soviet expansiveness, but in a 19th-century style. The hotel went from prestigious to seedy and is on its way back up to being a reliable, mid-range option. One wing is being renovated at a time, and rooms are qualified either as standard (meaning cramped and creaky) or upgraded (meaning fumigated, polished, and generally pleasant). The labyrinth of corridors is perplexing at first, so don't hesitate to ask for help. Units vary in size with no apparent logic, but all are comfortable. Service is sometimes begrudging—some old Soviet ways die hard—but it's forthcoming if you're persistent.

10 Ligovsky Prospekt. ⓒ 812/277-6330. Fax 812/315-7501. www.oktober-hotel.spb.ru. hotel@spb.cityline.ru. 563 units. $120–$150 double; from $170 suite. May–July $180–$200 double. $30–$40 extra bed. $20 children's bed. AE, MC, V. Metro: Mayakovskaya or Ploshchad Vosstaniya. **Amenities:** Cafes on each floor; concierge; tour desk; transport desk; business center; salon; room service; laundry service; nonsmoking rooms. *In room:* A/C, TV w/satellite, fridge, safe in some rooms.

INEXPENSIVE

Bed and Breakfast *Value*   The only true bargain on Nevsky, this seven-room hostel was once a communal apartment in an imposing Stalin-era building. The company also has a dozen apartments scattered around the city center that rent by the night for very reasonable rates. Rooms in the Bed and Breakfast range from a single with no window to a spacious triple with an expansive view. They are cheerfully decorated in IKEA-style furniture. Bathrooms are shared but have shower and tub and are well-maintained. A basic breakfast is offered—or can be made yourself—in the common kitchen. A washing machine is available. Guests range from European students to American seniors, who are generally happy to share advice and St. Petersburg experiences. Three friendly women take turns being in charge, though their English-language proficiency varies. The hostel's chief drawbacks are the dank and foreboding stairwell and the lack of an elevator to the third floor. Otherwise, this is an excellent, low-priced option.

74 Nevsky Prospekt. ⓒ 812/315-1917 or 812/315-0495. www.bednbreakfast.sp.ru. 7 units at Nevsky location, but other locations around town. $30 single; $40 double; $50 triple. No credit cards. Metro: Gostiny Dvor. **Amenities:** Tour and transport assistance; laundry service; common kitchen w/fridge, coffeemaker; iron, hair dryer, and safe available.

Moskva   A standard on the tour-group circuit since its appearance in the 1970s, the Moskva's most salient feature is its size. With 700 rooms (and scores more under renovation) rounding its semicircular facade overlooking the Neva River, the Moskva was made to accommodate Soviet-size congresses and conventions—and now its boosters say it's ideal for hosting "productive, solid business meetings." Today's guests include North American and European tour groups (especially Finns), groups from former Soviet republics, and a few contingents of Chinese businesspeople. At the bottom end of Nevsky Prospekt, the hotel is a few minutes on foot from dozens of restaurants and is on top of a metro station. The redesigned lobby glistens during the day but starts to feel seedy late at night. Renovation is taking place one floor at a time, so the older rooms are sometimes refused to Western visitors. Whether that's out of embarrassment at their sorry state or from a desire to make more money from the more expensive units, you're actually being done a favor—the upgraded rooms are well worth the higher rate with their proper plumbing, comfortable toilet seats, and double beds. The corridors are big enough to house a football field, reflecting Soviet disregard for property value. While the hotel is not charming or elegant, it's reasonably priced.

2 Alexander Nevsky Sq. (Ploshchad Alexandra Nevskogo). (C) **812/274-2052.** Fax 812/274-2130. www.hotel-moscow.ru. 700 units. $86–$120 double; from $200 suite. June–July $110–$150 double. AE, MC, V. Metro: Ploshchad Alexandra Nevskogo. **Amenities:** 3 restaurants; small creperie; bar; nightclub and casino; mini-coffee shops on each floor; indoor pool; health club; sauna; concierge; tour desk; transport desk; business center; shopping arcade; salon; room service; massage; laundry service; safe. *In room:* TV w/cable, fridge, minibar in some rooms.

Neva (R)   The heavy wooden door opens onto a mirrored, marble staircase that dates back to the 1860s, when the hotel was built. The door, staircase, and entire hotel have seen better days, and the building's last full renovation was in 1969, but the staff is accommodating and the price is low. The guest rooms have soaring ceilings and intricate molding, though beds are often creaky and windows lack modern insulation from street noise and drafts, making this a better summer than winter option. The less expensive rooms have showers with no stalls; the suites all have full modern bathrooms and enormous closets. The second-floor cafe serves breakfast in style, though for other meals you should opt for one of the several cafes and restaurants in the surrounding neighborhood, such as the next-door Lido dessert shop or the Bagration restaurant (p. 227). Several rooms with views of the Neva aren't any more expensive than rooms without Neva views.

17 Ulitsa Chaikovskogo. (C) **812/278-0500.** Fax 812/273-2593. www.nevahotel.spb.ru. 133 units. From $80 double; from $130 suite. AE, MC, V. Metro: Chernyshevskaya or Gorkovskaya. **Amenities:** Restaurant and bar; sauna and very small pool; tour and transport desk; business center; salon; room service; laundry and ironing service. *In room:* TV w/cable, fridge.

Floor Monitors

In a disconcerting holdover from the Soviet era, many older, larger hotels have a *dezhurnaya,* a sort of floor monitor, stationed outside the elevators who's charged with keeping track of everyone who lives on her floor. She (it's invariably a woman) knows when you come in and out, and with whom. Sometimes she's even in charge of your key: You leave it at her desk upon departure, then present a card upon your return to get it back. Don't let her presence intimidate you; in the post-Soviet world, her job is largely cleaning and maintenance coordinator. She can even be a source of help, making you a late night cup of tea or finding you discount theater tickets.

Rus   As long as you're inside the Rus you won't have to look at its exterior, which resembles a concrete spider. It was the ultimate in Soviet modernity when it opened in the 1970s. Holdovers from the Communist era include the "floor ladies" (see the "Floor Monitors" box below) and the antiquated barber shop. The rooms are in various states of renovation, with the cheaper ones offering narrow single beds and showers with no stalls, and the more expensive ones including fresh carpeting and blond wood wardrobes. The dizzying floor layout may mean a long walk from the elevator. The hotel is not far from the lively up-and-coming neighborhood around Chernyshevskaya metro station and Taurida Gardens.

1 Ulitsa Artillereiskaya. © **812/273-4683.** Fax 812/279-3600. 165 units. $70–$120 double; from $120 suite. AE, MC, V. Secure parking. Metro: Chernyshevskaya or Mayakovskaya. **Amenities:** Restaurant; cafes on each floor; sauna; concierge; tour and transport desk; business center; shops; salon; room service; laundry and ironing service, cellphone rental. *In room:* A/C in some units, TV w/cable, fridge.

4 South of Nevsky

EXPENSIVE

Alexander House 🕏🕏 *(Kids)*   It's a typical Russian story, with a twist: A television journalist and his wife decided to switch careers and open a mini-hotel, using only environmentally friendly building materials and furniture. That's no easy task in Russia, and they remain St. Petersburg's most eco-friendly hoteliers. The project was clearly a labor of love, with every item in each room chosen and placed with care. The rooms are named after different cities, and each is decorated uniquely. What they have in common are exposed brick and wood beams, double beds, and roomy wardrobes. There's no business center or other big-hotel services, but they can rent you a laptop and help you arrange for translators, tours, or other needs. They welcome kids and pets and make guests feel immersed in St. Petersburg. The hotel, the only one in its vicinity, inhabits a picturesque, tranquil spot overlooking the Krikova Canal. Yet it's just down the street from Mariinsky Theater and within walking distance of St. Isaac's Cathedral and Palace Square. You'll need to walk about 10 minutes to reach much commerce or dining, but the intimate charm of this hotel makes it well worthwhile.

27 Naberezhnaya Krikova Kanala. ©/fax **812/259-6877** or 812/334-3540. www.a-house.ru. 14 units. Oct–Apr $170 double, $220–$270 suite; May–Sept $190 double, $240–$290 suite. MC, V. Metro: Sadovaya or Sennaya Ploshchad. **Amenities:** Cafe; concierge; tour desk; transport desk; 24-hr. room service; laundry service; nonsmoking rooms. *In room:* TV w/satellite, dataport, minibar, fridge, hair dryer, iron.

MODERATE

Dostoyevsky Hotel 🕏   The Dostoyevsky Hotel feels worlds away from its namesake's haunted, mildewed, 19th-century St. Petersburg, instead occupying a spotless modern building atop one of the city's toniest shopping malls. The name refers to the surrounding neighborhood, where Dostoyevsky lived the last years of his life and wrote *The Brothers Karamazov.* The hotel, meanwhile, is aimed squarely at the 21st-century middle-class consumer. The soft lighting of the rooms feels cozy and inviting and takes the edge off the gleaming exterior of the building. Downstairs, the Vladimirsky Passage hosts nearly 200 shops, from designer boutiques to souvenir stands. If the shopping bustle is overwhelming, ask for a courtyard-facing room on a higher floor for some peace. Breakfast and taxes are included.

19 Vladimirsky Prospekt. ©/fax **812/331-3200.** 207 units. Double Nov–Mar $130, Apr–May and Aug–Oct $160, June–July $230. MC, V. Metro: Dostoyevskaya. **Amenities:** Cafe; health club; sauna; 24-hr. business center; concierge;

tour desk; transport desk; 24-hr. room service; laundry service; nonsmoking rooms. *In room:* A/C, TV w/satellite, data-port, minibar, fridge, hair dryer, iron.

Fifth Corner (Pyaty Ugol) *Kids* There's nothing historic about this fresh, roomy, and welcoming hotel—and that's just fine. Offering the best of modern conveniences at reasonable prices, Fifth Corner is two floors of rooms in an apartment building that opened as a hotel in 2003. The up-and-coming neighborhood, called "Five Corners" because of its confusing intersection, hosts an array of casual cafes, jeans shops, music stores, and more. The hotel's biggest drawback is the three-story climb up a wide, orange staircase to reach the lobby—no elevator is available. You could look at it as a mini-gym, since the hotel has no health club of its own. The hotel attracts both Russian and international visitors, but it's too small for tour groups. The young, eager staff are open to suggestions. Unlike most Russian hotels of comparable size and standard, this one offers baby beds and babysitting, and a child-friendly cafe. Some bathrooms have shower only, but all bathrooms are clean and spacious.

13 Zagorodny Prospekt. ℰ/fax 812/380-8181. www.5ugol.ru. 27 rooms. $150 double, from $180 suite; May to early July $170 double, from $200 suite. $20 extra bed. Breakfast included. AE, DC, MC, V. Metro: Dostoyevskaya or Vladimirskaya. **Amenities:** Cafe and bar; tour and transport desk; business center; room service; babysitting; laundry and ironing service; dry-cleaning; nonsmoking rooms. *In room:* TV w/satellite, dataport, minibar, fridge, hair dryer, safe.

Kristoff Hotels like this are ubiquitous in western European capitals, bigger than a bed-and-breakfast but small enough to make guests feel cared-for and part of the family. Russia has few such places, making Kristoff all the more precious. Housed in two renovated floors of an apartment building near the "Five Corners" (see previous review), the hotel is just far enough from Nevsky to escape the tourist crush but not so far as to feel isolated. Visitors range from students to seniors, first-time visitors to old Russia pros. The lobby is on the second floor, which is not immediately obvious from the street. Guest rooms are compact and decorated with plain but sturdy Russian furniture. The double rooms follow the Russian practice of two single beds pushed together instead of one large bed. All bathrooms have shower or bathtub. There's often only one person on duty, but service is attentive and individual. Breakfast is included, and the cafe-bar is open 24 hours.

9 Zagorodny Prospekt. ℰ 812/117-6643. Fax 812/117-3692. www.kristoffhotel.com. 15 units. $90–$110 double. MC, V. Metro: Dostoyevskaya or Vladimirskaya. **Amenities:** Restaurant; tour desk; transport desk; business center; laundry service; dry cleaning; nonsmoking rooms, safe. *In room:* A/C, TV w/satellite, Wi-Fi, fridge.

Rossiya The Rossiya soars over a square set back from the Stalin-era pomp of Moskovsky Prospekt. Its architecture and generous scale reflect the bland modernism of the 1960s, but inside it's gradually updating to a fresher style. A favorite with tour groups, the hotel is offering more and more services expected by Western tourists, such as nonsmoking rooms and babysitting. If you're on a higher floor (sixth or above), ask for a room with a view of downtown or of Victory Park across the street, since they cost the same as the courtyard-facing rooms. The unrenovated rooms are compact and mattresses are thin; the newer rooms are spacious, have firm mattresses, and include bidets. The park across the street serves as a monument to the Soviet victory in World War II, and is great for a morning walk. The hotel is far from Nevsky but near Park Pobedy metro and several buses that run to the center of town.

11 Ploshchad Chernyshevskogo. ℰ 812/329-3925. Fax 812/329-3939. www.rossiya-hotel.ru. 409 units. From $100 double; from $150 suite. AE, MC, V. Metro: Park Pobedy. **Amenities:** Restaurant; bar and dance club; cafes on most floors; health club; sauna; concierge; tour desk; car-rental desk; business center; shopping arcade; salon; 24-hr. room service; laundry and ironing service; nonsmoking rooms. *In room:* A/C, TV w/cable, fridge, minibar, iron and safe in some rooms.

5 Vasilevsky Island & the Petrograd Side

MODERATE

Litorin 🎭🎭 One of many appealing, reasonably priced mini-hotels opening on Vasilevsky Island, the Litorin stands out for its careful juxtaposition of modern art and 19th-century fireplaces. The hotel opened in 2003 and is still expanding. The staff pays individual attention to guests and to detail, which makes up for some of the standard hotel services it doesn't provide, such as laundry facilities. Not neglecting technology, it offers Wi-Fi and in-room Internet connections. Guest room furniture is unadventurous, but the art is intriguing. The bathrooms are large and fully renovated. Two of the rooms have balconies, and one has a king-size bed (unheard of in Russia). All rooms are quiet because the hotel faces an unremarkable side street between the island's two main avenues. It's a long walk to the nearest metro, though compensation is the less-frequented sights nearby, such as the cathedral on the embankment; the icebreaker *Krasin* docked nearby; and the Mining Institute, one of Russia's first universities.

12 Liniya 27 (Vasilevsky Island). ⓒ/fax **095/328-1946**. www.litorin.ru. 12 units. $125–$140 double. AE, MC, V. Metro: Vasileostrovskaya. **Amenities:** Restaurant; sauna; tour desk; transport desk; business center; Wi-Fi; room service. *In room:* A/C, TV w/satellite, dataport, safe.

Piter 🎭 Pronounced "peter" but spelled with an "i," this is the affectionate way residents refer to St. Petersburg. This small new hotel on the north side of the Neva River has a good quality-to-price ratio, and its proximity to the metro renders the distance from the heart of town almost irrelevant. Each guest room is decorated slightly differently, all in a basic Scandinavian style. The rooms are mid-size but the bathrooms are compact and offer showers only. On the ground floor, however, there's a sauna with Jacuzzi and small pool meant for a cool plunge after a hot steam—and a billiard table if you get a post-swim urge. European tourists fill the rooms much of the year. Local businessmen rent the billiard room and sauna for evening parties.

5/1 Ulitsa Dobrolyubova (entrance from Ulitsa Proviyanskaya). ⓒ **812/325-1518** or 812/325-1519. www.hotel-piter.spb.ru. 15 units. $90 double; $150 suite. DC, MC, V. Metro: Sportivnaya. **Amenities:** Cafe for breakfast; Jacuzzi; sauna; billiards; tour and transport desk; laundry service. *In room:* A/C, TV w/cable, fridge.

Pribaltiiskaya 🎭 *Kids* This three-paneled tower of steel and chrome is buffeted by winds from the Baltic Sea year-round, making it feel more like a pioneer outpost than a beachfront resort, despite its seaside location. Built in the 1970s as a joint Swedish-Soviet venture, it's a favorite of Scandinavian tour groups and business travelers not intimidated by its distance from the center of town. If you get a discount rate, it can be a good bargain, offering all major services and modern, if rather plain, rooms. Its style is late Soviet mixed with Scandinavian, meaning it has little in common with Nevsky's 18th-century opulence. This is a fine choice if you're with a tour group or have a car. Otherwise, the walk from the metro is long and windy in any season, and there's little nearby in terms of commerce or sightseeing, except for a decommissioned submarine around the corner now open for visitors. The Steak House on the seventh floor and the bar on the 13th are the highlights of the hotel's extensive dining options. Its pool, bowling alley, and planned indoor water park make it a good choice when traveling with kids.

4 Ulitsa Korablestroitelei. ⓒ **095/329-2686**. www.pribaltiyskayahotel.ru. 1,200 units. $110–$200 double, depending on time of year, with highest rates June–July; $200–$340 suite. $28 extra bed. AE, DC, MC, V. Metro: Primorskaya.

Amenities: 9 restaurants; 2 bars; nightclub and jazz bar; indoor pool; Jacuzzi; sauna; game room; tour desk; transport desk; 24-hr. business center; shopping arcade; salon; 24-hr. room service; massage; laundry service; dry cleaning; nonsmoking rooms; bowling. *In room:* TV w/satellite, fridge; minibar and hair dryer in newer rooms.

St. Petersburg   Built like a lonely fortress on the Neva River, the St. Petersburg hotel has great views, decent prices, and an unfortunately Soviet atmosphere. Luckily, its stark facade and interminable, dim corridors conceal several bright, comfortable rooms. Renovated rooms are decorated in muted colors and light woods; the unrenovated ones bear the deep reds and greens of standard-issue Soviet bed linens and wallpaper. Rooms with views of the Neva and the city cost slightly more, but the price is worth paying since the view is one of the key reasons to stay in this hotel. Tour groups often stay here, and are fed in the hotel's unimpressive restaurants. Few other culinary options are available in this largely residential and industrial neighborhood, so take a cab or the metro elsewhere.

5/2 Pirogovskaya Naberezhnaya. © **812/380-1909.** Fax 812/380-1906. 400 units. $60–$100 double facing courtyard; $100–$120 double with river view; from $160 suite. Breakfast included. AE, MC, V. Metro: Ploshchad Lenina. **Amenities:** 2 restaurants; bar; concert hall; small pool; health club; sauna; game room; concierge; tour desk; transport desk; business center; shopping arcade; salon; room service; laundry service; ironing room; safe. *In room:* A/C, TV w/cable, minibar in some rooms, fridge, hair dryer, safe.

6 Near the Airport

Pulkovskaya ⊛ ⟨Kids⟩   Pulkovo Airport has no airport hotels in the traditional sense; the closest equivalent is the Pulkovskaya, 10 minutes north on a straight highway toward the city center. Shuttles run from airport to hotel and back for a fee. Another Soviet-era giant, the hotel has renovated most rooms according to international standards. Russian and foreign tour groups fill up many rooms, but there are always plenty to spare. The casino and the marriage agency on the seventh floor aim at single male tourists, though the hotel also offers family-friendly holiday events and a dinner theater show. Guest rooms are mid-size, while generously spaced bathrooms offer both shower and tub. The Bread and Salt (Khleb-Sol) restaurant showcases a Cossack vocal and dance ensemble that's rather touristy but fun for older kids.

1 Ploshchad Pobedy (Victory Sq.). © **812/140-3900.** www.pulkovskaya.ru. 840 units. $180 double, $250–$300 suite; June–July $210 double, from $285 suite. AE, DC, MC, V. Secure parking. Metro: Moskovskaya. **Amenities:** 3 restaurants; 2 bars; casino; indoor pool; health club; 2 saunas; game room; concierge; tour desk; car-rental desk; business center; Wi-Fi; shopping arcade; salon; room service; laundry service; dry cleaning. *In room:* A/C, TV w/satellite, fridge.

14

Where to Dine in St. Petersburg

St. Petersburg's current dining scene reflects its seaside and river-crossed geography, with fresh- and salt-water fish on every menu. Its eye-on-Europe heritage means that traditional Russian dishes are often upstaged by French-inspired terrines and roasts, or by pastas and pizza. Cuisines from the former Soviet republics in central Asia and the Caucasus are well represented though less common than in Moscow. The sushi craze has definitely gripped the country's northern capital, too (see the "Sushi" box on p. 107).

Round-the-clock cafes and restaurants of all genres and calibers abound in the center of town. The farther you venture from Nevsky Prospekt, the cheaper your options will be—but they'll also be more limited and less likely to have menus in English. Exceptions are the ship-restaurants that line the north side of the Neva, most of which are gaudy and overpriced but very tourist-friendly. Overall, though, St. Petersburg restaurants have a very good quality-to-price ratio, with something for everyone on most menus. Keep an eye out for "business lunches," a good way to get a reasonably priced meal and

quick service at midday. Also try one of the surprising clutches of elegant restaurants on up-and-coming Vasilevsky Island.

Nonsmoking sections are becoming more and more common in St. Petersburg, but they are not yet a rule. Call ahead to check, if smoke concerns you. Hotel restaurants are spacious enough that you'll usually be able to find a table away from the smokers.

Menu prices can be confusing, since they're often pegged to either the dollar or the euro. Because of this practice, prices listed here are in U.S. dollars, though when the check comes you'll have to pay in rubles at the current exchange rate. See the "Currency Confusion" box on p. 83 for a fuller explanation. Credit cards are catching on quickly but are rarely accepted at small or inexpensive cafes.

Most restaurants listed here have menus in English. For those that don't, see the glossary of menu terms in appendix B. For an overview of Russian cuisine and dining customs, see appendix A. For tips for vegetarians, picnicking, and late-night dining, refer to chapter 6.

1 Restaurants by Cuisine

ARMENIAN

Kilikia ✿ (South of Nevsky, $$$, p. 229)

CENTRAL ASIAN

Karavan ✿ (South of Nevsky, $$, p. 229)

Key to Abbreviations: $$$$ = Very Expensive $$$ = Expensive $$ = Moderate $ = Inexpensive

EUROPEAN

Akademia ☆ (Vasilevsky Island, $$, p. 232)

Stroganovsky Dvor ☆ (Upper Nevsky, $, p. 226)

FRENCH/RUSSIAN

Staraya Tamozhnya ☆☆ (Vasilevsky Island, $$$, p. 232)

GEORGIAN

Bagration ☆ (Lower Nevsky-Smolny, $$$, p. 227)

Kavkaz Bar ☆☆ (Lower Nevsky-Smolny, $$, p. 228)

INTERNATIONAL

Flying Dutchman (Vasilevsky Island, $$$, p. 231)

Propaganda ☆☆ (Square of the Arts, $$, p. 227)

Tinkoff ☆☆ (South of Nevsky, $$, p. 230)

Triton ☆☆ (South of Nevsky, $$$$, p. 229)

ITALIAN/RUSSIAN

Park Giuseppe ☆☆ (Square of the Arts, $$$, p. 226)

MEDITERRANEAN

Porto Maltese ☆ (Lower Nevsky-Smolny, $$, p. 228)

RUSSIAN

Blindonalds (South of Nevsky, $$, p. 230)

Chainaya Lozhka (Upper Nevsky, $, p. 225)

Hermitage Cafe (Around Palace Square, $, p. 224)

Literaturnoye Café ☆ (Upper Nevsky, $$, p. 225)

Lucky Shot ☆ (Upper Nevsky, $$$, p. 224)

NEP ☆ (Around Palace Square, $$, p. 221)

Palkin ☆☆☆ (Upper Nevsky, $$$$, p. 224)

Park Giuseppe ☆☆ (Square of the Arts, $$$, p. 226)

Russkaya Rybalka ☆ (Vasilevsky Island, $$$, p. 231)

Stray Dog Cellar ☆ (Square of the Arts, $$, p. 227)

Street of Broken Lights ☆ (Lower Nevsky-Smolny, $, p. 228)

Stroganovsky Dvor ☆ (Upper Nevsky, $, p. 226)

RUSSIAN/EUROPEAN

Lenin's Mating Call ☆ (South of Nevsky, $$, p. 230)

Onegin ☆☆ (Upper Nevsky, $$$, p. 224)

Stray Dog Cellar ☆ (Square of the Arts, $$, p. 227)

Stroganovsky Dvor ☆ (Upper Nevsky, $, p. 226)

RUSSIAN/FRENCH

Hermitage Restaurant ☆☆☆ (Around Palace Square, $$$, p. 221)

RUSSIAN/INTERNATIONAL

Russky Kitsch (Vasilevsky Island, $$, p. 233)

RUSSIAN/SEAFOOD

Restoran ☆☆ (Vasilevsky Island, $$$, p. 231)

SERBIAN/RUSSIAN

Black Cat, White Cat ☆ (Lower Nevsky-Smolny, $$, p. 227)

VEGETARIAN

Idiot (South of Nevsky, $, p. 230)

Troitsky Most (Vasilevsky Island, $, p. 233)

2 Around Palace Square & the Hermitage

EXPENSIVE

Hermitage Restaurant ✹✹✹ RUSSIAN/FRENCH   The location right on Palace Square is what draws people here, but the inventive cuisine and atmosphere are what keep them coming back. Above a labyrinth of dining halls, the vaulted stone ceilings give the place the feel of a secret treasure cavern; works by local artists hang in the corridors. Each dining room is distinct in style, from the table sizes and shapes to the silverware and window coverings. When crowds are thin (more likely on a weekday or mid-afternoon) you can choose which room suits your mood. The menu combines imperial-era favorites like pikeperch grilled with cepe mushrooms from the surrounding forests, and more modern French-inspired favorites such as a delicately seasoned veal tartare. You can even get a $10 hamburger if nothing else on the extensive menu is appealing.

8 Dvortsovaya Ploshchad (Palace Sq.). ✆ **812/314-4772.** www.hermitage.restoran.ru. Reservations recommended. Main courses $14–$50. AE, MC, V. Daily noon–midnight. Metro: Nevsky Prospekt.

MODERATE

NEP ✹ RUSSIAN   Named after Lenin's New Economic Policy, an attempt at state-run capitalism in the 1920s that was crushed by Stalin's collectivization campaign, this restaurant is political only in name. Its prime location on the corner of Palace Square and the Moika River makes it rather touristy, but the fare is decent and filling and the prices not as high as they could be in this locale. Play it safe and order the ground beef cutlets—or go all out and try the venison filet with bilberry and juniper, a modern rendition of traditional northern Russian fare. Sadly, the restaurant doesn't offer a view of its surroundings, since it's in the basement, but the ambience is convivial. The service can be warm or cold depending on the day and the waitstaff. Any mushroom dish is worth sampling; they are best in late summer and fall.

18 Palace Sq. ✆ **812/312-6057.** Main courses $15–$20. No credit cards. Daily noon–11:30pm. Metro: Nevsky Prospekt.

Tea Traditions

The best tea is drunk in St. Petersburg, and generally throughout Russia. Since China has a common border with Siberia, tea need not be transported by water to reach Moscow or St. Petersburg. Sea voyages are very bad for tea.

—Alexander Dumas, *Dictionary of Cuisine*

Russian tea traditions date back to the 17th century, when Czar Mikhail I received a gift of tea leaves from the Mongol Khans. Herbal teas date back much further, as Russians have long used drinks of boiled forest herbs to cure their ills. Today, tea—*chai* in Russian—remains Russians' hot drink of choice, and they're far more likely to quench thirst with a cup of tea than a glass of water. The teabag and busier schedules have encroached on tradition, but tea—and its attendant cakes and sandwiches—is still the first thing you're offered upon entering any Russian home. In the countryside, the samovar remains as crucial a part of Russian kitchen culture as the tea it brews inside. If your time and money allow it, take tea at a historic hotel while in Russia.

Where to Dine in St. Petersburg

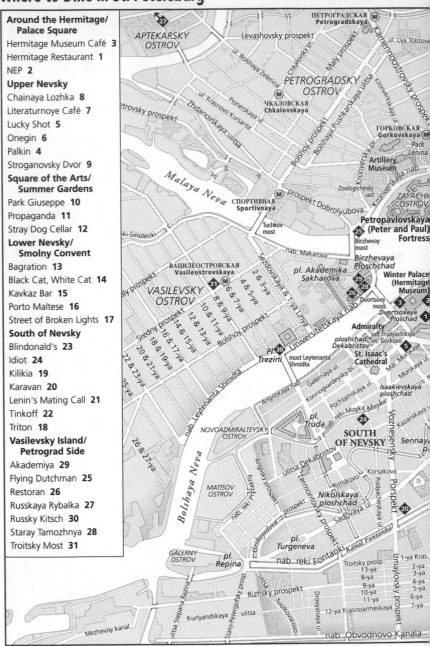

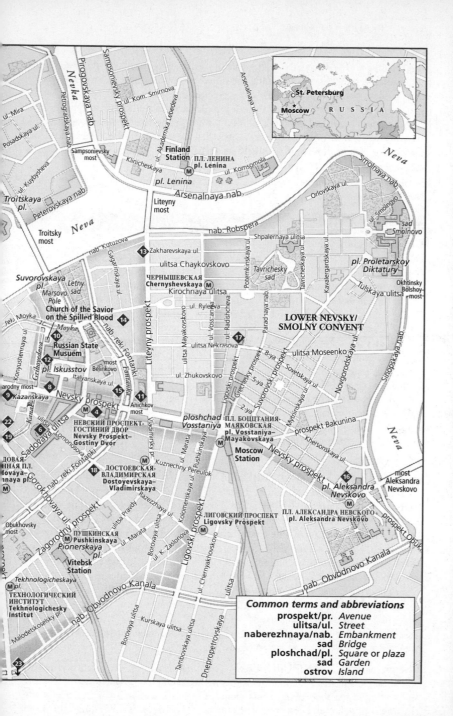

St. Petersburg

Moscow   R U S S I A

Nevka

Pirogovskaya nab.

Sampsonievsky prospekt

Petrogradskaya nab.

ul. Akademika Lebedeva

ul. Mira

Posadskaya ul.

Sampsonievsky most

Klinicheskaya

ul. Kuybysheva

Finland Station

ПЛ. ЛЕНИНА
pl. Lenina

ul. Komsomola

Arsenalnaya ul.

Troitskaya pl.

Petrovskaya nab.

pl. Lenina

Arsenalnaya nab.

Liteyny most

Neva

Troitsky most

Neva

nab. Kutuzova

nab. Robspera

Shpalernaya ulitsa

Orlovskaya ul.

Smolnaya nab.

Neva

ul. Smolnovo

sad Smolnovo

13 Zakharevskaya ul.

ulitsa Chaykovskovo

Potemkinskaya ul.

Tavrichesky sad

Tavricheskaya ul.

Kavalergardskaya ul.

pl. Proletarskoy Diktatury

Suvorovskaya pl.

Gagarinskaya ul.

ЧЕРНЫШЕВСКАЯ
Chernyshevskaya Ⓜ

Kirochnaya ulitsa

Parad naya ul.

Tulskaya ulitsa

Okhtinsky Bolshoy most

Letny sad

Marsovo Pole

reki Moyka

Church of the Savior on the Spilled Blood **14**

ul. Ryleeva

ul. Radishcheva

ul. Vossan ya

LOWER NEVSKY/ SMOLNY CONVENT

Sinopskaya nab.

Moyka

10

Russian State Museum

nab. reki Fontanki

ul. Mayakovskovo

Liteyny prospekt

ulitsa Nekrasova

17

 utitsa Moseenko

Konyushennaya ul.

Griboyedova

pl. Iskusstv

most Belinkovo

Italyanskaya ul.

ul. Zhukovskovo

ul. Vossanya

8-ya

5-ya

Suvorovski prospekt

Grechesky prospekt

Sovetskaya ul

ulitsa Moseenko

Novgorodskaya ul.

Mirtinskaya ul.

Neva

arodny most

9 **Kazanskaya**

Kanala

Sadovaya ulitsa

Nevsky prospekt

8

15

Fontanka

Anichkov most

11

2-ya

prospekt Bakunina

Khersonskaya ul.

22

6

19

4

Lomonosova

НЕВСКИЙ ПРОСПЕКТ- ГОСТИНЫЙ ДВОР
Nevsky Prospekt– Gostiny Dvor

Vladimirsky prospekt

ploshchad Vosstaniya

ПЛ. БОЩТАНИЯ- МАЯКОВСКАЯ
pl. Vosstaniya– Mayakovskaya

Ⓜ

Nevsky prospekt

most Aleksandra Nevskovo

ДОВАЯ- ННАЯ ПЛ.
novaya- naya pl.

Ⓜ

Sadovaya ul.

Gorokhovaya ul.

nab. reki Fontanki

18

ДОСТОЕВСКАЯ- ВЛАДИМИРСКАЯ
Dostoyevskaya– Vladimirskaya

Kuznechny Pereulok

ul. Marata

Pushkinskaya

Moscow Station

16

pl. Aleksandra Nevskovo

prospekt Obuk

Obukhovsky most

Zagorodny prospekt

ulitsa Pravdy

Razezzhaya ul.

Borovaya ul.

ul. K. Zaslonova

Kolomenskaya ul.

ПУШКИНСКАЯ
Pushkinskaya
Pionerskaya pl.

ul. Marata

ЛИГОВСКИЙ ПРОСПЕКТ
Ligovsky Prospekt Ⓜ

Ligovski prospekt

ПЛ. АЛЕКСАНДРА НЕВСКОГО
pl. Aleksandra Nevskovo

nab. Obvodnovo Kanala

Vitebsk Station

Tekhnologicheskaya

ТЕХНОЛОГИЧЕСКИЙ ИНСТИТУТ
Tekhnologichesky Institut Ⓜ

Malodetskoselsky pr.

Borovaya ulitsa

Kurskaya ulitsa

ul. Chernyakhovskovo

ulitsa

nab. Obvodnovo Kanala

Tambovskaya ulitsa

Dnepropetrovskaya ulitsa

23

Common terms and abbreviations

prospekt/pr.	*Avenue*
ulitsa/ul.	*Street*
naberezhnaya/nab.	*Embankment*
sad	*Bridge*
ploshchad/pl.	*Square* or *plaza*
sad	*Garden*
ostrov	*Island*

INEXPENSIVE

Hermitage Cafe RUSSIAN   This cafe is surprisingly small for the size of the museum, given that any visitor doing the museum justice will need a rest and a food stop at some point during the day. Once you get a seat (which can be a long wait), you'll see that the light, Art Nouveau hall is a pleasant place in which to eat. The cuisine is essentially Russian fast food, with limp mini-pizzas, roast chicken, and tasty little sandwiches. The Internet cafe across the hall offers hot drinks, sandwiches, and desserts, as well as dozens of terminals set up with links to museums of the world (along with regular Internet access).

Ground floor of Hermitage Museum in Winter Palace. Lunch plate $3–$8. No credit cards. Tues–Sun 11am–5:30pm. Metro: Nevsky Prospekt.

3 Upper Nevsky Prospekt

VERY EXPENSIVE

Palkin 🕷🕷🕷 RUSSIAN   If you want to splurge just once in St. Petersburg, do it here. The original Palkin opened in 1785 and became a mecca for aristocrats and intellectuals; today's reincarnation opened in 2002 on the same spot, displacing the movie theater that had stood here for decades. The interior today is at least as sumptuous as in the decadent days of Catherine the Great. A century after Catherine's reign, Tchaikovsky, Chekhov, and Dostoyevsky enjoyed generous servings and lively debates at Palkin. Today, members of Russia's 21st-century elite make it a frequent stop, including friends of St. Petersburg native (and Russian president) Vladimir Putin. Chefs research menus of past centuries, including wedding feasts for grand princes, to create dishes like sterlet baked in white wine with a sauce of cepes and crayfish. More standard fare includes a pot-au-feu of young chicken and vegetables cooked lightly enough to retain a rich flavor.

47 Nevsky Prospekt. ✆ 812/103-5371. Reservations required. Jackets preferred for men. Main courses $40–$60. AE, DC, MC, V. Daily 11am until last guest leaves. Metro: Nevsky Prospekt.

EXPENSIVE

Lucky Shot (Udachny Vystrel) 🕷 RUSSIAN   If you're feeling carnivorous, dedicate an evening to this urban version of a Russian hunting lodge. It offers a taste of the fruits of Russia's northern forests and its über-macho hunting culture. The reindeer and boar heads on the walls seem to encourage diners to regale their friends with tall tales of hunting adventures. The sauces made from wild mushrooms, nuts, bilberries, cranberries, and other forest delicacies are as good as—and sometimes better than—the meat. All ingredients are allegedly local, which means the meat menu varies by season. We had success with moose and boar, but it's always a good idea to ask your server or neighboring tables which meats are good that day. The "tender lard with fresh greens" is a delectable appetizer, despite its name. Lunchtime is calmer, with fewer tables of large, vodka-soaked parties.

3 Gorokhovaya Ulista. ✆ 812/140-1820. Reservations recommended. Main dishes $20–$40. AE, DC, MC, V. Metro: Nevsky Prospekt.

Onegin 🕷🕷 RUSSIAN/EUROPEAN   Avant-garde parties, 19th-century details, and a fashionista clientele combine in this popular restaurant. Much more accessible and serving tastier food than at first glance, Onegin is the brainchild of one of the city's most popular (and controversial) designers. The decor is a blinding mix of old and new, so whimsical it's almost too extreme for daytime viewing. The food is good

---

> **Tips**   **Street Smarts**
>
> Most street food in St. Petersburg is either inedible or risky, with one notable exception: the food at the triangular wooden shacks labeled TEREMOK (which looks like ТЕРЕМОК in Cyrillic, and means "little wooden house"). They sell Russian *bliny,* crepe-style pancakes made on the spot with a variety of fillings. Mushrooms with sour cream is a popular savory filling, and the numerous berry choices are winners for dessert. The huts are handy for satisfying mid-meal cravings or snacks for energetic children for $3 or less.

---

all day long, however, and the lunchtime crowd is less pretentious than the club crowd that takes over after dark. The Russian soups are as rich as anyone's grandmother could make, and the less traditional offerings, such as veal in lobster sauce with spinach puree, are similarly successful. If you just want a drink, sink into one of the lush dark couches and study the gravity-defying chandeliers. Prices are not as high as you'd expect at such a hip place. It's named after the hero of one of Pushkin's most-loved epics.

11 Sadovaya Ulitsa. ℰ **812/571-8384.** Reservations recommended on weekends. Main dishes $10–$40. AE, MC, V. Sun–Thurs 5pm–2am; Fri–Sat 5pm–5am. Metro: Gostiny Dvor.

MODERATE

Literaturnoye Café ℰ RUSSIAN   Sadly, a Kentucky Fried Chicken has taken over the original ground-floor hall of this 200-year-old standby, but the second floor remains a tribute to the 19th-century literary giants who dined and philosophized here. Alexander Pushkin's name has been most closely associated with the cafe, and his favorite dishes are listed on a separate menu page—*shchi* cabbage soup and baked creamed mushrooms top the list, both quite good. The rest of the menu is a rundown of standard Russian fare, satisfying but not stunning. The green lampshades lend romance to the evenings, but the cafe is also a good, calm spot for a quick cup of tea, coffee, or *sbiten,* a hot drink made from hot water, herbs, and honey. Residents still refer to the place as Beranger, the cafe's original 19th-century name. (The "literary" label came as a tourist draw much later.) Beware of the poor English translation of the menu, and don't be afraid to ask if something doesn't make sense. Live piano music is featured most evenings. On nice days, you can sit on the benches outside, which are close to Nevsky's bustle but slightly protected by greenery.

18 Nevsky Prospekt. ℰ **812/312-6057.** Main courses $12–$18. No credit cards. Daily noon–11:30pm. Metro: Nevsky Prospekt.

INEXPENSIVE

Chainaya Lozhka (Teaspoon) RUSSIAN   A sort of Russian cafeteria, this chain serves cheap, quick fare with a Russian emphasis. The beet-and-carrot salad, creamy ham-and-potato salad, marinated mushrooms, and cabbage soup are hardly haute cuisine, but they can satisfy midday hunger at unbeatable prices. Nothing is written in English, but the food is displayed at the counter, so you can just point to what you want. Despite its name, the teas are mediocre bag teas and the coffee is either watery or grainy, but all drinks are under a dollar. The place can get crowded, but turnover is quick. This is a safe, convenient choice if you're wandering Nevsky any time of day.

44 Nevsky Prospekt (among other locations). © 812/117-4657. Salads and main dishes $1–$5. No credit cards. Daily 7am–11pm. Metro: Nevsky Prospekt.

Stroganovsky Dvor (Stroganoff Courtyard) ⊛ RUSSIAN/EUROPEAN   This cafe is cool, cheap, and convenient, and the atmosphere is so bizarre it's worth experiencing. The two-story restaurant is housed in a huge transparent tent plopped in the courtyard of an 18th-century aristocratic mansion, and is decorated with statues and stylistic streetlamps. Heat lamps keep it toasty even in the subarctic winter, and the view of the recently renovated courtyard is delightful year-round. Customers can use special telephones placed at each table to call in orders—or to call occupants of other tables. Service is friendly and readily available. The Russky Ampir restaurant inside the mansion (run by the same company as the cafe) provides a more authentic and elegant way to appreciate this historic spot, but it's overpriced and overrated.

17 Nevsky Prospekt (inside courtyard). © 812/315-2315. Sandwiches $3–$5. No credit cards. Daily 24 hr. Metro: Nevsky Prospekt.

4 Square of the Arts up to Summer Gardens

EXPENSIVE

Park Giuseppe ⊛⊛ ITALIAN/RUSSIAN   The main reason to come here is the environment: You're almost inside Mikhailovsky Gardens, with a view of the Mikhailovsky Castle and the candy-colored domes of the Church on the Spilled Blood. The cozy, compact pink building has a delightful shaded terrace and artsy attic room. It's hard to imagine that in Soviet times this pavilion was a public toilet. Thankfully there's no remnant of that era left, and the only scents wafting out are those of hot tea and fresh flowers. The cuisine is Russian-style Italian, meaning thin-crust pizzas, Caesar salad with salmon, and plenty of fish. The service can be slow, so don't come here in a rush.

2B Canal Griboyedova (entrance across from church). © 812/571-7309. Main courses $8–$20. No credit cards. Daily 11am–3am. Metro: Gostiny Dvor.

Family-Friendly Restaurants

Because St. Petersburg children are usually fed at home by *Babushka* (Grandma) until adolescence, and few tourists come with small kids, few restaurants have been motivated to accommodate families. This is changing, thanks largely to international hotel and restaurant chains. The weekend brunch at **Corinthia Nevsky Palace** (p. 210) includes a playroom and kids' activities as well as many kid-palatable buffet options. **Russkaya Rybalka** has a children's play area and child's menu, and older kids may get a kick out of helping their parents fish off the pier. **Street of Broken Lights** is one of the few places local residents frequent with the whole family, and servers are child-accommodating. For quick food at all hours, Russian fast-food restaurant **Blindonald's** has a child's corner and familiar fare, with a focus on pancakes and mini-pies stuffed with jam, meat, or potatoes. **McDonald's, KFC,** and **Sbarro** are always safe bets for a highchair and baby-changing tables, though they don't generally have play equipment and are not as spacious as their outlets in American suburbs.

MODERATE

Propaganda *๕๕* INTERNATIONAL   This popular restaurant's name and Soviet-style decorations are decidedly tongue-in-cheek, concealing a relaxed, open, post-Communist atmosphere. It's an unbeatable lunch spot and a good choice for dinner, except on weekend nights when it gets crowded. The menu includes Russian favorites with a twist, such as the melt-in-your-mouth salmon *pelmeni* (like Russian ravioli), made with fresh fish blended with fresh greens and packed inside almost transparently thin dough. In a nod to the capitalist world, the menu also offers burgers with fries (pretty good for the Eastern bloc), as well as cheesecake made with Philadelphia cream cheese (mediocre). Healthy portions may leave you little room for dessert, anyway. Be sure to view the Lenin-themed restrooms. Books lining the back dining-room walls are yours for perusing, though they're in Russian only. The hall facing the Fontanka River offers an all-you-can-eat buffet lunch for less than $10.

44 Fontanka Naberezhnaya. ⓒ 812/275-4558. Main courses $8–$20. MC, V. Daily 24 hr. Metro: Mayakovskaya.

Stray Dog Cellar (Podval Brodyachy Sobaki) *๕* RUSSIAN/EUROPEAN   This was a mecca for Petersburg's artistic and literary ground-breakers in the early 20th century, who considered themselves "stray dogs" shunted aside by proper aristocratic society. The basement cafe reopened in 2001 after years of disrepair, and is again hosting poetry readings, one-act plays, sculpture shows, and live music. Anna Akhmatova hid here during the Civil War, and fellow poets Vladimir Mayakovsky and Oscar Meyerhold frequented the cafe early in their careers. History aside, this is a convenient place for a bite to eat, offering average Russian fare and a few departures. Stick to the Russian favorites, such as sturgeon, fresh or smoked salmon, and meat-based soups; avoid the adventurous dishes with exotic fruits. The back rooms get smoky at night.

5/4 Square of the Arts (Ploshchad Isskustv). ⓒ **812/315-7764.** Main courses $8–$14. No credit cards. Mon–Sat 11am–midnight. Metro: Gostiny Dvor.

5 Lower Nevsky Prospekt up to Smolny Cathedral

EXPENSIVE

Bagration *๕* GEORGIAN   This small, sleek hall is one of the nicest dining options in the gradually reviving neighborhood. The hall centers around an open grill sizzling with lamb kebabs and succulent spiced sausages. The fare is largely Georgian, with some Azerbaijani and Uzbek specialties available, such as regional variations on lamb-rice pilaf. The tasteful, silvery setting includes creative wine displays and Caucasus Mountain sabers mounted on the walls. The extensive selection of Georgian wines is worth sampling instead of the overpriced French offerings. Georgians often accompany meat with heavy, sweet wines, so if you'd prefer something else, make that clear to the server. Customers include neighbors stopping in for a quick *khachapuri* (a sort of sauceless, meatless pizza with a delicious mélange of Georgian cheeses), nouveau riche Georgians, and a few St. Petersburg–based Westerners.

5/19 Liteiny Prospekt. ⓒ **812/272-6046.** Reservations suggested. Main courses $13–$35. AE, MC, V. Daily noon–midnight. Metro: Chernyshevskaya.

MODERATE

Black Cat, White Cat (Chornaya Koshka, Bely Kot) *๕* SERBIAN/RUSSIAN   This is a top choice for lunch or dinner in the once-neglected neighborhood around Chernyshevskaya metro station, which now boasts numerous antiques stores and historic buildings undergoing long-overdue renovations. Named after a Serbian film that won a cult following in Russia, the restaurant offers cuisine with a Serbian focus as well as plenty of Russian and international standards. The good roasted meats are grilled on a spit in the middle of the hall. You can also sample rice-based salads and tangy sausages. At night the understated black-and-white hall turns disco, the black lights go on, and you can no longer tell what color your stuffed tomatoes are.

13/15 Ulitsa Pestelya. ℂ 812/279-7430. Main courses $7–$15. MC, V. Metro: Chernyshevskaya.

Kavkaz Bar ✿✿ GEORGIAN   For expats and visitors, this is St. Petersburg's most popular spot at which to sample cuisine from the former Soviet state of Georgia. Its Caucasus Mountain spices and fruits are not found in Russian cooking. Cozy and tastefully decorated with Georgian pottery and tapestries, the restaurant is just a block north of Nevsky but the atmosphere is relaxed. Garlic is used liberally, so if you'd prefer a dish without it, be sure to ask. Try the enormous *khinkali,* spiced meat dumplings you're supposed to eat with your hands; the tandoor-style chicken (chicken *tabaka*); or the eggplant slices slathered in walnut-garlic paste. Meat dishes come with *tkemali,* a sweet and spicy sauce made from Georgian sour plums; plus you get stalks of fresh cilantro, dill, and lemony *cheremsha* to munch on. The food is reasonably priced, but the wines, mostly Georgian and French, cost more than they should. If you want to try Georgian wine, stick with the dry reds. Don't be turned off by Kavkaz's cheesy ads in the local magazines and brochures found at most hotels.

18 Karavannaya Ulitsa. ℂ 812/312-1665. Main courses $6–$15. AE, MC, V. Daily 11am–10pm. Metro: Mayakovskaya.

Porto Maltese ✿ MEDITERRANEAN   The seafaring theme starts with the porthole in the door, which opens directly onto a fish counter spilling with octopus, lobster, sturgeon, and more. Though the restaurant is nominally Maltese and offers Mediterranean seafood, the menu favors fish caught in the rivers and lakes surrounding St. Petersburg, such as pikeperch and *som,* a kind of catfish. The octopus and squid are good but are shipped in and not as fresh as the local fare. The salad bar—a relative rarity in St. Petersburg—is also seafood-centered, with shellfish salads and several versions of Baltic herring. Fish is sold by weight and priced per 100 grams (3.8 oz.). Porto Maltese is one of the best dining options at this far end of Nevsky.

174 Nevsky Prospekt. ℂ 812/271-7677. Main courses $15–$50. MC, V. Daily noon–midnight. Metro: Ploshchad Alexandra Nevskogo.

INEXPENSIVE

Street of Broken Lights (Ulitsa Razbitykh Fonarei) ✿ (Kids) RUSSIAN   The main draw here is the extensive take-out menu, something unheard of elsewhere in town (other than at McDonald's). The decor and menu borrow from the popular Russian television series after which the restaurant is named, featuring cops and neighborhood dramas. The show and the restaurant are popular among families, and this is one of the few places Russians will take their kids. If the weather's nice, head to nearby Taurida Gardens after picking up a potato-and-ham salad *(salat Olivier);* small open-faced sandwiches *(buterbrody)* with cheese, cucumber, smoked meat, or fish; or a plate of grilled pork.

34 Ulitsa Radishcheva. ℂ 812/275-9935. Main courses $8–$20. AE, MC, V. Daily noon–midnight. Metro: Chernyshevskaya.

6 South of Nevsky

VERY EXPENSIVE

Triton 🐟🐟 INTERNATIONAL   Perhaps the city's most rarefied dining establishment, Triton is the place to go for a luxury seafood experience and for an evening out with the New Russian rich. The glass floor in the foyer reveals an aquarium beneath your feet, and a waterfall cascades tastefully down the main hall. Even the fish swimming in the transparent toilet tanks manage to look sophisticated instead of kitschy. The restaurant caters to the evolving New Russians, satisfying their need for extravagance but in a hushed atmosphere with subtle service—as opposed to the fawning servers and gaudy floor shows popular elsewhere. A harpist accompanies dinner service. Try one of the several kinds of caviar—they're pricy, but so is everything in this restaurant—and the lobster, surprisingly succulent given that it's shipped in. The foie gras is the finest choice if you don't want fish. Coffee is served with much ceremony. Be prepared for everyone from the maitre d' to the coat-check person to study your attire; you're expected to study their carefully designed, nautically inspired uniforms, too.

67 Naberezhnaya Fontanki (Fontanka Embankment). ℂ 812/310-9449. Reservations recommended. No dress code but a jacket for men is recommended. Main courses $28–$60. AE, MC, V. Mon–Sat noon–2am. Sometimes closes for special events. Metro: Dostoyevskaya or Vladimirskaya.

EXPENSIVE

Kilikia 🐟 ARMENIAN   For an elegant, nourishing, and leisurely dinner or hearty lunch, come to Kilikia. Even if you know nothing of Armenian cuisine, you're bound to find something familiar and satisfying. It resembles Middle Eastern cooking, with added fruits and spices found in the Caucasus Mountains. The grilled lamb and beef dishes are excellent, as is the stewlike *teva*. The vegetable-based appetizers can constitute a meal in themselves; try anything with eggplant or grape leaves. Don't tell the server it tastes like Turkish food, however—hostilities between the nations remain fierce nearly a century after the 1915 genocide of Armenians during the Ottoman Empire. Even the restaurant's name is controversial, referring to a traditionally Armenian region that's now in Turkey. The restaurant is a favorite of Petersburg's extensive Armenian community, particularly for special occasions. The business lunch is a cheaper option than dinner and quite popular, so you may have to wait for a table if you come after 1pm.

26/40 Gorokhovaya Ulitsa. ℂ 812/327-2208. Main courses $12–$20. AE, MC, V. Metro: Sennaya Ploshchad.

MODERATE

Karavan 🐟 CENTRAL ASIAN   This little taste of central Asia is a fun way to escape a rainy day in Petersburg and immerse yourself in foliage, spices, and fruits. The little streams running through the hall are more evocative of St. Petersburg's canals than of arid Uzbekistan, but they're a nice touch. They must be crossed by tiny bridges, so watch your feet. Diners lounge on deep couches piled with brightly patterned pillows, in a variation of the platform-style seating arrangement common in central Asia. The menu includes several Azerbaijani and Georgian dishes as well as the Central Asian *manty* (steamed dumplings stuffed with spiced ground lamb) and *plov* (rice pilaf of lamb, carrots, and raisins). Try the yogurt drinks or the *cutaby*— pancake-shaped pies of cheese, chopped greens, or ground meat stuffed into ultra-thin dough. Russians generally order several appetizers and a selection of grilled meats for the whole table to share.

46 Voznesensky Prospekt. ℂ 812/310-5678. www.carawan.ru. Reservations necessary on weekends. Main courses $8–$20. AE, MC, V. Daily 1pm–1am. Metro: Sadovaya.

Lenin's Mating Call (Zov Ilicha) ☞ RUSSIAN/EUROPEAN Soviet kitsch meets soft porn in this wacky restaurant and bar. It's divided into two halls: The "Soviet" room has busts of Lenin hanging from the ceiling like stalactites, some of them characteristically stern and some downright goofy, while the "anti-Soviet" room is full of parody posters, busts of the extravagant New Russian, and references to drugs and sex. The menu (the same in both rooms) offers Soviet choices—mostly Russian standards and a few items from the former Soviet republics—and anti-Soviet ones, featuring bourgeois dishes such as fondue and cracked crab. The Russian dishes such as marinated mushrooms and herring are especially tasty. TV screens throughout the restaurant (and in the bathrooms) show erotic films in the evening, so only those 18 and over are allowed in. If you feel daring, the restroom walls can be made translucent. There's live music Thursday through Saturday.

34 Kazanskaya Ulitsa. ℂ 812/117-8641. Main courses $11–$25. AE, MC, V. Daily 1pm–2am. Metro: Sadovaya or Sennaya Ploshchad.

Tinkoff ☞☞ INTERNATIONAL The brewery-restaurant concept didn't exist in Russia until Tinkoff came along in 1998, and now this cavernous space is the benchmark for copycat bars here and around the country. The lively dinner spot is popular among Russian and expat yuppies, with its sushi bar, beer hall, and dance hall, all offering an extensive Russian-German menu—and, of course, beer. Tinkoff's own brew comes in several unfiltered flavors and some filtered ones, from pale white to deep dark, and includes a nonalcoholic choice. The beer-based cocktails are potent stuff. If the Tinkoff brand doesn't impress you, try one of the German, Irish, or Japanese beers on offer. The Caesar salad, a trendy menu item in Russia of late, is copious and tasty, and the quail with figs is surprisingly subtle for such a larger-than-life restaurant. The German sausages are rather rubbery. The room containing the stage blares recorded music when no one is playing live, so it's loud any time of day; ask for a different room if that bothers you. The place fills up fast on weekend nights.

7 Kazanskaya Ulitsa. ℂ 812/118-5566. Reservations suggested on weekends. Main courses $12–$35. AE, DC, MC, V. Daily 11am–midnight. Seasonal closings. Metro: Sadovaya or Sennaya Ploshchad.

INEXPENSIVE

Blindonalds RUSSIAN The tacky name makes this place sound worse than it is. It's not really the Russian version of McDonald's; it's a cheap place to get quick food, for here or to go. Baked potatoes, small meat pastries, and the *bliny* (pancakes) that give the restaurant its name make this a low-budget way to try local fare. Don't expect friendly service or elegant presentation, but do expect to fill up fast. The *pelmeny* (meat ravioli) are a good cold-weather choice, steaming and heaped with the sauce of your choice (Russians prefer sour cream, or *smetana*). Two of its easily reached locations are listed below.

18 Zhukovskogo. ℂ 812/557-0350. Full meal $3–$5. No credit cards. Daily, noon until last guest leaves. Metro: Chernyshevskaya. Also at 186 Moskovsky Prospekt. ℂ 812/327-9755. Metro: Park Pobedy.

Idiot VEGETARIAN This bohemian basement on the foggy banks of Moika Canal, named after one of Dostoyevsky's novels, attracts a fair share of brooding, philosophical types of all nationalities. It bills itself as a vegetarian restaurant, and there is indeed no meat on the menu, but most people come here to warm up with a glass of mulled wine or the complimentary welcome shot of vodka, or to chill out with a book and a cool drink in the back room. The food is homey and satisfying, especially anything with the wild mushrooms that Russians are so expert at preparing, as well as the miniature pies *(pirozhki)* stuffed with cabbage, apricots, or potatoes. Idiot is a great place to stop while wandering the Moika, since there's nowhere else to eat nearby.

82 Moika Canal. (C) 812/315-1675. Main courses $3–$8. No credit cards. Daily, noon until last guest leaves. Metro: Sennaya Ploshchad or Nevsky Prospekt.

7 Vasilevsky Island & the Petrograd Side

EXPENSIVE

Flying Dutchman (Letuchy Gollandets) INTERNATIONAL   The most eccentric of the overpriced ship-restaurants along the north shore of the Neva, the Flying Dutchman has a 24-hour fitness center among its amenities so you can burn off your dinner, and a beauty salon to clean you up afterwards. The top-floor restaurant, the dance club downstairs, and the gym have floor-to-ceiling windows with views of the Peter and Paul Fortress or of the river and the Hermitage on the opposite bank. This is a good place for a big party or a special night out, but it's not very subtle or intimate. Though there's no official dress code, hosts may snub you in favor of better-dressed customers. Cuisine is all over the world map, from caviar on ice to duck à l'orange and the ubiquitous sushi. Quality is overall good, but mostly you're paying for location and atmosphere, not the food.

6 Mitnenskaya Naberezhnaya. (C) 812/336-3737. Reservations recommended weekends. Main courses $15–$40. AE, MC, V. Daily 24 hr. Metro: Gorkovskaya.

Restoran && RUSSIAN/SEAFOOD   This excellent restaurant achieves elegance in cuisine and decor through simplicity, a rare thing in this city of elaborate imperial tastes. The chefs focus on reinterpreting Russian classics with an emphasis on fish from the Baltic and nearby rivers. The unvarnished wood and the stone vaulted arches make the place feel medieval, but the food's presentation and preparation are fully modern. A table of homemade liqueurs made from cranberry, ginger, juniper, or garlic is the first thing you pass; farther along is a tea table with a samovar and homemade jams; and deeper inside is a salad bar focusing on marinated vegetables and pickled fish. The appetizers are extensive and can be combined to make a full meal. Otherwise, try the pike quenelles or the tender rabbit with braised vegetables. The staff is accommodating but not overbearing, and though they welcome tour groups, the restaurant doesn't feel at all touristy.

2 Tamozhenny Pereulok. (C) 812/327-8979. Reservations recommended on weekends. Main courses $12–$18. AE, DC, MC, V. Daily noon–midnight. Metro: Vasileostrovskaya.

Russkaya Rybalka (Russian Fishing Expedition) & (Kids) RUSSIAN   For a more hands-on dining experience, head to this island escape not far from the city center and catch your own meal. This restaurant took over a territory of ponds and now harvests local fish that customers can reel in themselves. The chefs then do the dirty work of cleaning, and prepare the fish for you to order. Catfish, eel, carp, crayfish, sterlet, and even sturgeon are among the offerings, but the choice depends on the season. Some months only one type of fish is big enough to eat, limiting you to the fish they bring in from outside. Ducks and swans populate the ponds, too, but are not on the menu. Among the dozens of homemade sauces, the garlic-almond cream sauce is the standout. You can sit on the sunny terrace, or you can rent out the little heated wooden huts that seat six to eight and have your food brought to you there—huts cost $55 for 1 hour, $70 for 2 hours or more. The restaurant itself is welcoming and offers a generous

---

Impressions

On the tray were herb-brandy, different kinds of vodka, pickled mushrooms, rye-cakes made with buttermilk, honey in the comb, still mead and sparkling mead, apples, plain nuts and roasted nuts, and nuts in honey. . . . preserves made with honey and with sugar, a ham and a fowl that had just been roasted to a turn.

—Leo Tolstoy, *War and Peace*

---

children's play area. The wooded location is a plus and a minus: You get to enjoy fresh air and exhaust-free outdoor eating, but you have to find your way here first. In a taxi or car, it's just 10 or 15 minutes from the city center, but on public transport you have to rely on a trolleybus ride from the metro stop that sometimes takes 30 minutes.

Krestovsky Island, 11 Yuzhnaya Doroga. ⓒ 812/323-9813. www.russian-fishing.ru. Reservations recommended, especially in summer. Fish sold by weight; main courses $15–$50. AE, MC, V. Daily 11am–midnight. Fishing ponds heated in winter but selection is better Apr–Oct. Metro: Krestovsky Ostrov, then trolleybus #6, 11, or 40; ask the driver for "Russkaya Rybalka."

Staraya Tamozhnya (Old Customs House) ⭑⭑ FRENCH/RUSSIAN   This top-notch restaurant is as ornate as its neighbor Restoran (above) is austere. Scarlet and gold plates are carefully set upon gold-embroidered table linens, furniture is artfully carved and polished, and even the flowery menu is constantly redesigned. The restaurant celebrates French culinary traditions the way Russian aristocracy of the 18th and 19th centuries did. Today it's popular with well-to-do Russian and foreign executives and visitors on a splurge. The menu is updated according to seasonal availability. A special truffle menu comes out in January, and the pot-au-feu with lobster pops up a few times a year. Keep an eye out for the pheasant with pine nuts and endive. The French cheeses and three-chocolate fondue are always divine. The wine cellar corner is cozy, and a light jazz ensemble plays most evenings. In a nod to its Russian location, the restaurant hosts vodka-tasting sessions.

1 Tamozhenny Pereulok. ⓒ 812/327-8980. Reservations required for dinner. Main courses $21–$45. AE, DC, MC, V. Daily noon–midnight. Metro: Vasileostrovskaya.

MODERATE

Akademiya ⭑ EUROPEAN   Though it can't seem to decide whether it's mass-market or elitist, Akademiya's food is consistently good. The place is not as stylish as the other restaurants on this corner (see Restoran and Staraya Tamozhnya, above), but it's less expensive. The vaulted brick ceilings provide good acoustics during live music performances on weekends. The shelves along the walls hold a haphazard collection of books, but they appear to be more for show than for actual reading. Menu highlights include the pikeperch and the T-bone steak, a cut of meat you don't find often in Russia. The pungent "hangover cabbage stew" is an acquired taste, but its fans insist it does the trick after a vodka-drenched night. The restaurant is sometimes closed for private parties, so it's a good idea to call in advance even though reservations are not necessary.

62 Birzhevoy Proezd. ⓒ 812/327-8949. Main courses $8–$50. AE, DC, MC, V. Daily, noon until last customer leaves. Metro: Vasileostrovskaya.

Russky Kitsch RUSSIAN/INTERNATIONAL   This over-the-top theme restaurant is primarily a way for wealthy New Russians to make fun of themselves, but it also has creative food and a stunning view across the Neva towards the Winter Palace and its environs. Many of the menu and decorative details are inside jokes that will be lost on non-Russians, but the overall effect is unmistakable. Ceiling frescoes imitate frescoes in imperial palaces but feature Russian pop icons and politicians of the past decade (including, inexplicably, Arnold Schwarzenegger). Menus are presented in tomes of Lenin's works, and include such un-Bolshevik items as kiwi juice (strange) and cauliflower saffron soup (delicious). Despite the extravagant atmosphere, prices are mostly reasonable. Ask for a seat on the glass-enclosed terrace overlooking the river. It feels airy and cheery even in the deepest of winter. The corner room has raspberry-colored walls in homage to the favored shade of sport jacket preferred by an entire class of Russian thugs-turned-businessmen.

25 Universitetskaya Naberezhnaya. ✆ 812/325-1122. Main courses $8–$16. AE, DC, MC, V. Daily noon–2am. Metro: Vasileostrovskaya.

INEXPENSIVE

Troitsky Most (Trinity Bridge) VEGETARIAN   This small, local chain specializes in clean living and meatless cuisine, regardless of which continent the food comes from. Indian, Italian, Georgian, and even Russian dishes make it to the menu, but no alcohol is served. The whole place is smoke-free, perhaps the only such venue in Petersburg. Try the fresh pastas or the mixed fruit-and-vegetable salads. The house specialty is a strange potato-tofu-cheese vegetable casserole. Decor is pseudo-Indian, the atmosphere is laid-back to the extreme, and the prices are low.

Troitsky Most has two locations north of the Neva, one on up-and-coming Vasilevsky Island, and the other near the Peter and Paul Fortress.

6th Liniya, Vasilevsky Island. ✆ 812/327-4622. Main courses $3–$7. No credit cards. Daily 11am–11pm. Metro: Vasileostrovskaya. Also at 2 Malaya Posadskaya Ulitsa. ✆ 812/232-6693. Metro: Gorkovskaya.

Exploring St. Petersburg

St. Petersburg is a coherent and carefully planned city, and the value of its individual buildings is best appreciated when you take a step back and view the ensemble to which the buildings contribute. Sculpted parks and curving canals are part of the plan, and well worth a detour—though be sure to have a map in English *and* Russian, because off the main roads, street signs are usually in the Cyrillic alphabet.

The city is Russia's principal port, and its geography and history make it immediately distinguishable from Moscow. St. Petersburg did not grow gradually from provincial backwater to major metropolis like its southern rival, and it was never the capital of world communism—this city was built up from the bogs, fast and furious, to be an imperial capital, and it served as such for 2 centuries. St. Petersburg is better at celebrating the past than at choosing a direction for the future, which means that museums, palaces, and ballet and opera houses are where its strengths lie; daring modern art and architecture are not. The Hermitage is a crucial stop but far from the only museum you should visit on this trip.

St. Petersburg's relative youth and the secular ideas of its founder, Peter the Great, mean that cathedrals play a less crucial and less religious role here than in 850-year-old Moscow. Still, your visit should include a church or two; the ones listed below are architecturally or historically notable. Some cathedrals remain museums as they were in Soviet days, but many are again functioning churches and hold services throughout the day. For hints on avoiding offense while visiting Orthodox cathedrals, see the box "Visiting Churches" on p. 129.

Museum entrance fees are often higher for foreign visitors than for Russians, but on par with those in western Europe. Be prepared to surrender your coat or jacket at the coat check any time of year (see the box "Cult of the Coat Check" on p. 134). Be aware that many museums are closed one day a month for "sanitary days"—especially important to note if you're only in town for a few days.

1 Hermitage & Environs

The State Hermitage Museum and the Winter Palace 🎨🎨🎨   The Winter Palace would be a museum itself even if it didn't hold the Hermitage Museum, one of the world's largest and most valuable collections of fine art. The patterned parquet flooring, dazzling chandeliers, and extravagant and turbulent history of the 1750s-era palace almost distract from the riches on display—but not quite. Most of the Hermitage's masterpieces lie in warehouses or the museum basement, but they're hardly missed; it's exhausting enough to view the permanent collection which, among other treasures, includes more French artworks than any museum outside France. Hall nos. 185 to 189 are worth a glance even if their labels RUSSIAN CULTURE and STATE ROOMS

The Siege of Leningrad

Nearly everyone in St. Petersburg today has a family member who lived through the 900-day siege of the city by Nazi forces, and mere mention of the humanity-crushing blockade still brings tears to the eyes of those who survived it. About 1 million people died during the siege of the city then known as Leningrad, most of them civilians who wasted away of hunger, cold, and disease. From September 1941 to January 1944, residents of this former imperial capital were reduced to eating leather belts, stray dogs, and even human corpses to survive. Antique furniture was stuffed into stoves to survive three winters without heat or electricity. All the while, shells from German aircraft rained down on the city's monuments, accompanying Leningraders' descent into desperation. The only source of supplies to the city was the Road of Life, a rough and remote ice road cut across Lake Ladoga during the first winter of the siege. Though Russians credit Stalin with breaking the back of Nazi forces, the Soviet dictator is also blamed for prolonging Leningrad's suffering by not doing more to end the blockade or to boost supplies to the city.

Today the politics of this period are largely forgotten, and the siege is viewed as evidence of the city's resilience and endurance. St. Petersburg has several museums about the *blokad,* as Russians refer to it, and monuments to victims of the siege; three are listed in this chapter. Even if you don't visit one (they're not for the weak-kneed), keep an eye out for shell wounds on city monuments such as St. Isaac's Cathedral, or for plaques around town showing residents which sides of city streets to favor to avoid shelling. Harrison Salisbury's book *The 900 Days* remains the most vivid and respected chronicle of the blockade in English, 40 years after it was first published.

I did not on this day forget
The bitter years of oppression and of evil
But in a blinding flash I understood
It was not I, but you who suffered and waited
...
My Motherland with the wreath of thorns
And the dark rainbow over your head
I love you—I cannot otherwise—
And you and I are one again, as before.

—Olga Berggolts, St. Petersburg poet, writing on the day of the German invasion, June 22, 1941, of her love for her country despite being imprisoned in Stalin's purges of the 1930s

don't enthrall you. The Pavilion Hall, with mosaic tables and floors, marble fountains, engineering marvels, and a wraparound view, is a favorite for the whole family. The Impressionist and more recent works, including two rooms of early Picasso, are a must-see, though they're in plainer rooms on the third floor that can be stuffy and

Exploring St. Petersburg

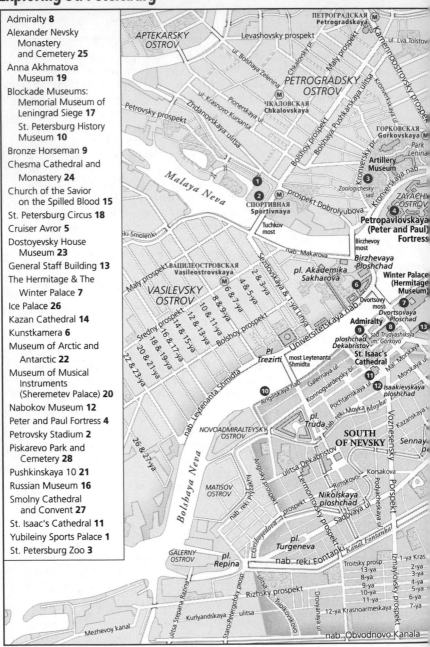

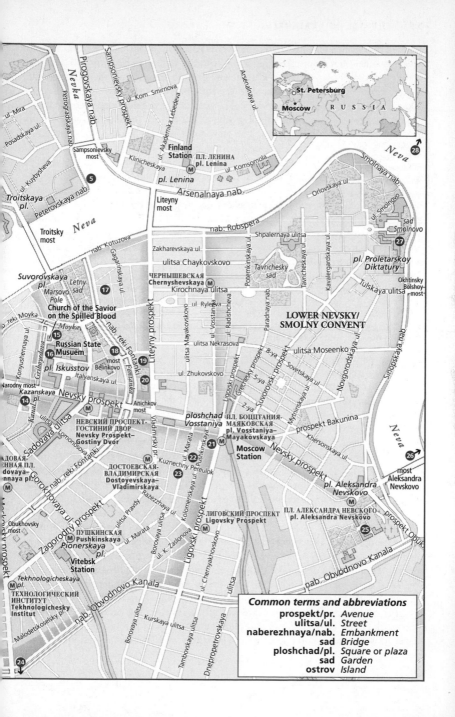

St. Petersburg

★ Moscow   R U S S I A

Nevka

Pirogovskaya nab.

ul. Mira

Sampsonievskiy prospekt

Petrogradskaya nab.

ul. Kom. Smirnova

ul. Akademika Lebedeva

Arsenalnaya ul.

Posadskaya ul.

ul. Kuybysheva

Sampsonievskiy most

Klinicheskaya

5

Finland Station
ПЛ. ЛЕНИНА
pl. Lenina
Ⓜ
ul. Komsomola

pl. Lenina

Troitskaya pl.

Peterovskaya nab.

Arsenalnaya nab.

Neva

Liteyny most

Smolnaya nab.

Neva

28

Troitsky most

nab. Kutuzova

Gagarinskaya ul.

nab. Robspera

Orlovskaya ul.

ul. Smolnovo

sad Smolnovo

27

Zakharevskaya ul.

ulitsa Chaykovskovo

Shpalernaya ulitsa

pl. Proletarskoy Diktatury

Suvorovskaya pl.

Letny sad

17

ЧЕРНЫШЕВСКАЯ
Chernyshevskaya Ⓜ
Kirochnaya ulitsa

Potemkinskaya ul.

Tavrichesky sad

Tavricheskaya ul.

Kavalergardskaya ul.

Tulskaya ulitsa

Okhtinsky Bolshoy most

Marsovo Pole

Church of the Savior on the Spilled Blood

ul. Ryleeva

ul. Vosstaniya

Radishcheva

LOWER NEVSKY/ SMOLNY CONVENT

o. reki Moyka

Moyka

15

nab. reki Fontanka

Liteyny prospekt

ulitsa Mayakovskovo

ulitsa Nekrasova

Paradnaya nab

ulitsa Moseenko

Novgorodskaya ul.

Sinopskaya nab.

Russian State Musuem

16

18

most Belinkovo

Fontanka

19

ul. Zhukovskovo

8-ya

Grechesky prospekt

Suvorovskiy prospekt

5-ya

Sovetskaya ul.

Myrinskaya ul.

pl. Iskusstov

Italyanskaya ul.

20

Narodny most

Kazanskaya pl.

14

Nevsky prospekt

Anichkov most

ploshchad Vosstaniya

ПЛ. БОЩТАНИЯ-МАЯКОВСКАЯ
pl. Vosstaniya–Mayakovskaya

2-ya

prospekt Bakunina

Kanal Gribyedova

Konyushennaya ul.

ulitsa Lomonosova

НЕВСКИЙ ПРОСПЕКТ-ГОСТИНИЙ ДВОР
Nevsky Prospekt–Gostiny Dvor Ⓜ

Vladimirsky pr.

Moscow Station

Nevsky prospekt

Khersonskaya ul.

Neva

26

Sadovaya ulitsa

АДОВАЯ-ЕННАЯ ПЛ.
dovaya-nnaya pl.

Gorokhovaya ul.

nab. reki Fontanki

ДОСТОЕВСКАЯ-ВЛАДИМИРСКАЯ
Dostoyevskaya–Vladimirskaya Ⓜ

Kuznechny Pereulok

ul. Marata

Pushkinskaya

21

22

23

Razezzhaya ul.

Kolomenskaya ulitsa

pl. Aleksandra Nevskovo Ⓜ

most Aleksandra Nevskovo

prospekt Obuk

Obukhovsky most

Zagorodny prospekt

ПУШКИНСКАЯ
Pushkinskaya Ⓜ
Pionerskaya pl.

ul. Pravdy

ul. Marata

Borovaya ulitsa

ul. K. Zaslonova

ul. Chernyakhovskovo

ЛИГОВСКИЙ ПРОСПЕКТ
Ligovsky Prospekt Ⓜ

Ligovskiy prospekt

ПЛ. АЛЕКСАНДРА НЕВСКОГО-
pl. Aleksandra Nevskovo

25

nab. Obvodnovo Kanala

Vitebsk Station

Tekhnologicheskaya Ⓜ pl.

ТЕХНОЛОГИЧЕСКИЙ ИНСТИТУТ
Tekhnologichesky Institut

nab. Obvodnovo Kanala

Kurskaya ulitsa

Borovaya ulitsa

Tambovskaya ulitsa

Dnepropetrovskaya

ulitsa

Malodetskoselsky pr.

24

Common terms and abbreviations
prospekt/pr.	Avenue
ulitsa/ul.	Street
naberezhnaya/nab.	Embankment
sad	Bridge
ploshchad/pl.	Square or plaza
sad	Garden
ostrov	Island

237

crowded in summer. Crowds are thinner in the Antiquities halls on the ground floor, which include relics from early, pre-Slavic tribes as well as riches from the Greeks, Romans, and Egyptians. Italian, Dutch, and Spanish masters are well represented, though Russia's greatest art is housed in the Russian Museum across town. Planning is key to any Hermitage visit, and an online tour can be a great preparation. Mornings tend to be full of Russian school groups except in July and August, which tend to be full of European tour groups. The audioguide is quite helpful, but the official English-speaking guides hovering around the entrance can offer more detail and nuance. Be sure to ask if you can set your own itinerary or if they will show you only specific rooms. It's worth checking the museum website before you go in order to get a sense of what you want to focus on, and to see which halls are closed for renovations. A bank machine and post office are available on the ground floor. Spread around the city are four other parts of the Hermitage Museum complex: The General Staff Building, Menshikov Palace, Winter Palace of Peter the Great, and the Museum of Lomonosov Porcelain Factory. Allow yourself a full morning or afternoon in the Hermitage itself—or a full day, if you can spare it. You won't regret it.

1 Palace Sq. Entrance to Hermitage main collection: through courtyard of Winter Palace, from Palace Sq. © 812/110-9079. www.hermitage.ru. Admission to Hermitage Museum $13 adults, $3 students with ID, free for those under 18. English tours for up to 5 people by official museum guides $55. Admission to other buildings in the Hermitage collection is $7.50 for each one, or you can buy a $25 ticket that allows entrance to the main museum and three others of your choice over the course of 1 day. Main museum Tues–Sat 10:30am–6pm; Sun and Russian holidays 10:30am–5pm. Ticket office closes 1 hr. before museum closing. Metro: Nevsky Prospekt.

2 Around Palace Square

The Winter Palace forms just one element of the magnificent architectural ensemble of **Palace Square (Dvortsovaya Ploshchad)** ✸✸✸ , the city's most important plaza. Shaped like a truncated piece of pie, this square isn't large by Russian standards, but it is certainly grand. It was not part of Peter's original plan for the city, but grew up over the 18th and 19th centuries to accommodate the Winter Palace and the curved General Staff Headquarters, while opening up at an angle toward the Admiralty and the Neva beyond. It achieves a perfect sense of balance despite its unusual form, and offers a stunning—and intentional—vista of the city's elegant lines from any given point. Its architectural beauty did little to protect it from the city's political upheavals, and the square became a center of fermenting dissent in the century leading up to the Russian Revolution. The unrest culminated in the Bolshevik seizure of the Winter Palace via the square that quashed all hope of retaining aristocratic rule. For decades after the seat of Russian power was moved to Moscow, Palace Square was the staging ground for obligatory displays of Communist solidarity and might—until the end of the Soviet regime saw it again become a forum for anti-government expression. Politics rarely touch the square today; instead, it fills with in-line skaters and tour buses. For a calmer experience of the square, show up early in the morning. Stand in front of the Alexander Column—a 600-ton monolith topped by a cross-carrying angel, built under Czar Alexander II to celebrate Russian victory over Napoleon—and imagine all that this square has seen.

Exploring St. Peter and Paul Fortress

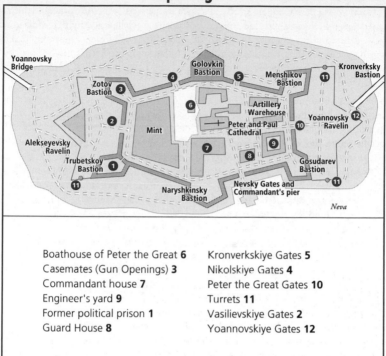

Boathouse of Peter the Great **6**

Casemates (Gun Openings) **3**

Commandant house **7**

Engineer's yard **9**

Former political prison **1**

Guard House **8**

Kronverkskiye Gates **5**

Nikolskiye Gates **4**

Peter the Great Gates **10**

Turrets **11**

Vasilievskiye Gates **2**

Yoannovskiye Gates **12**

The square's chief element after the Winter Palace is the **General Staff Building** (**Generalny Shtab;** ✆ **812/110-9079**). Its facade, bending around the square for nearly half a mile, was designed to enclose several facilities, the army's General Staff Headquarters being just one of them. The czarist-era Ministry of Finance and Foreign Ministry were housed on the left as you look from Palace Square, linked to the General Staff Building by an unusual, three-piece triumphal arch celebrating Russia's victories against Napoleon, Turkey, and Sweden. The Library of the General Staff is still housed there and is closed to the public; its collection was once considered among the world's best military libraries. The left wing is now part of the Hermitage and houses temporary exhibits. The city hopes to link the buildings with the Winter Palace via an underground passageway, and the Guggenheim Museum hopes to open a St. Petersburg museum in the General Staff Building in the future. Admission to exhibits is $7 adults and children over 7. It's open Tuesday through Saturday from 10:30am to 6pm; Sunday from 10:30am to 5pm.

Overlooking Palace Square from a distance to the west is the **Admiralty (Admiral-teistvo)** ⭐⭐⭐ , once a fortified shipyard. It is now a naval academy that sadly is not open to the public. It's such a crucial St. Petersburg monument, however, that it's worth spending a few minutes admiring its 61m-high (230-ft.) spire, topped by a weathervane in the shape of a ship. Stand on the plaza beneath the spire and look

Peter and Paul Fortress (Petropavlovskaya Krepost)

Reserve a morning or afternoon for a visit to the fortress that overlooks the Neva's busy traffic, and was originally meant to serve as the city's nucleus. Although today's St. Petersburg is centered on the south bank of the Neva River, Peter had planned to base it on the north side, and the Peter and Paul Fortress was one of his greatest masterpieces. The citadel occupies small Hare's Island (Zaichy Ostrov) across from the Winter Palace, and contains a notable cathedral, the Museum of City History, a mint, an old printing house, a former political prison, and a long stretch of sandy beach packed with bathers in the summer. **Peter and Paul Cathedral** ⭐⭐⭐ , named after the city's patron saints and erected in 1723, was St. Petersburg's first stone church. The spire made the cathedral the city's tallest building until the 20th century. It became the burial place of all Russian czars and their families from Peter's day until the end of the Romanov empire. The remains of Czar Nicholas II and his family, executed by the Bolsheviks in 1918, were moved here in 1997 from the Siberian city where they were killed, after painful debate over whether the remains were authentic. In another cruel chapter from Russia's history, the Trubetskoi Bastion housed political prisoners for centuries, including Peter the Great's son Alexei, Fyodor Dostoyevsky, Leon Trotsky, and Vladimir Lenin's brother.

The fortress can be reached from bridges on either side, though the ticket office is closer to the eastern bridge, just inside the gates on the right. Two highlights are **walking along the fortress's southern walls** (tickets can be purchased for about 50¢ at the stairs on either end); and watching (and hearing) the **daily cannon blast** at noon. The city museum is rather disappointing and not enough exhibits are explained in English. In summer the sandbar on the Neva side of the island hosts a sand sculpture competition. In winter ice fishermen camp out on the shore—and a few brave souls plunge into the icy water to cure their ills. On the facing embankment is the small house where Peter lived while building his capital.

The fortress is on **Zaichy Ostrov (Hare's Island;** ✆ **812/230-0340**; metro: Gorkovskaya). Entrance to the fortress grounds is free. Admission to cathedral and other museums on the grounds costs $4.25 adults, $2 children. From 6 to 7pm, cathedral admission is free. The complex is open daily from 10am to 10pm. The museums and cathedral are open Thursday through Monday from 11am to 6pm.

toward the city: You're at the nexus of three major avenues—Nevsky Prospekt, Gorokhovaya Ulitsa, and Vosnesensky Prospekt—that shoot out from the Admiralty like a trident. This is no accident, and is one example of the city's careful design. The building was one of the first in St. Petersburg, built to feed Peter the Great's dream of making Russia into a naval power.

3 Cathedrals, Monasteries & More

Alexander Nevsky Monastery and Cemetery (Lavra Aleksandra Nevskogo) ℛ The reason most visitors come to this complex is for its two cemeteries, which hold the remains of some of Russia's leading cultural figures, whose gravestones are works of art themselves, often reflecting the trade of those buried beneath. The monastery was built in 1710, named by Peter after the 13th-century Grand Duke Alexander Nevsky, who defeated the Swedes in a decisive 1240 battle. Nevsky's remains were brought here; his grave was later joined by those of Dostoyevsky and Tchaikovsky; fellow composers Rimsky-Korsakov, Glinka, and Mussorgsky; the architects of St. Petersburg's key monuments; and the brilliant and remarkable founder of Russia's first universities, Mikhail Lomonosov. Cross the bridge over tiny Chornaya Stream to the central monastery courtyard, before you visit the incongruously cheerful Church of the Annunciation. The churches here are more baroque and neoclassical than the medieval monasteries in Moscow. The ticket desk is just inside the arched entrance; ask for a map of the cemeteries. Allow at least an hour and a half to see the grounds and Lazarus and Tikhvin cemeteries (also known as the Cemetery of Masters of Art).

1 Naberezhnya Reki Monastirka. ℂ 812/274-1612. Admission $2. Grounds daily 6am–8pm. Cathedrals open Fri–Wed 11am–6pm. Metro: Ploshchad Alexandra Nevskogo.

Buddhist Temple (Budisky Khram)   The red portico of this temple immediately catches your eye as you drive along the otherwise nondescript avenue. At once eastern and western, it is a blend of Tibetan Buddhist features and Russian Art Nouveau, built in 1909. Construction was led by Czar Nicholas II's personal doctor, a Buddhist, who rallied funds from open-minded sponsors in Russia and even from the Dalai Lama. It has enjoyed renewed attention in Russia in recent years thanks to the eclectic Russian rock legend Boris Grebenshchikov, a devout visitor. It's now run by monks from Buryatia, one of Russia's primarily Buddhist republics, near Lake Baikal. Inside, the red-and-yellow prayer hall and smell of incense transport you far from 21st-century St. Petersburg.

91 Primorsky Prospekt. ℂ 812/430-1341. Free admission. Daily 10am–7pm; services at 10am and 5pm. Metro: Chernaya Rechka.

Chesma Cathedral and Monastery   This Gothic, candy-cane cathedral is only worth a visit if you're already in the neighborhood around Victory Park (Park Pobedy), since it's well south of the city center. Architecture buffs will be fascinated by the cathedral's pink-and-white vertical stripes and unusual column construction. The monastery across the street is now an aviation construction institute, where students perform lab work in the former monks' cells. The church was abandoned in Soviet times, when children climbed through broken stained glass to romp through its chapels. It's now a functioning church once again.

Lensoveta St. ℂ 812/373-6114. Free admission. Daily 9am–7pm.

Impressions

It was always known in advance when the students would riot in front of Kazansky Cathedral. Every family had its student informer. The result was that these riots were attended—at a respectful distance to be sure—by a great mass of people.

—Osip Mandelstam, St. Petersburg poet and author
who fell victim to Stalin's secret police

Church of the Savior on the Spilled Blood (Tserkov Spasitelya Na Krovi) ♠ St. Petersburg's most-photographed church, this cathedral is a mountain of blindingly bright, beveled domes topped by glistening gold crosses. Its architects sought to revive medieval Russian architectural styles, but the cathedral's bold cheeriness lacks the brooding mysticism of similar churches in Moscow, instead reflecting the renewed nationalism and material prosperity of late-19th-century Russia. It was built on the site where Czar Alexander II was assassinated in 1881, prompting residents to come up with the Spilled Blood reference. Its official name is Church of the Resurrection of Christ. Alexander II was the forward-thinking czar who finally freed Russia's serfs in 1861, but he grew conservative in his later years and was targeted by a group of revolutionaries demanding more reform. The church's interior mosaics were created by Russia's top artists of the day, including Art Nouveau master Mikhail Vrubel.

2b Naberezhnya Kanala Griboyedova (embankment of the Griboyedov Canal). ℂ 812/315-1636. Admission $10 adults, $6 children over 7. Permission to take photos $2, video $4. Thurs–Tues 11am–7 pm. Metro: Nevsky Prospekt or Gostiny Dvor.

Kazan Cathedral (Kazansky Sobor) ♠♠ This prominent landmark on Nevsky Prospekt is an example of nontraditional Russian Orthodox architecture adapted to satisfy church tradition. To fit with the city's careful design, the cathedral's columned, curved facade faces Nevsky—but Orthodox custom requires that the nave run east-west, so the entrance to the cathedral is actually around the side. Completed in 1811, the cathedral was partly inspired by St. Peter's Basilica in Rome. Its centered single dome, horizontal line, and gray color scheme have little in common with the more vibrant, vertical cathedrals typical of previous centuries. The cathedral was named after the icon of Our Lady of Kazan, whose intriguing tale is the first item in church brochures. For more than 60 years it housed the State Museum of Atheism and Religion, and for a while in the 1990s it managed to be simultaneously a functioning church and a museum to godlessness. The museum has since moved and dropped the "atheism" from its name.

2 Kazanskaya Ploshchad. ℂ 812/318-4528. www.kazansky.ru Free admission. Daily 10am–8pm. Services every day at 10am and 7pm. Metro: Nevsky Prospekt.

St. Isaac's Cathedral (Isaakevsky Sobor) ♠♠ St. Isaac's mighty, somber facade rose only in the mid–19th century but has become an indelible part of St. Petersburg's skyline since then. Critics of the day called it "The Inkwell" because of its boxy shape topped by a single enormous gray dome, in contrast to the multilayered and multicolored domes and towers of most Orthodox churches. Its massive hall can accommodate

14,000 people, though it probably never has. More popular with tourists than believers, the church earned residents' respect during World War II, when it endured Nazi shelling and its grounds were planted with cabbage to help residents survive the 900-day Nazi blockade. Its interior is as awesome as its exterior, with columns made of single chunks of granite, malachite, and lazurite; floors of different-colored marble; and never-ending frescoes. If the viewing balcony around the dome is open, it's well worth a climb for the view of the city and of the cathedral from on high. However, ticket prices for this activity are rising at an alarming pace. Allow an hour, more if you visit the balcony.

Isaakevskaya Ploshchad. ℂ 812/315-9732. www.cathedral.ru. Admission $8 adults, $4 children. To climb colonnade, an additional $4 adults, $2 children. Thurs–Tues 11am–6pm; colonnade closes at 5pm. Metro: Nevsky Prospekt.

St. Petersburg Mosque (Mechet)   Built in 1910, the mosque's enormous blue-tiled roof was modeled after the striking complex of tiled buildings in Samarkand, Uzbekistan, housing the mausoleum of medieval Muslim conqueror and thinker Tamerlane. The mosque was a gift to St. Petersburg from the emir of the Silk Road city of Bukhara, then part of the Russian empire. Closed down by the Bolsheviks, it was used as a medical equipment warehouse during World War II. It was the largest mosque in the Soviet Muslim world—even larger than the Uzbek ones it emulated—and is still a major symbol for Russia's 20 million–plus Muslims. Its gray granite walls contrast vividly with the sky-blue mosaics covering the dome and minarets. Inside, columns of green marble break up the vast prayer spaces.

Kamennoostrovsky Prospekt. ℂ **812/233-9819.** Free admission. Daily 10am–7pm, with major service on Fri. Metro: Gorkovskaya.

Smolny Cathedral and Convent (Smolny Sobor)   ℱ   You're unlikely to wander past the vibrant robin's-egg blue walls of the Smolny complex, because of its distant location in a barren district tucked in a curve in the Neva. But it's worth a visit if you have a guide who can interpret its architecture and history, or if you can attend one of its organ and chamber music concerts. The convent was originally designed in the 18th century for Peter the Great's daughter Elizabeth, but she later abandoned her plans for monastic life and became empress after a palace coup. It is one of the masterpieces of Italian architect Bartolomeo Rastrelli, also responsible for the Winter Palace. Unfortunately, most of the grounds are closed to the public (having been converted into insurance offices and city government annexes) or under renovation. Allow a couple of hours if you have a guide.

3/1 Ploshchad Rastrelli. ℂ **812/271-7632.** Admission $7 adults, $4 students, free for children under 7. Permission to take photos $1, video $2. Fri–Wed 10am–5pm. Concert tickets available at cathedral ticket office. Metro: Kropotkinskaya.

Synagogue (Sinagoga)   This Moorish temple was consecrated in 1893, during a lull in the pogroms that were decimating Jewish populations elsewhere in Russia. Even more remarkable than its construction was its survival throughout the next century, when atheist (and anti-Semitic) Soviet leaders razed cathedrals and other architectural monuments with impunity. The dome and corkscrewlike towers are covered with handmade carvings. Services are held in the red-brick Small Synagogue (Malaya Sinagoga). The Grand Synagogue (Bolshaya Sinagoga) is reserved for festivals, but through the doors you can see its yellow-and-white interior. It's located in a neighborhood behind the Mariinsky Theater called Kolomna, which housed many prominent Jewish families at the turn of the 20th century. Only the most highly educated and professionally trained Jews were allowed to live in St. Petersburg during that period; the rest were confined to the Pale of Settlement, a zone stretching from Poland to western Russia. If you visit, skullcaps are required for men, and are available at the shop at the entrance.

2 Lermontovsky Prospekt. ⓒ 812/113-8975. Free admission. Sun–Fri 9am–6pm; services at 10am. Metro: Sadovaya.

4 Major Museums

Russian Museum (Russky Muzei)   This museum should be on every visitor's itinerary, even those who know or care little about Russian art. It's as much an introduction to Russian history, attitudes, and vision as it is a display of artistic styles. Housing 32,000 art works from the 12th to 20th centuries, the museum is best viewed with a tour guide or by using the English-language audioguide to ensure that you get the most out of its collection before you drop from exhaustion. The most popular rooms are in the Benois Wing, where works by Avante Garde artists Malevich and Kandinsky attract international crowds. Chronologically, they're at the end of the exhibit, so save time and energy if you want to see them. The Old Russian Wing deserves a good look, too, offering perspective on the evolution of Orthodox icon painting that helps you better appreciate any cathedrals you visit later. The rural scenes of Russian village life by Alexei Venetsianov and the soothing forestscapes of Ivan Shishkin, both on the ground floor, are often unfairly overlooked. Note the Art Nouveau paintings and sketches of set designs for Diaghilev's Ballet Russe. Take a few moments to appreciate the museum's exterior before you go in. It was built in the 1820s for the brother of Czar Alexander I and Czar Nicholas I, Grand Duke Mikhail. The museum owes many of its riches to private collections seized by the Soviets, or "volunteered" by wealthy collectors hoping to avoid persecution. Allow at least 2 hours, more if you have an enthusiastic guide.

4/2 Inzhenernaya Ulitsa. ⓒ 812/595-4248 or 812/314-3448. www.rusmuseum.ru. Admission $12 adults, $6 students with ID, free for children under 18. English-language tour for up to 5 with official museum guide $65 plus entrance fee. Wed–Sun 10am–6pm. Metro: Gostiny Dvor or Nevsky Prospekt.

Kunstkamera   Officially called the Peter the Great Museum of Anthropology and Ethnography, this museum was created back in Peter's day to study the human body and fight superstition rampant in 18th-century Russia. The 300-year-old building itself is in a rather sorry state, with its stone staircases uneven from wear, and moldings flaking off. The real reason people visit is the repulsion and attraction of its "naturalia" collection of anatomical specimens, including deformed animals, bottled human body parts, and diseased babies preserved in jars for nearly 300 years. This is not for those with weak stomachs, or for very young or sensitive children (older ones love the "gross-out" factor of the exhibits). It was aimed at advancing Peter's fascination with modern science, which struck horror in most Russians at the time. Many of today's scientists credit Peter with laying the groundwork for the institutions that later produced Mendeleyev (creator of chemistry's periodic table) and the Nobel Prize–winning scientists of the 20th century. The museum also holds a collection of coins and artifacts from around the world, which were more remarkable when Russia remained largely cut off from the rest of the world, but are still impressive for their variety.

3 Universitetskaya Naberezhnaya (entrance from Tamozhenny Pereulok). ⓒ 812/328-1412. www.kunstkamera.ru. Admission $4 adults, $3 students and children. $2 to take photos, $4 video. Tues–Sun 11am–6pm; closed last Wed of every month. Metro: Vasileostrovskaya.

Blockade Museums   Two exhibits, both of them eye-opening and tear-jerking, trace the city's experience enduring 900 days of siege and isolation by Nazi forces from 1941 to 1944 (see the box, "The Siege of Leningrad," earlier in this chapter). Try to squeeze in an hour-long visit to one of these sobering museums. The **Memorial Museum of the Leningrad Siege** ⓚ is the more commonly visited, hosting tour groups in the afternoons and Russian school groups in the mornings. The small two-story museum gets crowded leading up to Victory Day on May 9, when Russians celebrate the victory over Nazism. Less frequented but no less impressive is **"Leningrad During the Great Patriotic War"** ⓚⓚ, a permanent exhibit at the **St. Petersburg History Museum** in a riverside mansion. The hall of children's photos and diaries is especially moving. The exhibits aren't marked in English, but each room has a panel in English describing its contents. The last hall shows a video in English and Russian about the blockade, with plenty of chairs to rest in while you watch. Exhibits include posters for Shostakovich's Seventh Symphony, composed and first performed during the siege; a chronicle of the Road of Life; and a metronome that played on Leningrad radio during the blockade, its speed indicating the level of danger of shelling on a given day. Both exhibits gloss over Stalin's role in exacerbating the city's struggle and the country's wartime losses, but even the Soviet propaganda doesn't overshadow the very real horrors presented by the museums. For an even more powerful but less intimate way to remember the blockade victims, see the Piskarevo Cemetery review in the "Monuments, Memorials, & Cemeteries" section below.

Memorial Museum of Leningrad Blockade. 9 Solyanoi Pereulok. ⓒ 812/579-3021. Admission $2.50 adults, $1 students and children over 7. Thurs–Tues 10am–5pm; closed last Thurs of each month. St. Petersburg History Museum. 44 Angliiskaya Naberezhnya. ⓒ 812/117-7544. Admission $3.50 adults, $2 students and children over 7. Thurs–Tues 11am–5pm. Metro: Nevsky Prospekt.

Museum of Musical Instruments (in the Sheremetev Palace) ⓚⁱᵈˢ   If you play a musical instrument and have a free hour or so, this museum is a fun opportunity to discover inventive ways Russians and others have made music over the centuries. If you're lucky, one of the museum guides will let you use the computer program that reproduces the sounds of the museum's instruments. One of Tchaikovsky's pianos stands in a second-floor hall packed with harpsichords, early mechanical pianos, and spinets. Note the elegant display of the evolution of harp design from the 16th to 20th centuries, and the Arctic tribal instruments. Children with some knowledge of music will enjoy the quirkier exhibits, such as the glass harmonica on the first floor, a piano-size contraption of glass cups stacked horizontally and played with wet hands to produce an airy, wind instrument sound. The museum's setting, the resplendent 18th-century Sheremetev Palace by architect Savva Chevakinsky, is part of the reason to visit.

34 Naberezhnaya Fontanka. ⓒ 812/272-4441. Admission $5.50 adults, $2.75 students and children over 7. Wed–Sun 10am–5pm; closed last Wed of each month. Metro: Mayakovskaya.

Museum of Arctic and Antarctic (Muzei Arktiki I Antarktiki)   This curious collection of artifacts brought back from polar expeditions is not for everyone, but if you're fascinated by snow, northern cultures, or geology, stop in. It's also a nice way to cool off (at least mentally) on a hot afternoon. It's only logical that Russia, whose northern border spans much of the Arctic, would have a museum dedicated to the Far North. The Antarctic exhibits were added after a series of Soviet-era expeditions there. Housed in an early 19th-century church, the museum has a dome inlaid with a mosaic map of Antarctica engraved with the Soviet-sounding phrase CONTINENT OF PEACE AND FRIENDSHIP. The English-language brochures are good but not free. Canadians in particular seem to appreciate this museum. Allow an hour.

24a Ulitsa Marata. ⓒ 812/113-1998. www.polarmuseum.sp.ru. Admission $3.50 adults, $2 students and children over 7. Tues–Sun 10am–5pm. Metro: Dostoyevskaya.

Pushkinskaya 10 𝓰   Anyone interested in modern art, experimental performance, or alternative music should visit this art complex. Its galleries showcase artists who use a wide variety of media, and its performance spaces host lectures, "sound experiments," and other hard-to-define modern cultural events. See the website for listings. The alley leading up to it is covered in graffiti, mostly of questionable artistic merit, but past the dodgy courtyard, the art center is a haven of creativity. The gift shop is a good source of unusual gifts.

10 Pushkinskaya Ulitsa (entrance from 53 Ligovsky Prospekt, through the arch). ⓒ 812/764-5371. www.p10.non-museum.ru. Admission varies with exhibit or performance. Galleries and museum open Wed–Sun 3–7pm. Metro: Moskovskaya.

5 Parks & Gardens

Summer Gardens (Letny Sad) 𝓰𝓰   This is the place to rest on a bench after a day of visiting museums, or to escape from the crush of city sidewalks—or to imagine how Peter the Great spent his summer afternoons. The lush greenery (at least for a few months of the year) almost makes you forget that these gardens were entirely planned, designed for Peter's pleasure walks and adhering to the city's rules of classicism. Peter brought in marble Renaissance-era statues from Italy to give the park a more European feel. He and his successors threw grand receptions here with dancing, drinking, and fireworks under the endless sun of the White Nights. The statues and fountains serve as landmarks in case you get disoriented. The shrubbery was once carefully trimmed but now its groomers allow trees to take on more abundant forms. The Summer Palace is open to visitors, its rooms re-created as they would have been in Peter's time. The small two-story building was not heated, so it was a summer treat. Glance inside the Coffee House and the Tea House, too. The park closes for a few weeks in spring, usually in April, for a "drying out" period as the slush melts.

Entrance from Kutuzov Embankment (Naberezhnya Kutuzova) or Panteleimon Bridge (Panteleimonovsky Most). Park daily 10am–10pm; admission charged during festivals. Summer Palace Wed–Sun 10:30am–5pm. Tickets $2. Metro: Gostiny Dvor or Gorkovskaya.

Taurida Gardens (Tavrichesky Sad) 𝓚𝓲𝓭𝓼   This park is gradually returning to its past splendor, when its ponds were thronged with boaters, and aristocratic families strolled its winding lanes and rolling hills. Now it's one of the few good places to take kids near the city center, with a skating rink and sledding slopes in winter, a carousel and

Island Pursuits

For a taste of nature within St. Petersburg that few foreign tourists seem to know about, venture out to the three island-parks north of the Neva. The nobility used them for outdoor pursuits in the 18th century, but they were opened to the proletariat in the 20th. Today Russians of all classes wander their peaceful paths.

The most pleasant of the three is **Yelagin Island (Yelaginsky Ostrov),** officially named the Central Park of Culture and Rest. Stroll its traffic-free, oak- and chestnut-lined roads, float in a canoe on its boating ponds, and tour its classical royal palace. Yelagin Palace, built in 1812, was the first major building by Carlo Rossi, who later left his mark on much of the city. Note the patterned parquet floors and mahogany doors with gilded fittings. **Yelagin Palace Museum (℗ 812/430-1131)** is open Wednesday through Sunday from 10am to 6pm. Watching the sun set on the far west end of the island, over the Gulf of Finland, is an honored tradition, though it's a long walk. Several rides and other attractions for children are available, some sturdier than others. To get to Yelagin Island, head to metro station Krestovsky Ostrov, then walk over one of the footbridges or take bus no. 411 or no. 416 to the end of the line.

Kamenny Island (Kamenny Ostrov) became a private refuge of the nobility soon after it was forcibly relocated to Peter the Great's new capital in the 1700s. Catherine the Great bought it for her son at one point, and commissioned a palace for him on its eastern point. The neoclassical **Kamennoostrovsky Palace** is now a veterans' hospital that is largely off limits to visitors. The west side of the island is more accessible and once housed the summer mansions of the aristocracy, and later the Soviet elite (particularly top KGB generals). It now is home to Russia's nouveau riche. Seeking security, they've built fences so high that the elaborate homes are not visible to outsiders. A few of the older homes are still visible and worth admiring. The main pursuit here, however, is wandering the tranquil, wooded roads. This can be combined with a visit to one of the other islands. To get to Kamenny Island, get off at the Chernaya Rechka metro station and walk south across the river (about 10 min.).

Krestovsky Island (Krestovsky Ostrov) is the largest and least romantic of the three. It's more a sporting center, with tennis courts, yacht clubs, and enormous Krestovsky Stadium. Seaside Victory Park (Primorsky Park Pobedy) was planted by survivors of the World War II siege of Leningrad in memory of those who died, and in celebration of the victory over the Nazis. Two popular restaurants are boosting the island's reputation—Russkaya Rybalka (p. 231) and the German-style beer hall Karl I Friedrich—though they're hard to reach without a car. To get to the island, take the metro to Krestovsky Ostrov. Most of the sights are west of there, reachable on foot or by bus no. 134 from the metro.

other rides, and plenty of woodland to frolic in. Some of the grounds are in disrepair, with chipped alleys and rusted fences. The park, originally a private garden for Catherine the Great's adviser and lover Grigory Potemkin, reflects Catherine's informal landscaping style, in contrast to the rigidity of Peter's Summer Gardens. The gardens host open-air jazz festivals during the White Nights and other concerts throughout the summer.

2 Ulitsa Potemkinskaya. Daily 7am–10pm. Metro: Chernyshevskaya.

Victory Park (Park Pobedy) *Kids*   Built to celebrate the victory over Nazi Germany in World War II, this extensive city park is far from the city center but has its own metro stop. If you're staying nearby or are traveling with children, it's worth a visit. It suffers from the forced triumphal feeling of many Soviet parks, but if you ignore the massive monuments, the many outdoor attractions make it feel human-sized again. Its ponds offer skating and sledding in winter, and boating and water bikes in summer (though they're rather rickety). Elsewhere you can find tennis courts, flower gardens, and an amusement park. On a sobering note, the park was built on the site of a brick factory whose ovens were used to burn corpses of victims of the 900-day Nazi siege.

Moskovsky Prospekt. Daily 10am–9pm. Free admission to park, with small charge for park rides. Metro: Park Pobedy.

6 Monuments, Memorials & Squares

St. Petersburg is full of unforgettable architectural moments, if you take a minute—or 15—to stop and look around. Of the city's chief monuments, at the top on your list should be the **Bronze Horseman (Medny Vsadnik)** *ເເ*. This most famous of St. Petersburg's monuments is best viewed from a boat in the Neva River, where you can feel the ferocity of Peter the Great and his stallion rising above you and the city he created. It's worth visiting on foot, too, to enjoy a walk through Decembrists' Square and watch newlyweds pay their respects to the city's founder. Commissioned by Catherine the Great in honor of her grandfather-in-law and designed by French sculptor Etienne Falconet, the monument was unveiled in 1782. It depicts Peter in control of his wild steed (representing Russia), his hand reaching out over his masterpiece of a metropolis. The rearing horse is perched on a wavelike chunk of granite, its hoof stepping on the snake of Treason. The monument took on a deeper and more sinister significance for Petersburg residents after Pushkin's epic poem "The Bronze Horseman," in which the unfortunate protagonist imagines the statue coming to life and pursuing him.

Pushkin himself is the subject of another monument, at the center of the **Square of the Arts (Ploshchad Isskustv)** *ເເ*. The square is the real architectural masterpiece here, forming a nucleus of cultural institutions, while the Pushkin statue, built in 1957, is little more than a landmark. Originally designed by Carlo Rossi, an Italian-Russian architect, the square acquired many of its buildings in later years, but they all adhered to his original vision. Take a moment on one of its benches to appreciate its lines, then walk around the square to take in Mikhailovsky Palace (now the Russian Museum), the Ethnography Museum delicately and elegantly added later, the Mussorgsky Theater, the Operetta Theater, and the Philharmonic. The closest metro stop is Gostiny Dvor.

Impressions

Behind him, to the darkness wedded,
Lit by the moon's pale ray and slight,
One hand in warning raised, the dreaded
Bronze Horseman galloped through the night.

—Alexander Pushkin, *The Bronze Horseman*, 1833

Ostrovsky Square (Ploshchad Ostrovskogo) ⊛ rests at the heart of another of St. Petersburg's impressively planned districts, and is an ideal spot at which to rest your feet after exploring Nevsky. The square separates Pushkin Theater from Nevsky Prospekt, allowing the theater to line up and incorporate with Lomonosov Square on the Fontanka River beyond. The square, designed by the ever-present Italian Carlo Rossi, centers around a statue of Catherine the Great, represented at her most elegant and regal. The base of the statue is carved with Catherine's advisers, envoys, and consorts, some silly enough to be caricatures. Look behind the Pushkin Theater at **Rossi Street (Ulitsa Zodchego Rossi),** an example of St. Petersburg's relentless sense of proportion: It is 22m (72 ft.) wide and 220m (720 ft.) long, and it's flanked by matching buildings 22m (72 ft.) tall.

Anyone interested in naval history or ship construction should visit the **Cruiser Avrora,** moored on the embankment on the Petrograd side across from the St. Petersburg Hotel. The cruiser, built in 1897, took part in the Russo-Japanese war of 1905. It has been a city landmark since the Russian Revolution, when the ship bellowed out a blank shot to announce the Bolshevik storming of the Winter Palace in 1917. It's now a free public museum and training ground for cadets. In Soviet times the city's Pioneers, a sort of Communist Boy Scouts (and Girl Scouts), were brought here for their swearing-in ceremonies. The exhibits are mostly in Russian, but the cadets speak some English and can serve as informal tour guides. The decks are a bit treacherous in icy weather and the stairs are quite steep. Spend half an hour here before continuing along the embankment for more ship-gazing. Admission is free. The cruiser is open Wednesday to Sunday 10:30am to 6pm (metro: Gorkovskaya).

Impressions

Amid thickets of exotic shrubs, a fountain threw up a column of fresh and sparkling water; its spray, illumined by innumerable wax lights, shone like the dust of diamonds and refreshed the air, always kept in agitation by the movement of the dance. It seemed like the palace of the fairies: all ideas of limits disappeared.

—French ambassador Marquis de Custine, about a
ball at the Mikhailovsky Palace in 1839

In sharp contrast to the reverent, almost decadent monuments in the center of town is **Piskarevo Park and Memorial Cemetery (Prospekt Nepokorionnikh** ℱ), open daily sunrise to sunset. The mass graves in this vast and somber park hold the bodies of about half a million people who died during the 900-day Nazi siege of Leningrad during World War II. Most were civilians who died of cold, starvation, and disease. St. Petersburg residents, nearly all of whom have a relative who perished during the blockade, come here regularly to lay flowers and remember. It's far from the center and most tourist sights, but several tours include a stop here. The long central alley leads to a Soviet-style statue of a grieving woman representing the Motherland, and the rest of the graves are uniform and extend far into the park. An exhibit of photographs and documents related to the siege is housed in a pavilion; for a fuller story, visit the St. Petersburg History Museum's blockade exhibit (see description earlier in this chapter). It's far from public transport, so take a taxi if you're on your own. Allow 2 hours with transport time.

7 Literary St. Petersburg

Dostoyevsky House Museum ℱ Fyodor Dostoyevsky's native city, which obsessed and oppressed him, was a central theme in his work; it's only logical to honor him by visiting one of the houses where he lived. This corner house in a gentrifying neighborhood is one of the best-displayed and most tourist-friendly of the city's many house museums. This is because Dostoyevsky is perhaps the most world-famous of the legions of poets and writers who sprang from the intellectual and political ferment of 19th-century St. Petersburg, even if Alexander Pushkin is more fondly admired within Russia. For followers of the desperate characters of *Crime and Punishment* and *Notes From Underground,* Dostoyevsky's house may seem unusually middle-class and almost cheery. Closer examination reveals signs of the ups and downs that beset the writer throughout his career, from debts to imprisonment for revolutionary activity. After finishing the *Brothers Karamazov* in his study, with his wife Anna's unwavering assistance, Dostoyevsky died here of lung disease. In an unsettling reference to his demise, the exhibit includes cigarettes he stuffed himself. A note from one of his sons slid under the door while the author was at work strikes a chord with any busy parent: "Daddy, give me a candy. –Fedya." Take advantage of the English-language audioguide, which lasts about an hour.

4 Kuznechny Pereulok. ℂ 812/571-4031. Admission $3.50 adults, $1.75 students and children over 7. Audioguides in English $2.50. Tues–Sun 10:30am–5:30pm. Closed last Wed of the month. Metro: Dostoyevskaya.

Impressions

I make no claim
on this illustrious house,
But it has turned out that almost all my life
I have spent under the notable roof
Of the Fontanka Palace . . . I destitute
Came and destitute leave . . .
      —Anna Akhmatova, *Sochineniye v Dvukh Tomakh (Works in Two Volumes)*

Anna Akhmatova Museum 🕏🕏 One of St. Petersburg's most eloquent and prolific chroniclers, Akhmatova watched her city survive revolution, civil war, political terror, and world war. From the 1920s to the 1950s, she lived in this apartment in the "Fountain House" (Fontanny Dom), a former palace with a history as troubled as her own. The four-room museum is rich in detail despite its small size, and English-language printouts in each room provide the depth and context you need to make this a worthwhile visit. The audioguide provides more ambience but not much more information. The museum is hard to find: Enter through the arch on Liteiny Prospekt and head for the small park; turn left and head to the apartment entrance at the southwest corner of the park. Akhmatova struggled here to write freely under the budding Soviet state while avoiding arrest. From here she prepared the care packages she sent to her son when he was imprisoned for political reasons, some of which are on display. Her tangled love triangle with Nikolai Punin and his wife played itself out here, with all three sharing the apartment at one point. The most vivid part of the museum is the photo album through which visitors can leaf, showing Akhmatova and her family growing up through the turbulence of early 20th-century Russia. The building, which once belonged to the family of Count Sheremetev, was transferred to the state after the revolution. It became an Arctic research institute, and though some residents were allowed to continue living here, they could enter only with special ID cards. Akhmatova's is shown here, with her profession listed as "resident." Allow an hour for the visit.

53 Liteiny Prospekt. ℂ 812/272-2211. www.akhmatova.spb.ru. Admission $7 adults; $3.50 students and children over 7. English-language audioguide $3.50. Tues–Sun 10:30am–6pm. Metro: Mayakovskaya.

Nabokov Museum 🕏 Vladimir Nabokov lived here from his birth in 1899 to 1917, when he fled the revolution with his family, first for Crimea and ultimately for the United States. The museum is a small but revealing look at the man who produced some of the 20th century's most searing, daring works (and not just *Lolita*). The family once occupied all three floors of this neoclassical building, but now their remaining belongings are crowded into the ground floor (the upper floors host a local newspaper office). Exhibits include some of Nabokov's first poems, penned in his school years, and notes or gifts from family visitors such as H.G. Wells.

47 Bolshaya Morskaya Ulitsa. ℂ 812/315-4713. Admission $3.50. Tues–Fri 11am–6pm; Sat–Sun noon–5pm.

8 Especially for Kids

St. Petersburg doesn't seem like a child-friendly place at first, with its business-oriented service industry and surfeit of strip clubs and casinos, but a little perseverance can make your child's visit unforgettable. Russia's world-famous **circus** traditions wow children and adults alike, particularly the acrobatics, though anyone sensitive to animal rights should probably stay away. **St. Petersburg Circus** (**Tsirk Cinizelli;** ℂ 812/312-4411) performs at 3 Naberezhnya Fontanki (Fontanka Embankment). Tickets cost $14 to $35 (including a hefty $10 foreigner surcharge) for adults and children over 7. The closest metro station is Gostiny Dvor. Performances are at 3 and 7pm.

St. Petersburg Zoo, 1 Alexandrovsky Park (ℂ 812/232-8260; metro: Gorkovskaya), is a perennial child-pleaser, though it's in need of an upgrade. It's open Tuesday through Sunday from 10am to 5pm.

Boat rides along the Neva River or the city's canals (see "Organized Tours" below), or simply boat-watching along the embankment, are good ways to give kids a sense of the city's marine geography and history. The **Peterhof** palace and grounds (see chapter 18) are well worth the journey if you're with kids and it's summertime. They can play in the musical fountains, explore the grotto beneath the main cascade, and clamber through the extensive park. For older kids with an interest in science or just in being grossed out, visit the **Kunstkamera** (reviewed earlier in this chapter), with its bottled body parts. **Victory Park**'s many attractions include a Ferris wheel and other rides, though some are in sorry repair. Victory Park and **Taurida Gardens** (both covered earlier in this chapter) also offer skating rinks in winter and paddle boats in summer.

9 Organized Tours

The best tours of St. Petersburg are those done by **boat.** The smaller boats that cruise the canals give a closer view of the city's insides than the ferries that go up and down the Neva River. The ferries and hydrofoils are the ideal mode of transport to visit out-of-town sights such as **Peterhof** and **Pushkin/Tsarskoye Selo** (see chapter 18 for details). Water cruises are of course only available when the city's waterways aren't iced over, roughly May through October. You can pick up a canal tour on Griboyedov Canal just north of Nevsky Prospekt, and on the Fontanka River just north of Nevsky Prospekt; prices run $3.50 to $7 for a 1-hour tour. River cruises to Peterhof and along the Neva and Finnish Gulf start from the embankment in front of the Winter Palace. The **Vodokhod** company (Dvortsovaya Naberezhnaya; ✆ **812/380-9011**) is cheaper, but **Russian Cruises** (Dvortsovaya Naberezhnaya; ✆ **812/974-0100;** www.russian-cruises.ru) offers more enthusiastic service and English-speaking staff. Most companies offer a special White Nights tour in late evening during June and July.

English-language tours of museums or other city sights are often organized by the hotels. Companies to seek out for individual or group tours are **Davranov Travel,** which runs bus trips to the key sights out of town and offers several museum tours (17 Italianskaya Ulitsa; ✆ **812/117-8694;** www.davranov.ru); **Russian Holiday** (78 Nevsky Prospekt; ✆ **812/327-3023;** www.rusholiday.com); and **Eclectica,** offering tours of the city and outskirts (44 Nevsky Prospekt; ✆ **812/110-5579**).

10 Outdoor Pursuits

See the "Parks & Gardens" section above for more suggestions.

BIKING

Biking is a daring undertaking anywhere in Russia, where drivers are unaccustomed to sharing the road with nonmotorized vehicles and where bike paths are nonexistent. Half the year the roads are too slushy or icy for pleasant biking, but in summer, a cruise along any one of the city's embankments is delightful for experienced bikers. Try **Rent-a Bike** (3 Glinka St., inside the Kitsport store; ✆ **812/114-6587;** www.renatabike.ru). Bikes are available for as little as $10 per day; bike tours are also available.

BOATING

This is a city of canals and rivers, and in the months when they're not iced over they offer a variety of boating options. See "Organized Tours," above. Numerous private

boats also ply the canals, offering rides for groups from 2 to 10 people. Rates are negotiable and vary widely, from $20 to $100 an hour, so it's worth your while to bargain
or find a Russian speaker to help out. Safety features are generally good in the big
tourist ferries and hydrofoils, but they can be negligible in the smaller boats.

FISHING

Ice-fishing is the sport of choice for Russian men of a certain age and temperament in
the winter. You can catch a glimpse of them sitting motionless on the Gulf of Finland.
Unless you have lots of ice-fishing experience, this is a better spectator sport than par-
ticipatory one.

GYMS

St. Petersburg is just catching on to the gym concept, and only the biggest hotels will
have a Western-style health club. If your hotel doesn't, **Planeta Fitness** is a Russian
chain with branches around town offering daily passes ((C) **812/275-1384;** www.
fitness.ru; before 5pm $20; after 5pm $30).

ICE SKATING

Russian children often skate before they can read. Watching a determined grandfather
guide his grandkids along an icy pond in the winter can be just as fun as watching a
big tournament. Any pond turns into an informal rink during the freezing season.
Victory Park and Taurida Gardens (both covered earlier in this chapter) have real rinks
as well, and rent basic skates.

JOGGING

A White Nights jog along the Neva River is an unforgettable experience—but your
feet may never forgive you. St. Petersburg's stone streets, treacherously crooked and
cracked sidewalks, and drivers unused to dodging speedy pedestrians make jogging a
challenge. Your best bet is to hit the larger parks, such as Victory Park; even the smaller
parks closer to the center of town such as Taurida Gardens or Summer Gardens can
make for pleasant runs. Running during daylight hours is recommended, which is not
a problem in the spring and summer. Russians are not big on casual jogging, viewing
it as the domain of athletes and not amateurs, so be prepared for perplexed looks.

SKIING

The forests around St. Petersburg are a paradise for cross-country skiers, but downhill
options are limited to resorts a few hours out of town. Some dedicated city residents
skate-ski through the lanes of the bigger city parks, such as Victory Park. Cross-country
ski rentals are available adjacent to the palace at Tsarskoye Selo, for royal rural sightseeing (see chapter 18 for details).

11 Spectator Sports

In addition to the venues mentioned below, check the schedules of **Yubileiny Sports
Palace,** 18 Prospekt Dobrolyubova ((C) **812/293 4049;** metro: Sportivnaya); and
Krestovsky Sports Complex, Primorsky Park Pobedy, with its main entrance on
Krestovsky Ostrov (island) ((C) **812/235-5435;** Metro: Krestovsky Ostrov) for a vari-
ety of sporting events throughout the year.

FIGURE SKATING

Russia is one of the world's premier figure-skater factories and St. Petersburg has produced many of the country's top skaters. Check out the schedule at the **Ice Palace (Ledovy Dvorets),** 1 Prospekt Pyatiletok (© **812/118-6620;** www.newarena.spb.ru; metro: Ledovy Dvorets). Otherwise, come during one of the figure-skating tournaments, which are held in January and February. See the International Skating Union website for details (www.isu.com).

HOCKEY

Ice hockey is a crucial sport in this northern city. Viewing the big matches became a lot more pleasant with the construction of the Ice Palace/Ledovy Dvorets (see above for contact information) for the 2000 Hockey World Cup. For more casual viewing pleasure, come in winter and visit the bigger city parks, where a match is nearly always underway on the ponds. Tickets for the Ice Palace are available at the palace itself or at theater ticket kiosks around town (called *kassa,* spelled KACCA in Russian).

SOCCER

Soccer is Russians' favorite sport. St. Petersburg's premier soccer club, Zenit, is finally emerging from the shadows of its Moscow rivals. If you're in town during a Zenit match, head for **Petrovsky Stadium,** 2 Petrovsky Prospect (© **812/323-9361;** metro: Sportivnaya), and be prepared for some raucous behavior. City parks host informal soccer (called *futbol* here) matches year-round—even in the snow. See www.uefa.com for European League matches in St. Petersburg.

TENNIS TOURNAMENTS

The St. Petersburg Open, held at rather run-down **Peterburgsky Sport Complex,** 8 Ulitsa Gagarina (© **812/103-4040;** www.spbopen.ru; metro: Park Pobedy), is the main venue at which to catch top-ranked Russian ATP stars on their homeland's courts. The Davis Cup also sometimes comes here (www.daviscup.com).

WALKING TOUR	ST. PETERSBURG HIGHLIGHTS

Start:	Palace Square.
Finish:	Gostiny Dvor.
Time:	About 2 hours.
Best Times:	Any weekday or Sunday morning, when the crowds are thinner.

This tour links key St. Petersburg sights with less important ones. The side streets and embankments are just as crucial to understanding the city as are the palaces, so look at everything, even between stops.

---

❶ Palace Square

Stand at the Alexander Column in the center and turn around slowly, a full 360 degrees. Each building on the asymmetrical square emerged in a different era but they combine to create a flawless ensemble.

Nothing in this view, or this city, is accidental. Imagine the royal equipages pulling into the square, the czarist army processions, the revolutionaries' resentment of all the square stood for—and the Communist-era appropriation of the square

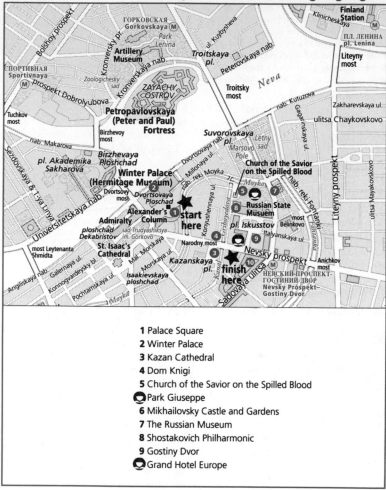

1 Palace Square
2 Winter Palace
3 Kazan Cathedral
4 Dom Knigi
5 Church of the Savior on the Spilled Blood
○ Park Giuseppe
6 Mikhailovsky Castle and Gardens
7 The Russian Museum
8 Shostakovich Philharmonic
9 Gostiny Dvor
○ Grand Hotel Europe

for holiday parades. The column itself is not attached to the ground—its weight keeps it upright.

Walk north from the column to the courtyard of the:

❷ Winter Palace

The palace's now tranquil courtyard bustled with court activity in Empress Elizabeth's and Catherine the Great's days, and with revolutionary activity 150 years later. It was closed to visitors until recently, visible only from inside the Hermitage Museum. You can pick up a museum plan while you're here, though a visit to the Hermitage deserves at least an afternoon or a full day to itself.

As you leave the courtyard, take in the view of the curved General Staff building across the square.

Head left toward the Moika Canal, then turn right and follow it down to Nevsky Prospekt. Note the uniformity of the buildings along the canal, all in various shades of yellow, and the odd proportion of the wide bridges crossing the narrow waterway. Cross Nevsky and head left, until you reach the columned gray facade of:

❸ Kazan Cathedral

Walking the length of the cathedral's concave colonnade gives you a stepped-back view of Nevsky on one side and a sense of the cathedral's scale on the other. Its modern, secular lines are almost reminiscent of the Capitol Building in Washington, built just 2 decades earlier. Compare this to other Orthodox churches you see around Russia. Marshal Kutuzov, who led the Russian victory over Napoleon, is buried here. Even if you don't go in, note that the church's entrance is on the east side instead of facing the street, to satisfy Orthodox church canon.

Cross the avenue again and stop at the corner of Nevsky and Griboyedov Canal to admire:

❹ Dom Knigi

This Art Nouveau treasure is just another building along Nevsky, but worth noting are its glass dome and mystical mosaics. It once belonged to the Singer sewing machine company, whose name is still engraved on the facade, between the second and third floors. For decades it was Dom Knigi, or House of Books, Leningrad's main bookstore. Currently under renovation, it's slated to become an upscale shopping mall.

Cross Griboyedov Canal and head north along it, past the boatmen hawking canal tours, toward the dizzying domes of the:

❺ Church of the Savior on the Spilled Blood

Built 7 decades after Kazan Cathedral, this church sprang from an entirely different era and worldview. Though constructed during Russia's industrial and economic boom of the late 19th-century, the Church of the Savior harkens back to the piled, etched, color-coated domes of medieval Russian churches, and is slathered with gold and precious stones—a much more Russian style of church-building than the reasoned lines of European-style Kazan Cathedral. Inside the Church of the Savior, note the spot where Czar Alexander II was assassinated by a revolutionary. This politicized location is part of the reason for the church's nationalist design.

Walk around the cathedral along the outer edge of Mikhailovsky Gardens, stopping to study the undulating patterns of the cast-iron fences surrounding the gardens. This could be a good moment for coffee, or something more substantial.

TAKE A BREAK
The one-story pink pavilion in Mikhailovsky Gardens was once a public toilet, but don't let that deter you. The **Park Giuseppe** restaurant (𝄐 812/117-7309) now has a splendid terrace overlooking the gardens and the Church of the Savior. Good pizzas (by Petersburg standards), strong coffee, and a good selection of teas and desserts are the menu highlights.

Continue to follow the fence around to the entrance to the gardens.

❻ Mikhailovsky Castle and Gardens

The warm coral of the castle makes it look almost inviting despite its grim history. The paranoid Czar Paul I had it built because the Winter Palace made him feel too exposed to threats from without and within his court. (Paul was right about the threats, but not about the security of his new home: He was assassinated by advisers soon after he moved in.) Compare the high fences enclosing the gardens and the inaccessibility of this castle courtyard to the more sociable Winter Palace, facing the Neva River and opening onto Palace Square. Mikhailovsky Castle was later an engineering school and is now the Engineering Museum.

Circle the palace and turn right onto Italianskaya Ulitsa, heading straight until you reach the Square of the Arts. Take a rest on a bench in this small rectangular plaza, then wander its circumference to study its components:

❼ The Russian Museum

This museum is housed in the triumphantly classical Mikhailovsky Palace (Dvorets), not to be confused with the Mikhailovsky Castle (Zamok) that you just saw. The optimism of the period when the palace was built (1819–25) is reflected in the mock war trophies that top its gates and victorious frieze. The royal family made it a museum in 1898, as their belated effort to create a gallery of Russian art to rival Moscow's Tretyakov Gallery.

Walk around the square past the Mussorgsky Theater (check out its repertoire of ballet and opera performances on the way), around the Grand Hotel Europe and across Mikhailovskaya Ulitsa to the:

❽ Shostakovich Philharmonic

Built in the 1830s, Russia's premier music hall has staged the country's leading works, from Tchaikovsky's concertos to Rachmaninoff's symphonies. It has hosted conductors including Sviatoslav Richter, Mstislav Rostropovich, and of course Dmitry Shostakovich.

Continue down Mikhailovskaya Ulitsa to Nevsky Prospekt. Turn around and look at the Square of the Arts one more time from this perspective. Then turn left down Nevsky and continue to the underground walkway at the next intersection. Cross Nevsky through this passage, noting its lively commerce in pirated CDs, DVDs, and software. You'll emerge at:

❾ Gostiny Dvor

This 19th-century shopping mall has gone through several incarnations. Picture its early years, when it was a gathering place for the nobility looking for gifts to take to balls at the Winter Palace. It was also a place to come after lighting a candle at an icon at Kazan Cathedral. Its current customers include the city's new middle class, as well as some members of the nouveau riche who made fortunes in the privatizations and economic chaos of the 1990s.

WINDING DOWN
To stay in an aristocratic, 19th-century mood after this walk, stop at the **mezzanine of the Grand Hotel Europe**, back on Mikhailovskaya Ulitsa (✆ **812/329-6622**). The plush armchairs in this peaceful atrium make you feel like an escapee from modern St. Petersburg, especially when the harpists play. Tea, pastries, and small sandwiches are available.

Shopping in St. Petersburg

Shopping in St. Petersburg can produce precious porcelain or a bag full of cheap lacquer boxes, depending on your energy level, resourcefulness, and pocketbook. The *matryoshka* nesting dolls are so plentiful and ubiquitous that you probably won't be able to leave without one. For more original ware, visit Lomonosov Porcelain Factory, which has a museum and shop featuring imperial china patterns. Soviet banners and Red Army gear are a draw for some, though Moscow features more of a selection, since St. Petersburg prefers to emphasize its royal heritage rather than its Soviet past. Amber from the Baltic region is a bargain compared to what you'd pay anywhere else, and the selection is much broader. St. Petersburg is fast on its way to competing with Moscow as a luxury shopping capital, with plenty of French, Italian, and local haute couture aimed at the *nouveau riche.* The city's dearth of multinational retail chains is likely to change in the coming decade, for better or for worse. Tips on purchasing traditional Russian gifts are outlined below; for more on Orthodox icons, *matryoshka* dolls, Russian linen, and the porcelain style known as Gzhel, see chapter 8.

1 The Shopping Scene

The chief challenge in finding unique souvenirs and gifts in Russia is determining whether you're allowed to bring them home. See "Entry Requirements & Customs" in chapter 2 for an explanation of the export regulations of Russia's Culture Ministry, which affect Orthodox icons, samovars, and many artworks.

Hotel gift shops and the souvenir stands on Nevsky have higher prices than elsewhere. The outdoor markets are a better bet, such as the one across from the Church of the Savior on the Spilled Blood (see "Vernisazh" below). Be ready to bargain, and beware of counterfeiting. If something sounds suspiciously cheap, there's a reason. The monasteries and cathedrals have the richest selection of icons.

St. Petersburg has no sales tax, but be clear with the vendor about what currency is being cited. In shops most prices will be printed in rubles. Street vendors will sometimes cite in dollars or euros, though they're technically forbidden from accepting anything but rubles. VAT is included in the price, but it is not refundable at the border as it is in some European countries.

If you want to ship home large items such as paintings or carpets, try **DHL,** 4 Izmailovsky Prospekt (© **812/326-64-00**); or **UPS,** 51 Shpalernaya Ulitsa (© **812/**

Box That Up

Lacquer boxes have become a staple of Russian souvenir shops, but with a little context they take on a greater meaning. The practice of painting on papier-mache boxes started in the village of Danilovka outside Moscow in the 1700s, and quickly spread to surrounding towns. Today, the towns of Palekh, Fedoskino, and Mstera are among the leading lacquer-art producers. The boxes sold now are made of several layers of papier-mache pressed together, cut, and oven-dried. Generally painted on a black background, the colors are primarily scarlet- and gold-based, and the finished product is lacquered in clear varnish, often multiple layers, for radiance and durability. The images usually represent scenes from Russian fairy tales or legends, and can vary widely depending on the artist's interpretation. Study several before buying a lacquer box. The box should be lightweight, and the detail should be impeccable, since the better artists spend up to 2 months painting them using special magnifying glasses.

For a gift for a whole family, buy a lacquer box together with the English-language translation of the fairy tale depicted (on sale at many souvenir shops and bookstores).

327-8540). These companies can take care of any Customs clearances you need. Also, **Alla Art Agency** (© 812/304-4098) will arrange Culture Ministry approvals of valuable artwork and ship it to you, for a fee.

Shops and shopping centers are generally open 7 days a week from around 10 or 11am until 7 or 8 pm, and a very few still take an hour off for lunch between about 1 and 2pm. Most are closed on Russian holidays.

2 Great Shopping Areas

Nevsky Prospekt is the city's commercial lifeline, offering an almost repetitive abundance of souvenirs, clothing, and snacks. **Gostiny Dvor** shopping arcade concentrates all of Nevsky's riches in one two-story pre-revolutionary mall. The facades on Nevsky tell only part of the story, since many lead back into passages of luxury boutiques, discount clothing stores, or jewelry shops. Commerce thins out at Nevsky's extremities. **Upper Nevsky** holds the posher shops, while **Lower Nevsky** (east of Moskovsky Train Station) is calmer and less pretentious. Souvenir and art stands clog the thoroughfare and adjacent courtyards, and seem to multiply in summer.

The area from St. Isaac's to Palace Square is a shopper's wasteland but an architectural paradise. The Summer Gardens and adjacent areas are similarly commerce-barren, except for the **Vernisazh**—the city's most convenient, reliable, and extensive gift bazaar.

St. Petersburg Shopping

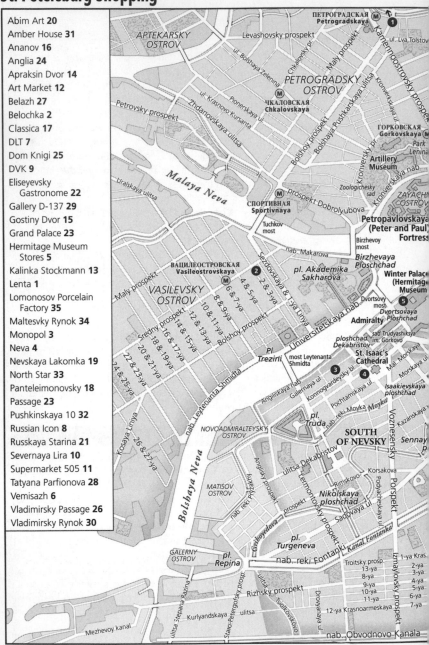

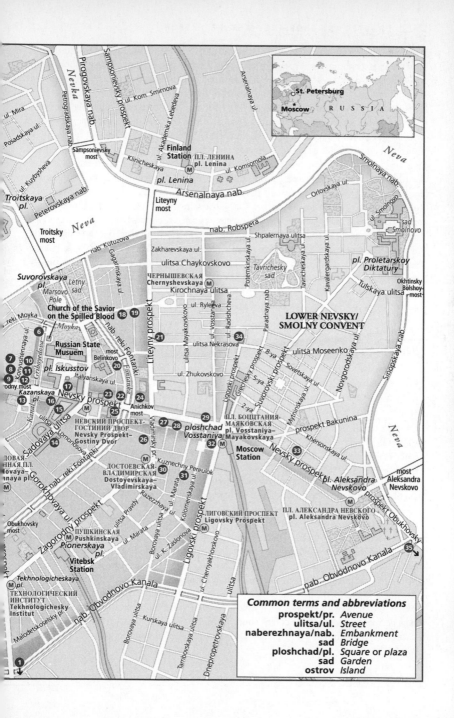

RUSSIA

St. Petersburg
Moscow

ul. Mira
Posadskaya ul.
Pirogovskaya nab.
Neuka
Petrogradskaya nab.
Sampsonievskiy prospekt
ul. Kom. Smirnova
ul. Akademika Lebedeva
Arsenalnaya ul.

Sampsonievskiy most
Klinicheskaya
Finland Station ПЛ. ЛЕНИНА
pl. Lenina
ul. Komsomola

ul. Kuybysheva

pl. Lenina

Troitskaya pl.
Peterovskaya nab.
Arsenalnaya nab.
Orlovskaya ul.
Smolnaya nab.
Neva
ul. Smolnovo

Troitsky most
Neva
Liteyny most

nab. Kutuzova
nab. Robspera
sad Smolnovo

Zakharevskaya ul.
Shpalernaya ulitsa

Suvorovskaya pl.
Letny sad
ulitsa Chaykovskovo
Tavrichesky sad
pl. Proletarskoy Diktatury

Marsovo Pole
ЧЕРНЫШЕВСКАЯ
Chernyshevskaya
Kirochnaya ulitsa
Potemkinskaya ul.
Tavricheskaya ul.
Kavalergardskaya ul.
Tulskaya ulitsa
Okhtinsky Bolshoy most

Church of the Savior on the Spilled Blood 18 19
reki Moyka
6
Moyka
ul. Ryleeva
ul. Vosstania
Radishcheva
Paradnaya nab.

LOWER NEVSKY/ SMOLNY CONVENT

7 10
8 11
9 12
Konyushennaya ul.
Griboyedova
Russian State Musuem
most Belinkovo
21
ulitsa Mayakovskovo
ulitsa Nekrasova
34
ulitsa Moseenko

odny most
13
pl. Iskusstov
20
Italyanskaya ul.
ul. Zhukovskovo
Novgorodskaya ul.

17
23 22
Nevsky prospekt
24
Anichkov most
Ligovski prospekt
Grechesky prospekt
Suvorovski prospekt
6-ya
7-ya
8-ya
5-ya
Sovetskaya ul
Mytninskaya ul
Sinopskaya nab.
Neva

Kazanskaya pl.
16 15
25
27 28
НЕВСКИЙ ПРОСПЕКТ-ГОСТИНИЙ ДВОР
Nevsky Prospekt-Gostiny Dvor
29
Vladimirsky pr.
ploshchad Vosstaniya
26
32
ПЛ. БОЩТАНИЯ-МАЯКОВСКАЯ
pl. Vosstaniya-Mayakovskaya
prospekt Bakunina
Khersonskaya ul
33
Nevsky prospekt
pl. Aleksandra Nevskovo
most Aleksandra Nevskovo

14
Sadovaya ulitsa
Kanala
Lomonosova
Moscow Station

ДОВАЯ-ННАЯ ПЛ.
ovaya-naya pl.
Gorokhovaya ul prospekt
nab. reki Fontanki
ДОСТОЕВСКАЯ ВЛАДИМИРСКАЯ
Dostoyevskaya-Vladimirskaya
30
31
Kuznechny Pereulok
Razezzhaya ul.
ul. Marata
Ligovsky Prospekt
prospekt Obukhovsky
35

Obukhovsky most
ПУШКИНСКАЯ
Pushkinskaya Pionerskaya pl.
Vitebsk Station
ul. Marata
Borovaya ulitsa
ul. Pravdy
ul. K. Zaslonova
Kolomenskaya ul.
ЛИГОВСКИЙ ПРОСПЕКТ
Ligovsky Prospekt
ul. Chernyakhovskovo
Ligovsky Prospekt
ПЛ. АЛЕКСАНДРА НЕВСКОГО
pl. Aleksandra Nevskovo

Zagorodny prospekt

Tekhnologicheskaya pl.
ТЕХНОЛОГИЧЕСКИЙ ИНСТИТУТ
Tekhnologichesky Institut
nab. Obvodnovo Kanala
Kurskaya ulitsa
Tambovskaya ulitsa
Dnepropetrovskaya ulitsa
nab. Obvodnovo Kanala

Malodetskoselsky pr.
Borovaya ulitsa

1

Common terms and abbreviations	
prospekt/pr.	*Avenue*
ulitsa/ul.	*Street*
naberezhnaya/nab.	*Embankment*
sad	*Bridge*
ploshchad/pl.	*Square or plaza*
sad	*Garden*
ostrov	*Island*

With Nevsky so saturated, the area around Chernyshevskaya metro station is emerging as a calmer, less expensive shopping alternative. Several antiques shops have opened here, along with an increasing number of hotels and cafes centered around Ulitsa Pestelya, in this neighborhood north of Lower Nevsky.

Russians do most of their shopping at **farmers' markets** and **open-air bazaars,** most of which are outside the center of town. These lively and pungent markets offer a fun if intense way of experiencing the real Russia, and quickly make you forget those Gorbachev-era images of bread lines and shortages. In the food markets, pomegranates and kiwis spill from fruit stands, rows of lamb carcasses line the meat stalls, and familiar American coffees and candies rise high in the dry goods section. In the non-food markets (which Russians call the "things" market, or *veshchevoi rynok*) you can find fur coats, Turkish leather jackets, 20¢ Russian-made underwear, Chinese-made plastic chess sets, and just about anything else, at prices below what shops charge. Two food markets near the center worth checking out are **Vladimirsky Rynok** (Kuznechny Pereulok, just outside Vladimirskaya metro station) and **Maltevsky Rynok** (Ulitsa Nekrasova, not far from Chernyshevskaya metro station). Both are cleaner and slightly more expensive than average. The main "things market" downtown is **Apraksin Dvor** (Sadovaya Ulitsa, south of Nevsky Prospekt and near Gostiny Dvor metro station), with throngs of shoppers morning to night, 7 days a week. Pickpocketing is common, so keep one eye on your wallet.

3 Shopping Centers

St. Petersburg's premier shopping center since the 1760s has been **Gostiny Dvor (Guest Courtyard),** a triangular arcade of shops on two floors on Nevsky Prospekt. In the Soviet era the long, doorless corridors were flanked by shop after shop carrying the same limited selection of gray suits, uncomfortable shoes, and two-ring binders. Today the shopping center holds just about everything, though most of it is priced beyond the means of the average Russian. Boutiques selling $1,000 dresses abut shops with Italian briefcases and French fountain pens. At the back edge of the arcade, facing Ulitsa Lomonosova, are a few cheaper clothing shops. Souvenir shops are sprinkled throughout the center, as are several little cafes that offer very cheap Russian-style open-faced sandwiches and savory pies for an energy boost and a chance to rest your feet.

St. Petersburg's other shopping centers fall into two categories. The *passazh,* an enclosed row of shops leading back from a main street, is a concept left over from the pre-revolutionary years when they were usually reserved for the aristocracy. Today some have been beautifully restored and house designer boutiques and posh beauty salons. The main row of shops to check out is **Passage** (48 Nevsky Prospekt); the view of inside and out from the second-floor cafe is exceptional. Nearby is the newer **Grand Palace** (44 Nevsky Prospekt), with rows of Italian and French couture boutiques and a staggeringly expensive chocolate shop. Only slightly less decadent is **Vladimirsky Passage** (19 Vladimirsky Prospekt). The less appealing but more affordable type of shopping center is the *torgovy tsentr*. These glass-and-chrome constructions have sprung up around Russia in recent years, feeding Russians' hunger for consumer goods. There's little historic or unique about these centers, but they're your best bet for basic needs such as shampoo, camera batteries, or umbrellas, and it's one way to see how city residents spend their money.

4 Shopping A to Z

A few personal shopping ideas and hints:

AMBER

The Baltic Sea coast from Kaliningrad up toward St. Petersburg holds nearly all of the world's amber. This strange gem of petrified tree sap is ubiquitous in Russia's imperial capital. Rings, necklaces, brooches, cigar holders, pens, and other souvenirs made of amber are widely available. Although they're not cheap, they cost much less than in other countries farther from the source. Any souvenir market, crafts store, or jewelry shop is bound to have a decent selection (see reviews below). Keep an eye out for the more unusual shades of pale green or yellow.

Amber House (Yantarny Dom)   A broad and reliable but pricy selection of jewelry made from amber and Siberian stones can be found here. The really unusual items are usually the better buys. 28 Ulitsa Marata. ✆ 812/112-3013. Metro: Vladimirskaya.

ANTIQUES & COLLECTIBLES

Abim Art   This spacious and eclectic gallery on the Fontanka embankment offers paintings, china, and knickknacks. 5 Fontanka Naberezhnaya. ✆ 812/314-0080. Metro: Gostiny Dvor.

Belazh   This is an old standby on Nevsky, whose prices are higher because of its location but whose quality and selection of artworks and porcelain remain good. 57 Nevsky Prospekt. ✆ 812/310-6688. Metro: Gostiny Dvor.

Panteleimonovsky   Paintings, furniture, and tabletop collectibles may be found here, with an emphasis on Art Nouveau objects. 13/15 Ulitsa Pestelya. ✆ 812/279-7235. Metro: Chernyshevskaya.

Russkaya Starina   Its focus is on Russian crafts and antiques, as opposed to the western European collectibles carried by most other antiques shops. 6 Nekrasova Ulitsa. ✆ 812/318-6481. Metro: Chernyshevskaya.

ART

Art Market   This informal market in front of the Lutheran Church on Nevsky has been almost institutionalized in its many years parked here. A broad selection of paintings, watercolors, sketches, and photos are on display by the artists. The more original and less expensive pieces are usually displayed at the booths in the back. Prices are negotiable, and range broadly. Vendors speak English. 32–34 Nevsky Prospekt. Metro: Nevsky Prospekt.

Gallery D-137   This small gallery houses works by several daring and respected local artists, in a renovated brick basement. 90/92 Nevsky Prospect. ℂ 812/275-6011. Metro: Mayakovskaya.

Hermitage Museum Store   While not as extensive as they could be, the various stalls in the Hermitage sell art prints and postcards of many sizes, as well as other museum memorabilia. Palace Sq. ℂ 812/110-9079. Metro: Nevsky Prospekt.

Pushkinskaya 10   One of the functions of this all-purpose, counterculture arts center is to sell art, though it doesn't seem obvious at first. Galleries hold rotating exhibits featuring local artists, whose styles range from naturalism to nihilism. See the review for Pushkinskaya on p. 246. 10 Pushkinskaya Ulitsa. ℂ 812/164-4857. Metro: Mayakovskaya.

Vernisazh   This is the compact but rich outdoor market across from the Church of the Savior on the Spilled Blood. Hand-painted tea sets, mountains of lacquer boxes and *matryoshka* dolls, Soviet maps, wooden Christmas ornaments, decorative eggs, hand-knit wool shawls, fur hats, malachite chess sets, flasks with the hammer and sickle, and amber brooches are among the multitude of wares here. In sharp contrast to the market's haphazard, earlier days, the vendors now are neatly organized and registered, and many take credit cards. Prices, often quoted in dollars, are very negotiable. Vernisazh is run by the Center for the Support of Art and Entrepreneurship. 1 Canal Griboyedova. ℂ 812/167-1628. Metro: Nevsky Prospekt.

BOOKS

Most hotels and museums also have books about the city in English.

Anglia British Bookshop   The Anglia has the best selection of books in English, with an emphasis on travel guides, picture albums, and classic and modern fiction. However, it's more expensive than its Russian counterparts selling all of the above. 38 Fontanka. ℂ 812/279-8284. Metro: Mayakovskaya or Gostiny Dvor.

Dom Knigi   The relocated "House of Books" still has a good selection of English-language books. 62 Nevsky Prospekt. ℂ 812/314-1422. Metro: Chernyshevskaya.

DVK (Dom Voyennykh Knig)   One of the world's few 24-hour bookstores, this three-story emporium has replaced the landmark Dom Knigi as the city's premier bookstore. Though the name means "house of military books," this store has every kind of reading material imaginable, with a small selection of English-language guides and novels on the first floor, near the main entrance. 30 Nevsky Prospekt. ℂ 812/312-3946. Metro: Nevsky Prospekt.

CAVIAR

Kalinka Stockmann   This Finnish-Russian supermarket chain sells all classes of caviar at prices higher than you'll find in the bazaars but lower than in the hotels— and much lower than you'll find at home. 25 Nevsky Prospekt. ℂ 812/326-2638. Metro: Nevsky Prospekt.

Lenta   The cheapest caviar in town outside the bazaars (where quality is dodgy) is found at the many hypermarkets in the suburbs, such as Lenta. Both of the following are open 24 hours. 11 Vyborgskoye Shosse, near metro Ozerki. ℂ 812/380-6130. Also at 33 Pulkovskoye Shosse, on the way to the airport. ℂ 812/103-3000.

CHINA & PORCELAIN

Lomonosov Porcelain Factory   You'll see china from this factory all around town, or you can buy it at the source. The factory was opened in 1744 by Peter the Great's daughter, Empress Elizabeth I. Its craftspeople designed china for the royal family and nobility. After the revolution it was nationalized and produced plates with Constructivist Soviet art and propaganda slogans. Today it's been re-privatized, and sells both imperial and Soviet patterns. Check out the factory museum while you're there, which is part of the Hermitage Museum's holdings. 151 Obukhovsky Oborony Prospekt. ℭ 812/560-8300. Metro: Lomonosovskaya.

CHOCOLATE

Russian chocolate has come a long way from the waxy stuff sold in Soviet shops, though it's still sweeter than what you'll find in Switzerland or Belgium. A few ounces of the cheerfully wrapped chocolates is a sure way to please any underage friends or family back home (though you might want to sample them first, since a few are made with liqueurs). The big supermarkets also usually have small wrapped chocolates for very reasonable prices. Try **Belochka,** 28 Sredny Prospekt, on Vasilevsky Island (ℭ 812/323-1763; Metro: Vasileostrovskaya); or **Nevskaya Lakomka,** 17/25 Ulitsa Pestelya (ℭ 812/271-2070; Metro: Chernyshevskaya).

CRAFTS

See the review for Vernisazh under "Art," above.

DISCOUNT SHOPPING

Apraksin Dvor   This 200-year-old shopping mall has lost its aristocratic elegance and become a jumble of cheap clothing stalls, seedy gaming halls, electronics markets, and lowbrow bars and cafes. It's slated for a cleanup, but in the meantime it's got plenty of low-priced clothes, shoes, toys, and CDs. Watch your pocket. 30 Sadovaya Ulitsa. Metro: Gostiny Dvor.

FASHION

CHILDREN'S

DLT   This shopping center is full of shops selling imported and Russian goods with an emphasis on children's stores. 21 Bolshaya Konyushennaya Ulitsa. ℭ 812/312-2627. Metro: Nevsky Prospekt.

WOMEN'S & MEN'S

Gostiny Dvor   This arcade has mostly international brands but in a Russian atmosphere. See description under "Shopping Centers" earlier in this chapter. Hours are daily 10am to 10pm. 35 Nevsky Prospekt. ℭ 812/110-5408. Metro: Gostiny Dvor.

Tatyana Parfionova   Arguably St. Petersburg's most famous fashion designer, Parfionova creates unforgettable, original clothes and accessories. Her shows are the hottest ticket in town and her pieces are displayed in the Russian Museum. For something you definitely won't find at home, stop at her boutique. Excellent service. 51 Nevsky Prospekt. ℭ 812/113-1415. Metro: Gostiny Dvor.

FOOD

Also see the listings under "Caviar" and "Chocolate," above.

Eliseyevsky Gastronome   Like its Moscow counterpart, this reincarnation of a czarist-era shop has a rich selection of teas, sweets, and Russian treats, beneath crystal chandeliers and surrounded by stained-glass windows. 56 Nevsky Prospekt. © 812/311-9323 or 812/311-4657. Metro: Nevsky Prospekt.

GIFTS/SOUVENIRS

See Vernisazh under "Art," above.

ICONS

Also see chapter 8 for history and advice on Orthodox icons.

Russian Icon   An extensive array of icons is on display in this convenient boutique. They're all recently made, meaning you'll have no problem taking them out of the country, but they follow the same rules icon-painters have adhered to for centuries. The icons are more expensive than those at the monasteries, but the selection is larger. 15 Bolshaya Konyushennaya. © 812/314-7040. Metro: Nevsky Prospekt.

JEWELRY

See also review under "Amber" and the review for Vernisazh under "Art."

Ananov   This exclusive shop exhibits some original designs using unusual stones and gems, at high prices. 31 Nevsky Prospekt. © 812/110-5592. Metro: Vladimirskaya.

North Star (Polyarnaya Zvezda)   A more mid-range selection (and more mid-range prices) of gold, silver, and gems is offered here, including Siberian emeralds and amber. 158 Nevsky Prospekt. © 812/274-8525. Metro: Ploshchad Alexandra Nevskogo.

MUSIC

Classica   You'll find a great selection of classical, choral, and Russian folk music, mostly labeled in English as well as Russian. 2 Mikhailovskaya Ulitsa. © 812/110-4428. Metro: Nevsky Prospekt.

Severnaya Lira   This treasure trove of cheap sheet music emphasizes Russian composers. 26 Nevsky Prospekt. © 812/312-0796. Metro: Nevsky Prospekt.

Supermarket 505   The huge market sells CDs, DVDs, and CD-ROMs for as little as $2. The line between what is licensed and what is pirated is hazy. 10 Bolshaya Konyushennaya Ulitsa. © 812/318-6481. Metro: Nevsky Prospekt.

TOYS

See **DLT,** listed above under "Fashion," for modern, international toys. **Vernisazh,** listed above under "Art," offers more original toys like wooden Russian puppets and unusual chess sets.

VODKA & WINE

See **Kalinka Stockmann** and **Lenta** above under "Caviar." Both have good, inexpensive selections of Russian vodkas and wines from Georgia, Crimea, and Moldova that you're unlikely to find at home. The spirits sold in the ubiquitous kiosks around town are sometimes counterfeit and not worth risking despite their lower prices. Two others to try are:

Monopol   Extensive selection of wines, vodkas, brandies, and other liquor from around the world. 9 Konnogvardeisky Bulvar. © 812/312-0319. Metro: Gostiny Dvor.

Neva   Wine gallery catering to nouveau riche Russians and tourists. Ignore the French offerings and opt for an Armenian brandy or dry Georgian red. 13 Isaakevsky Sq. © 812/315-4731. Metro: Nevsky Prospekt.

St. Petersburg After Dark

Most of St. Petersburg's liveliest and richest cultural events take place during the magical summer weeks when there is no "after dark," under the soft, elongated sunset of the White Nights. Its 18th-century palaces throw open their doors for midnight music concerts, its regal parks and squares host open-air jazz festivals, and much of the city seems to be wandering the bridges and quays or floating down the canals until morning.

Of course, this city that considers itself Russia's cultural capital is alive with performances the rest of the year as well, and city boosters increasingly fill the calendar with events to even out the tourist flow, and to remind visitors that its northern latitude is not the only reason to visit St. Petersburg.

What was known for decades as the Kirov Ballet and Opera Company has again adopted its pre-revolutionary name of the Mariinsky Company, and performs at the magnificent Mariinsky Theater when it's not touring internationally. Its reputation, funding, and talent suffered during the decade following the Soviet Union's collapse, as many of its best dancers went abroad. But its standards remain world-class, and the theater and the city have benefited from growing competition by smaller companies. See chapter 9 for tips on buying Russian theater tickets.

The city's club and bar scene hasn't reached the superlative debauchery of Moscow's, but St. Petersburg's discos and casinos still offer plenty to shock and stimulate a Western visitor.

English-language listings for theater, music, and movies are best found in *The St. Petersburg Times* (www.sptimes.ru). Bar and club reviews can be found in the free, bilingual listings magazines found at restaurants and hotels.

1 The Performing Arts

This is the city where Maurice Petipa invented ballet, so it would be a shame not to pay homage by watching some of the world's top stars interpret this most classical of dance forms. Yet watching the *Nutcracker* in a Russian theater or hearing a Shostakovich concerto in a Russian symphony hall are only the most obvious ways to appreciate St. Petersburg's performing arts. Flawless dancing and searing melodies grace lesser-known works, too. St. Petersburg offers you an opportunity to explore operas and ballets less common outside Russia, such as Tchaikovsky's *Eugene Onegin* or Rimsky-Korsakov's *Imperial Bride*. Classical music venues are conservative in their repertoires but produce consistently rigorous performances—at surprisingly low prices. ***Take note:*** Most theaters close down after the White Nights until the season

---

Tips   **Where to Go During White Nights**

Several festivals claim to be St. Petersburg's "official" White Nights event, but in fact there are so many entertainment options that it doesn't matter who's more official than whom. The city government defines the period as the 50 days when the sun never gets more than 9 degrees below the horizon, roughly from late May to mid-July. The biggest events run for 2 weeks in late June and early July, centered around the summer solstice. Some festivals with the name "White Nights" in them start as early as May, so even if you're not in town on the longest day of the year, you have plenty of performances to choose from. See the Mariinsky Theater website (www.mariinsky.ru) for details of its **Stars of the White Nights** festival, considered the most prestigious in town. For schedules of the **White Nights Jazz** festival, another top draw, see www.jazz.ru/eng. The Shostakovich Philharmonic hosts a June music festival. Film festivals, fashion festivals, and beer festivals fill up any space left on the White Nights calendar. See www.cityguide.spb.ru for details. Once you arrive, consult your hotel concierge or English-language *The St. Petersburg Times* for more listings.

The main all-night, outdoor party scene is along a stretch of **Angliiskaya Naberezhnya (English Embankment)** on the south bank of the Neva, not far from the Hermitage, with street musicians, food stands, and throngs of people. Elsewhere, most official events are held in the evening, starting around 8 or 9pm, except at the dance clubs, where the partying starts and ends much later. Outdoor music festivals fill up stages at the **Summer Gardens** and **Taurida Gardens,** good for walks and picnics before or after the concerts. The imperial palaces outside St. Petersburg put on summer music performances, with the festival at **Peterhof** especially impressive, including concerts around the fountains and in the ballrooms. The towns of Vyborg and Tsarskoye Selo (Pushkin) also host music concerts; see chapter 18 for details. A few cruise companies and dozens of private boats ply St. Petersburg's canals in the wee hours during the White Nights, offering an excellent way to celebrate the city's overall beauty.

---

re-opens in September, so if you're here in late July or August, your options will be slim. See "The Performing Arts" in appendix A for a brief history of Russian ballet, opera, theater, and classical music.

DANCE

Alexandrinsky Theater   Also called the Pushkin Theater, the Alexandrinsky hosts performances by the acclaimed Russian Ballet and visiting dance companies, as well as dramatic plays (in Russian only). It is an impressive alternative to the Mariinsky if tickets there are not available or are out of your price range. Designed in the 1820s by Carlo Rossi, the Alexandrinsky is an important part of the surrounding architectural

St. Petersburg After Dark

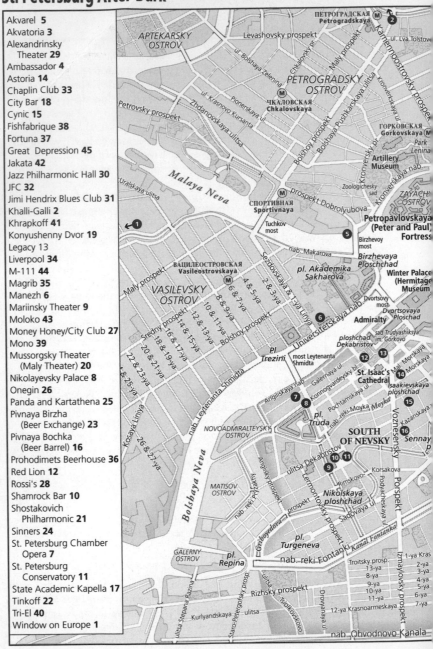

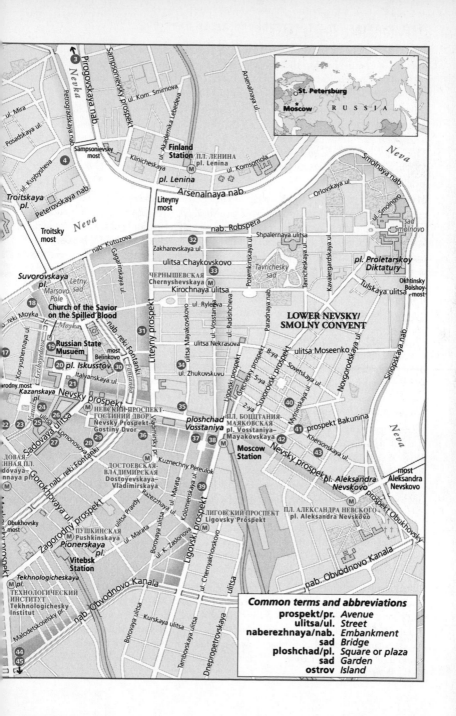

Common terms and abbreviations

prospekt/pr.	*Avenue*
ulitsa/ul.	*Street*
naberezhnaya/nab.	*Embankment*
sad	*Bridge*
ploshchad/pl.	*Square* or *plaza*
sad	*Garden*
ostrov	*Island*

271

ensemble. Sip champagne at intermission on the columned balcony for the full experience. It's one of the rare theaters that stays open in summer, offering top-quality performances when other theaters are shuttered or the troupes are on tour. Tickets run from $12 to $40. 2 Ploshchad Ostrovskogo. ℂ 812/315-4464. Metro: Gostiny Dvor.

Hermitage Theater   This exclusive viewing hall created for Catherine the Great is an intimate way to appreciate some of the world's top dancers and musicians. The hall's small size means tickets are expensive and limited, but the splurge is worthwhile. Tickets are available at the Hermitage Museum ticket office. Ticket prices run from $35 to $60. 34 Dvortsovaya Naberezhnya (Neva River side of the Winter Palace). ℂ 812/311-9025. Metro: Nevsky Prospekt.

Mariinsky Theater ⟨R⟩⟨R⟩⟨R⟩   Viewing anything in this theater makes you feel regal, even if the performance is limp and you're in sneakers. The sea-green exterior encloses a five-tiered theater draped, embroidered, and gilded in blue and gold. Top-floor seats have a dimmer view of the performers but a close-up view of the ceiling frescoes that draw you right into their pillowy clouds and floating angels. The snack bar offers champagne and small, cheap, open-faced sandwiches topped with caviar or smoked salmon. The reason visitors come, however, is to see the renowned and rigorous Mariinsky (formerly Kirov) Ballet. Director Valery Gergiev still prefers the classics such as *Sleeping Beauty* and *La Bayadere,* but the repertoire includes the occasional anthology or less well-known Russian ballets. The higher balconies can get stuffy in summer, and the restrooms are well below the standards of the rest of the building. The theater closes in August and early September, though visiting troupes occasionally perform during this period. Tickets purchased at the box office are cheaper than those bought through your hotel, but availability is often limited, since travel agencies buy up huge blocks of tickets in advance. 1 Teatralnaya Sq. ℂ 812/114-5264. www.mariinsky.ru/en Tickets $6–$18 for 3rd balcony seats; $100–$150 for orchestra. Metro: Sadovaya or Sennaya Ploshchad.

Mussorgsky Theater (aka Maly Theater or State Academic Opera and Ballet Theater) A cultural landmark since its first performance n 1833, this theater's repertoire includes Russian classics such as the *Nutcracker* and Prokofiev's *Romeo and Juliet,* international favorites *Barber of Seville* and *Carmen,* and a few small anthology-style performances. The theater itself is an only slightly less grand version of the Mariinsky, with the same open orchestra surrounded on three sides by four levels of balconies, all of which offer good views. A faithful miniature model of the theater next to the ticket office, aside from being a work of art, is useful for determining which seats you want. Much more convenient than the Mariinsky, this theater is right on the elegant Square of the Arts. It is closed late July to early September. 1 Square of the Arts (Ploshchad Isskustv). ℂ 812/314-3758. Tickets $5–$30 for matinees; $10–$60 for evening shows. Metro: Gostiny Dvor.

Nikolayevsky Palace   The "Feel Yourself Russian" folk show at this 18th-century palace is aggressively promoted at many hotels, and is extremely tourist-oriented. The traditional costumes are superb if overly bright, and the dancers are strong, but the whole performance is almost stereotypical. It's cheery and accessible to non-Russian speakers, and unlike many similar shows around town that toss in a topless number at the end, this one is kid-friendly. Tickets run about $35. 4 Ploshchad Truda. ℂ 812/312-5500. Metro: Sadovaya.

CLASSICAL MUSIC

Peter and Paul Cathedral   The cathedral inside the Peter and Paul Fortress is the main hall of the St. Petersburg Men's Choir, which carries on the tradition of its czarist-era founders. A stunning setting for some stunning voices, with performances Monday and Friday nights. Tickets run from $15 to $22. Peter and Paul Fortress (Hare's Island/Zaichy Ostrov). ℃ 812/767-0865. Metro: Gorkovskaya.

St. Petersburg Conservatory (Rimsky-Korsakov St. Petersburg State Conservatory)   This training ground for classical musicians across from the Mariinsky is no longer the coveted and cosseted institution it was in days past. The theater needs renovations, the musicians need to be better paid, and the ticket office could be friendlier, but performances here are still impressive. If you buy directly from the ticket office, you'll pay less than you would through your hotel, but you're still stuck with the $15 "tourist fee" on top of each ticket for foreigners. Primarily Russian composers and performers are featured. Tickets cost $2 to $6 (plus the $15 "tourist fee"). 4/31 Triumfalnaya Sq. ℃ 812/299-0378. Tickets $2–$6 plus a $15 "tourist fee." Metro: Mayakovskaya.

Shostakovich Philharmonic   Two halls, the Bolshoi (Grand) and Glinka (Small), stage symphonies, solo piano concerts, international festivals and competitions, and more, featuring music by Russian and international composers. The Grand Hall is home to the St. Petersburg Philharmonic but shares its stage with visiting performers. Both halls boast ornate and intricate interiors and superb acoustics, though they're in need of renovation. The building itself contributes to the ensemble of the Square of the Arts. 2 Mikhailovskaya St. ℃ 812/110-4164. www.philharmonia.spb.ru. Tickets $20–$35 in Bolshoi Hall; $5–$15 in Glinka Hall. Metro: Gostiny Dvor.

Smolny Cathedral and Convent   The acoustics of the central cathedral in what was once an elite convent make for unforgettable organ and chamber music concerts. They're staged several nights a week at varying times; some start in mid- or late afternoon. See p. 243 for more details on the Smolny Complex. 3/1 Rastrelli Sq. ℃ 812/271-7632. Tickets $5–$20. Metro: Chernyshevskaya.

State Academic Kapella   Housed in a classical building just across the canal from Palace Square, this music academy houses a renowned chorus and symphony orchestra. It hosts international music festivals, including excellent organ festivals. In 2005 it underwent a much-needed renovation of its 18th-century stage and practice halls. 20 Moika Embankment. ℃ 812/314-1034. Tickets $5–$20. Metro: Nevsky Prospekt.

Beyond the White Nights

Some festivals to watch out for during the off season include the **Autumn Marathon Jazz Festival** in October, run by the city Jazz Philharmonic; the **White Days** festival in January, with performances at all the major ballet and concert halls; and the **New Year's Festival** of dance and music late December to early January.

Theater Dining

St. Petersburg's theaters are too spread out for a theater dining scene, and performances tend to be too early (7pm as a rule) for pre-theater meals. The area around the Mariinsky Theater is surprisingly devoid of good dining options, so many visitors head for the rather incongruous Shamrock Irish restaurant and pub across the street, or the Russian coffee shop Yest around the corner. A better but slightly farther option is **Ob'ekt,** a Russian-European cafe-bar with a casually elegant atmosphere and reliable food, at 32 Moika Canal (© **812/312-1134;** Metro: Sadovaya).

OPERA

Mariinsky Theater   Its repertoire includes international favorites such as *The Marriage of Figaro* and *Carmen* performed in their original languages, as well as Russian favorites *Sadko* (a colorful and whimsical interpretation of a Russian fairy tale) and Mussorgsky's historical opera *Boris Godunov,* about the family dramas and tumultuous politics of 16th- and 17th-century Russia. Closed late July to early September. 1 Square of the Arts (Ploshchad Isskustv). © **812/314-3758.** Tickets $5–$30 matinees; $10–$60 evening shows. Metro: Gostiny Dvor.

Mussorgsky Theater (aka Maly Theater)   The fairly predictable international-Russian repertoire is performed in their original languages. See review under "Dance," above. Closed late July to early September. 1 Square of the Arts (Ploshchad Isskustv). © **812/ 314-3758.** Tickets $5–$30 matinees; $10–$60 evening shows. Metro: Gostiny Dvor.

St. Petersburg Chamber Opera   A range of Russian and international operas grace the stage of an 18th-century mansion. It's more intimate and less expensive than the Mariinsky. Tickets cost $30 to $35. 33 Galernaya Ulitsa. © **812/312-3982.** Metro: Sennaya Ploshchad.

THEATER

English-language theater performances are rather rare in St. Petersburg, though the choices multiply during the White Nights. See *The St. Petersburg Times* (www. sptimes.ru) for listings.

2 The Club & Music Scene

Someone is playing live music or spinning dance tracks somewhere in St. Petersburg any time of day, any time of the year. The city claims to be the birthplace of Russia's post-Soviet rock scene, spawning such bands as **Pep-see, Tequilajazz,** and the raspy, raunchy **Leningrad,** which went on to spawn others. Dance clubs run the gamut from freaky to haute couture to retro. Even the most mainstream of nightclubs or bars is bound to have topless entertainment, which has become such a staple of Russian nightlife that most Russians don't seem to watch.

St. Petersburg's jazz clubs underestimate the population's keen interest in the genre. Most people prefer to appreciate jazz at home, but a few venues are worth visiting for the peculiar Russian form of jazz. The White Nights Jazz Festival is one of the highlights of the summer season. See www.jazz.ru for details and listings.

DANCE CLUBS & DISCOS

Akvarel Several of the ship-restaurants along the north side of the Neva offer dance clubs at night, but this all-glass dockside restaurant/club is by far the sleekest way to party on the water. Vladimir Putin came here to sample its nouveau Italian cuisine and check out his native town's thriving nightlife. Door control gets fierce after 11pm; if you come for dinner and stay for the party you'll have no problem passing muster. 14a Prospekt Dobrolyubova. © 812/320-8600. Metro: Sportivnaya.

Jakata Consistently hip, and playing a mix of lounge, techno, and trance, this is the city's most authentic and least pretentious dance club. Open daily 24 hours, but don't bother showing up before midnight. 5 Bakunina Ulitsa. © 812/346-7461. Metro: Ploshchad Vosstaniya.

Khalli-Galli It's rather out of the way and definitely not for kids, but if you want a glimpse at the inhibition-free Russian party scene and some of its most dedicated practitioners, grab a taxi and head here. Open Tuesday through Saturday from 6pm to 4am, with strip shows after 11pm. 23 Lanskoye Shosse. © 812/246-9910. Cover $15 and up.

Khrapkoff If you fancy Latin dance lessons after a day of Russian sightseeing, come here. It's especially appealing when you want to warm up after a chilly day. The dance lessons start at 10pm Friday and Saturday. After lessons the place turns into a mainstream dance club, open until 6am. Other nights it's a bar (Sun–Thurs 10pm–2am). 12 Mytninskaya Ulitsa. © 812/274-4368. Metro: Ploshchad Vosstaniya.

Magrib This cafe-club is ostensibly North African, with embroidered pillows to lounge on and hookahs placed liberally around the hall. But people come here for the lively dance floor and people-watching. The restaurant side is overpriced but the cafe in front is a good place to relax before or during the party. DJs rotate and mix a blend of trance, house, and techno. Closed Monday. 84 Nevsky Prospekt. © 812/275-1255. Cover $7 women, $11 men, Tues free, Wed free for women. Metro: Mayakovskaya.

Onegin Russian models and fashion designers make the clientele here among the most beautiful in town. Also a popular, chic restaurant (reviewed on p. 224), this club seems harder to get into than it really is. A bit of attitude and persistence (and some decent togs) should be all you need to join this rarefied crowd. Music varies widely, and starts around 11pm. 11 Sadovaya Ulitsa. © 812/571-8384. Cover $5 after 10pm. Metro: Gostiny Dvor.

ROCK & POP

Konyushenny Dvor A hillbilly bar with an urban edge, this bar attracts Russian yuppies and foreign tourists who have little in common with the cowboy paraphernalia on its walls. Its small dance floor gets packed by midnight and music is mainstream but always dance-friendly. The balcony seats are much more fun, but watch out for the crooked, dim stairwell if you've been sampling Russian vodka. 5 Canal Griboyedova. © 812/315-7607. Cover $5 after 9pm. Metro: Nevsky Prospekt.

Liverpool   The Beatles had an especially devoted following in the Soviet Union, where their music made it to the masses only through bootleg LPs and underground fan clubs. At the Liverpool pub, live (Russian) bands play Beatles covers and other music of their era most nights. This is a weird and worthwhile stop for any Beatles fan. 16 Ulitsa Mayakovskaya. ✆ 812/279-2054. www.liverpool.ru. Metro: Mayakovskaya.

Money Honey/City Club   One of the more democratic clubs in' town, this place can be rough and rowdy on weekend nights. Live rockabilly music is on offer nearly every night, along with cheap beer. Closes early (11pm) on Monday. 13 Apraksin Dvor. ✆ 812/310-0549. www.moneyhoney.org. Cover charged for major shows. Metro: Sadovaya.

Rossi's   Once you get past the scary metal dragon-bird skeleton gateway and the metal detector, Rossi's is a lively and welcoming basement bar and music club. The low, vaulted ceilings of exposed brick and wood beams mean the place gets smoky at night. If that's a problem, make it an early evening stop for a beer or cocktail. 1/3 Ulitsa Zodchego Rossi. ✆ 812/110-4016. Cover $8 after 9pm Thurs–Sun. Metro: Gostiny Dvor.

JAZZ & BLUES

Jazz Philharmonic Hall   For more traditional shows, head to St. Petersburg's jazz shrine, whose large hall offers balconies and a nostalgic atmosphere. Performances are consistently excellent, with classically trained performers. Shows start at 7pm daily. Check out the Museum of Petersburg Jazz on the second floor. 3 Fontanka Naberezhnya. ✆ 812/164-8565. Tickets $5–$10. Metro: Vladimirskaya.

JFC   Elegant yet relaxed, this venue features Russian and foreign musicians and is a favorite among expats and Russian jazz connoisseurs. 33 Shpalernaya Ulitsa. ✆ 812/272-9850. Cover $2–$5. Metro: Chernyshevskaya.

Jimi Hendrix Blues Club   This basement bar inhabits a building that Russians know better as the house of poet Sergei Yesenin. It's the best place in town to hear blues, both authentic (by visiting performers) and with a Russian twist. Despite the exposed brick walls and torn posters, the place would have been too classy for Hendrix, but the atmosphere is pretty laid-back, the food is good, and the prices are reasonable. 33 Liteiny Prospekt. ✆ 812/279-8813. Cover $3. Metro: Mayakovskaya.

FOLK & ALTERNATIVE

Cynic (Tsynik)   This fun and funky venue stayed hip even after expanding to a three-room space with room enough to dance (unlike its minuscule original locale). Students, expats, and anyone with steam to blow appreciate its spontaneous shows by underground bands and its cheap beer and food. It's famous for its *grenki,* garlic toast, but you get used to the smell fast. Open Sunday through Thursday from 11am to 3am; Friday and Saturday from 10am to 7pm. 4 Antonenko Pereulok. ✆ 812/312-1526. Metro: Sennaya Ploshchad.

Fishfabrique   Part of the Pushkinskaya 10 art complex (p. 246), this is the hippest and most creative place for alternative bands, though perhaps the smallest. It's called "Fishka" by locals. Check out the gallery of experimental sound and other wonders in this countercultural cavern of performance and gallery spaces. Open daily from 3pm

to 6am; concerts usually take place Thursday through Saturday. 10 Pushkinskaya Ulitsa.
© 812/164-4857. Cover $2–$8 for concerts. Metro: Ploshchad Vosstaniya.

Moloko   Unpretentious and authentically alternative, this club is following in the footsteps of the Tamtam Club, where many of St. Petersburg's biggest stars got their break. Now it features local and international (especially German) punk and alternative bands, as well as cheap drinks. 12 Perekupnoi Pereulok. © 812/274-9467. Cover $2–$3. Metro: Ploshchad Vosstaniya.

NIGHTCLUBS & CABARET

Unfortunately, most nightclubs in St. Petersburg have become synonymous with bordellos, and the stage shows are little more than strip acts. The nightclubs in the more expensive hotels are somewhat cleaner, though they tend to be stale and not worth the high drink prices. The bars and dance clubs are a better way to feel the city's nighttime pulse. One exception, perhaps the only cabaret in town, is the **Chaplin Club,** which puts on pantomime shows, comedy shows, or jazz performances at 7:30pm every night for about $2. The shows are in Russian but visually enjoyable, and the atmosphere is relaxed and arty with a vaudevillian feel. During the day, children's parties are staged and a generous all-inclusive Russian-European lunch is offered for $7. The club is at 59 Chaikovskogo Ulitsa (© 812/272-6649; metro: Chernyshevskaya).

3 The Bar Scene

St. Petersburg's bar scene is less extensive than Moscow's, but it's more compact—largely jammed up along Nevsky Prospekt—and perhaps more creative. Nevsky's bar-restaurants are open until the wee hours, or all night. During the White Nights, the taps flow steadily till dawn. The brewing industry has blossomed in and around St. Petersburg in recent years, and many of the country's favorite brands are based here. Be sure to try out local beers Tinkoff, Baltika (no. 7 is the most accessible), and Nevskoye at some point during your stay.

City Bar   This bar is run by an American and attracts a mixed Russian-expat crowd for its "Amerikansky Biznes Lunch" at midday and its lively bar at night. Beer, martinis, and a Sunday all-you-can-drink champagne brunch for just $12 are among its highlights. 10 Millionaya Ulitsa. © 812/314-1037. Metro: Nevsky Prospekt.

Great Depression   It calls itself "the bar to honor the working classes," though it's more popular with students and sports fans who come here to watch international soccer matches. The bar is not at all centrally located, but if you're staying in the adjacent Rossia Hotel or are visiting Victory Park across the street, it's worth a stop. 157a Moskovsky Prospekt. © 812/371-6989. Metro: Park Pobedy.

Manezh   Sometimes it's a sports bar, sometimes a bierstube, sometimes a concert space. Enormous screens make Manezh great for watching big soccer matches or Olympic games. 13 Universitetskaya Naberezhnaya. © 812/327-8947. Metro: Vasileostrovskaya.

Pivnaya Birzha (Beer Exchange)   There are no set prices for beer in this friendly bar-cafe—you bid for brew as at a stock exchange. The 15 or so beers on tap include local brews, locally brewed international brands like Carlsberg and Heineken, and some imports. The $3 business lunch is good. 25 Canal Griboyedova. (C) 812/571-5659. Metro: Nevsky Prospekt.

Pivnaya Bochka (Beer Barrel)   Russian beer on tap and basic Russian cuisine at low prices are the main draws here. This is a good after-dinner spot but it only stays open until 11pm. 39 Kazanskaya Ulitsa. (C) 812/312-7253. Metro: Gostiny Dvor.

Prokhodimets Beerhouse   This is a friendly spot for porter, lager, and unfiltered beer in the section of town known as the Five Corners (Pyat Uglov). Its name translates as something like "rascal." 8 Ulitsa Rubinshteina. (C) 812/117-1243. Metro: Vladimirskaya.

Red Lion   Its ideal location (inside the Senate building across from the Bronze Horseman) is reason enough to check out this British-style pub. Food is mediocre but a plate of late-night fish and chips is hard to resist. Free admission, occasional live bands, and periodic rounds of free champagne add to its appeal. Open daily 24 hours. 1 Decembrists Sq. (Ploshchad Dekabristov). (C) 812/117-4526. Metro: Nevsky Prospekt.

Shamrock Bar   Oddly, this Irish pub is the only place to get a bite to eat or drink on the square near the Mariinsky Theater. It's cozy and friendly, and about as culturally distant from the imperial ballet theater as you can get. There's live Irish music most nights, and lots of beer on tap. 27 Ulitsa Dekabristov (Teatralnaya Sq.). (C) 812/318-4625. Metro: Sadovaya.

Tinkoff   This brewery houses a lively sports bar, sushi bar, and music club, and is among the city's most consistently popular hangouts. See review for Tinkoff restaurant on p. 230. 7 Ulitsa Kazanskaya. (C) 812/118-5566. Metro: Sadovaya or Sennaya Ploshchad.

Window on Europe   One of the best spots in town to watch a midnight sunset is the glass-enclosed terrace on the Finnish Gulf. The restaurant is as unwieldy as the Pribaltiiskaya Hotel that looms above it, with more than 1,000 seats. But that means you'll always have a good view. The food is mediocre but the drink selection broad. Open 24 hours. Ploshchad Evropa (behind the Pribaltiiskaya Hotel). (C) 812/327-8947. Metro: Primorskaya.

4 The Gay & Lesbian Nightlife Scene

The gay scene in Petersburg, as elsewhere in Russia, really only emerged over the past decade after Soviet-era laws against homosexuality were scrapped. Now the city's gay club scene is like its counterparts in any major metropolis: fickle. Today's hot spot may be too mainstream—or may have gone straight—by next season. Many of the city's top dance clubs have gay nights, and nearly all clubs are gay-friendly. See www.gay.ru/english for up-to-date listings.

Mono   Essentially a two-room apartment, Mono serves as a decent gay venue, with transvestite shows and dance music. 4 Kolomenskaya Ulitsa. (C) 812/164-3678. Cover up to $3 for men; up to $6 for women. Men only Mon; women accepted Sat only accompanied by 2 men. Metro: Mayakovskaya.

Sinners (Greshniki)   Four floors of an old mansion host one of the city's best mixed party spots. Sometimes it's gay-dominant, sometimes simply gay-friendly, but it's always good for dancing. Paint and brushes are often available for body art. 28 Canal Griboyedova. ✆ 812/219-4291. Cover $2–$3 men; $8–$12 women. Metro: Nevsky Prospekt.

Tri El (Three Ls)   Hip and friendly lesbian club. Petersburg's—and perhaps Russia's—first lesbian club, this is slowly opening up to a broader public. Its cozy lounge and inexpensive bar draw in visitors as much as its lesbian strip shows and transvestite performances. 45 Pyataya Sovietskaya Ulitsa. ✆ 812/110-2016. Cover $2–$5. Women only Sat–Wed. Metro: Ploshchad Vosstaniya.

5 More Entertainment

CASINOS

St. Petersburg's high-brow history hasn't kept out the flood of gaudy gambling establishments embraced by post-Soviet Russia. Slot machines are found in places you least expect them, including upscale restaurants and shops. At the casinos, minimum stakes are often quite high (as much as $100); be sure to ask about this before you even check your coat.

Astoria   It has nothing to do with the nearby Astoria Hotel, but this casino imitates some of the hotel's historical ambience and is definitely one of the most glamorous places to part with your money at roulette, poker, or blackjack. Daily 24 hours. 20 Malaya Morskaya Ulitsa. ✆ 812/313-5020. Metro: Nevsky Prospekt.

Fortuna   This casino is as convenient and high-rolling as befits this stretch of Nevsky. Daily 2pm to 6am. 71 Nevsky Prospekt. ✆ 812/164-2087. Metro: Nevsky Prospekt.

BOWLING

To prepare for the trendy disco atmosphere of most Russian bowling alleys, see "More Entertainment" in chapter 9.

Akvatoria   An uninspiring gray office building well beyond the center houses this entertainment complex on the ground floor. Daily noon to 6am. 61 Vyborgskaya Naberezhnya. ✆ 812/245-2030. Lanes $12 per hour and up. Metro: Vyborgskaya.

M-111   This multistory amusement zone offers some of the hippest bowling in town, with black light and club music after 9pm. Daily noon to 6am. 111 Moskovsky Prospekt. ✆ 812/320-4400. Lanes $8–$30 per hour, depending on time of day (around midnight on weekends the price peaks). Metro: Moskovskiye Vorota.

BILLIARDS

See "More Entertainment" in chapter 9 for a description of Russian "piramida" vs. English billiards and American pool.

Ambassador   A good source of cheap beer and pool near the upscale Astoria and Angleterre hotels. 31 Ulitsa Kuibisheva. ✆ 812/232-8506. Tables $2–$5 depending on the hour (before 6pm is cheapest). Metro: Nevsky Prospekt or Sadovaya.

Legacy (Naslediye)   Legacy, located on Decembrists' Square overlooking the Neva River and St. Isaac's Cathedral, boasts two halls for Russian billiards and American pool. It also has an extensive bar, a dance floor, and a nightly strip show after 11pm. 1 Decembrists' Sq. ✆ 812/315-3153. Tables $6 per hour and up. Metro: Nevsky Prospekt.

Panda and Kartathena This nightspot houses a casino favored by Petersburg's nouveau riche, as well as billiards and pool tables. No informal dress is allowed, but if you want an atmospheric way to shoot some balls, come here. 26 Griboyedov Canal. ℭ **812/312-8896.** Metro: Nevsky Prospekt.

18

Side Trips from St. Petersburg

Anywhere you go outside St. Petersburg will give you new perspective on the city's geography and its place in Russia's history. Whether you want to breathe fresh air, delight in country palaces of the nobility, or see rural architecture, branching out from the city is well worth a day or so of your trip.

Peterhof, Pavlovsk, and Pushkin (Tsarskoye Selo) house three of the most spectacular summer estates of the Romanov czars, and most tour groups and individual tourists visit at least one of them. We recommend the same, though avoid them on rainy days. The extensive, landscaped parklands around the palaces are as much a part of the trip as the overly gilded interiors. The towns, charming in their own right, remind you why Peter chose to base his capital elsewhere, on the river-crossed delta opening to the Baltic Sea.

The other destinations listed here reflect entirely different chapters in Russian history. Vyborg is a 13th-century town that has been Swedish, Finnish, and Karelian (an ethnic group based in what is now northwest Russia and eastern Finland) as well as Russian, and its architecture and mindset are nothing like those of Peter the Great's Enlightenment-era capital. Kronshtadt is an island fortress that once served as a Viking rest stop but later became a major Soviet naval base closed to outsiders. It's now open to tourists and makes for a fascinating day trip.

These destinations are best appreciated with a tour guide unless you know a lot about them before you go. Peterhof and Kronshtadt are fairly easy to reach on your own, and both can be accessed by boat in the warmer months. The other destinations require multiple modes of transportation, making them better candidates for an organized tour.

1 Peterhof (Petrodvorets) ✶✶✶

30km (18 miles) W of St. Petersburg

Unquestionably the number-one day trip from St. Petersburg, Peterhof lures visitors with its Versailles-inspired palace, which overlooks a cascade of fountains and gardens opening onto the Baltic Sea. This scene is much better appreciated from April to October, when the Grand Cascade is flowing and the park is in bloom. Going to Peter the Great's summer palace by ferry or hydrofoil enhances the pleasure of the experience, giving you a sense of Peter's maritime ambitions and of the region's role as Russia's western frontier. The boat ride and extensive park make this a great summer outing for kids.

Side Trips from St. Petersburg

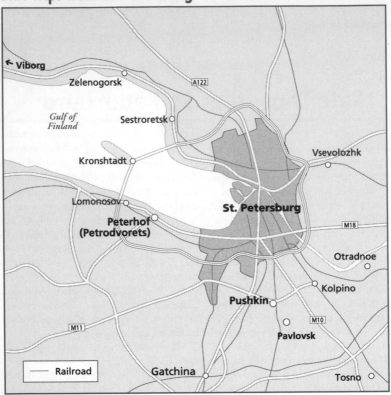

ESSENTIALS

You'll get much more out of Peterhof if the weather is good, since a major part of the experience is seeing the fountains (Apr–Oct) and wandering the grounds. The trip can easily be handled on your own, though organized tours are readily available. Tours offer two main advantages: no worries about transport, and detailed descriptions of the sights. The disadvantages are that you may be stuck in a crowded, touristy restaurant for lunch, and you won't get to explore the grounds freely. Tour costs are not much higher than paying for transport and museum tickets on your own. Check with your hotel about tours, or try **Davranov Travel** (17 Italianskaya Ulitsa; © **812/117-8694;** www.davranov.ru).

Boat trips are the best way to get here from mid-May to early October, not least because of the breathtaking view of the palace as you pull up to the Peterhof pier. Two companies run hydrofoils from the docks on the Neva River in front of the Winter Palace. **Russian Cruises** (© **812/974-0100;** www.russian-cruises.ru) is the better equipped and offers English-language commentary. The **Vodokhod** company (© **812/380-9011**) is cheaper but more rudimentary. The trip whizzes along the forested banks of the Baltic Sea and takes about 45 minutes. Boats run several times a day. When you disembark, head up the canal for the palace; the entrance is on the opposite side. Organized tours will often take you there on a boat and back home on a bus.

From October to May the best way to go is by bus. Russian vendors hawk trips on direct buses from Nevsky Prospekt metro station. They cost about $20 round-trip and take an hour and a half.

WHAT TO SEE & DO

The palace and grounds offer enough to fill a day, or at least an afternoon. Start with the **Great Palace,** and be prepared to squint at all the gold inside. The rooms run in a long line facing the park, which can make for bottlenecks if visitors reverse direction or when there are large groups. Many visitors say the palace feels too magnificent to live in—and Peter felt the same, preferring **Monplaisir,** a small baroque bungalow close to the water's edge that was the first building in the Peterhof complex.

Peter chose Peterhof's location for his summer residence based on its proximity to Kronshtadt, the island fort that housed his fledgling Russian navy (see review later in this chapter). Built in 1715 by Jean Baptiste Leblond, the Great Palace came to be known for its grand summer fetes, in which everyone was invited to explore the czar's domain. The palace was occupied by the Nazis during World War II and suffered severe damage; its painstaking renovation became the region's pride. Note the Throne Room, with its dizzying light and portraits of the Romanovs; the neighboring Ladies-in-Waiting Room; and the intricate wooden floors of the Western Chinese Study.

In the lush park, the Monplaisir house, the small red-and-white Hermitage, and the **Marly Palace** (with a carved wood desk that Peter himself made) are well worth exploring, too, and more atmospheric than the Great Palace. Before heading down into the park, spend a moment on the palace balcony to take in the view of the greenery and the **Grand Cascade** from above. If it's open, explore the **grotto** beneath the fountain to see the 18th-century engineering feats that helped pipe in water from springs in the surrounding Ropsha Hills and make the cascade's 64 water jets work in synchronicity.

The most elaborate statues and fountains are along the axis from the palace to the pier. Be sure to see **Samson Fountain,** with the biblical strongman tearing apart the jaws of a lion, symbolizing Peter's victory over Sweden in 1709. Off to one side are the musical staccato fountains that shoot up at unpredictable intervals, where children love to drench themselves in warm weather while trying to guess which one will go off next. The park also includes a labyrinth of paths and ornate iron footbridges, as well as several small pavilions and gazebos. Park pavilions have opening days and admission fees different from those of the palace; weekends are the only time everything is open.

Peterhof (Petrodvorets) Palace and Park is at 2 Razvodnaya Ulitsa (© **812/427-9527**). Admission to the palace costs $12 adults, $6 college students and children; admission to the park alone costs $7 adults, $3.50 students and children. The palace is open Tuesday through Sunday from 10:30am to 5pm (closed last Tues of each month). Monplaisir and other buildings on the grounds have different hours.

WHERE TO DINE

The most convenient dining options are on the grounds of the park itself. **Imperatorsky Stol,** in the orangerie near the Triton Fountain, is a cozy place for tea, snacks, or a full meal of decent and inexpensive Russian-European cuisine (© 812/427-9106). The **Standart** restaurant (© 812/427-9281), at the center of the Lower Park near the canal, has more elegantly and expertly prepared Russian fare, for a higher price. It's housed in the former Illumination Yard, which was used to store pyrotechnic equipment for the palace's extravagant balls. Outside the grounds are a few restaurants playing up the town's imperial heritage for the benefit of rich Russian and foreign tourists, with servers in period costume and ornate dining halls. One of these is **Ofitserskoye Sobraniye** (25 Ulitsa Konstantinovskaya; © 901/307-6457)**,** housed in a former club for pre-revolutionary royal officers. Its extensive appetizer selection is more successful than the main courses.

2 Tsarskoye Selo (Pushkin)

25km (16 miles) S of St. Petersburg

For an intimate view of imperial country living during St. Petersburg's rise to world prominence, visit baroque Catherine's Palace at Tsarskoye Selo (formerly called Pushkin). This is almost always viewed together with a trip to nearby Pavlovsk to see Czar Paul I's classical castle and sculpted gardens (see the next section). It was here that Russian engineers laid the country's first railway line connecting these two royal resort towns, in order to shuttle nobles between palaces for summertime balls. Today anyone can ride the train, a 5-minute, 50¢ ride, and view a model of the original train that took Czar Nicholas I and his family on their first ride. The world-famous **Amber Room**—gutted by the Nazis and recently meticulously reconstructed—is the major draw at Catherine's Palace; the rest of its rooms are marginally less impressive.

ESSENTIALS

Tsarskoye Selo and Pavlovsk each can be visited on its own, but their proximity to each other and convenient transport between them make for a pleasant dual-destination trip. Nearly all organized tours combine the two. You could fit both into 1 day, extend the trip over a weekend, or visit each separately. If you're visiting both, it makes most sense to hit Tsarskoye Selo in the morning, then head to Pavlovsk for a picnic lunch in the park before visiting the palace there.

Many St. Petersburg hotels offer tours, as do **Davranov Travel** (17 Italianskaya Ulitsa; © 812/117-8694; www.davranov.ru) and **Frigate Tours** (© 812/331-3333; www.frigate-tour.com). You can also get a riverboat to Tsarskoye Selo from the pier in front of the Winter Palace in St. Petersburg during the warmer months. Getting there on your own is not too difficult, but getting around once you're there requires a great deal of walking. A good tour guide or detailed book about the palaces (available at bookstores in St. Petersburg; see "Books" in chapter 16) is recommended. Organized tours usually take you by bus to Tsarskoye Selo first, then to Pavlovsk.

If you're on your own, Russian tour buses run direct to Tsarskoye Selo from in front of Nevsky Prospekt metro station; the trip takes about 40 minutes and costs about

$20 round-trip. You can also take a suburban train *(elektrichka),* which leaves Vitebsk station in St. Petersburg for Tsarskoye Selo, then continues on to Pavlovsk. The ride costs less than $5 and takes about 45 minutes, then another 5 minutes to Pavlovsk, but you must be able to read the names of both towns in Russian to make sure you don't miss your stop (see appendix B). The train station at Tsarskoye Selo is a sight in itself, with its Art Nouveau sweep and murals showing stations along the route, as well as the Royal Waiting Room upstairs. The walk to the palace takes a good 15 minutes, or you can hire a taxi.

WHAT TO SEE & DO

The town's original name, Tsarskoye Selo (Tsar's Village) comes from the palaces and parks built by empresses Catherine I (Peter the Great's second wife) and Elizabeth I (their daughter). The electric-blue, white, and gold **Catherine's Palace (Yekaterinsky Dvorets)**—the world's longest palace, at nearly 300m (1,000 ft.)—is the town's central star. In the Soviet era, the town was named after the adored Russian poet Alexander Pushkin, who studied at the *lycée* here for 6 years in the early 19th century and later had a *dacha* (country house) in town. The Pushkin-related sights are only worth visiting if you speak Russian. The town has since readopted its pre-revolutionary name, but many Russians and much literature about the town still refer to it as Pushkin.

Although the palace was named after Catherine I, it was Catherine II (the Great) who was responsible for much of its interior design. It was built in stages, each of which reflects the character of the empress in charge at the time. Its baroque, festive features come from Elizabeth's favored court architect Bartolomeo Rastrelli, who later designed St. Petersburg's Winter Palace, while the simpler, neoclassical interiors came from Catherine the Great's English architect Charles Cameron. The facade of the palace is as sunny as the muted green face of the Winter Palace in Petersburg is misty, and much of the interior of Catherine's Palace glares even more brightly than its exterior. The gold cupolas of the palace church rise above one end of the facade, and a flowery, ornamental "E" (the Russian initial for Yekaterina) tops its entrance.

The palace's masterpiece, the **Amber Room,** is a crucial part of every tour. Museum guards sometimes restrict visitors' time there to control crowds. Its unrivalled concentration of amber, its unusual concept, and its dramatic history make it worth all the hype. The room actually feels small compared to others in the palace. It takes you a moment to realize that its walls are lined in amber panels, using nearly a ton of stone (technically, petrified sap). Florentine mosaics portraying the five senses combine a staggering array of shades of amber, from milky green to deep rust brown. Furniture inlaid with amber occupies the room. Many of the works, however, are copies of long-lost originals. The original engraved wall panels were a gift to Peter the Great from the king of Prussia in 1716, then were stolen by Nazis who occupied the palace during the siege of Leningrad. One of the mosaics, *Smell and Touch,* is an original, discovered in private hands in Bremen, Germany, in 1997. The palace itself suffered even more widespread damage when the Nazis retreated—they blew up many of its masterpieces on their way, and the reconstruction took decades.

The other chief highlight of the palace is the **Great Hall,** a grand ballroom lined with two tiers of windows interspersed with mirrors, much like Versailles' Hall of Mirrors. When the sun shines, the hall sparkles with reflections off the mirrors—perfect for balls on sunny midsummer nights. The palace holds chamber music concerts during the White Nights. The Grand Hall's ceiling painting runs nearly the length of the room, and depicts Russian military victories and accomplishments in the sciences and arts.

Similarly luxurious halls elsewhere in the palace are the **Agate Pavilion,** a bathhouse of polished Siberian stone; and the **Blue Drawing Room, Blue Chinese Room,** and **Choir Anteroom,** all of which have intoxicating silk wall coverings. The **Green Dining Room** is one of the first imperial rooms in Russia to incorporate a fireplace and marble mantelpiece; until then, the preference had been for Dutch-tiled corner ovens.

Leave plenty of time to explore the grounds, in particular the **Marble Bridge** over the Great Pond, and the **Pyramid,** where Catherine the Great's favorite dogs were buried. The pavilion on the island was built for the musicians who accompanied royal boat trips on the pond.

Catherine's Palace (Yekaterinsky Dvorets) is located at 7 Ulitsa Sadovaya, Pushkin (© 812/465-5308; www.tzar.ru). Admission to the park is free; admission to the palace costs $13 adults, $7.50 for college students and for children over 7. The park is open daily sunrise to sunset; the palace is open Wednesday through Monday from 10am to 6pm (closed last Mon of each month).

WHERE TO DINE

Cafe Tsarskoye Selo in the palace itself is the most convenient but least interesting lunch option in the vicinity, with hot and cold drinks and small open-faced sandwiches. (Its entrance is opposite the *lycée;* © 812/465-5308). A more picturesque spot is the **Admiralty (Admiralteistvo),** on the second floor of the pavilion of the same name on the shore of the Baltic Sea, at the other side of the Great Pond from the palace (Yekateriinsky Park; © 812/465-3549). The cuisine is primarily Russian, and service is friendly. Slightly farther from the palace, along the park's edge, is **Staraya Bashnya (Old Tower)** restaurant, concealed in the cluster of buildings called Fyodorovsky Gorodok (14 Akademichesky Pereulok; © 812/466-6698). Russian items such as garlicky beef dumplings *(pelmeni)* and beef stroganoff are particularly worthwhile. The restaurant is small, so reservations are a good idea before you make the trek out there.

3 Pavlovsk

30km (19 miles) S of St. Petersburg

The park at Pavlovsk outshines even its impressive palace, and is perfect for picnicking on a clear day. Several enclaves dot the grounds, representing more human-size architecture of the 18th and 19th centuries. The town is named after the palace's original ruler, Czar Paul I (Pavel in Russian). In a reflection of their characters, Paul's summer home is as restrained and classical as his mother Catherine the Great's summer getaway at Tsarskoye Selo is extravagant and baroque. Comparing the two is a key reason to combine visits to them in a single day.

ESSENTIALS

This trip is often combined with a journey to Tsarskoye Selo (see review above). If you want to view it separately, you can try to arrange an individual tour through your hotel or a travel agency. Otherwise, you can take a suburban train *(elektrichka)* from St. Petersburg's Vitebsk Station. The train takes about 50 minutes, and goes through Tsarskoye Selo first; Pavlovsk is the next stop. You must be able to read the name in Russian (see appendix B). The trip through town to the palace is about a 15-minute walk or ride on a local bus; it's not marked, but any resident can direct you.

WHAT TO SEE & DO

Here, as in Tsarskoye Selo, the town's palace is the central attraction. More an imitation of a Roman villa than a royal residence, the yellow-and-white Grand Palace at Pavlovsk was built in 1782 on a bluff overlooking the Slavyanka River. The Nazis also occupied this palace, but curators managed to save many of its masterpieces by hiding them in niches behind false walls.

A who's-who of Russian architects had a hand in the palace's interiors, including Charles Cameron, Jacomo Quarenghi, and Carlo Rossi. You'll notice the split personality this produced in the contrast between the extravagant **Throne Room** and the simple, dignified **Corner Drawing Room,** lined in lavender marble and Karelian birch furniture. Note the table settings in the **Dining Room,** ready for imperial guests. **Paul's Library** includes tall tapestries given to him by Louis XVI soon before the French Revolution.

Paul's wife Maria Fyodorovna lived here another 27 years after his death, and her quarters constitute a separate little museum within the palace. The **Dowager Empress Rooms,** as they're named, feel lived-in, unlike the rest of the palace, with its cold ornamentation. The rooms especially come alive after you look at palace portraits of Maria and at her own artworks.

The 607-hectare (1,500-acre) park is a winding labyrinth of wooded lanes, shady glades, and pavilions, but it's well planned enough that you never feel lost no matter how far you wander. Highlights include the Circle of White Birches at the end of the Rose Pavilion Alley, Centaur Bridge, and the partly crumbled Apollo Colonnade on the riverbanks on the palace side.

Admission to the **Grand Palace (Veliky Dvorets),** 20 Ulitsa Revolutsii (© **812/470-2156;** www.pavlovsk.org) and grounds is $11 for adults, $5.50 for college students and for children over 7. You'll pay an additional $3 to visit the Dowager Empress Rooms. The palace is open Saturday through Thursday from 10am to 5pm (closed 1st Mon of each month).

WHERE TO DINE

The grounds here are so ideal for picnicking that the best dining suggestion is to stop in the **Great Column Hall (Bolshoi Kolonny Zal)** restaurant and order food to go. (You can even get a bottle of champagne—or technically, Russian sparkling wine.) Housed in the former servants' quarters, the restaurant has a cafeteria-style section and a full-menu section as well, in case the weather is dreary. The Russian dishes are more successful, though you can order international favorites like Caesar salad. Another charming but basic option in the park is **Cafe Slavyanka,** across Centaur Bridge from the palace and to the left.

For an enthusiastic, satisfying, and almost kitschy taste of Russian country dining, stop at **Podvorye** restaurant (16 Filtrovskoye Shosse; © 812/465-1399) on your way to or from Pavlovsk. The hunting-lodge-style restaurant is on the main highway leading to St. Petersburg, so you need a bus or taxi to get there. Wild boar steak, elk cutlets, and even bear meat are among your options; vegetarians should try the pickled garlic and mushrooms, or pretty much anything with garlic or wild mushrooms. Guests are greeted with free vodka samples. A milder drink choice is *mors,* a delicious cranberry juice made from stewed local berries.

4 Kronshtadt

30km (18 miles) SW of St. Petersburg

For a place that was closed to outsiders just a decade ago, this island is remarkably accessible today, and is perhaps the easiest day trip outside St. Petersburg. The island was first mentioned as a 12th-century rest stop for Viking expeditions to Greece, later became a fortress buttressing Peter the Great's new capital from attack, and later still became a key Cold War naval outpost. Today it's open for tourist business but still appears to be casting about for its modern role. Head here to wander the carefully planned harbor, the immaculate boulevards, the neo-Byzantine Naval Cathedral, and the naval history museum—or simply to gaze at the restless Baltic Sea around you.

ESSENTIALS

Kronshtadt is one of the few side trips manageable without a group or a tour guide. If you prefer a tour, check with your hotel; most places can arrange an individual or group tour. You can also try travel agencies such as **Davranov Travel** (17 Italianskaya Ulitsa; © 812/117-8694; www.davranov.ru) and **Frigate Tours** (© 812/331-3333; www.frigate-tour.com).

The most appropriate way to travel to a naval outpost is, of course, by boat. From May to October, ferries head here several times a day from the piers behind the Hermitage Museum and from in front of Kunstkamera Museum on the other side of the Neva River. The ride takes about 1 hour and costs about $8.

You can also take a bus. Russian vendors hawk group bus trips at the corner of Nevsky Prospekt and Griboyedov Canal for about $10 round-trip (the ride takes about an hour). Or take minibus no. K-45 from metro station Chernaya Rechka, for about a 40-minute ride that costs less than $2.

Once you arrive, it couldn't hurt to buy a map from a newspaper kiosk. They're not always available, but the island is too small for you to get lost. The map helps you focus on specific spots and saves you time wandering through the bleaker neighborhoods of Soviet apartment blocks.

WHAT TO SEE & DO

The chief sights are the Naval Cathedral, which houses a good naval history museum, and the harbor. Much of the architecture and port infrastructure dates from Peter the Great's time, when he ordered a base built on Kotlin Island for Russia's fledgling navy, to block enemies from approaching his new capital. After victory over Sweden in the decisive Battle of Poltava in 1709, Peter launched large-scale construction of the island, and the first harbor and adjacent warehouses appeared. Some chronicles suggest

Peter originally wanted to put the new capital on the island, but he never went further than building one of his many palaces here. It later burned down, but the palace of his chief adviser Alexander Menshikov still stands—it's an impressive Italian-designed mansion on the southern shore. The town itself is clearly planned, in the style of St. Petersburg, with broad, straight avenues and large squares. The **harbor** still feels more like a utilitarian military base than a romantic island boardwalk, but it's worth a wander nonetheless, if only to see the aging warships and port infrastructure.

The broad, etched dome of the **Naval Cathedral** dominates the skyline and looms over otherwise empty Yakornaya Ploshchad (Anchor Sq.). The anchor is incorporated into the cathedral's door carving, and pops up around town in grillwork, signage, and restaurant decor. Built in 1902 in a pseudo-Byzantine style, the cathedral is covered with intricate carvings and seems out of place in this otherwise rational, reserved city. The church's interiors have largely been turned over to the **Kronshtadt Museum of Naval History,** which is worth a visit if you have an English-speaking guide; otherwise, it may prove frustrating since most exhibits are in Russian only. The museum is packed with models of ships, weaponry through the centuries, seascapes by Russian artists, and unusual items such as anti-submarine netting. While it recounts the history of the island, the museum is rather awkward in its handling of the bloody mutiny that most Russians have come to associate with the name Kronshtadt. When the island's entire battalion staged an uprising against repressive Bolshevik leaders in 1921, the Soviet government responded swiftly and fiercely, massacring almost the whole battalion. The city remained a closed naval base for the rest of the Soviet era, and was only opened in 1996. The museum (© **812/236-4713**) is open Wednesday to Sunday from 11am to 5pm.

WHERE TO DINE

Kronshtadt has no bustling beach boardwalk, but it has several mediocre restaurants within walking distance of the cathedral, museum, or harbor. None is particularly outstanding or particularly risky, though few have English-language menus. This is starting to change, and any place with a menu in English will be more expensive and probably offer somewhat better food and service. One pleasant spot for lunch is **Stary Gorod (Old Town),** 7 Ulitsa Grazhdanskaya (© **812/236-2238**), offering Russian and European standards such as borscht and baked salmon in a simple, homey setting. Seafood dishes are in the majority, though the selection is not as broad as you'd expect for an island town. The "business lunch" is just $3. Decent Russian beer is on tap.

5 Vyborg

130km (78 miles) NW of St. Petersburg

For a journey into an entirely different era and mindset from St. Petersburg and the imperial estates on its outskirts, head to Vyborg. This 13th-century, cobblestoned city near the Finnish border has less glamour but more depth than Peter the Great's capital. Vyborg's architecture reflects its history, which tossed it back and forth among Swedes, Russians, Finns, and Karelians native to the region. The couple of hours it takes to get there can be thought of as journeying into Scandinavia for a day; then the trip doesn't seem so long at all. The distance is a good reminder of how close to the edge of his empire Peter the Great based his new capital.

ESSENTIALS

Organized tours to Vyborg are rarer than those to Peterhof or Pavlovsk, but a hotel concierge or tour guide can help you find one. Vyborg is on the main highway between St. Petersburg and Finland, which can get clogged on Russian holiday weekends and on which traffic slows down considerably during the blustery winter months. A summer weekday is an ideal time to go if you're in a car or on a tour bus. Trains also run three times a day from St. Petersburg's Finlandsky Vokzal Station; the trip takes 2 hours one-way.

For a provincial city, Vyborg is unusually international, with menus in several languages and service staff usually eager to speak English. That's largely because of its proximity to Finland, and its popularity among Finnish tourists who come to buy cheap vodka, beer, and cigarettes. Russian vendors may speak to you in Finnish before they try English. If you're traveling on your own, buy a map at a newspaper kiosk; the city can be unwieldy if you don't know where you're going.

WHAT TO SEE & DO

The city inhabits a peninsula and several small islands on the northeast Baltic coast. The area was initially a trade settlement of Karelians, an ethnic group native to a region in what is now eastern Finland and northwest Russia. The Swedes came along and founded a city here in 1293 to use as a base for raids into neighboring Russia. Peter the Great conquered the city in 1710 during his 40-year war with Sweden. A century later, in 1811, it went to the Grand Duchy of Finland under Russian sovereignty. The city and surrounding region were part of the fledgling, independent nation of Finland from 1917 to 1940, and Vyborg (called Viipuri in Finnish) was Finland's second-largest city. The Winter War between Finland and the Soviet Union left Vyborg again in Russian hands, where it has remained since. Karelians remained the primary inhabitants until World War II, when many were evacuated to western Finland or forced out by Soviet troops.

Vyborg Castle, on a rocky island in the center of town, was the Swedes' first major project here, built in the 1290s. The stone castle saw many additions in subsequent centuries, and now houses a small museum whose exhibits include archaeological finds from the area and some curious items confiscated by 20th-century border guards. The island itself is an almost mystical outpost that lends itself easily to imagining what it looked like 700 years ago. The castle hosts St. Petersburg's White Nights events such as jazz or classical music concerts. The castle (© **81378/21515** or 81378/25186) is open Tuesday through Sunday from 10am to 5pm.

Be sure to wander through the **Old Vyborg district,** which boasts architecture from the 14th to 17th centuries that is markedly more Scandinavian in style than the Russian palaces that later popped up around town. Catholic and Protestant churches are more plentiful than Orthodox ones. **Market Square (Rynochnaya Ploshchad)** includes the only remaining tower of the 16th-century fortress wall built by the Swedes; the market itself dates from 1905 and shows hints of the Russian obsession with Art Nouveau. The **Central Library,** designed by Alvar Aalto in the 1930s, is a highlight of Finnish design during this fruitful architectural period. The architectural and nature reserve at **Monrepos Park** is well worth a stroll or picnic if the weather is fine. The romantic landscaping of the island park includes gardens and sculptures favored by the aristocracy and architects of Peter the Great's day. **Progonnaya Ulitsa (Driving St.),** once used for driving sheep and cows to pasture, now boasts several unusual buildings as it stretches toward the Gulf of Finland.

WHERE TO DINE

Cheap restaurants and beer halls abound in Vyborg, largely aimed at Finnish students and bargain hunters who come for the day or weekend. Two better-than-average places to eat are Igorika and Atlantik. **Igorika,** a 5-minute walk from the castle at 2 Severny Val (© **81378/21388**), describes itself as a bistro with fusion cuisine, which means its primarily Russian menu includes international standards such as chicken curry. It's open around the clock for those taking night trains to or from Finland, and the atmosphere is friendly and lively. Near the castle, **Atlantik,** 9 Ulitsa Podgornaya (© **81378/24776**), is in a drab stone building that conceals a cozy, wood-dominated interior. It offers mostly Russian standards with an emphasis on Baltic Sea fish—fresh, smoked, or pickled. The restaurant fills up with groups on weekends.

Appendix A: Russia in Depth

Russia fills out Europe's right flank and reaches across the top of Asia to wade in the Pacific, making it European, Asian, Arctic, and none of the above. Its struggle for identity, association, and empire has defined it since the Vikings formed the state of Rus nearly 1,200 years ago. Blood and repression have marred this struggle, right up to today. Russia's leaders have been expert at inflicting ugliness on their people, and Russians have become expert at putting up with it. Yet the country has survived and thrived, producing some of the world's best science, music, and literature. More remarkably, Russians are among the most festive and giving people on the planet, always ready to put their last morsel of food and last drop of drink on the table to honor an unexpected late-night guest with toasts, more toasts, and laughter. Moscow has dominated the country's political, economic, and cultural life for most of the past 900 years; St. Petersburg, during the 2 centuries when it assumed the role of Russia's capital, plunged Russia at long last into the modern world. The two distinct, yet distinctly Russian, cities remain the pride of this unfathomably vast country.

1 History

IN THE BEGINNING

Early tribes of nomadic Scythians first settled what are now Russian lands in the 7th century B.C., but it wasn't until the 6th century A.D. that Slavic tribes from southeastern Europe advanced into the neighborhood. It was not the Slavs, however, but the Viking Rurik from nearby Scandinavia who established the first Russian state, based in Novgorod, in the 9th century A.D. The population remained primarily Slavic, though its leaders claimed descent from Rurik for the next 700 years.

The young state's power base soon shifted to Kiev, now the capital of Ukraine. The era of Kievan Rus, as it was called, saw the flowering of a major European

Dateline

- 7th c. B.C. Scythian tribes settle lands in what is now Russia.
- 862 Viking Rurik establishes state at Novgorod.
- 988 Prince Vladimir adopts Orthodox Christianity for Russian lands.
- 888 Monks Cyril and Methodius invent Cyrillic alphabet.
- 1326 Russian capital moved to Moscow. Muscovite prince achieves first major defeat of Mongols at Kulikovo Pole.
- 1480 Ivan III (the Great) ejects Mongol Tatars, freeing Russia from "the Mongol Yoke."
- 1547 Ivan IV (The Terrible) named first czar of all Russians.
- 1605–1613 "Time of Troubles."
- 1613 Mikhail Romanov crowned czar.
- 1703 Peter the Great founds St. Petersburg, and later moves the capital there from Moscow.
- 1755 Russia's first university, Moscow University, established.
- 1780s Catherine the Great expands Russian lands to Crimea, Georgia, deeper into Siberia.

entity, whose territories stretched across present-day Belarus, Ukraine, and much of western Russia. As Kievan Rus, the country gained a religion and an official language and developed the distinctive architectural styles seen across the region today.

Kievan Rus cast its lot with the Orthodox Christian world in 988, during the reign of Vladimir. Orthodoxy became the foundation of Russian life for nearly 800 years, and remains a crucial part of the Russian identity, even after 70 years of Soviet state-enforced atheism. In the 9th century, two monks, Cyril and Methodius, developed what became known as the Cyrillic alphabet, which Russia still uses today. Largely an agricultural economy, Kievan Rus developed substantial trade with Byzantium and Scandinavia, using the resulting riches to build the cathedrals and fortresses that protected and symbolized the empire.

Internecine battles gradually weakened Kievan Rus, and the invasion of its eastern lands by Genghis Khan's Mongol hordes in 1237 made things worse. Moscow, meanwhile, had matured from a hilltop village into a substantial principality by 1147, the official year of its founding, and became the seat of Russian authority in 1326. The Russian state remained feeble, however, and fell to repeated invasion by Mongol Tatars from the east. The Tatars kept Russia's princes under their thumbs until Ivan III (Ivan the Great) came to power in the late 1400s, and refused to pay the Mongols any more tribute. His reign saw Muscovite-controlled lands spread north to the Arctic and east to the Urals. It was Ivan the Great who launched construction of the Kremlin's magnificent cathedrals and its current walls.

His grandson Ivan IV was the first Russian crowned "czar" (a variation on "Caesar") but became better known as Ivan the Terrible. He further strengthened the state and was considered an enlightened leader until the death of his wife plunged him into paranoia and despotism. He instituted Russia's first secret police force, persecuted former friends as enemies, and killed his own son and pregnant daughter-in-law in a fit of rage. The country and his dynasty were devastated by the time Ivan IV died in 1584.

The ensuing decades were wrought with bloody, corrupt struggles for succession that came to be known as the "Time of Troubles." Boris Godunov (1598–1605) was the most legendary of this era's leaders, a *boyar* (nobleman) elected in an unusual experiment with democracy called the *zemsky sobor* (national assembly), which was made up of nobles, church leaders,

- **1805–07** First war with Napoleon.
- **1812** Napoleon reaches Moscow but leaves in defeat.
- **1814** Triumphant Russians reach Paris.
- **1825** Decembrist Uprising by progressive generals quashed by Nicholas I.
- **1853–56** Crimean War pits Russia against Britain, France, and Turkey.

- **1850s** Caucasus Wars end with Russian armies subduing Chechnya and other mountain regions.
- **1861** Czar Alexander II abolishes serfdom.
- **1881** Czar Alexander II assassinated by revolutionary.
- **1880s–1903** Series of pogroms against Russian Jews.
- **1904–05** War with Japan.

- **1905** Striking workers revolt, forcing czar to allow first elected parliament.
- **1914** Russia joins World War I against Germany; Petersburg residents change the city's name to the less German-sounding Petrograd.
- **1916** Royal favorite Rasputin murdered.

continues

Selected List of Russian Leaders

Rurik 862–879 Viking prince who founded state of Rus, based in northern city of Novgorod and populated by eastern Slavs.

Vladimir I 978–1015 Prince who chose Orthodox Christianity as the Russian state religion, launching widespread cathedral construction. Oversaw emergence of Kievan Rus as major European state.

Ivan III (The Great) 1462–1505 Ended 3 centuries of Mongol dominance over Russian lands, expanded Russian territories east and north, ordered construction of the Kremlin's greatest cathedrals.

Ivan IV (The Terrible) 1533–1584 First Russian crowned "czar." Initially a reformer, he later introduced Russia's first secret police force and terrorized political opponents.

Boris Godunov 1598–1605 *Boyar* (nobleman) elected czar by a national assembly amid a power vacuum in the Kremlin. His death led to another crisis of succession.

Mikhail I 1613–45 Son of noble Romanov family, elected czar. Romanov dynasty would stay in power for the next 300 years, until Soviet rule. His coronation ended the "Time of Troubles."

Peter I (The Great) 1698–1725 Moved Russian capital to St. Petersburg, a city he built on a delta on the Baltic Sea. Turned Russia westward, introducing European architectural styles, art, and attitudes to his isolated nation. Founded Russian navy.

Elizabeth I 1741–61 Built many of Petersburg's greatest palaces, including the Winter Palace that houses the Hermitage.

Catherine II (The Great) 1762–96 A German princess who married into the Romanov dynasty and became one of Russia's most influential leaders. Expanded Russian territory south and west, oversaw construction of many crucial Petersburg buildings and institutions.

Alexander I 1801–25 Led Russian army against Napoleon, eventually driving the Grande Armée back to Paris.

Nicholas I 1825–55 Suppressed uprising by reformist generals (later dubbed "Decembrists") soon after his coronation; maintained hard line against dissent.

Alexander II 1855–81 Abolished serfdom, freeing the majority of the population and allowing land ownership. Later grew more conservative and was assassinated by an anarchist.

Alexander III 1881–94 Reactionary leader whose reign was fraught with revolutionary activity that he sought to suppress.

Nicholas II 1894–1917 Russia's last czar. Resisted increasing calls for reforms until 1906, after disastrous war with Japan and striking workers led to creation of Russia's first parliament. Led Russia against Germany in World War I; abdicated amid revolutionary activity in 1917; was executed along with his wife and five children in 1918.

Vladimir Lenin 1917–24 Founder of Soviet state. After years abroad studying Marxist theory and plotting revolution, returned to Russia to lead Bolsheviks. Led "red" Communist forces during civil war; established Soviet secret police. His embalmed body is on Red Square.

Josef Stalin 1924–53 Seminary-student-turned-dictator who forcibly collectivized Soviet land, purged Soviet leadership of purported enemies in "The Great Terror," and executed or repressed millions of Soviet citizens for real and imagined crimes. Led the Soviet Union to victory in World War II at the cost of 27 million lives.

Nikita Khrushchev 1955–64 Congenial leader who denounced many of Stalin's policies and oversaw period of "thaw" in arts and political life. Nearly came to nuclear conflict with U.S. in Cuban Missile Crisis. Deposed by conservative Communist Party colleagues.

Leonid Brezhnev 1964–82 Long-serving leader who came to embody stagnation of late Soviet period. Oversaw crackdown on "Prague Spring," expulsion of dissidents. Launched war in Afghanistan.

Yuri Andropov 1982–84 Influential former KGB chief who sought to stem corruption and introduce minor reforms.

Konstantin Chernenko 1984–85 Conservative Brezhnev protégé who escalated Cold War military spending.

Mikhail Gorbachev 1985–91 Last Soviet leader. Reformer who introduced *glasnost* and *perestroika* but later tried to rein in the independence movements spawned by these policies. Briefly ousted by hard-liners in failed coup attempt; 3 months later the Soviet Union collapsed.

Boris Yeltsin 1991–1999 First Russian president. Orchestrated end of USSR, freed prices, and oversaw privatization of state companies. Launched war in Chechnya; sent tanks against recalcitrant lawmakers; opened Russia to foreign investors.

Vladimir Putin 2000–present Second Russian president. Former KGB agent who assumed power when Yeltsin resigned. Has overseen economic boom, suppressed free media, and squeezed out political rivals.

Unorthodox Beginnings

Whether legend or fact, the story of how Russians chose Orthodox Christianity hardly sounds holy: Grand Prince Vladimir I of Kievan Rus was deciding which of the world's religions would best suit his burgeoning state. He rejected Judaism for its prohibition of pork, a crucial Russian food source; and dismissed Islam because no Russian (even in the 10th c.) would heed a ban on liquor—a lesson Mikhail Gorbachev learned a millennium later after launching a disastrous anti-alcohol campaign. Prince Vladimir finally settled on Orthodox Christianity, allegedly because of his envoys' rave reviews of the Hagia Sophia in Constantinople.

and commoners. Godunov's death left a power vacuum that led to the appearance of the first False Dmitry, a Polish-backed prince who claimed to be Ivan the Terrible's son Dmitry, whose death 15 years earlier remained shrouded in mystery. The False Dmitry and his Polish entourage made it to the Kremlin but he was soon executed by angry opponents. Remarkably, another Polish-backed False Dmitry was among the several ill-fated leaders to take over the Kremlin in the ensuing years.

At last the 16-year-old Mikhail Romanov, a distant relative of Ivan the Terrible, was elected czar in 1613 by another national assembly. It took him 2 years to establish himself securely and put an end to the Time of Troubles. Ultimately, Mikhail was able to establish a new dynasty, one that would last until Czar Nicholas II was executed by Bolsheviks 300 years later.

THE WINDOW TO EUROPE

Although Russians through the ages have debated whether to look to western Europe or to their Slavic roots for inspiration, Peter the Great had no doubts: Europe on the verge of the Enlightenment held the future. His early years were fraught with hostilities within the royal family, and once he attained the throne, he abandoned the medieval Moscow Kremlin. Peter traveled to western Europe and upon his return moved to a swamp on the Baltic Sea, ultimately transforming it into a grand capital of columned, Italian-designed palaces along broad avenues and sculpted canals.

- **1917** February Revolution; Czar Nicholas II abdicates afterwards; in October, Vladimir Lenin's Bolsheviks storm St. Petersburg's Winter Palace and depose provisional government.
- **1917–19** Civil war ravages Russia, ending in victory for Lenin; capital is moved back to Moscow.
- **1922** Union of Soviet Socialist Republics (USSR) officially founded, eventually growing to 15 republics.
- **1924** Death of Lenin.
- **1930s** Stalin's collectivization kills millions; purges of party and military leadership take place.
- **1939** Nazi-Soviet nonaggression pact divides eastern Europe into spheres of influence.
- **1941** Hitler's army invades the Soviet Union; Nazi siege of Leningrad begins, lasting 900 days.
- **1943** Battle at Stalingrad proves turning point in World War II.
- **1945** Soviet army liberates Auschwitz; Hitler defeated; war ends; Yalta conference.

St. Petersburg's beauty came at a great price: Thousands of people died fulfilling Peter's sometimes impossible building orders, and the damp climate just below the Arctic circle weakened and sickened many of its new residents.

Peter's policies dragged Russia out of its insularity and planted it firmly in the world of European diplomacy and modern thought. Yet he was as authoritarian as any Russian leader, and even had his own son sentenced to death. Russia's next exceptional leader was Catherine the Great (1762–96), a German princess who married into the Romanov family and conspired to oust her husband to attain the throne. She greatly expanded Russia's territory to the east and south, and her foreign policies won her and Russia great respect in the rest of Europe. Russia's aristocracy came to speak French better than Russian, a trend that continued for generations.

Russia's love affair with France collapsed under Napoleon, who gave Russia its biggest military challenge in centuries. The French made it into Moscow in 1812—but only after the Russians had set fires in the city, stripped it bare, and fled, leaving Napoleon's army without food and shelter on the eve of winter. The *Grande Armée* retreated, and the Russians' victorious drive into Paris 2 years later was immortalized in poems, songs, and children's rhymes.

RUSSIA'S ARTISTIC APEX

Until the 19th century, Russia's artistic developments were little known abroad and underappreciated at home. That changed after the Napoleonic Wars, as Russia's confidence in its place in Europe led to greater support and recognition of local composers, writers, and choreographers in the emerging art of ballet. Alexander Pushkin became Russians' best-loved poet, with his direct, melodic use of the Russian language—and his liberal political leanings, which ran him afoul of the czars. Fyodor Dostoyevsky's fiction delved into innermost existential depths in response to repression from without. Pyotr Tchaikovsky's symphonies gave voice to the terror and triumph of war with France. Writer Leo Tolstoy, playwright Alexander Griboyedov, and artist Isaak Levitan were among the legions of cultural heroes who found success in their uniquely Russian ways of expression.

READYING FOR REVOLUTION

Much of Russia's 19th century was defined by pre-revolutionary struggle, as radicals studied the revolutions in the United States and France, and the czars sought to stamp out dissent even where it didn't exist. The Decembrist uprising of

- **1948** Soviets develop atomic bomb.
- **1953** Death of Stalin.
- **1956** Nikita Khrushchev denounces Stalin's policies in a secret Politburo speech; Hungarian uprising crushed.
- **1961** Soviets send first man into space (Yuri Gagarin); Berlin Wall built.
- **1962** Cuban Missile Crisis.
- **1968** "Prague Spring" quashed by Soviet troops.
- **1979** Soviet forces invade Afghanistan; war against U.S.-funded Islamic guerrillas lasts 10 years.
- **1985** Mikhail Gorbachev appointed General Secretary of the Communist Party; launches *glasnost* and *perestroika*.
- **1986** Chernobyl nuclear reactor explodes in world's worst nuclear accident.
- **1989** Berlin Wall falls.
- **1990** Baltic states declare independence; Boris Yeltsin elected president of the Russian Federation, the biggest Soviet republic.

continues

And Make It Snappy!

The term "bistro" is purported to have come from hungry Russian soldiers descending on Paris in 1814, who demanded their meals fast—*bystro* in Russian—from harried servers in Montmartre's cafes.

1825, led by reformist generals in the royal army, was quashed by Czar Nicholas I, who then bolstered the censors and the secret police. Czar Alexander II freed the serfs at last in 1861, but society remained starkly unequal and most of the population was still poor and uneducated. The thriving merchant class helped fuel Russia's industrial advances in the late 1800s. Alexander II grew increasingly conservative and suspicious of opposition in his later years; he was assassinated in 1881 by anarchists. The next 2 decades were marred by a series of pogroms against Russia's substantial and influential Jewish population; Jews were massacred and their property seized. Since Catherine the Great's time, Jews other than select professionals were banished from St. Petersburg and elsewhere in the empire to the Pale of Settlement, a swath of land in what is now Poland, Belarus, Ukraine, Lithuania, and western Russia.

Alexander II's grandson Nicholas II—the last of the Romanov czars—assumed the throne in 1894 with few plans for reform. From 1904 to 1905, Russia fought a war with Japan over territory in the Far East, which left the czarist navies humiliated and laid bare the weaknesses of the imperial government. Nicholas stifled an uprising of striking workers in January 1905 on what is known as Russia's Bloody Sunday. Under increasing pressure from the population and his court, the czar allowed the creation of a limited parliament, Russia's first ever, elected in 1906.

All this was setting the stage for 1917. Fighting the Germans in World War I had further weakened Nicholas's shaky hold on the country, and with revolution in the air, he abdicated in February 1917. An aristocrat-led provisional government jockeyed for power with the revolutionary parties of Vladimir Lenin and Leon Trotsky. Lenin's more extremist Bolshevik Party, claiming support among exploited workers and peasants, emerged the victor. Nicholas, his wife Alexandra, and their five children were exiled to Siberia and then executed in 1918, as civil war

- **1991** Hard-liners attempt a coup against Gorbachev but fail; Leningrad residents vote to change the city's name back to St. Petersburg; Yeltsin and the leaders of Ukraine and Belarus declare the USSR defunct; Gorbachev resigns.
- **1993** Opposition lawmakers revolt against Yeltsin, who attacks them with tanks.

- **1994** Yeltsin sends troops into Chechnya to quash rebellion; 20 months later, Russian troops withdraw in humiliation and Chechnya enjoys semi-autonomy.
- **1998** Russia's reviving economy hit by global financial crisis; government defaults on debt and ruble crashes.

- **1999** Russian army re-enters Chechnya and remains there today.
- **Dec. 31, 1999** Yeltsin unexpectedly resigns, appointing Prime Minister Vladimir Putin his successor.
- **2000** Putin easily wins election.
- **2004** Putin easily wins re-election.

engulfed the nation. Years of chaos, famine, and bloodshed followed, before the Union of Soviet Socialist Republics was born.

SOVIET RUSSIA

After Lenin died in 1924, Josef Stalin, a former seminary student from Georgia, worked his way to the top of the Communist Party leadership. Stalin reversed Lenin's late attempts at liberalization, instead ushering in a campaign to collectivize all land into state hands—no small task in a nation so vast. The brutal drive, combined with a drought, led to famine that left 5 to 10 million dead. Stalin crafted a dictatorship by gradually purging his rivals, real and imagined. His repression reached a peak in the late 1930s and decimated the party and military leadership. Millions were executed or exiled to prison camps across Siberia and the Arctic, referred to by their Russian initials GULAG, or State Agency for Labor Camps.

Stalin tried to head off war with Germany through a secret pact with Hitler, known as the Molotov-Ribbentrop pact after the foreign ministers who signed it. The pact promised Soviet food supplies to the Nazis and set out a plan for dividing eastern Europe between the two powers. Hitler invaded anyway, plunging the Soviet Union into a war that would cost the country 27 million lives, more losses than any nation suffered in World War II. The Great Patriotic War, as Russians call it, brought the 900-day siege of Leningrad (see the sidebar "The Siege of Leningrad" in chapter 15) as well as gruesome battles at Stalingrad and Kursk that helped break the back of Hitler's forces.

Rasputin: Mystic, Sinner, Healer, or Spy?

In 1907, Czar Nicholas II and his empress Alexandra, desperate to help their hemophiliac son and only male heir, Alexy, turned to a wandering healer named Grigory Rasputin. The decision was to have consequences for the whole country. The facts around Rasputin's life remain clouded in contradiction and controversy, but his influence on the royal household in the years leading to up to the Russian empire's demise are indisputable. Nicholas and Alexandra remained loyal to him for his apparent success in easing Alexy's suffering, which they were trying to keep from the Russian public. But Rasputin's personal life—including energetic sexual exploits and drunken binges—sullied his reputation as an Orthodox mystic, especially among the czar's advisers and aristocracy. Some claim Rasputin was a member of the *khlisty* sect, who believed in salvation through sin (the name comes from the Russian word for "whip").

The royal couple's increasing alienation from Russian reality was blamed on Rasputin's twisted advice, and he was accused of acting as a German spy during World War I. Nicholas's inner circle grew so worried about Rasputin's influence on national policies that they murdered him in 1916. Even his death is steeped in legend: His killers reported that they poisoned him, shot him, and beat him before tossing him into an icy canal—and that he was still kicking under water. Alexandra, devastated, ordered his remains dragged out a few days later. Within 2 years, Nicholas's rule had collapsed and his whole family had been executed.

Genuine grief mixed with nervous relief gripped the country when Stalin died in 1953, as many feared that life without this frightening father figure would be even worse than with him. Nikita Khrushchev's eventual rise to power brought a thaw; political prisoners were released and there was a slight relaxation of censorship amid continued postwar economic growth. But after putting down protests in Hungary in 1956 and nearly provoking nuclear war in the 1962 Cuban Missile Crisis, Khrushchev was eventually ousted by more conservative colleagues in a bloodless coup. Soviet space successes during this time—including sending the first satellite, first man, and first woman to space—awed the world and fueled the Cold War arms race.

Khrushchev's replacement, Leonid Brezhnev, is largely remembered for the era of stagnation that marked the Soviet Union in the 1960s and 1970s—but it was also an era of the peace and stability so elusive for Russians for so long. This era ended with the Soviet invasion of Afghanistan in 1979, leading to an inconclusive, unpopular 10-year war with U.S.-backed Islamic guerrillas. Brezhnev's death brought two quick successors in the early 1980s, Yuri Andropov and Konstantin Chernenko, who both died in office before the relatively young Mikhail Gorbachev took over.

THE SOVIET COLLAPSE & AFTERMATH

Gorbachev's name became synonymous with the policies of *glasnost* (openness) and *perestroika* (restructuring) that he tried to apply to the Soviet system. But he underestimated how deeply the country's economy and political legitimacy had decayed. The reforms he cautiously introduced took on a momentum that ultimately doomed him and the Soviet Union. After the fall of the Berlin Wall in 1989 and the peaceful revolutions around the Communist bloc of eastern Europe, Gorbachev aligned with hard-liners at home to cling to power.

The hard-liners thought he wasn't doing enough, however, so they tried to overthrow him in a desperate, poorly executed coup attempt in August 1991. They were defeated by defiant generals and a buoyant Boris Yeltsin, then president of the Russian part of the USSR, who was cheered on by thousands of pro-democracy demonstrators. Three months later, Gorbachev resigned and the Soviet Union splintered into 15 new countries.

When Yeltsin freed the ruble from its state controls, he wiped out millions of people's savings, and his popularity plummeted. Yeltsin and his administration couldn't keep up with the economic transition from a planned economy to the free market, and crime, corruption, and

Calendar Confusion

Russia used the Julian calendar until February 1918, well after the rest of Europe switched to the Gregorian calendar, which at that point was 13 days ahead. When the Bolsheviks stormed the Winter Palace, it was still October 1917 in Russia but was already November in the rest of Europe; hence, for the next 7 decades, the Soviets celebrated "Great October Revolution Day" on November 7. The Russian Orthodox calendar ignored the switch, and Russians still celebrate Christmas on January 7 instead of December 25. Some also celebrate the "Old" New Year on January 13 and 14, as well as the traditional New Year's bash on December 31 and January 1.

The Great Russian Spying Tradition

You've heard of the KGB, that ultimate of Cold War villains. Yet it represents just one chapter in Russia's rich history of spying, snooping, informing, rooting out conspiracies, and all-around paranoia. Most of this activity has been aimed not at outsiders, but at Russians themselves. Ivan the Terrible (1533–1584) was the first Russian leader to establish a secret office to spy on his subjects, and his successors kept up the tradition. Undercover agents and counter-espionage thrived amid the revolutionary activity of the late 19th century. When the Soviets took over, they formalized the secret police into a pillar of the government that became notorious for torturing or murdering suspects or sending them to prison based on flimsy or nonexistent evidence.

Soviet spy agencies were labeled with a succession of double-speak acronyms. Felix Dzerzhinsky, considered the father of Soviet espionage, established the Cheka, an abbreviation for the Extraordinary Commission for the Struggle against Counter-revolution, Speculation and Sabotage, in 1917. Later, the NKVD (People's Committee for Internal Affairs) ruled over labor camps and prisons for political enemies under Stalin. It then became the MGB (Ministry of State Security), before morphing into the better-known KGB (Committee of State Security). Its many departments snooped on every aspect of Russians' lives, from workplace tardiness to personal correspondence. The system shrank considerably after the Soviet collapse, but the "gebeshniki," or "state security guys," have enjoyed a bit of a comeback under Vladimir Putin, an ex-KGB operative who ran the post-Soviet intelligence agency, the FSB (Federal Security Service) in the late 1990s. While the FSB is in charge of domestic snooping, foreign spies are tracked by the honestly named Foreign Intelligence Service (SVR).

poverty flourished. The 1990s saw a few Russians make exorbitant sums by buying up state property on the cheap, while workers at thousands of schools, hospitals, and factories lost their jobs or went months, even years, without pay. The global financial crisis hit Russian in 1998. As its burgeoning markets collapsed, the government defaulted on debt, and the ruble, which had finally steadied, again tumbled.

Politically, Yeltsin grew increasingly intolerant, like so many Russian leaders before him. He faced a showdown with opposition parliament deputies in 1993 that he ended by sending in tanks after his opponents tried to seize the country's main television tower. Meanwhile, separatist-led violence in the southern province of Chechnya prompted Yeltsin to send in troops in 1994. This led to a deeply unpopular war that exposed the shoddy state of the Russian army, which withdrew in defeat 2 years later. Chechnya's status remained murky, however, and the region fell to lawlessness and an economy based on embezzling and kidnapping for ransom. A series of apartment bombings in Moscow and other Russian cities in 1999 was blamed on Chechens, and offered a pretext for a new war.

This second war was championed by Vladimir Putin, who had just been named prime minister in Yeltsin's fourth government reshuffle in a year and a half. This time, terrorism-scarred Russians supported the war, and the man leading it. Putin's law-and-order image from his years as a KGB agent worked in his favor, as did Russians' weariness of the capricious, ailing Yeltsin. On December 31, 1999, the eve of the new millennium, Yeltsin unexpectedly resigned and handed power to his protégé Putin.

TODAY

Russia under Putin, who was overwhelmingly elected president in 2000 and just as enthusiastically re-elected in 2004, is undoubtedly a calmer and richer place than it was under his predecessor. He cut income taxes to a flat 13%, allowed the sale of land for the first time since Lenin's days, and has presided over the greatest growth in Russia's economy in decades. But he's been able to do all this largely because he's disabled his political opposition. The well-financed pro-Kremlin party, United Russia, broke the Communists' hold on parliament and squeezed out the liberal parties as well, leaving few independent voices in the legislative branch. Feisty television stations have been shuttered under Putin, for what prosecutors call financial reasons and journalists call political ones. Russia's richest man, Mikhail Khodorkovsky, was sentenced in 2005 to 10 years in prison on tax evasion charges that he says were punishment for his support of opposition parties; his Yukos oil empire is being dismantled by the state. The case turned many foreign investors and Western governments against Putin.

Small-scale crime has gone down under Putin, partly thanks to his increased use of KGB-style security services. Many Russians welcome this new order after the 1990s, when residents and business owners felt victimized by organized crime. Still, Putin's security policies have failed to solve the bigger problems of corruption and terrorism. The Russian army continues to wage a war in Chechnya whose casualty figures are a secret. Chechen suicide bombers have targeted Moscow and terrified the world with their siege of a school in the southern city of Beslan in 2004. Car bombings and other violence plague southern provinces surrounding Chechnya.

Although Russia as a whole is a graying country with a relatively low standard of living, Moscow and St. Petersburg are its glaring exceptions. Both cities, especially the capital, are experiencing a genuine economic boom that has brought them in line with some of the world's richest cities. Much of their prosperity is linked to rising oil prices, since Russia is the world's second-largest oil producer. But although a drop in oil revenue would be painful, Russia's overall stability is not a myth—inflation is at last under control and exchange rates are predictable.

Despite reservations about Putin's policies, for tourists there's never been a better time to visit Russia. Russians are finally free to contact foreigners, and vice versa, which is evident at the uninhibited pick-up scenes in Moscow and St. Petersburg bars. Visitors are no longer assigned "minders," and Russians no longer need permission to leave their country. Surly Soviet service is giving way to smiling efficiency, as more and more Russians travel abroad and bring home higher expectations of service and options at home. New restaurants open in Moscow almost daily, and fashions are as fresh as in Milan. Cash machines are ubiquitous and English is increasingly widespread. Russia has, at last, opened its doors to the world.

2 Food & Drink

Dining in Russia can be delectable or dangerous, dismal or divine. Caviar and vodka are readily available, as are melt-in-your-mouth *bliny* (similar to crepes), wild mushrooms, and succulent lamb dumplings. The range and number of restaurant options keeps expanding. Hotel dining, alas, has changed little from the bland Soviet era, except in the top-end spots, where luxurious brunches recall the decadence of pre-revolutionary aristocracy.

Breakfast is served from about 7 to 10am, and although Russians at home usually eat heartily in the morning, hotels often offer just rolls and jam with tea or coffee. Lunch has traditionally been the major meal of the day, and includes appetizer, soup, main course of meat or fish, and dessert. It can be eaten any time after noon. The pace of today's Moscow and St. Petersburg has popularized the smaller, quicker "business lunch," served around noon to 2pm. Dinner can be anything from a light sandwich to another four- or five-course meal, and is usually not eaten before 7 or 8 pm. These are rough guidelines, since most restaurants in Moscow and St. Petersburg serve continuously.

Russia's lively restaurant scene is all the more impressive when you realize that the country had no casual restaurant culture before the 1990s. Dining out was reserved for special occasions, and always involved formalwear, endless courses, and some kind of entertainment.

It almost never included children, who were not considered mature enough for such an event. The food and service, especially in the Soviet era, were generally bleak. Even now, most Russians prefer to eat at home. If you're invited to someone's home, be prepared for an endless stream of food, most of it rich and well-salted. Alcohol will invariably be served, and to avoid offense it's a good idea to at least sip or sample everything, though you don't have to drain your glass. As a foreigner you will be the star of the show, doted upon and offered the best cuts of meat and the juiciest berries. And you will not be allowed to lift a finger to help; that would be an insult to your hosts, a suggestion that they are somehow inadequate at satisfying you.

Pelmeni, dumplings filled with ground beef, pork, or lamb and spices and boiled in broth (a bit like overstuffed ravioli), are a Siberian specialty. *Varenniki* are a larger, flatter version of these dumplings, filled with potatoes or berries. The Georgian version, *khinkali,* are larger and spicier; the central Asian version, *manty,* are steamed instead of boiled. *Piroshki* are small baked pies filled with ground meat, cabbage, or fruit, and are eaten with your hands; *pirogi* are large dessert pies. Buttery *bliny,* thin crepelike pancakes, are spread with jam or savory fillings such as ham and cheese and rolled up. Tiny round *olady* are the pancakes eaten with caviar. Russian soups done right are delightfully flavorful, such as the refreshing summer sorrel soup *zelyoniye shchi* or the hearty winter meat stew *solyanka.*

Vodka—whose name means "little water" in Russian—is ubiquitous and demands a complex ritual of imbibing if Russians are at your table. (See the "Vodka" sidebar above.) Local beers are improving rapidly; Baltika and Nevskoye are cheap and tasty choices. Russian-made versions of Belgium's Stella Artois and Czech pilsner are also available. French and Californian wines are quite expensive, but simpler wines from the former Soviet republic of Georgia are available at most Russian restaurants. At business meals, wine or even vodka is common at lunch or dinner. If you're

Vodka

Russians call it a blessing and a curse. No Russian family is untouched by vodka, for better or for worse. Your trip to Russia will invariably involve at least a taste of the national drink. Even its name is fundamental: It's a diminutive of the Russian word for "water" *(voda)*.

EVOLUTION OF A SPIRIT

Some credit (or blame) the Genoans for introducing the concept of distilled alcohol to Russia in the late 1300s, not long after western European alchemists discovered its wonders. Monks in Moscow's Kremlin were soon brewing "bread wine," using grain, which was ubiquitous in Russia, instead of grapes. Though it was initially intended as a medicine, the drink became so popular that Ivan III (The Great) introduced the first vodka monopoly soon afterward. His grandson Ivan IV (The Terrible) recognized its dangers as well as its power, and introduced the first of several unsuccessful attempts by Russian leaders to ban the drink.

Vodka was absorbed into Russian court ceremony, and by the 17th century, Russian merchants and nobles were exporting their vodkas across Europe. Recipes expanded to include vodkas scented with cherries, apples, pears, blackberries, acorns, caraway seeds, dill, and sage, and the drink gradually grew stronger. The Russian chemist Mendeleyev—the author of chemistry's Periodic Table of Elements—played a key role in establishing vodka standards used to this day. In his late-19th-century doctoral dissertation, he determined what he considered the scientifically ideal proportion of alcohol to water (40%). Most vodkas today are 40% alcohol (80 proof), twice as strong as the 40-proof vodkas of the 16th and 17th centuries.

Czar Nicholas II tried to ban alcohol during World War I to keep the troops clear-headed, and Lenin kept the ban in place after taking over in 1917. Stalin reversed this policy, expanding state-run vodka production and including a glass of low-quality vodka in the daily rations for construction workers, road workers, and dock workers. Reviving a tradition that dated back to Peter the Great's time, the military brass added vodka to Red Army rations in World War II. The pendulum swung back in the 1980s under Mikhail Gorbachev, whose anti-alcohol campaign was disastrous to his reputation and to government coffers, which had enjoyed substantial revenues from state-run distilleries. Boris Yeltsin had no such distaste for vodka, personally or politically. His free-market reforms encouraged innovation and competition, but also flooded stores with cheap, poorly regulated, and often dangerous new spirits.

THE MAGIC BEVERAGE TODAY

Today rules are tighter than in the 1990s, and rich Russians are demanding ever-purer and more innovative vodkas. Most vodkas are distilled from wheat, rye, or barley malt or some combination of the three, though village distillers prefer cheaper sources such as corn and potatoes. The traditional restaurant serving size is a *ryumka* (shot glass) of 50 grams (1.8 oz.). Rural Russians largely prefer the cheaper *samogon,* a milky homemade brew guaranteed to set your throat on fire. Bathtub distilleries are a common sight in villages, and are the butt of many a Russian joke, but the humor is tinged with tragedy. Making and drinking *samogon* is increasingly the only occupation available in Russian villages, with employment and opportunity nearly nonexistent outside the big cities. Alcohol poisoning is a leading cause of death.

Most Russians, however, know how to celebrate vodka without abusing it. To join in this national pastime, stick to the brands served in restaurants or sold in supermarkets. **Stolichnaya, Russky Standart,** and **Flagman** are safe and excellent choices. A 750-milliliter bottle of high-quality vodka purchased in a Russian store costs 30% to 50% less than it would abroad, though domestic Russian prices are rising rapidly. Other brands to try are the popular Ukrainian vodka **Nemiroff,** either straight or pepper-flavored; and the simpler, wheat-based **Pshenichnaya.** Avoid purchasing from street kiosks—their rock-bottom prices often conceal liquids of dubious quality.

HOW TO DRINK VODKA

If you want to appreciate a good vodka the way Russians do, follow these guidelines:

- Drink it well chilled and straight, preferably in 50-gram shots. No ice or vodka cocktails are allowed. Ignore anyone who tries to get you to mix it with beer.
- Down it in one gulp. No sipping allowed.
- Don't drink until someone proposes a toast. (If you're really eager, propose a toast yourself; your hosts will be stunned but impressed.)
- Always chase it with something to eat. Russians prefer pickles, a clove of garlic, marinated herring, or a slice of lard, but really, whatever's on the table will do. Connoisseurs can neutralize the vodka's power just by sniffing a slice of the rich, brown bread ubiquitous at Russian meals.

If you pace yourself, vodka can be like a good wine, a pleasant accompaniment to a rich table but not necessarily the prelude to a dreadful hangover. If you do go overboard, the Russians have a surefire, if noxious, morning-after cure: Drink a potful of cabbage brine. The dread of that should be enough to keep you in check the night before.

For a closer view at vodka's role in Russian history, visit the **Vodka Museum** in St. Petersburg, at 5 Konnogvardeisky Bulvar (© **812/312-9178;** metro: Nevsky Prospekt). The small exhibit includes paraphernalia for producing and imbibing, and they even offer you a free sample (Tues–Sun 11am–9pm).

Impressions

If only there was vodka,
and with it selyodka *(herring),*
Then everything would be all right

—Traditional Russian saying

feeling adventurous, try *kvas,* a thirst-quenching beverage made from fermented bread. Available only in summer, it's very mildly alcoholic, and Russians consider it something between a Coke and a beer.

Russians' drink of choice, however, is tea *(chai),* ideally served from a samovar: a small pot of strong tea base *(zavarka)* sits brewing on top and is diluted to taste with the hot water from the belly of the samovar *(kipitok).* Coffee *(kofye)* is often instant or resembles thick Turkish coffee, unless the menu specifically says espresso or cappuccino.

A service charge is usually included in the restaurant bill, but a nominal tip is welcome.

3 Etiquette & Customs

APPROPRIATE ATTIRE

Anything goes in today's Russian cities: full-length furs, baseball caps, pierced navels, or see-through gowns from Versace's spring show. Generally, Russian women dress up rather than down, with heels and lipstick de rigueur. Athletic shoes are reserved for the gym for both genders unless they're from a famous designer, and baggy sweatshirts are a sure sign of a tourist. In Orthodox churches, men should bare their heads and women should cover theirs; keeping a small kerchief in your purse or backpack is a good idea. Women should also cover knees and shoulders, though this rule is often ignored in the more touristed sites. The main thing to remember is weather: Boots are a must October through April, as are a hat, scarf, and gloves. Layers are essential year-round.

GESTURES

Russians greet acquaintances with kisses on both cheeks, though upon meeting someone the first time, a handshake (between men) or a simple nod is standard. Russians may at first be reserved, but upon later meetings they can be physically friendly, and their sense of personal space is smaller than what Anglo-Saxons are used to. Common gestures include spitting over the left shoulder (to ward off bad luck), and flicking the middle finger onto the chin (meaning anything having to do with getting drunk).

AVOIDING OFFENSE

Russian superstitions run deep, and even a "Westernized" Russian teenager will probably cringe if you whistle indoors or greet someone across a threshold, both believed to bring bad tidings. Touching or even getting too close to a newborn baby is unwelcome. Never give a Russian an even number of flowers; this is reserved for funerals. The KGB's successors won't report—or deport—you if you criticize Russian leaders, but you might be in for some heated debate if you want to discuss Chechnya, Stalin, or the Putin administration.

4 The Performing Arts

You don't have to know a word of Russian to delight in its ballets and symphonies, and its operas are worth viewing for the spectacle and drama even if the language escapes you. Russians take great pride in their cultural heritage, and in the Soviet era nearly everyone, factory worker and collective farmer included, made regular visits to theater, concert hall, or opera house. The generous Communist subsidies that made such widespread cultural appreciation possible shriveled in the 1990s, but both performers and theatergoers are now climbing out of the post-Soviet slump and finding a balance between honoring the classics and testing new artistic directions.

Russia's rigorous **ballet** traditions have relaxed little in the past 200 years, and that commitment to physical perfection carries over into every form of dance represented in today's Russia. Even strippers often have classical training. The wave of departures by Russian ballet prodigies for richer Western companies has ebbed in recent years, and a new generation is carrying on the traditions of Baryshnikov, Nureyev, and Nijinsky in their homeland. Russia's reputation makes it a top destination for dance festivals, offering a great opportunity to see international superstars or smaller European and Asian companies.

For **classical music** fans, there's no better way to pay tribute to the homeland of Tchaikovsky, Rachmaninoff, Mussorgsky, Scriabin, Shostakovich, and Rimsky-Korsakov than to hear their works played in a Russian conservatory by their dedicated heirs. Russia's musicians—like its athletes and dancers—are trained from preschool age, with strict discipline and devotion to classicism. Even though musicians remain dreadfully underpaid and many have left for more lucrative jobs, theirs remains a highly selective profession. Any concert you hear in Russia is bound to be of top quality.

Devotees of playwright **Anton Chekhov** and the **Stanislavsky acting method** may appreciate a visit to the **Moscow Art Theater,** where both found fame. However, it's difficult to celebrate their contributions to theater traditions in Moscow or St. Petersburg without a good command of Russian. A relatively new phenomenon in the Russian performance scene is the musical; fans of the originals may find it amusing to watch the Russian-language version of *Chicago* or *The Hunchback of Notre Dame.*

What Russian **opera** lacks in subtlety, it makes up for in spectacle. Opera tickets generally cost less than ballet tickets, and seeing Mussorgsky's historical saga *Boris Godunov* is a dramatic way to dose up on Russian culture and see the interior of a monumental theater like the Bolshoi at the same time.

5 Russian Art & Architecture

Russian art and architecture remain a mystery to most outsiders, even as the country itself has opened up to the world. Knowing just a little about the evolution of Russian fine and applied arts, and about the political movements that often drove them, will make your trip less overwhelming and more eye-opening.

For a millennium, from Russia's 9th-century conversion to Orthodox Christianity until the 19th century, Russian art was almost exclusively defined by **icon-painting.** This Byzantine practice of painting saints or biblical scenes on carved wooden panels was guided rigidly by church canon, so the icons appear much more uniform and repetitive than western European religious art of the Renaissance, for example. The best advice for a novice viewer is to pick one or two icons in a room and study their lines and balance— don't look for realism or classic proportion, or to be uplifted. They're meant to be somewhat haunting and introspective.

Some Russian icon painters managed to infuse originality into their work, but it takes a trained eye to notice the distinctions. Andrei Rublev was the most famous and most controversial medieval icon painter, and brought the genre to a new level in the 14th century. His works are best appreciated at Tretyakov Gallery in Moscow (p. 131) and Trinity Monastery at Sergiev Posad. Spaso-Andronnikov Monastery in Moscow (p. 175), where he lived and worked, has none of his original work but does contain an informative exhibit about him. For tips on purchasing Russian icons, see the box "Russian Orthodox Icons" in chapter 8.

Russian art fell out of favor after Peter the Great transferred the capital to St. Petersburg in the early 1700s and adorned it with French and Italian masterpieces, or imitations thereof. It wasn't until the mid–19th century that the Slavophile movement brought real success to Russian painters. The **Wanderers,** or *peredvizhiki,* broke from the St. Petersburg Academy of Arts and its Western-style traditions to focus on portraying Russian village life. Standouts of this period include Ivan Kramskoi and Ilya Repin, whose works are well displayed at Tretyakov Gallery (p. 131) and at the Russian Museum in St. Petersburg (p. 244).

The late 19th century saw Russia's version of the **Arts and Crafts** movement, relying on traditional Russian applied arts. Russian artists also embraced what they call Style Moderne, or **Art Nouveau.** Stunning interpretations of this style can be found in Mikhail Vrubel's *Dream*

Princess mosaic around the top of the Metropol hotel's facade (p. 82) and in a related, room-size mosaic by him in Tretyakov Gallery.

The political upheaval of the early 20th century was a major engine of Russian artistic growth. Vibrant colors, angular shapes, and the intensity of urban life replaced the bucolic rural scenes, and the Russian **Avante-Garde** movement flourished. Kasimir Malevich and Mikhail Larionov explored the genres of Futurism, Rayonism (Russia's only truly abstract art), and Suprematism. Belarusian Marc Chagall produced surreal and surprising paintings during this period. Many of these works are on display at Tretyakov Gallery in Moscow (the old and new wings) and at the Russian Museum in St. Petersburg.

Early Soviet leaders initially harnessed the creativity of free-thinking artists for propaganda purposes, and the posters, sculptures, and public spaces designed by Russian artists in the 1920s are among the world's most stirring artworks. The **Constructivists,** including Vladimir Tatlin, Alexander Rodchenko, and Varvara Stepanova, incorporated technological and industrial themes and energy into their work. Their works are only beginning to emerge from museum storehouses, and some are on display at Tretyakov Gallery and at St. Petersburg's Russian Museum. Russia's Avante-Garde contributed more to world art than is usually appreciated, largely because the Soviet government so effectively erased or discredited their work by the 1930s, championing instead the bold images but less daring ideas of Socialist Realism.

The **propaganda poster** came to replace the icon as Russia's chief canvas for most of the Soviet era, until freedom from artistic constrictions in the late 1980s and 1990s produced a wave ofbold, experimental art. Today, Russia's artists seem to be casting about for a new role.

Russian architecture, too, was church-centric and followed Orthodox stricture for centuries. Churches were built in the shape of a Greek cross, with few windows and steep roofs. The onion domes became a prominent feature in the 11th century. The iconostasis, a screen in front of the altar with a careful hierarchy of icons, is the key object to look for inside a church.

Medieval architects took more risks than their icon-painting colleagues. The cathedrals in the Kremlin are the most coherent examples of the slow encroachment of Italian influences upon Russian tradition in the 15th and 16th centuries. Venetian scallops edge the roofs, though the buildings include the *kokoshniki* (pointed arches) and *zakomari* (semicircular gables) typical of the era's architecture in Moscow. St. Basil's Cathedral in Moscow is one of the last churches to so boldly use beveled domes and the *shatyor,* or tent-roofed tower later banned by Orthodox leaders—no other church in Russia today looks quite like it.

Peter the Great's Western-looking ideas overturned Russian architecture, and the capital he built adhered to Enlightenment ideas and a relentless symmetry. The rococo Winter Palace (p. 234) and Smolny Cathedral (p. 243), as well as the neoclassical Mikhailovsky Palace and Admiralty (see the walking tour in chapter 15), look almost nothing like the twisted domes of medieval Moscow. Visit any square in St. Petersburg and turn around 360 degrees, and you'll have a sense of how consistent and secular the city's designers were, even those who came well after Peter's death.

The Revivalist movement of the 19th century saw the return of traditional Russian church features such as the decorated cupolas seen in St. Petersburg's Church of the Savior on the Spilled Blood (p. 242). After the victory over Napoleon, the Empire style caught on for Russian aristocratic residences, proof of which can be found around the streets of Prechistenka and Ostozhenka in Moscow.

Early Soviet architecture was as creative and energized as the period's art, with architects such as Konstantin Melnikov forging functional, elegant buildings that made the Soviet idea (of a progressive, egalitarian state) seem the pinnacle of modernity. (His most famous house is near the Arbat at 6 Krivoarbatsky Pereulok.) Lenin's Mausoleum on Red Square (p. 126), for all its morbid function, is one of the last surviving examples of Constructivist architecture. The Moscow metro system was designed by the country's top architects and is an excellent place to view the juxtaposition of tradition (flowery capitals) with Soviet politics (statues of the proletariat). It's also one of the most beautiful subway systems in the world. (See p. 130 for more information.)

Later, the "Stalin Gothic" style appeared in dozens of towering buildings around Moscow (spreading as far as Warsaw and Prague), with turrets and spires on administrative or residential buildings. Two prime examples are the Ukraina hotel and Moscow State University. (See the box "Stalin's Seven Sisters" in chapter 4.) Architecture after Stalin descended into the bleak, boxy towers that mar the skyline of any Russian city. Today's architectural trends are set by the nouveau riche Russians building multimillion-dollar "cottages" on the outskirts of Moscow and St. Petersburg. The guiding principle often seems to be "as big and extravagant as possible." They make for amusing viewing, though many are surrounded by tall walls and security systems to stop you from doing just that.

6 Russian Literature

Dense, fatalistic, philosophical, lyrical, haunting, bleak, passionate. . . . These stereotypes cling to Russian literature and often scare newcomers away. But even a little knowledge of the country's greatest authors will help you make sense of the many literary museums, monuments, and slogans you'll run across during your trip. Russians are extremely well read, and take any opportunity to celebrate their literary traditions (and they may know more about your country's authors than you do).

Russian writing didn't really blossom until the 19th century, long after most European cultures had well-established literary traditions. In the early 1800s, serfdom was still enshrined in law, and literacy remained the luxury of the upper classes, who preferred to read European literature to demonstrate their Western mindset. But a burst of nationalism following the victory over Napoleon began to change Russia's literary habits, much as it affected Russian art of the same period. A growing class of students in universities and academies took up their pens. **Alexander Pushkin** is the most important of these, revered by Russians as the father of modern Russian literature for applying day-to-day language to poetic forms. This made his work more accessible than any other Russian writer's work before his. His death in a duel in 1837 at the age of 37 elevated him to icon status.

If Pushkin's romantic epics such as *Eugene Onegin* and *Ruslan and Ludmila* reflected the more hopeful, ironically playful side of Russian life, **Fyodor Dostoyevsky**'s work revealed its darker, more troubled side. *Crime and Punishment* traces the inner turmoil of a poor student who murders a pawnbroker. No character is really likable, but each is disturbingly believable. *Notes From Underground*'s account of a man expressing his free will by sinking into desperation leaves the reader ready to jump off a bridge.

Nikolai Gogol chose satire over solemnity, portraying the complacency and petty concerns of the rural gentry and urban clerical classes in short stories such as "The Nose and The Overcoat" and in his novel *The Inspector-General.* **Mikhail Lermontov** carved a name for himself with *A Hero of Our Time* and other tales about the Caucasus Mountains and Russia's efforts to subdue warrior clans there.

Nineteenth-century writers also took on Russian politics, often incurring the wrath of czarist governments: Pushkin was exiled from St. Petersburg, and Dostoyevsky was jailed for taking part in a radical intellectual discussion group.

The next crucial figure in the Russian literary pantheon was **Leo Tolstoy.** His writing career spanned 6 decades, starting with *Sevastopol Sketches* about his time serving in the Crimean Wars. He won

Impressions

I climb a ladder called progress, civilization, culture. I keep climbing, not knowing precisely where I'm going, but in fact the wonderful ladder alone makes life worth living.

　　—Anton Chekhov, *My Life,* in a treatise that served as Chekhov's rebuttal to Tolstoy's rejection of intellectual activity for a simpler life.

fame for *War and Peace,* his careful and complex account of the Napoleonic Wars, and for *Anna Karenina,* about the fall of a married woman suffocated by her bourgeois world. Tolstoy later abandoned the aristocratic, intellectual realm for a form of Christian anarchism and asceticism at his farm at Yasnaya Polyana outside Moscow.

Anton Chekhov countered Tolstoy's rejection of modern life with an unflagging faith in progress. Originally a doctor, Chekhov began writing short stories before discovering widespread success as a playwright. His preference for progress underpinned plays such as *The Seagull, The Three Sisters,* and *The Cherry Orchard,* in which stagnation and the emptiness of rural life are recurrent themes.

The political turmoil of the early 20th century fueled literary expression before Soviet ideology crippled it or sent it fleeing abroad. Some writers managed to produce masterpieces amid this repression and fear. **Anna Akhmatova** thrived in the heady years before the revolution, then spent decades producing subtle yet wrenching commentary on the transformation of her beloved hometown into Soviet Leningrad. The Communist leadership was notoriously fickle in its loyalties. **Vladimir Mayakovsky** was hailed as the voice of the revolution but by the late 1920s was ostracized. **Mikhail Bulgakov** staged several plays in the 1920s; his *Dog's Heart,* in which a bourgeois surgeon puts a dog's heart in a decidedly proletariat patient, became a much-loved film. However, most of his works were banned or censored, including his masterpiece *Master and Margarita,* a complex novel that invokes Pontius Pilate and has the devil stalking one of Moscow's most prestigious neighborhoods. **Vladimir Nabokov** fled Russia after the revolution but continued publishing in Russian and translating his own works into English. His stylized allegories on art and life include *The Luzhin Defense, Invitation to a Beheading,* and his most notorious novel, *Lolita.*

Of Russia's living writers, **Alexander Solzhenitsyn** is the most iconic. Imprisoned in a labor camp in the 1950s for his dissident views, he emerged even more determined to fight the Soviet system. His *Gulag Archipelago* chronicled the network of labor camps in exhaustive and exhausting detail. He earned a Nobel Prize but was afraid to collect it; he was eventually exiled in 1974. He returned to post-Soviet Russia in 1994 and continues to write essays critical of Russia's direction and moral decay.

Post-Soviet Russia's most successful writer is **Boris Akunin** (a pseudonym), who has tapped into a mass-market hunger for accessible historical fiction that satirizes Russian faults without ridiculing them. A more highbrow modern author is **Tatyana Tolstaya,** a great-grand-niece of Tolstoy's and acerbic commentator on Russian and Western life. **Viktor Pelevin**'s cynical and philosophical novels toy with fantasy and the dangerous combination of Russian fatalism and modern technology.

Appendix B:
Useful Russian Terms & Phrases

The Cyrillic alphabet scares off most tourists from trying to pick up any useful Russian, and that's a great shame. The 33-letter alphabet is really not hard to learn, since many of the letters are the same as in English. Knowing how to read those dizzying signs will make your trip through Russia much less mysterious and more comfortable. Kids are remarkably quick at picking out the new letters, and can turn the learning process into a family game of who can read that street sign faster. If you have any experience with college fraternities or sororities, you'll note that Cyrillic shares many letters with Greek, too.

Most Russians in hotels, restaurants, and shops will speak some English, especially those of the younger generations. Any effort to speak Russian will be welcomed, and in smaller establishments even a few words of Russian may get you out of a bind or improve service. Below is a rough guide to the alphabet, with phonetic English equivalents, followed by useful words and phrases with which to navigate Russian streets and restaurant menus. Words are printed in Russian followed by a pronunciation guide.

1 Alphabet

Russian	Pronunciation
А а	ah
Б б	b
В в	v
Г г	g (hard g)
Д д	d
Е е	yeh
Ё ё	yö
З з	z
Ж ж	zh (like "s" in measure)
И и	ee
Й й	ee (slightly harder than above)
К к	k
Л л	l
М м	m
Н н	n
О о	o
П п	p
Р р	r (rolled r, like the Spanish or Scottish)

Russian	Pronunciation
С с	s
Т т	t
У у	u
Ф ф	f
Х х	kh (guttural)
Ц ц	ts
Ч ч	ch
Ш ш	sh
Щ щ	shch (like "fresh cheese")
Ъ ъ	hard sign (always silent)
Ы ы	between "y" and "we"
Ь ь	soft sign (always silent)
Э э	eh
Ю ю	yu
Я я	ya

2 Basic Vocabulary

KEY WORDS

English	Russian	Pronunciation
Yes/No	да, нет	da, nyet
Hello	здравствйте	*zdras*-tvoo-tye
Hi	привет	pree-*vyet*
Good morning	доброе утро	*do*-bro-ye *oo*-tra
Good day	добрый день	*do*-bry dyen
Good evening	добрый вечер	*do*-bry *ve*-cher
Good-bye	до свидания	da svi-*da*-nya
See you later	пока	pa-*ka*
Thank you	спасибо	spa-*see*-ba
Please/You're welcome	пожалуйста	pa-*zha*-li-sta
Excuse me	извините	eez-vee-*nee*-tye
Sorry	простите, пожалуйста	prah-*stee*-tye, pa-*zha*-li-sta
How are you?	как дела?	kak deh-*la*
Fine, good	хорошо	kho-ro-*show*
Bad	плохо	*plo*-kha
When	когда	ka-*gda*
Today	сегодня	se-*vohd*-nya
Yesterday	вчера	vche-*ra*
Tomorrow	завтра	*zav*-tra
Open	открыто	ot-*kree*-ta

English	Russian	Pronunciation
Closed	закрыто	za-*kree*-ta
Watch out	осторожно	os-toh-*rozh*-no
Help!	помогите	pa-ma-*gee*-tye
Stop	стоп, стой	stop, stoi
Entrance	вход	vkhod
Exit	выход	*vy*-khod
Danger	опасно	o-*pas*-no
Hospital	больница, госпиталь	bol-*nee*-tsa, *gos*-pee-tal
Police	милиция	mee-*lee*-tsee-ya
Fire	пожар	po-*zhar*
Ambulance	скорая помощь	*sko*-ra-ya *po*-moshch
Pharmacy	аптека	ap-*teh*-ka
Currency exchange	обмен валюты	ob-*men* vah-*lyoo*-tee
Bank	баик	bahnk
ATM/cash machine	банкомат	bahnk-o-*mat*
Ticket	билет	bee-*lyet*
Post office	почта	*poch*-ta
Postage stamp	марка	*mar*-ka
Postcard	открытка	ot-*kreet*-ka
Airport	аэропорт	ah-air-o-*port*
Subway/metro	метро	me-*tro*
Bus	автобус	av-*toh*-bus
Tram	трамвай	tram-*vai*
Taxi	такси	tahk-*si*
Shop	магазин	ma-ga-*zeen*
Museum	музей	moo-*zay*
Park	парк	park
Church	церковь, храм	*tser*-kov, khram
Embassy	посольство	pah-*sohl*-stva
Coat check	гардероб	gard-yeh-*robe*
Admission fee	вход	vkhod
Free of charge	бесплатно	bes-*plaht*-no

HANDY PHRASES

English	Russian	Pronunciation
Do you speak English?	Вы говорите по-английски?	vy go-vo-*ree*-te po ang-*lee*-skee?
I don't speak Russian	Я не говорю по-русски	ya nee guh-vuh-*ryoo* pa-*roo*-skee
I speak a little Russian	Я немного говорю по-русски	ya ne-*mno*-go guh-vuh-*ryoo* pa-*roo*-skee

English	Russian	Pronunciation
How much does it cost?	Сколько стонт?	*skol*-ka *sto*-eet?
Expensive	дорого	*do*-ra-ga
Cheap	недорого	ne-*do*-ra-ga
Where is...	Где находится...	gde na-*kho*-dee-tsa...
a hotel	гостиница	gos-*tee*-nee-tsa
the metro station	станция метро	*stan*-tsee-ya me-*tro*
the restroom/WC	туалет	tua-*let*
To the right	направо	na-*pra*-vo
To the left	налево	na-*le*-vo
Straight ahead	прямо	*prya*-mo
What time is it?	сколько времени?	*skol*-ka *vre*-me-nee?
I would like to order...	мне, пожалуйста...	mnye, pah-*zha*-li-sta
I would like the check please	принесите счет, пожалуйста	pree-ne-*see*-te shyot, po-*zha*-li-sta
Service charge/tip	за обслуживание	za ob-*sloo*-zhee-va-nee-ye
VAT (tax)	НДС (налог)	en-de-es

SOME KEY PLACE NAMES

English	Russian	Pronunciation
Moscow	Москва	mosk-*vah*
Kremlin	Кремль	kreml
Red Square	Красная Площадь	*kras*-nay-a *ploh*-shchad
Tverskaya Street	улица Тверская	*oo*-li-tsa tvcr-*sky*-ah
St. Petersburg	Санкт-Петербург	sankt pe-tehr-*burg*
Hermitage	Эрмитаж	er-mee-*tazh*
Nevsky Prospekt	Невский проспект	*nev*-ski pros-*pekt*
Palace Square	Дворцовая площадь	dvar-*tsoh*-va-ya *ploh*-shchad
Street	улица	*oo*-li-tsa
Avenue	проспект	pros-*pekt*
Boulevard	бульвар	bool-*var*
Embankment	набережная	*na*-ber-ezh-nya
Lane	переулок	peh-reh-*oo*-luk
Underground walkway	переход	peh-reh-*khod*

NUMBERS

1	один (ah-*deen*)	7	семв (syem)
2	два (dva)	8	восемв (*voh*-syem)
3	три (tree)	9	девять (de-vyat)
4	четыре (chuh-*tee*-reh)	10	десять (de-syat)
5	пять (pyat)	11	одинадцать (ah-*deen*-uh-tsat)
6	шесть (shest)	12	двенадцать (dve-*na*-tsat)

13 **тринадцать** (tree-*na*-tsat)
14 **четырнадцать**
  (chuh-*teer*-nah-tsat)
15 **пятнадцать** (pyat-*na*-tsat)
16 **шестнадцать** (shest-*na*-tsat)
17 **семнадцать** (syem-*na*-tsat)
18 **восемнадцать** (voh-syem-*na*-tsat)
19 **девятнадцать** (de-vyat-*na*-tsat)
20 **двадцать** (*dva*-tsat)

30 **тридцать** (*tri*-tsat)
40 **сорок** (*so*-rok)
50 **пятьдесят** (pyat-deh-*syat*)
60 **шестьдесят** (shest-deh-*syat*)
70 **семьдесят** (*sem*-deh-syat)
80 **восемьдесят** (*voh*-syem-deh-syat)
90 **девяносто** (deh-vya-*no*-sta)
100 **сто** (sto)
1000 **тысяча** (*ty*-sya-cha)

DAYS

Monday **понедельник** (pon-e-*del*-nik)
Tuesday **вторник** (*vtor*-nik)
Wednesday **среда** (sre-*da*)
Thursday **четверг** (chet-*vairg*)

Friday **пятница** (*pyat*-nee-tsa)
Saturday **субота** (soo-*bo*-ta)
Sunday **воскресенье** (vos-kre-*seh*-nya)

MONTHS

January **январь** (yan-*vahr*)
February **февраль** fev-*rahl*)
March **март** (mart)
April **апрель** (ah-*prel*)
May **май** (ma-ee)
June **июнь** (ee-*yun*)

July **июль** (ee-*yul*)
August **август** (ahv-*goost*)
September **сентябрь** (sent-*yahbr*)
October **октябрь** (ahkt-*yahbr*)
November **ноябрь** (no-*yahbr*)
December **декабрь** (dek-*yahbr*)

3 Russian Dining Savvy

BASICS

English	Russian	Pronunciation
menu	**меню**	men-*yoo*
breakfast	**завтрак**	*zahv*-trak
lunch	**обед**	o-*byed*
dinner	**ужин**	*oo*-zhin
smoking/nonsmoking	**курящий-некурящий**	koo-*rya*-shee, ne-koo-*rya*-shee
appetizers	**закуски**	za-*koo*-skee
salad	**салат**	sa-*laht*
soup	**суп**	soop
first courses	**первые блюда**	*per*-vee-yeh *blyoo*-da
main dishes	**вторые блюда**	vto-*ree*-yeh *blyoo*-da
dessert	**дессерт**	deh-*sairt*
bread	**хлеб**	khleb
butter	**масло**	*mas*-loh
salt	**соль**	sol
pepper	**перец**	*pe*-rets
sugar	**сахар**	*sah*-khar
honey	**мед**	myod

English	Russian	Pronunciation
jam	**варенье**	var-*en*-ye
mustard	**горчица**	gar-*chee*-tsa
ketchup	**кетчуп**	*keh*-choop
cold	**холодный**	kho-*lohd*-nee
hot	**горячий**	go-*rya*-chee

SOUP (СУПЫ)

English	Russian	Pronunciation
borscht	**борщ**	borsh
cabbage soup	**щи**	*she*
cold sorrel soup	**зеленые щи**	zel-*yon*-i shchi
tangy stew (meat- or fish-based)	**солянка**	sol-*yan*-ka
fish-based stew	**уха**	*uk*-ha
broth	**похлебка**	pokhl-*yob*-ka

DAIRY PRODUCTS (МОЛОЧНЫЕ ПРОДУКТЫ)

English	Russian	Pronunciation
milk	**молоко**	ma-la-*koh*
cream	**сливки**	*sleev*-kee
sour cream	**сметана**	sme-*tah*-na
cheese	**сыр**	syr
farmers' cheese	**творог**	*tvor*-ug
kefir	**кефир**	keh-*feer*
eggs	**яйца**	*ya*-ee-tsa
hard-boiled egg	**крутое яйцо**	kroo-toh-ye ya-ee-*tso*
soft-boiled egg	**яйцо в смятку**	ya-ee-*tso* v *smyat*-koo
scrambled eggs	**омлет**	om-*lyet*

MEAT (МЯСО)

English	Russian	Pronunciation
beef	**говядина**	gov-*ya*-dee-na
pork	**свинина**	svee-*nee*-na
chicken	**курица**	*koo*-ree-tsa
lamb	**баранина**	ba-*ra*-nee-na
veal	**телятина**	tel-*ya*-tee-na
ham	**ветчина**	vet-chee-*na*
cold cuts, sausage	**колбаса**	kohl-ba-*sa*
hot dog–type sausage	**сосиска**	sah-*see*-ska
ground meat grilled on skewer	**кебаб**	ke-*bahb*

English	Russian	Pronunciation
chunks of meat, usually lamb, grilled on skewer	шашлык	shash-*leek*
duck	утка	*oot*-ka
turkey	индейка	in-*day*-ka
ground meat–filled dumplings	пельмени	pel-*me*-nee
ground-meat cutlets	котлеты	kot-*leh*-tee
rabbit	кролик	*kroh*-leek
liver	печень	*pe*-chyen
aspic	студень	*stoo*-dyen
rare	с кровыо	s *kroh*-vyoo
medium	прожаренный	pro-*zhar*-eh-nee
well-done	хорошо прожаренный	kho-ro-*show* pro-*zhar*-eh-nee

FISH (РЫБА)

English	Russian	Pronunciation
caviar (black)	икра (черная)	eek-*ra* (*chor*-na-ya)
beluga/sevruga/osetra	белуга/севрюга/осетра	
red caviar (salmon roe)	красная икра	eek-*ra* (*kras*-na-ya)
salmon	лосось-семга	lah-*sohs*, *syom*-ga
sturgeon	осетрина	ah-se-*tree*-na
trout	форель	fa-*rel*
pikeperch	судак	soo-*dak*
herring	сельдь	syeld
catfish	сом	som
tuna	тунец	too-*nets*
eel	угорь	*oo*-gor
crayfish	раки	*ra*-kee
sterlet	стерлядь	*ster*-lyad
sushi	суши	sushi

VEGETABLES (ОВОЩИ)

English	Russian	Pronunciation
tomato	помидор	po-mee-*dor*
cucumber	огурец	ah-goo-*rets*
cabbage	капуста	ka-*poo*-sta
carrots	морковь	mar-*kov*
potatoes	картошка	kar-*toh*-shka
lettuce	салат	sa-*laht*

English	Russian	Pronunciation
radish	редиска	reh-*dee*-ska
mushroom	грибы	gree-*bee*
beets	свекла	*svyo*-kla
eggplant/aubergine	баклажан	bah-klah-*zhan*
spinach	шпинат	shpee-*nat*
sweet pepper	перец	*pe*-rets

FRUIT (ФРУКТЫ)

English	Russian	Pronunciation
apple	яблоко	**ыa**-blo-ko
banana	банан	bah-*nahn*
orange	апельсин	ah-pel-*seen*
plum	слива	*slee*-va
peach	персик	*pear*-seek
strawberry	клубника	kloob-*nee*-ka
cherry	вишня	*vee*-shnya
wild cherry	черешня	che-*re*-shnya
raspberry	малина	mah-*lee*-na
grape	виноград	vee-no-*grad*
currant	смородина	smo-*ro*-dee-na
melon (usually a sweet cantaloupe)	дыня	*dee*-nya
watermelon	арбуз	ar-*booz*
grapefruit	грейпфрут	grayp-*froot*

DESSERTS, ETC. (ДЕССЕРТ)

English	Russian	Pronunciation
ice cream	мороженое	mo-*ro*-zhe-no-ye
cake	торт	tort
cookies	печенье	pe-*che*-nye
candy	конфеты	kon-*fyet*-ee
pie (savory or sweet)	пирог	pee-*rog*
bliny (crepelike pancakes)	блины	blee-*nee*
mini-pancakes	оладьи	oh-*la*-dee
chocolate	шоколад	sho-ko-*lad*

DRINKS (НАПИТКИ)

English	Russian	Pronunciation
tea	чай	chai
coffee	кофе	*ko*-fye

English	Russian	Pronunciation
water	вода	vah-*da*
still/sparkling	без газа/с газом	bez *ga*-za, s *ga*-zom
juice	сок	sok
milk	молоко	ma-la-*koh*
vodka	водка	*vohd*-ka
beer	пиво	*pee*-va
red wine	красное вино	*kras*-no-ye vee-*no*
white wine	белое вино	*bel*-o-ye vee-*no*
brandy	коньяк	kon-*yak*
whiskey	виски	*vis*-kee
cocktail	коктейль	kok-*tail*
Coca-Cola (or any cola-type drink)	кока-кола	ko-ka-*ko*-la
any sweet carbonated drink	лимонад	li-mo-*nad*

Appendix C:
Useful Toll-Free Numbers
& Websites

AIRLINES

Air Canada
© 888/247-2262
www.aircanada.ca

Air France
© 800/237-2747 in the U.S.
© 800/667-2747 in Canada.
© 0845/0845-111 in the U.K.
www.airfrance.com

Air-India
© 800/223-2250 (first class) or 800/
223-7776 (economy class)
www.airindia.ca

Alitalia
© 800/223-5730 in the U.S. and Canada
© 0870/544-8259 in the U.K.
www.alitalia.com

Alaska Airlines
© 800/252-7522
www.alaskaair.com

Austrian Airlines
© 800/843-0002 in the U.S. and Canada
© 020/8897-3037 in the U.K..
www.aua.com

British Airways
© 800/247-9297 in the U.S. and Canada.
© 0870//850 9 850 in the U.K.
www.british-airways.com

Delta Air Lines
© 800/221-1212 in the U.S. and Canada
© 0800/414-767 in the U.K.
www.delta.com

KLM (a Northwest Airlines partner)
© 800/225-2525 in the U.S. and Canada
© 08705/074074 in the U.K.
www.klm.com

LOT Polish Airlines
© 800/223-0593
www.lot.com

Lufthansa
© 800/645-3880 in the U.S.
© 800/399-LUFT in Canada.
© 0845/773-7747 in the U.K.
www.lufthansa.com

Malév Hungarian Airlines
© 800/223-6884 in the U.S.
© 800/665-6363 in Canada
© 020/7439-0577 in the U.K.
www.malev.hu

MAJOR HOTEL & MOTEL CHAINS

Best Western International
© 800/528-1234 or 1-800-780-7234
www.bestwestern.com

Holiday Inn
© 800/HOLIDAY
http://www.ichotelsgroup.com

Inter-Continental
Hotels & Resorts
© 888/567-8725
http://www.ichotelsgroup.com

ITT Sheraton
© 800/325-3535
www.starwood.com or www.sheraton.
com

Le Meridien
© 800/543-4300
www.lemeridien.com

Marriott Hotels
© 800/228-9290
www.marriott.com

Novotel
© 800/NOVOTEL (668-6835)
www.novotel.com

Radisson Hotels International
© 800/333-3333
www.radisson.com

Renaissance
© 800/228-9290
www.renaissancehotels.com or www.
marriott.com

Sheraton Hotels & Resorts
© 800-325-3535
www.sheraton.com

Index

See also Accommodations and Restaurant indexes, below.

A Guide for Every Type of Traveler

FROMMER'S® COMPLETE GUIDES

For independent leisure or business travelers who value complete coverage, candid advice, and lots of choices in all price ranges.

These are the most complete, up-to-date guides you can buy. Count on Frommer's for exact prices, savvy trip planning, sightseeing advice, dozens of detailed maps, and candid reviews of hotels and restaurants in every price range. All Complete Guides offer special icons to point you to great finds, excellent values, and more. Every hotel, restaurant, and attraction is rated from zero to three stars to help you make the best choices.

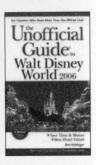

UNOFFICIAL GUIDES®

For honeymooners, families, business travelers, and anyone else who values no-nonsense, *Consumer Reports*–style advice.

Unofficial Guides are ideal for those who want to know the pros and cons of the places they are visiting and make informed decisions. The guides rank and rate every hotel, restaurant, and attraction, with evaluations based on reader surveys and critiques compiled by a team of unbiased inspectors.

FROMMER'S® IRREVERENT GUIDES

For experienced, sophisticated travelers looking for a fresh, candid perspective on a destination.

This unique series is perfect for anyone who wants a cutting-edge perspective on the hottest destinations. Covering all major cities around the globe, these guides are unabashedly honest and downright hilarious. Decked out with a retro-savvy feel, each book features new photos, maps, and neighborhood references.

FROMMER'S® WITH KIDS GUIDES

For families traveling with children ages 2 to 14.

Here are the ultimate guides for a successful family vacation. Written by parents, they're packed with information on museums, outdoor activities, attractions, great drives and strolls, incredible parks, the liveliest places to stay and eat, and more.

Visit Frommers.com

WILEY
Now you know.

FROMMER'S® COMPLETE TRAVEL GUIDES

Alaska
Amalfi Coast
American Southwest
Amsterdam
Argentina & Chile
Arizona
Atlanta
Australia
Austria
Bahamas
Barcelona
Beijing
Belgium, Holland & Luxembourg
Belize
Bermuda
Boston
Brazil
British Columbia & the Canadian
 Rockies
Brussels & Bruges
Budapest & the Best of Hungary
Buenos Aires
Calgary
California
Canada
Cancún, Cozumel & the Yucatán
Cape Cod, Nantucket & Martha's
 Vineyard
Caribbean
Caribbean Ports of Call
Carolinas & Georgia
Chicago
China
Colorado
Costa Rica
Croatia
Cuba
Denmark
Denver, Boulder & Colorado Springs
Edinburgh & Glasgow
England
Europe
Europe by Rail

Florence, Tuscany & Umbria
Florida
France
Germany
Greece
Greek Islands
Hawaii
Hong Kong
Honolulu, Waikiki & Oahu
India
Ireland
Italy
Jamaica
Japan
Kauai
Las Vegas
London
Los Angeles
Los Cabos & Baja
Madrid
Maine Coast
Maryland & Delaware
Maui
Mexico
Montana & Wyoming
Montréal & Québec City
Moscow & St. Petersburg
Munich & the Bavarian Alps
Nashville & Memphis
New England
Newfoundland & Labrador
New Mexico
New Orleans
New York City
New York State
New Zealand
Northern Italy
Norway
Nova Scotia, New Brunswick &
 Prince Edward Island
Oregon
Paris
Peru

Philadelphia & the Amish Country
Portugal
Prague & the Best of the Czech
 Republic
Provence & the Riviera
Puerto Rico
Rome
San Antonio & Austin
San Diego
San Francisco
Santa Fe, Taos & Albuquerque
Scandinavia
Scotland
Seattle
Seville, Granada & the Best of
 Andalusia
Shanghai
Sicily
Singapore & Malaysia
South Africa
South America
South Florida
South Pacific
Southeast Asia
Spain
Sweden
Switzerland
Texas
Thailand
Tokyo
Toronto
Turkey
USA
Utah
Vancouver & Victoria
Vermont, New Hampshire & Maine
Vienna & the Danube Valley
Vietnam
Virgin Islands
Virginia
Walt Disney World® & Orlando
Washington, D.C.
Washington State

FROMMER'S® DOLLAR-A-DAY GUIDES

Australia from $60 a Day
California from $70 a Day
England from $75 a Day
Europe from $85 a Day
Florida from $70 a Day

Hawaii from $80 a Day
Ireland from $90 a Day
Italy from $90 a Day
London from $95 a Day

New York City from $90 a Day
Paris from $95 a Day
San Francisco from $70 a Day
Washington, D.C. from $80 a Day

FROMMER'S® PORTABLE GUIDES

Acapulco, Ixtapa & Zihuatanejo
Amsterdam
Aruba
Australia's Great Barrier Reef
Bahamas
Berlin
Big Island of Hawaii
Boston
California Wine Country
Cancún
Cayman Islands
Charleston
Chicago

Disneyland®
Dominican Republic
Dublin
Florence
Las Vegas
Las Vegas for Non-Gamblers
London
Los Angeles
Maui
Nantucket & Martha's Vineyard
New Orleans
New York City
Paris

Portland
Puerto Rico
Puerto Vallarta, Manzanillo &
 Guadalajara
Rio de Janeiro
San Diego
San Francisco
Savannah
Vancouver
Venice
Virgin Islands
Washington, D.C.
Whistler

FROMMER'S® CRUISE GUIDES

Alaska Cruises & Ports of Call

Cruises & Ports of Call

European Cruises & Ports of Call

FROMMER'S® DAY BY DAY GUIDES

Amsterdam
Chicago
Florence & Tuscany

London
New York City
Paris

Rome
San Francisco
Venice

FROMMER'S® NATIONAL PARK GUIDES

Algonquin Provincial Park
Banff & Jasper
Grand Canyon

National Parks of the American West
Rocky Mountain
Yellowstone & Grand Teton

Yosemite and Sequoia & Kings
 Canyon
Zion & Bryce Canyon

FROMMER'S® MEMORABLE WALKS

Chicago
London

New York
Paris

Rome
San Francisco

FROMMER'S® WITH KIDS GUIDES

Chicago
Hawaii
Las Vegas
London

National Parks
New York City
San Francisco

Toronto
Walt Disney World® & Orlando
Washington, D.C.

SUZY GERSHMAN'S BORN TO SHOP GUIDES

Born to Shop: France
Born to Shop: Hong Kong, Shanghai
 & Beijing

Born to Shop: Italy
Born to Shop: London

Born to Shop: New York
Born to Shop: Paris

FROMMER'S® IRREVERENT GUIDES

Amsterdam
Boston
Chicago
Las Vegas
London

Los Angeles
Manhattan
New Orleans
Paris

Rome
San Francisco
Walt Disney World®
Washington, D.C.

FROMMER'S® BEST-LOVED DRIVING TOURS

Austria
Britain
California
France

Germany
Ireland
Italy
New England

Northern Italy
Scotland
Spain
Tuscany & Umbria

THE UNOFFICIAL GUIDES®

Adventure Travel in Alaska
Beyond Disney
California with Kids
Central Italy
Chicago
Cruises
Disneyland®
England
Florida
Florida with Kids

Hawaii
Ireland
Las Vegas
London
Maui
Mexico's Best Beach Resorts
Mini Las Vegas
Mini Mickey
New Orleans
New York City

Paris
San Francisco
South Florida including Miami &
 the Keys
Walt Disney World®
Walt Disney World® for
 Grown-ups
Walt Disney World® with Kids
Washington, D.C.

SPECIAL-INTEREST TITLES

Athens Past & Present
Cities Ranked & Rated
Frommer's Best Day Trips from London
Frommer's Best RV & Tent Campgrounds
 in the U.S.A.

Frommer's Exploring America by RV
Frommer's NYC Free & Dirt Cheap
Frommer's Road Atlas Europe
Frommer's Road Atlas Ireland
Retirement Places Rated

FROMMER'S® PHRASEFINDER DICTIONARY GUIDES

French

Italian

Spanish

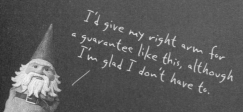

IF YOU BOOK IT, IT SHOULD BE THERE.

Only Travelocity guarantees it will be, or we'll work with our travel partners to make it right, right away. So if you're missing a balcony or anything else you booked, just call us 24/7. **1**-888-TRAVELOCITY.

travelocity

You'll never roam alone